OUR NATION UNHINGED

OUR NATION UNHINGED

THE HUMAN CONSEQUENCES
OF THE WAR ON TERROR

Peter Jan Honigsberg

FOREWORD BY ERWIN CHEMERINSKY

UNIVERSITY OF CALIFORNIA PRESS

BERKELEY   LOS ANGELES   LONDON

University of California Press, one of the most
distinguished university presses in the United States,
enriches lives around the world by advancing scholar-
ship in the humanities, social sciences, and natural
sciences. Its activities are supported by the UC Press
Foundation and by philanthropic contributions from
individuals and institutions. For more information,
visit www.ucpress.edu.

University of California Press
Berkeley and Los Angeles, California

University of California Press, Ltd.
London, England

Library of Congress Cataloging-in-Publication Data

Honigsberg, Peter Jan.
   Our nation unhinged : the human consequences of
the War on Terror / Peter Jan Honigsberg ; foreword
by Erwin Chemerinsky.
      p.   cm.
   Includes bibliographical references and index.
   ISBN 978-0-520-25472-5 (cloth : alk. paper)
   1. Prisoners of war—Legal status, laws, etc.—
United States. 2. Detention of persons—United States.
3. Human rights—Government policy—United States.
4. War on Terrorism, 2001—Prisoners and prisons.
5. Prisoners of war—Legal status, laws, etc.—Cuba—
Guantanamo Bay Naval Base. 6. Prisoners of war—
Legal status, laws, etc.—Cuba—Guantanamo Bay
Naval Base—Cases. 7. Combatants and noncom-
batants (International law) I. Title.
KF9625.H66   2009
345.73'056—dc22   2008052272

Manufactured in the United States of America

18 17 16 15 14 13 12 11 10 09
10 9 8 7 6 5 4 3 2 1

This book is printed on Natures Book, which contains
30% post-consumer waste and meets the minimum
requirements of ANSI/NISO Z39.48–1992 (R 1997)
(Permanence of Paper).

In praise of the lawyers who stood up for human rights, the rule of law, and the Constitution and in tribute to the Cuban iguana for its role in establishing human rights at Guantanamo Bay

Injustice anywhere is a threat to justice everywhere. We are caught in an inescapable network of mutuality, tied in a single garment of destiny. Whatever affects one directly, affects all indirectly.

Martin Luther King, Jr.
"Letter from Birmingham Jail," *April 16, 1963*

Thank You

Lee Ryan: law librarian extraordinaire, Erwin Chemerinsky, Alexa Koenig, Richard Leo, Carlos Castresana, Jeffrey Brand, Mark Denbeaux, Thomas Wilner, Candace Gorman, Mary Louise Zernicke, Christopher Honigsberg, Liam Honigsberg, Colleen Honigsberg, Karlene Navarro, Susan Freiwald, Maya Manian, Connie de la Vega, Scott Handleman, John Shafer, John Denvir, Alice Kaswan, Pelonomi Khumoetsile-Taylor, Marina Hsieh, Tiffanie Jower, Jody Taliaferro, Jennifer Roden, Stephanie Smith, Brendan Sanchez, Elizabeth Zaninovich, Marie Montesano, Maria Lampasona, Angela Fitzsimons, Elizabeth Goya, Sarah Michael, Abby Conzatti Nichols, Ada Yu, Elizabeth Berg, Naomi Schneider.

Please see Cubaniguana.net for updates to this book.

Contents

The Cuban Iguana
and American Jurisprudence

In fall 2003, attorney Tom Wilner needed to persuade the justices of the Supreme Court that it was in their interest to take the case of a dozen Kuwaiti detainees being held in isolation in Guantanamo Bay, Cuba, without charges, without a hearing, and without access to a lawyer.

Wilner used three arguments in his elegant petition to the Court. He argued that, under the Constitution, the courts have a critical role in striking a balance between the president's need to protect our nation's security and the people's need to protect the fundamental right to a fair hearing, with a lawyer present, before a neutral decision maker.

Wilner further argued that the administration's mistreatment of the detainees and the denial of their rights under law had become an international embarrassment. Here was an opportunity for the Supreme Court to make it right.

In his third argument, Wilner referred to the example of the Cuban iguana. When the Cuban iguana crosses the Cuban border into Guantanamo, it is protected by American law, under the Endangered Species Act. However, the human beings held prisoner at Guantanamo were not protected under American law. Wilner concluded that if the Supreme Court did not review his clients' cases, the Cuban iguana would have greater safeguards than human beings at Guantanamo.

The Supreme Court agreed to hear the case.

Cuban iguana in Guantanamo. Courtesy Chris Maluszynski, Moment Agency.

Foreword

As I write this in August 2008, some men have been kept prisoners in Guantanamo Bay, Cuba, for six and a half years. They are essentially held in solitary confinement. They have been prisoners longer than World War II, longer than World War I, longer than the Civil War. Only one has received a trial.

A particularly shameful aspect of a truly shameful episode of American history is that no one except the lawyers representing these men—not the United States, not its courts—seems to feel the slightest urgency in determining whether these men should continue to be held as prisoners. No court has granted expedited review for any of the proceedings concerning these men and their legal claims. The Bush administration has won in its claim of power to detain individuals without due process simply by endlessly protracting the proceedings. Each day, the men who are held captive at Guantanamo are denied the chance to see their children and their loved ones; each day, they are denied freedom even though they have never been tried or convicted of any crime.

I have been representing one of these men, Salim Gherebi, for over six years now. He grew up in Libya and is married and a father of three. He has never met his youngest child, because his wife was pregnant at the time he was apprehended. Gherebi is in his late forties but looks older. He is under six feet and slight in build. I can say in all honesty, without revealing any classified information, that I have no idea why he is there. He may be a very dangerous man and deserve to be incarcerated, or he may be there by mistake. That is what a trial is supposed to determine.

Professor Peter Jan Honigsberg has written a magnificent book telling the story of what has occurred since September 11, 2001, and how the Bush administration has betrayed the most basic principles of constitutional law and international human rights protections. He tells the story of Guantanamo in moving, human terms, and he also shows how it relates to the other abuses that have occurred over the last seven years.

To appreciate the events that Professor Honigsberg describes, it is important to see them in a historical context. Throughout American history, the response to crisis—especially foreign-based crisis—has been repression. In each instance, we realize in hindsight that the nation was not made any safer because of the government's action. In this way, some of the worst aspects of American history repeat themselves.

The legacy of suppression in times of crisis began early in American history. In 1798, in response to concerns about survival of the country, Congress enacted the Alien and Sedition Acts, which made it a federal crime to make false criticisms of the government or its officials.[1] These laws were used to persecute the government's critics, and people were jailed for what would be regarded today as the mildest of statements. Within a few years, after the election of 1800, Congress repealed most of these laws and President Thomas Jefferson pardoned those who had been convicted. The right to freedom of speech had been lost and nothing was gained.

During the Civil War, President Abraham Lincoln suspended the writ of habeas corpus. Additionally, dissidents were imprisoned for criticizing the way the government was fighting the war. There is no evidence that this aided the war effort in any way. Ultimately, the Supreme Court declared unconstitutional Lincoln's suspension of the writ of habeas corpus.[2]

During World War I, the government aggressively prosecuted critics of the war. One man went to jail for ten years for circulating a leaflet arguing that the draft was unconstitutional;[3] another, Socialist leader Eugene Debs, was sentenced to prison for simply saying to his audience, "You are good for more than cannon fodder."[4] At about the same time, the successful Bolshevik revolution in Russia sparked great fear of communists here. The attorney general, Mitchell Palmer, launched a massive effort to round up and deport aliens in the United States. Individuals were summarily deported and separated from their families without any semblance of due process.

During World War II, 110,000 Japanese Americans were forcibly interned in what President Franklin Roosevelt called "concentration camps."[5] Adults and children, aliens and citizens, were uprooted from their lifelong homes and placed behind barbed wire. Not one Japanese American was ever charged with espionage, or treason, or any crime that threatened security. There is not a shred of evidence that the unprecedented invasion of rights accomplished anything useful. Nonetheless, the Supreme Court, in *Korematsu v. United States,* expressed the need for deference to the executive in wartime and upheld the removal of Japanese Americans from the West Coast.[6]

The McCarthy era saw enormous persecution of those suspected of being communists. Jobs were lost and lives were ruined on the flimsiest of allegations. In the leading case of the era, *United States v. Dennis,* the Court approved twenty-year prison sentences for the crime of "conspiracy to advocate the overthrow of the government" for teaching works by Marx and Lenin.[7]

In this way, the abuses by the Bush administration since September 11, so powerfully described in this book, are a continuation of a tragic history that has replayed itself throughout American history. But in some ways, what has occurred since September 11 is even worse than what this nation previously experienced. I do not make this statement as hyperbole, and I am not unmindful of the extent of past wrongs. Thankfully, nothing in the war on terrorism begins to approach the deprivation of rights that occurred for the 110,000 Japanese Americans who were interned in concentration camps during World War II.

But no administration in American history has shown the profound disregard for the Constitution and basic principles, such as separation of powers and due process of law, as has occurred during the presidency of George W. Bush. Professor Honigsberg's book provides the details and the documentation.

The war on terrorism is of indefinite duration. The president has told us that it will last long beyond our lifetime, and he is surely right on this. In part, this is because the enemy—and I do not dispute in any way that there is a serious enemy—is not going away. I believe that the most important world development in the last quarter century has been the rise of fundamentalism. The terrorism of September 11 is unquestionably a product of this. There is no sign that the desire of these violent fundamentalists to harm the United States is in any way abating. Quite the contrary, I fear that one consequence of our misguided war in Iraq is the further radicalizing of many against the United States.

There is another, more subtle way in which the war on terrorism poses an indefinite threat to civil liberties. There never will be a formal end to it, so the loss of liberties it entails will seemingly continue forever. There is no single defined enemy, and no concession or peace treaty will end the war and the loss of liberties.

William Rehnquist wrote a prescient book a few years before September 11, in which he advanced the thesis that civil liberties are restricted in wartime but then restored after the completion of the wars.[8] Descriptively, this is an accurate statement, though I very much disagree with his normative conclusion that the deprivations of rights were justified or necessary. The widespread assumption since September 11 has been that this pattern would be followed once again, that the loss of liberties would be temporary. But there is no indication that this will be so. The Bush administration has not backed off a single repressive action.

Moreover, it must be remembered that much of the deprivation of rights is occurring outside the United States and thus is largely invisible and immune from scrutiny. No one knows how many individuals the government is detaining in foreign camps as part of the war on terrorism.

In fact, the threat to civil liberties is particularly insidious because so much of what the government is doing is completely secret. It is impossible for the democratic process, or the courts, to provide any check when actions are invisible. How many individuals were arrested and detained by the federal government after September 11? How many individuals are now being detained? Who are the detainees and why are they being held? Astoundingly, the answers to these questions remain unknown. The Bush administration and the Justice Department have steadfastly refused to answer these basic inquiries, so that no one knows how many people have been held in custody and for what reasons. The simple reality is that there are no checks against secret violations of rights. There is no way to know what else this administration has done to restrict liberties that has not yet come to light.

But what is known and described in this book is terribly troubling. As I have spoken on this to countless audiences over the last seven years, I have been repeatedly struck that those who agree most with my message are people who have served in the military or who have loved ones in the military. They ask how the United States can expect foreign nations to comply with international law regarding their American captives if this country so blatantly disregards international law when it has foreign prisoners. In this way, the Bush administration has done incalculable damage to this country's ability to lead the world in advancing and protecting basic human rights. Guantanamo has become the shameful symbol of this.

All of this is told in Professor Honigsberg's terrific book. My hope is that it will help change the course of events and help to make sure that these events are never repeated by the American government in the future.

Erwin Chemerinsky
Dean and Distinguished Professor of Law
University of California, Irvine, School of Law

NOTES

1. 1 Stat. 596, Act of July 14, 1798.
2. *Ex parte Milligan*, 71 U.S. 2 (1866).
3. *Schenck v. United States*, 249 U.S. 47 (1919).
4. *Debs v. United States*, 249 U.S. 47 (1919).
5. William Manchester, *The Glory and the Dream* (1974), 300.
6. U.S. 214 (1944).
7. U.S. 494 (1951).
8. William Rehnquist, *All the Laws but One: Civil Liberties in Wartime* (1998).

Opening

Jose Padilla's lawyers have in their possession a photo of him wearing goggles and headphones. The thick, blackened goggles wrap around Padilla's head, covering much of his forehead. They are designed not only to obstruct his vision but also to block all light,  natural and artificial. According to one of his lawyers, they resemble paint goggles.[1] The goggles sit very low on his nose.

Conical headphones lock out all sounds. There seems to be a strap hanging loosely around his chin. He wears a short-sleeved orange jumpsuit, the kind that prisoners wear. His is open at the collar, exposing a white t-shirt underneath. Three military guardsmen, wearing what appears to be riot gear, with full helmets, gloves, kneepads, and plastic shields covering their faces, stand very near, perhaps gripping him at the waist.

Padilla's lips are sealed. His expression seems to speak submission. However, it could also be read as abject terror, numbness, or even hopelessness. But who is to say what this man is truly experiencing in the depths of his soul and which, if any, emotions are actually reflected in the photograph?

Jose Padilla is on his way to the dentist.

This photograph is a still taken from a video, and it is grainy. The military shot the video while Padilla was in a naval brig in Charleston, South Carolina. The videos of Padilla in the brig, except for a handful of slides taken from this video, are classified and require a security clearance.

In the previous still, Padilla's bare feet stick out of an opening cut into the bottom part of his cell door. His feet are about to be shackled

Jose Padilla at the naval brig in South Carolina. Courtesy U.S. government.

Jose Padilla being prepared for a trip to the dentist. Courtesy U.S. government.

with leg irons. In the preceding still, Padilla places his hands, palms together, through a slot, known as a bean hole, in the middle of the door in preparation for shackling. The guards stand erect outside the door to his seven-by-nine-foot cell, number 103.

President Bush designated Jose Padilla an enemy combatant in 2002. Padilla is an American citizen, born in 1970 in Brooklyn, New York. He lived in cell 103 for three and a half years. For twenty-one months, he was held in total isolation. He was allowed no contact with his family—either personal visits or communication via letters or phone calls. He was not allowed to speak to a lawyer. The only people who spoke to him were government interrogators and guards.

Video cameras monitored Padilla twenty-four hours a day, seven days a week. The cameras operated when he slept, when he ate, and when he went to the bathroom. They were also on when he was interrogated. Tapes for all but seventy-two hours of his entire incarceration exist. If there are tapes covering the remaining seventy-two hours, those tapes are missing. According to Padilla's lawyer, the military claims it has lost the tapes, but he believes otherwise. However, he would not discuss or speculate on what might have happened to them or on why they are missing.[2]

Black paint covered the windows in Padilla's cell in the brig. There was no natural light, and for most of the time, Padilla did not know whether it was day or night. He had no clock or timepiece to tell the time. He had no mirror, and hence no idea how he looked or how he might be changing. He lived in a unit composed of five cells on each of two tiers, all empty except for his. Sometimes he was hooded and required to stand in stress positions. Other times the guards or interrogators subjected him to harsh lights, or noxious odors were pumped into his cell.[3] His interrogators threatened him with execution. He was shackled to the floor and his wrists chained to his belly.

The guards shoved his meals through the bean hole in the door. Sometimes interrogators served his meals cold as part of the interrogation plan. Padilla sat on a metal bed with the tray balanced on his knees. There was no table in the cell. He always ate alone. He was never permitted to share a meal with another human being.

The bed was a raised steel plate attached to the concrete wall in his cell. There was no mattress or pillow. At random times, the jailers clanged the steel doors of the vacant cells open and shut. According to a therapist who interviewed him, Padilla underwent "forcible showering."[4] Padilla was required to submit to an intensively detailed procedure whenever he was permitted to shower. However, his lawyer, Andrew Patel, would not disclose the particulars, leaving it to our imagination.

Staff at the brig informed Padilla's attorney that his "temperament was so docile and inactive that his behavior was like that of 'a piece of furniture.'"[5] The brig's technical director, Sanford E. Seymour, testified at Padilla's competency hearing that he had twice seen Padilla weeping.[6]

After three and a half years in the brig, the administration removed Padilla to a federal prison in Miami, Florida. The government gave his lawyers copies of the tape from which the stills are taken. The lawyers used this tape, along with other evidence, to argue that Padilla had become unbalanced, if not unhinged, by being drastically deprived of sensory stimulation and human contact for such an extended period. As an example, when his mother encountered problems visiting him in the Miami federal prison, Padilla suggested that she write to President Bush for assistance.[7]

Padilla's lawyers had argued to the federal judge in Florida that because of his mistreatment while in the South Carolina brig, Padilla was no longer able to assist in his own defense. He was incompetent to stand trial due to mental instability, they asserted. The lawyers explained that Padilla did not trust them; after years of being utterly dependent on government authorities for every physical and mental need and comfort, and believing, perhaps on the suggestion of his interrogators, that he had been abandoned by his lawyer and family, he came to depend on and even sympathize with the people who fed, clothed, and minimally "cared" for him: the government and its interrogators.[8] The government responded to the lawyers' complaints that Padilla had come to identify with the government by arguing that Padilla was indeed competent to stand trial demonstrated by his ability to inform his attorneys of the cruel and inhumane treatment he received in the brig.

Jose Padilla may be an extremely bad guy. In fact, when officials arrested him on May 8, 2002, after he disembarked from a flight from Zurich at Chicago's O'Hare International Airport, the government considered him a great threat to our security. He was accused of planning to detonate a dirty bomb, which uses explosives to release nuclear material. (The extent of the damage depends on the type of radioactive material used and the skill employed in constructing the bomb.) At the time he was picked up, however, the government did not know whether he had the skill and wherewithal to produce the bomb. After his capture at O'Hare Airport, the administration moved Padilla to New York and held him as a material witness to a government investigation regarding 9/11. One month later, President Bush declared him an enemy combatant, and the government whisked him off to the naval brig.

During the years that Padilla was housed in the brig, he was never charged with a crime. He never had any kind of hearing before or while he was in the brig. In spring 2006, the government dropped the claim that Padilla had planned to detonate a dirty bomb. No explanation was given. Instead, the government accused him of plotting to blow up apartment buildings. The prosecution changed its position again in fall 2006, when it declined to pursue the apartment building accusation. Padilla was then moved to the criminal justice system in Florida, where he was finally, after nearly four years, charged with the amorphous crime of conspiracy: he was accused of being part of a North American cell that supported jihadist causes overseas.

This book is not only about Jose Padilla. The issues we face today are more far-reaching than one man's guilt or treatment. This book is about the Bush administration's manipulation of American and international law and its enormous human consequences. In detaining alleged terror suspects, the administration ripped apart the fabric we have respected for over two hundred years as the rule of law. Under the rule of law, we are governed by legitimate laws and not the dictates of leaders who ignore, manipulate, or even make up the law. Since September 11, 2001, we have abandoned our adherence to the rule of law and to our core values of due process and justice.

Due process sounds like a dry and boring term. It is not. It is vibrant and pulsating, a concept of justice and liberty. Due process ensures a defendant such essential rights as the right to a lawyer, to be informed of the charges against him, to confront the evidence and witnesses against him as well as to present witnesses and evidence on his own behalf, and to appear before a neutral decision maker. Due process defines who we are as a nation. Without it, America would not be the guardian of individual rights. When we are stripped of our right to due process, the government could mistakenly imprison any one of us without recourse.

No matter what we think about our nation's actions in the aftermath of 9/11, we should all know what responses our nation chose. We read and hear media catchphrases such as *waterboarding, dirty bomb, enemy combatant, extraordinary rendition, hunger strikers,* and *torture memos.* But these dark terms are only snapshots of what has changed since 9/11. They do not give the picture writ large.

This book lays out the big picture. It connects the dots from 9/11 to the present, documenting how our nation has betrayed and abandoned our founders' commitment to due process and the rule of law.

It did not have to be this way. We did not have to detain people here at home in the continental United States, in Guantanamo Bay, and in little-known and faraway CIA "black sites" around the world, denying them due process so as to protect our great and powerful nation. We did not have to abandon our grand legal system, a system that has contributed to making the United States the most esteemed nation in the world. We could have applied the rule of law to the people we have held since 9/11 and still protected ourselves and our nation from terrorists. We could have charged accused terrorists with specific federal crimes or with war crimes and provided them a fair and meaningful hearing on the accusations. It would not have been hard to do the right thing. After all, we had been doing the right thing for over two hundred years.

We have provided due process to terrorists and enemies in the past. We provided Nazi war criminals in World War II with lawfully constituted military tribunals and due process protections. We provided captured Vietnamese soldiers with minimum due process hearings, on the battlefield in Vietnam, to determine whether they were POWs pursuant to the Geneva Conventions. We provided similar due process combatant status hearings to captives in the Persian Gulf War. We provided a due process hearing to terrorist Timothy McVeigh, who blew up the Oklahoma Federal Building in April 1995, killing 168 Americans. If we had provided due process to the people we captured and held since 9/11, we would have, as in the past, preserved our integrity and honor. Instead, we abandoned values that we have carried with us throughout our more than two centuries of nationhood and that have made us proud to be Americans. We could have applied the rule of law to those we captured and treated those we detained with dignity and humanity.

This book is a narrative of the recent past. It is part law and legal analysis, part original investigation, and part account of the human condition. The investigations include observations and conversations with military officers and personnel during my visit to Guantanamo, interviews with over a dozen lawyers who represent detainees, and interviews with two fathers whose sons are forever entwined in the War on Terror. This narrative also includes the voices of the detainees. The book evokes the times, distills the events, and weaves together the circumstances on a seven-year journey to today. This moment in time—seven years of manipulation of the law, unlawful detentions, and violations of human rights—must be fully told. Much of what I recount has been skirted or not reported in the popular press. This book is a witness to history.

The people I describe have been largely invisible to us, but they were not invisible to their mothers or to their wives. They were not invisible to their children, their friends, or their communities. They were not invisible to the courageous lawyers who have stood up on their behalf. And after reading this book, they will no longer be invisible to you. The voices and stories in this book stand as a historical record and a chronicle for the future. This book speaks to the humanity in us all.

The narrative also recounts how a very few courageous lawyers first stood up to the government after 9/11, when no one else would. At that time, advocating for the detainees was unpopular and often considered unpatriotic. These gutsy lawyers who represented the first wave of enemy combatants—men described by the administration as "the worst of the worst"—received hundreds of pieces of hate mail, including death threats. Lawyers who worked in powerful firms suffered financial retribution for agreeing to represent detainees. Through sheer grit and persistence, this small band of lawyers convinced the Supreme Court to hear their cases on behalf of the detainees. And, in June 2004, these spirited lawyers did what few people expected: they convinced the justices to issue two historical rulings establishing that the detainees are entitled to the American right to a fair and meaningful hearing. This book is dedicated to those lawyers.

On the first day of my law school seminar on terrorism, I ask students to recall where they were on the morning of 9/11. It can get emotional. But we cannot fully understand why the Bush administration responded as it did in the War on Terror without recalling how we felt that morning, as the planes collided with the World Trade Towers in New York City and the Pentagon in Washington, D.C., killing almost three thousand people.

The Bush administration feared that America's safety and security were at high risk. So did we. We were all frightened that another attack was imminent. Where would it hit next, and could we possibly protect ourselves? Would a bridge be bombed, would our water system be poisoned, would a suicide bomber enter a restaurant where we were eating? Would anthrax come in the mail? Would our children and our grandchildren carry on in the world as we knew it?

Nevertheless, fear of loss and even death does not justify tossing aside the dedicated rights and protections for which the founders fought so fiercely over two hundred years ago. There is a balance between national security and individual freedom and liberty. That balance is expressed in our Constitution. Our Constitution has protected us throughout our nationhood. It is there to serve us today.

In spite of our due process heritage, there have been times during America's two-hundred-year history when our leaders have made mistakes and violated the Constitution. They have argued that they needed to violate the law to save the nation. Abraham Lincoln suspended habeas corpus in his fight to keep the nation unified, although under the Constitution only Congress can suspend this right.

In 1942, during World War II, President Franklin Delano Roosevelt, with the support of Congress, required 110,000 Japanese Americans to leave their homes and relocate to internment camps. We were at war with Japan, and the administration feared that Japanese Americans who were living on our western shores might act as saboteurs on behalf of Japan. A significant proportion of the Japanese Americans sent to the camps were American citizens. The U.S. Supreme Court upheld the actions of the president and the Congress. Later, we realized that we had been wrong.[9]

President Bush, in violating the civil liberties and human rights of American citizens and foreign nationals, argued that he was protecting the nation. However, he did not have to manipulate the law and at times even make up the law, disregarding human rights and liberties, to save our country. He could have provided fundamental due process protections to all prisoners under the Constitution and the Geneva Conventions. He could have held limited fair hearings to determine the status of the prisoners, as we did in Vietnam. We could then have freed those who were innocent.

As explained in part 1, those determined to be legitimate prisoners of war, known as "lawful combatants" under the Geneva Conventions, could be lawfully held to keep them from returning to the battlefield. Those determined to be "unlawful combatants," including spies and saboteurs, could be tried for war crimes in legitimately constituted military commissions. The administration introduced the category of *enemy combatants,* a classification that has never been recognized by the Geneva Conventions, as a way to circumvent the conventions and provide cover to mistreat and torture detainees.

Instead of holding Jose Padilla and others in the naval brig for years without charges and in violation of due process, the administration could have done what it did with other accused terrorists, such as John Walker Lindh, the American Taliban; Richard Reid, the shoe bomber; and Zacarias Moussaoui, at one time considered the twentieth hijacker. Although there are serious questions as to the military's treatment of Lindh when he was first captured—treatment that cannot be condoned[10]—ultimately these men were provided due process rights under the Constitution, including the assistance of competent counsel and fair and meaningful hearings. Lindh, Reid, and Moussaoui were given long prison sentences in a rule of law system. Ironically, even Jose Padilla—after nearly four years of sensory deprivation and torture in the naval brig without charges ever being filed—was finally removed to the criminal justice system in Florida federal court where he was charged, provided a due process trial, convicted of conspiracy, and sentenced to prison. This shows that the administration could have tried him under a rule of law system at the beginning of his detention.

The administration has argued that it had no choice but to move to the "dark side,"[11] because we were experiencing a "new kind of war."[12] National security justified extreme actions, the administration declared. However, was it really a new kind of war? People have argued that the War on Terror was not a war at all but rather a criminal action, more like the metaphorical war on drugs, and worthy of a criminal justice system response rather than a military response. But even as a new kind of war, the War on Terror does not give our nation's leaders permission to unilaterally ignore the Constitution, established rules of war, and international norms. No war should create a legal vacuum where the administration may define the law unto itself and permit cruel and inhumane actions.

There are five parts to this book. Part 1 looks at three major instances where the Bush administration manipulated, and at times even made up, the law. In each of these three critical arenas, the administration's underlying premises promoted policies that led to terrible human consequences. The three manipulations of law are:

1. Introducing the term *enemy combatant* for the express purpose of circumventing the Geneva Conventions and the U.S. Constitution
2. Justifying the use of harsh interrogations—a euphemism for torture—as an instrument of national policy
3. Asserting that the Constitution gives the executive absolute and unrestricted power as commander in chief to disregard Congress and the courts

The next three parts describe the terrible damage in the wake of the administration's manipulations of law: the lawless detentions and reckless abandonment of due process across venues in the continental United States, Guantanamo Bay, and foreign prisons or CIA black sites. Firsthand accounts identify the extent of the administration's cruel and gratuitous treatment of detainees. You may know parts of one story or another. But when you read these stories in their entirety, you will fully appreciate that we went too far.

Specifically, part 2 looks at lawless detentions in continental America. It focuses in depth on Jose Padilla's circumstances; on Yaser Hamdi, another American citizen; and on Ali al Marri, a lawful American resident. All three were accused of terrorism, classified as enemy combatants, and housed in the naval brig in Charleston, South Carolina. All three were held without charges and without access to lawyers or their families, while subjected to prolonged sensory deprivation and other cruel and inhumane treatment. At times they were tortured. This part also analyzes the preventive detention program for immigrants and material witnesses. The program was authorized by the administration immediately following the 9/11 attacks and focused nearly entirely on Arab and Muslim men. Somewhere between 1,500 and 2,000 men were detained, without charges and without due process, under a agenda whose guiding principle was "hold until cleared."

Part 3 probes in depth the lawless detentions at Guantanamo Bay naval base. This part reviews the chronology and treatment of the over eight hundred detainees for nearly seven years—from the time the first group of prisoners arrived on January 11, 2002, to fall 2008. The detainees and their lawyers have sought access to fair and meaningful hearings to challenge their detentions before neutral decision makers throughout these years. Twice the Supreme Court ruled in favor of the detainees and granted their requests for habeas hearings as provided by statute; both times the administration attempted to circumvent the rulings by enacting federal legislation. In December 2007, the Supreme Court heard the detainees' pleas for habeas hearings a third time. History was made on June 12, 2008. In a momentous 5–4 decision, the Court ruled that the enemy combatants held outside the continental United States in Guantanamo, Cuba, have not only a statutory right but a constitutional right to habeas.

Part 4 explores the extent of brutality and lawless detentions in prisons further away from America's shores—in countries such as Egypt, Syria, and Jordan and prisons in remote CIA black sites. Under a CIA-driven program known as extraordinary rendition, men considered high-value detainees were stripped, diapered, beaten, drugged, hooded, short-shackled, hauled onto planes, and flown to foreign, likely filthy, prisons to be tortured for intelligence information. Some of these men were captured by mistake but were still subjected to torture.

Part 5 describes a different approach. It examines the circumstances of nine individuals who were also accused of supporting terrorism since 9/11. However, these nine defendants were provided due process protections relatively soon after their arrests. Included in this part is a detailed account of John Walker Lindh, along with Richard Reid,

Zacarias Moussaoui, and the Lackawanna Six, characterized as an al Qaeda "sleeper cell" living in America. (People in a sleeper cell live their "ordinary lives" until they receive instructions to commit a terrorist act.) The successful prosecution of these nine people demonstrates that it would have been possible to apply the rule of law to all defendants caught up in our War on Terror, to imprison them if they are found guilty, and to keep our nation safe—without torture and without derogation of due process.

If more attorneys and others had stood up to the administration during these years since 9/11, this book would not have had to be written. Because we allowed our executive to act unlawfully, the disgraceful events described here came to pass. We must bear witness to what has happened to our great nation and our Constitution. We cannot repeat it.

Jose Padilla's first lawyer, Donna Newman, said it well: "Who wouldn't stand up? Who doesn't want to do the right thing? We believe in the system, we were fighting for the system."[13] Unfortunately, she spoke for a very tiny segment of the legal profession.[14]

PART ONE

MANIPULATING THE LAW

IN THREE MAJOR AREAS DESCRIBED IN THIS PART, the Bush administration manipulated the Constitution, federal statutes, and international laws and treaties. In some instances, it even appears that the administration made up the law. However, whether it manipulated the law or made it up, the result was the same. The administration's cynical attitude toward the rule of law led to policies that had terrible human consequences.

INTRODUCING THE TERM *ENEMY COMBATANT*

After 9/11, for the first time in American history, the government placed two American citizens, Yaser Hamdi and Jose Padilla, and a lawful American resident, Ali al Marri, in isolation, keeping them incommunicado for nearly three years in a naval brig, subjecting them to prolonged sensory deprivation and torture, and holding them without charges, without a hearing, and without access to a lawyer. The administration's justification for the treatment of these American citizens and a lawful resident—in violation of due process and the Constitution—was that these men, just like the men held in Guantanamo, were "enemy combatants" in the War on Terror.

Enemy combatant sounds like a legal term, but it is not. *Enemy combatant* has no meaning in international law. The term did not meaningfully exist in American law before the administration introduced it in spring 2002 as a descriptor of the men captured after September 11, 2001. Until then, the universe of combatants, as recognized by the Geneva Conventions and international law, consisted of two categories: lawful combatants—those entitled to prisoner of war (POW) status—and unlawful combatants, who were not so entitled. That is all.

Since 9/11, the term *enemy combatant* has become part of our American lexicon. And because the administration and the media have repeated this term so often, it has gained a life of its own. Thus, what began as a generic term describing someone who fights for the other side or a synonym for the legally recognized term *unlawful combatant*[1] has been used to circumvent the Geneva Conventions and the rule of law. *Enemy combatant* is a weasel term,[2] introduced by the administration to manipulate the law.

Of course, one could say that the administration was acting not like a weasel but like a fox in introducing a new term as a substitute for the legitimate terms *lawful combatant* and *unlawful combatant*. Certainly, the administration would argue that national security required bold moves to save the nation, and we could not have interrogated the captives as harshly as we needed to obtain necessary intelligence if we had continued to use the established terminology. However, the United States has always taken pride in adhering to the rule of law. Nations around the world looked to us to take the high moral ground when it came to the treatment of others. Either we are a nation of laws or we are a nation of men and women. If we are to be a nation of laws, we must follow the rule of law consistently and not abandon it when times get tough.

The United States is a signatory to the Geneva Conventions (GC), the humanitarian law that protects combatants. The conventions were designed to create a legal framework for the humane treatment of all combatants. The conventions lay the foundations for the laws of war. The Third Geneva Convention (GC3) sets out the rights and protections of what are universally recognized as lawful combatants, or prisoners of war (POWs). While on the battlefield, lawful combatants may kill and be killed. A nation may not prosecute or punish a lawful combatant for a lawful act of war. However, a nation may prosecute and convict a lawful combatant who commits a war crime, such as rape, provided the combatant receives a fair trial.[3]

The Fourth Geneva Convention sets out the rights and protections of "civilians," a term of art that describes combatants who are not lawful combatants and thus by default would be unlawful combatants. The term *unlawful combatant* does not appear in the GC but is widely understood as covering all combatants who are not lawful combatants. Unlawful combatants are not authorized to be on the battlefield. An example of an unlawful combatant is a spy or saboteur. This category also includes civilians who have taken a direct part in hostilities on their own without being integrated into the regular armed forces or into militias or volunteer corps that meet the requirements for POWs. Guerrillas, insurgents, terrorists, or members of a terrorist group in a war zone would be considered unlawful combatants under this definition,[4] although the administration could choose to treat them as criminals and prosecute them in the criminal justice system. Unlawful combatants enjoy fewer protections than do lawful combatants (POWs). But they, like lawful combatants, must be treated humanely.

According to GC3, a member of a nation's armed forces is a lawful combatant and would be considered a prisoner of war if captured. Thus, a U.S. soldier who is captured on the battlefield during war would be a lawful combatant, or POW. Similarly, a member of the armed forces of any other nation, such as Germany, Japan, China, Vietnam, Iran, and Iraq, would be a lawful combatant.

Prisoner of war is the favored status for detainees. Nations are required to treat prisoners of war with care. POWs are not required to reveal more than their name, rank, serial number, and date of birth. They have the right to be quartered in accommodations equal to those of the detaining nation's armed forces and to be provided with sufficient food, water, and clothing. They are also permitted to retain articles of personal use and to receive medical care and access to mail, among other things. We Americans would expect, even demand, that any of our soldiers who are captured be treated as POWs.

We could assume that a Taliban soldier who was a member of the armed forces of Afghanistan would also be a lawful combatant. In fact, immediately following 9/11, Secretary of State Colin Powell and members of the State Department urged the administration to treat Taliban soldiers as lawful combatants and, accordingly, prisoners of war.[5] However, President Bush took his cues from other members of the administration, including the Department of Justice and the Office of the Vice President, and initially designated Taliban soldiers as unlawful combatants.[6]

The reasoning the administration used in claiming that the Taliban soldiers did not qualify as lawful combatants was based on a reading of Article 4 of the Third Geneva Convention. The third convention defines who is a lawful combatant or prisoner of war. It reads, in essential part, as follows:

A. Prisoners of war, in the sense of the present Convention, are persons belonging to one of the following categories, who have fallen into the power of the enemy:

    (1) Members of the armed forces of a Party to the conflict as well as members of militias or volunteer corps forming part of such armed forces.

(2) Members of other militias and members of other volunteer corps, including those of organized resistance movements, belonging to a Party to the conflict and operating in or outside their own territory, even if this territory is occupied, provided that such militias or volunteer corps, including such organized resistance movements, fulfill the following conditions:

   (a) That of being commanded by a person responsible for his subordinates;
   (b) That of having a fixed distinctive sign recognizable at a distance;
   (c) That of carrying arms openly;
   (d) That of conducting their operations in accordance with the laws and customs of war.[7]

A reading of the first paragraph of Article 4 indicates that prisoners of war are "persons belonging to one of the following categories," and includes members of the armed forces, such as the Taliban who fought for Afghanistan. However, the administration has argued that for someone to qualify as a lawful combatant he must qualify under both parts (1) and (2). But, as one can see, there is no conjunction—there is no *and*—between (1) and (2), and the first paragraph says quite clearly "one of the following categories."

A reading of the next paragraph indicates that members of a militia or other volunteer corps, including organized resistance movements, who are not formally members of a nation's armed forces may also qualify as lawful combatants if they fulfill certain additional legal requirements: being commanded by a person responsible for subordinates, having a fixed distinctive sign identifying them as combatants, carrying arms openly, and conducting their operations in accordance with the laws and customs of war.

Historical context and treaty language appear to support the view that members of the regular armed forces are entitled to protection without regard to the four criteria. However, the position has not been unanimous. International law commentators, scholars, and governments have at times disagreed as to whether members of the armed forces, by virtue of being members of the armed forces, are POWs as defined by subsection (1) or whether they must also meet all four of the criteria under subsection (2).[8] Unfortunately, countries change their stance when it serves their interests.

Because it suited its position, the Bush administration argued that the requirement of meeting these four additional requirements was a necessary part of the definition of lawful combatant and that Taliban and al Qaeda combatants did not meet all four of these elements. The administration pointed particularly to (b), arguing that Taliban and al Qaeda combatants did not have a fixed distinctive sign recognizable at a distance. That is, they did not wear uniforms, and their turbans were not unique to the combatants because all men in the country wore turbans. The administration also contended that the combatants, particularly the al Qaeda soldiers, did not meet requirement (d), conducting their operations in accordance with laws and customs.

Designating the Taliban as unlawful combatants could have been a reasoned legal position, since people disagree on how GC3 should be interpreted and whether the four additional conditions apply. But months later, the administration went much further, entering territory where there was no law to support its position. With no official notification or explanation, the administration substituted the term *enemy combatants* for *unlawful combatants* as a descriptor of the detainees at Guantanamo Bay. Beyond the fact that the term *enemy combatant* was not a recognized legal term, the administration never officially acknowledged the inconsistency between its initial designation of the captives as unlawful combatants and its subsequent designation of the same captives as enemy combatants.

As unlawful combatants, the Taliban would still have recognized protections under the GC. But in classifying them as enemy combatants, the administration intended that these men be put outside the reach of the GC. Consequently, any protections the administration gave them would be by largesse alone and not guaranteed under the GC.

Unlike Taliban soldiers, members of al Qaeda are not the armed forces of any country. Accordingly, many scholars who interpret the GC characterize al Qaeda members as unlawful combatants without even reviewing the four other conditions. Of course, al Qaeda members who land on our shores could also be tried as common criminals.[9] Initially, President Bush declared that al Qaeda members were comparable to Taliban soldiers and would be designated unlawful combatants.[10] A few months later, the administration reclassified al Qaeda members as enemy combatants, like the Taliban.

Under Article 5 of the Third Geneva Convention (GC3), if there is doubt as to whether a combatant qualifies as a lawful combatant, the person must be treated as a lawful combatant and POW until a competent tribunal determines his status.[11] President Bush declared that there was no doubt as to the status of either the Taliban soldiers or the al Qaeda members. Hence there was no need for a hearing to determine whether the detainees qualified as POWs or even as unlawful combatants. Instead, they were all designated as enemy combatants.[12] Accordingly, although we held Article 5 hearings during the Vietnam War and the Persian Gulf War, the administration never held hearings pursuant to GC3 Article 5 when it captured combatants, including Taliban soldiers, in Afghanistan.[13]

Lawful and unlawful combatants constitute the universe of combatants. There is nothing else.[14] There are no black holes. *Enemy combatant* has never existed as a legal term in international law. The term has no legal meaning under the Geneva Conventions. The International Committee of the Red Cross (ICRC), the protective body and foremost interpreter of the GC, wrote that the GC apply to all the detainees "regardless of how such persons are called."[15]

Under the GC, a nation may hold both lawful defendants and unlawful defendants until hostilities have ended. The logic behind this requirement is that the country wants to be certain that the combatants do not return to the battlefield. Thus, had the administration followed the rule of law and adhered to the GC—whether it classified the detainees as lawful or unlawful combatants—the administration could have held all of them until the end of the War on Terror.[16] It is uncertain when the war will end, but the administration was certainly entitled to hold the detainees during ongoing combat operations and hostilities.

The administration also hoped to avoid the application of Common Article 3 (CA3) of the GC. The article is called a common article because it is common to all four Geneva Conventions. CA3 requires that all detainees be treated humanely. Outrages upon personal dignity, cruel, humiliating, and degrading treatment, and of course, torture are forbidden by CA3. The Supreme Court recognized the critical importance of applying, at minimum, CA3 to all detainees, when it ruled in 2006 that the minimum protections of CA3 applied to al Qaeda fighters.[17] CA3 also requires a due process trial and sentencing by a "regularly constituted court affording all the judicial guarantees which are recognized as indispensable by civilized peoples."

In manipulating or even making up the law by introducing the term *enemy combatant,* the administration intended not only to circumvent the GC and thereby mistreat detainees without legal consequences. High officials in the administration had a more personal motivation: powerful administration officials believed that denying that the detainees were protected by the GC would shield them from liability should future prosecutors charge them with war crimes. That is, the officials figured that if there was no law to protect the detainees, mistreating them would not be a violation of law. In an in-house memorandum, Attorney General John Ashcroft wrote: "[A] Presidential determination against treaty applicability [i.e., that the Geneva Conventions did not apply to the detainees] would provide the highest assurance that no court would subsequently entertain charges that American military officers, intelligence officials, or law enforcement officials violated Geneva Convention rules relating to field conduct, detention conduct or interrogation of detainees."[18]

On January 25, 2002, Alberto Gonzales, the White House counsel at the time, wrote a similarly self-serving statement to the president regarding the protection of administration officials: "The consequences of a decision to adhere to what I understand to be your earlier determination that the GC3 does not apply to the Taliban . . . substantially reduces the threat of domestic criminal prosecution under the War Crimes Act."[19] Gonzales explained that some language in the conventions, such as "outrages upon personal dignity" and "inhuman treatment," was "undefined . . . and it is difficult to predict with confidence what actions might be deemed to constitute violations of the relevant provisions of GC3." He was further concerned that "it is difficult to predict the motives of prosecutors and independent counsels who may in the future decide to pursue unwarranted charges based on Section 2441 [the War Crimes Act, which made it a crime to treat detainees inhumanely or commit an outrage upon personal dignity]. Your determination [that GC3 does not apply] would create a reasonable basis in law that Section 2441 does not apply, which would provide a solid defense to any future prosecution."[20]

Gonzales's fear was well justified. After the Supreme Court ruled in 2006 in *Hamdan v. Rumsfeld* that Common Article 3 applied to the treatment of detainees,[21] Gonzales contacted Republican lawmakers. He asked them to pass legislation that would shield U.S. personnel from detainee lawsuits and other possible prosecutions that might seek to enforce Common Article 3 violations through the federal War Crimes Act.[22] The Military Commissions Act of 2006 included a provision, drafted by the administration, that retroactively protects American officials from prosecution under the War Crimes Act for any crimes they may have committed after 9/11, including certain "cruel, inhuman or degrading treatment" that might have been a crime under the earlier version of the War Crimes Act.[23]

The first time that the term *enemy combatant* officially appeared in a government document was in the February 2002 federal district court decision in *Coalition of Clergy v. Bush*.[24] In dismissing the habeas petition, Judge Matz described the detainees as "aliens" and "enemy combatants."[25] It is not apparent where Judge Matz found the term *enemy combatant* to use in his opinion, or why he used it. A search of the documents filed in the case failed to reveal any document that used this term to describe the detainees. Erwin Chemerinsky, the lawyer for the Coalition of Clergy, does not recall that the government attorneys ever used the term during legal arguments. During the oral arguments, the government described the detainees as "enemy aliens," but not as enemy combatants. Perhaps the judge's clerks or even the judge himself had independently decided to use the term, since it was present in the zeitgeist at that time, including in the local popular press.[26]

That spring, administration officials began describing all captives and detainees as enemy combatants. The media embraced the term without question. From the time the administration first used the term *enemy combatant* in spring 2002 until fall 2006, the term was a moving target. The Department of Defense and the administration strapped disparate, even inconsistent, definitions to the term depending on litigation strategies and other executive requirements.[27] The administration gave it one definition in arguing a case to the Supreme Court, another when defining the men in Guantanamo, and a third when arguing a later case before the Supreme Court. During these first four years of use, Congress never legally sanctioned the term.

The term *enemy combatant* did not receive congressional legislative recognition until October 2006, when Congress enacted the Military Commissions Act. In the act, Congress pasted the words *lawful* and *unlawful* to the term *enemy combatant,* as in "lawful enemy combatant" and "unlawful enemy combatant."[28] Nevertheless, the term *enemy combatant* continues to haunt these times. The congressional definitions are not equivalent to the internationally recognized terms—*lawful combatant* and *unlawful combatant*—that are defined by the Geneva Conventions and accepted and valued by the international community.

JUSTIFYING HARSH INTERROGATIONS AND TORTURE

The Fifth Amendment to the Constitution provides that the government may not deprive a person of liberty without due process of law. *Liberty* is a key term here. The government may not divest an individual of his or her liberty without first affording that person a fair hearing before an impartial judge. In other words, the government must prove its accusations before punishing the defendant.

The right to liberty also appears in another context. If the government engages in behavior toward an individual that "shocks the conscience," it has violated that individual's liberty. The 1952 case *Rochin v. California* sets the standard. After breaking into a man's bedroom, three Los Angeles sheriff deputies found the partly dressed man sitting on his bed, his wife lying beside him. The deputies spied two capsules on a nightstand. When they asked what the capsules were, the man put them in his mouth. The officers jumped on him and attempted to extract the capsules. When that did not work, they handcuffed him and took him to a hospital. At the direction of one of the officers, a doctor forced an emetic solution through a tube into the man's stomach. The man vomited up the capsules, which contained morphine.[29] The Supreme Court ruled that the means the deputies used to extract the capsules from the defendant "shocks the conscience" and is "bound to offend even hardened sensibilities." The Court described the sheriff deputies' behavior as "close to the rack and screw" and indicated that it is "offensive to human dignity." In noting that the "Constitution is intended to preserve practical and substantial rights, not to maintain theories," Justice Frankfurter concluded that the officers' conduct clearly violated due process of law. That U.S. Supreme Court decision over fifty years ago reflected what we, as Americans, have always believed: we care how we treat others, even bad people.

The Eighth Amendment to the Constitution forbids cruel and unusual punishment. Beheading or quartering a defendant would be both cruel and unusual. The Supreme Court has banned the execution of juveniles and the execution of the mentally retarded because nearly all civilized nations in the world have banned the execution of such individuals, and hence it would be cruel and unusual. Another meaning of *cruel and unusual* is that the "punishment should fit the crime." The Supreme Court has banned the death penalty for rape, ruling that the penalty is not proportional to the crime.

While housed in the naval brig in Charleston, South Carolina, Jose Padilla, along with American citizen Yaser Hamdi and legal resident Ali al Marri, was subjected to prolonged sensory deprivation and profound long-term isolation, hooded, short-shackled, and kept in stress positions for lengthy periods, deprived of sunlight for months, and observed by cameras around the clock. This treatment violates the

Fifth Amendment due process clause because it shocks the conscience of most individuals. It also amounts to cruel and unusual punishment under the Eighth Amendment, although the Eighth Amendment applies to punishment *after* conviction, and these detainees were not charged, much less tried and convicted, before being subjected to this abusive behavior.

In 1984, the U.S. government signed and ratified the Convention against Torture and Other Cruel, Inhuman, or Degrading Treatment or Punishment (CAT).[30] This treaty makes no distinction between torture and cruel, inhuman, and degrading treatment. However, when President Reagan signed the treaty, he reserved the right to interpret the section on cruel, inhuman, and degrading treatment in light of the prohibitions in the Constitution, particularly the Fifth and Eighth Amendments.[31] As a result of the reservation, the government can now make, and has made, the argument that in the United States' interpretation of the law, there is a difference between torture and cruel, inhuman, and degrading treatment. Consequently, although torture is always expressly forbidden both by the CAT treaty and by federal statutes enacted pursuant to the treaty, not all cruel, inhuman, and degrading treatment is unlawful and expressly forbidden under American law. Only cruel, inhuman, and degrading treatment that violates the Fifth Amendment (treatment that shocks the conscience) or the Eighth Amendment (cruel and unusual punishment) is in violation of the treaty as understood by American law.[32] The Bush administration pounced on this distinction, stretching it to irrational limits.

In addition, the federal laws enacted pursuant to the treaty that make it a crime for Americans to torture someone outside the country do not refer to cruel, inhuman, and degrading treatment; they only prohibit torture.[33] The administration thus asserts that since the statute only bars torture and says nothing about cruel, inhumane, and degrading treatment, American agents—such as the CIA—are not necessarily bound by any laws other than the requirement not to torture. Since the definition of torture is malleable, CIA agents have had lots of room to mistreat a detainee. The administration argued that although it conducted harsh, or "enhanced," interrogations, these interrogations did not constitute torture.

Moreover, since there is no clear test for what constitutes "shocking the conscience," a case-by-case determination is required. Thus, when someone accuses the administration of cruel, inhuman, and degrading treatment, the administration can respond that its conduct does not shock the conscience—especially when it is dealing with the "worst of the worst." That is, what shocks the conscience for an average detainee does not necessarily do so when the detainee is a terrorist. Shocking the conscience becomes a relative test.

Immediately after September 11, 2001, the administration was intent on securing the nation from further attack and, in the process, catching and disarming terrorists. But when the military seized suspected terrorists and others, the administration had no specific policies in place as to how to effectively interrogate the captives. Instead, they looked elsewhere for assistance.

A program created by the air force and funded by the Pentagon at the end of the Korean War taught pilots how to withstand torture if captured. It was known as SERE, an acronym for Survival, Evasion, Resistance and Escape.[34] The government expanded the program to the army and navy after the Vietnam War. Following the attacks of 9/11, psychologists who were familiar with SERE "sought to reverse-engineer" the program.[35] That is, rather than teaching how to defend against these techniques, the new training program was designed to apply these harsh techniques to detainees. The psychologists trained interrogators in the SERE techniques, who then applied the techniques in Guantanamo.[36] The administration also looked to countries like Egypt and Syria for advice on harsh interrogation techniques.

The Torture Memos

The issue of how to interrogate for intelligence information had come to a head on March 28, 2002, when the administration caught Abu Zubaydah, believed to be a senior lieutenant to Bin Laden, in Pakistan.[37] The administration considered Zubaydah a pipeline to al Qaeda, and the CIA intended to mine him for as much intelligence as they could gather. The administration was considering interrogation techniques that might be regarded as torture. To protect its personnel from engaging in unlawful practices, the administration asked the Department of Justice to identify permissible interrogation techniques and to authorize the interrogators' conduct.[38]

Lawyers in the Office of Legal Counsel (OLC) in the Department of Justice drafted memoranda that officially justified and approved torture techniques. Military lawyers signed off on a list of acceptable harsh or enhanced interrogation techniques, many of which could be interpreted as not only cruel and inhumane but torture.

The interrogation techniques authorized by the DOD included prolonged interrogations (up to twenty hours a day); prolonged standing; sleep deprivation (allowing a detainee to rest briefly then repeatedly awakening him for up to four days in succession); stomach slaps; face slaps; use of dogs and other "aversions" to create increasing anxiety;[39] placement of a hood over the detainee's head during questioning; and holding a detainee in isolation for up to thirty days.[40] The OLC narrowly defined torture to permit an additional range of undisclosed practices, including waterboarding.

John Yoo, a University of California Berkeley law professor, was the deputy assistant general in the DOJ's Office of Legal Counsel immediately following September 11. In response to a request from Alberto Gonzales, counsel to the president, and other administration officials, Yoo drafted a letter and a memorandum that narrowly defined torture as rising to the level of organ failure or death under U.S. law[41] and international law pursuant to the CAT treaty. In essence, the letter and memo were designed to provide official and legal authority for the CIA to conduct harsh interrogations, even torture of detainees. John Yoo signed the letter. His supervisor, Jay Bybee, signed the memorandum. Both were dated August 1, 2002. Yoo also drafted and signed a second memorandum, written to William J. Haynes, the general counsel of the Department of Defense. This memo, dated March 14, 2003, was designed to provide the military with legal authority similar to that provided in the earlier documents for the CIA.[42]

The OLC is the legal arm of the Department of Justice. Lawyers in the OLC provide legal opinions for the attorney general, the president, and necessarily, the nation. The opinions can be canceled or terminated only by the president, the attorney general, or the OLC itself. Consequently, the two memos provided exactly the kind of legal cover and powerful defense that the military and the CIA required. If ever the interrogators or their superiors were prosecuted for violating federal laws in torturing or otherwise harshly treating detainees, they could argue that they were adhering to the law of torture as defined and explained by their counsel, the OLC.

These documents have become known as the "torture memos." (Yoo and others may have written additional memoranda on torture that have not yet surfaced.) The torture memos are so named because their most egregious statements give license to torture in nearly every circumstance. Torture is defined in the August 1 memo as "the level that would ordinarily be associated with a sufficiently serious physical condition or injury such as death, organ failure, or serious impairment of body functions."[43] Anything less is not torture. The March 14 memo has similar language.

The torture memos further argue that as long as the interrogator's specific intent is not to torture, the torturer does not violate U.S. laws or treaties. "Thus," the August 1 memo reads, "even if the defendant knows that severe pain will result from his actions, if causing such harm is not his objective, he lacks the requisite specific intent even though the defendant did not act in good faith. Instead, a defendant is guilty of torture only if he acts with the express purpose of inflicting severe pain or suffering on a person within his custody or physical control."[44] Under this extraordinary interpretation, torture as a by-product of the act of gathering intelligence is not actually torture. Only torture for its own sake would be forbidden. The March 14 memo has similar language.[45]

Yoo also wrote in the March 14 memo that the torture statute "does not preclude any and all use of drugs." He argued that mind-altering substances that do not "rise to the level of 'disrupting profoundly the senses or personality'" would not be precluded by interrogators unless the drugs or procedures "produce an extreme effect."[46] Over the years, detainees in Guantanamo have claimed that they were injected with drugs before interrogations. The military has denied these claims.[47]

The torture memos were approved by the Department of Justice, lawyers from the National Security Council, key congressional leaders, and CIA director George Tenet, who authorized the interrogation methods used by his agents.[48] The August 1 memo was in effect for nearly two years. The March 14 memo lasted a little over a year. On June 30, 2004, the new head of the Office of Legal Counsel, Jack Goldsmith, now a Harvard law professor, withdrew the memoranda as vastly overreaching in their analyses of the law. However, in condemning the memos, Goldsmith did not condemn the types of treatment used by the interrogators. The interrogation tactics continued.

On December 30, 2004, acting assistant attorney general Daniel Levin quietly posted a revised memo on the administration's website.[49] The new memorandum rejected torture. However, it included a footnote indicating that the CIA's previous actions were not illegal, thereby assuring the interrogators that their previous, and even present, conduct would continue to be protected.[50] A few weeks before the new memo was posted, the president had appointed Alberto Gonzales, formerly the president's legal counsel, to replace John Ashcroft as attorney general. Gonzales was scheduled to appear before the Senate Judiciary Committee, which was to consider his appointment. The administration did not want the torture memo to be a point of contention in the confirmation hearings.

However, after Gonzales was confirmed as attorney general, the Department of Justice (DOJ) replaced the Yoo and Bybee letter and memorandum with a memorandum that endorsed an expanded version of the CIA's harsh treatment of detainees. The new memorandum "provided explicit authorization to barrage terror suspects with a combination of painful physical and psychological tactics, including head-slapping, simulated drowning and frigid temperatures." Later in 2005, the DOJ issued a second memorandum.[51] This second memo declared that none of the methods used by the CIA violated "cruel, inhumane and degrading treatment," the standard that was outlawed by international laws and treaties, including the Geneva Conventions, the Convention against Torture, and the International Covenant on Civil and Political Rights, as well as the McCain Amendment to the Detainee Treatment Act of 2005.[52]

Steven G. Bradbury, who was acting chief of the Office of Legal Counsel at the DOJ from summer 2005 through spring 2008, signed the memoranda. As the *New York Times* pointed out, "Never in history had the United States authorized such tactics."[53] One question that concerned interrogators was whether the approved techniques could be combined, since even approved techniques had such a "painful, multiplying effect when combined that they might cross the legal line."[54] Although we will not know until the administration releases these memoranda, it is not unlikely that, given the interrogators' concern, combining approved techniques may have been an acceptable practice.

In testimony before a House subcommittee in February 2008, Bradbury reiterated that pain needed to be both severe and long-lasting to be considered torture. "Something can be quite distressing, uncomfortable, even frightening," but "if it doesn't involve severe physical pain, and it doesn't last very long, it may not constitute severe physical suffering. That would be the analysis."[55]

As of June 2008, the two Bradbury memoranda were still in effect and had been confirmed by several recent memoranda. Over the years following the disclosure of the first torture memos, President Bush has repeatedly proclaimed that we do not torture.[56] In addition, the administration has announced that it has suspended or discontinued the most severe or extraordinary interrogation techniques.[57] Such statements by President Bush and the administration are in profound conflict with these two recently disclosed memoranda, as well as all the earlier torture memos.

Is Torture Ever Justified?

Although the CAT treaty specifies that no "exceptional circumstances whatsoever," including a state of war or any other public emergency, may be invoked as a justification for torture,[58] the administration has argued that there may be times when "harsh interrogations" save lives. During his administration, President Bush has alluded to circumstances where American lives have been saved by the capture and harsh interrogation of high-level detainees. However, he has not provided the public with any fact-based account of potentially violent acts halted as a result of harsh interrogation by American agents. The administration argued that it would not reveal intelligence information because it was classified. Certainly, the government should not reveal classified information, but classified information consists of the sources and the methods used to obtain the information. The events themselves are over. The administration could and should reveal what might have happened if we had not captured the terrorists. However, the Bush administration has kept such information, to the extent it exists, secret.

Advocates for torture in limited circumstances point to the superficially persuasive "ticking-time-bomb" scenario in support of their position that torture is sometimes necessary in the modern state: the police capture a suspected terrorist who allegedly knows of a bomb about to go off in Manhattan. At minimum, the advocates argue, we must be permitted to torture him to save thousands of lives. That trade-off in lives seems compelling, and many people are convinced. However, there are much larger and more fundamental issues at stake. We are not talking about whether we as individuals will torture; we are talking about state-sanctioned torture. If our child was kidnapped and we had the kidnapper in hand, many of us would do whatever is necessary to find our child and return her home safely. In the ticking-time-bomb scenario, more than one child is at stake. But unlike the parent who acts individually, the ticking-time-bomb example requires the participation of state actors. The question then is, Who will be the state actors and who will give them permission? Will there be specially trained interrogators supervised in a chain of command? Perhaps something like a "torture police" squad? And who will monitor the torture to ensure that the policy is implemented "fairly"?[59]

Other problems arise when torture is sanctioned by the state. Undoubtedly, some people reveal genuine information when they are tortured. It is equally true that many people will say anything to stop the torture. Torturers know to go slowly, to give the victim time to feel the torture before he passes out from the pain. As the torture progresses, the victim tends to break down. Ironically, the longer it takes to obtain the information, the less immediate the ticking-time-bomb scenario becomes.

Professor Alan Dershowitz at Harvard argues for "torture warrants": If we are holding a suspected terrorist, the police apply to the local judge for a torture warrant, similar to the police applying to a local judge for a search warrant. If the judge does not issue the torture warrant, the police officer is not lawfully permitted to torture. Dershowitz's argument is that, as with search warrants, this procedure brings the rule of law into play so that the torture is not done outside the system. However, in his scenario you still have the situation where the state is sanctioning torture through its judges.

Moreover, judges may not provide an adequate defense against unnecessary torture. Even if the judge is uncomfortable with the situation, what judge wants to be the one who did not "save the nation" because he or she refused to issue a warrant? Judges tend to trust the police and the policy makers, since the police and policy makers have access to the critical evidence necessary to make these decisions. Even if one concludes that torture is sometimes necessary, will judges provide an unyielding line of protection to guarantee that torture is not applied to the wrong person? In addition, to legitimately torture someone, we must pass legislation that authorizes torture. And the legislation must be able to withstand challenges of being in violation of the Fifth Amendment (due process, right to liberty) and the Eighth Amendment (cruel and unusual punishment). Finally, are we prepared to say that in the United States, a country that espouses freedom and liberty, torture is no longer considered morally wrong?

The key issue that underlies these questions is this: have we reached a point in our evolution where it is legitimate to torture suspected terrorists in the belief that we are saving civilized society? We are not merely talking about one person who holds the code to a bomb. As soon as we permit him to be tortured, we open the door to a slightly different scenario where torture may again seem acceptable. Ultimately, civilized society declines in direct relation to the ascendancy of torture.

ASSERTING ABSOLUTE POWER
AS COMMANDER IN CHIEF

John Yoo and others in the administration, at the urging of top policy makers, asserted in the torture memos the absolute, unrestricted, unlimited powers of the executive, in his role as commander in chief, to torture if necessary. In justifying the administration's power to authorize torture when necessary, John Yoo operated on a principle that is fundamental to the theory of government espoused by the Bush-Cheney administration: unlimited and unconstrained executive power. This theory of executive power served the administration well in validating its actions post 9/11, underlying John Yoo's definition of torture in the torture memos. In his memos, John Yoo promoted the administration's core belief that the executive branch is first among equals when it comes to separation of powers. In his view, the other two branches of government, Congress and the judiciary, must defer to the executive, especially in times of war. In that vein, Yoo wrote, any effort by Congress to apply U.S. laws that prohibit torture and inhuman treatment "in a manner that interferes with the President's direction of such core war matters as the detention and interrogation of enemy combatants would be unconstitutional."[60]

In fact, both the August 1 and March 14 memos assert that "Congress may no more regulate the President's ability to detain and interrogate enemy combatants than it may regulate his ability to direct troop movements on the battlefield."[61] The March 14 memo added, "Even if an interrogation method arguably were to violate a criminal statute, the Justice Department could not bring a prosecution because the statute would be unconstitutional" in its application to the executive.[62] It is believed that David Addington, Vice President Dick Cheney's close associate and chief of staff, collaborated with Yoo on the August 1 memo.[63] Cheney was the architect of the administration's executive power theory.

To many constitutional scholars, Yoo and others who worked with him on the memo were overreaching, providing an extreme view and an incorrect analysis of presidential power. In fact, as constitutional scholars understand, Congress has many more wartime powers, enumerated in the Constitution, than the president. Congress alone has the power to declare war. Congress is authorized to raise, support, and maintain the army and navy. The president would be helpless to command his military without monies from Congress. In addition, Yoo's theory of the unitary power of the executive has no foundation in the Constitution or in any Supreme Court decision. In fact, the opposite is true: the Supreme Court has issued decisions that hold against his position. But Yoo's memos ignore those decisions in trying to create law and analysis consistent with the administration's overriding belief in executive power and executive privilege.

Indeed, the torture memos are not the only instances where the administration has asserted the supremacy of the executive. Although many other instances are not directly related to the War on Terror, they nevertheless reflect the administration's pervasive belief that it has the power to do whatever it wants without interference from the courts or Congress, a belief that has informed the administration's actions throughout its tenure, including the War on Terror. An example related to the War on Terror is the president's belief that he has the executive authority to eavesdrop on the telephone calls and e-mails of American citizens inside the United States without obtaining court-approved search warrants, the usual process required under federal statutes and the Fourth Amendment.[64] Prior to the attacks on 9/11, federal agencies were required to obtain warrants from a specialized and historically secret Foreign Intelligence Surveillance Court, created under the 1978 Foreign Intelligence Surveillance Act (FISA), before conducting domestic surveillance.[65] However, in 2002, President Bush signed a secret order permitting the National Security Agency to monitor the international phone calls and e-mails of people, including American citizens, inside the United States without the required warrants. The Bush administration argued that it needed to act quickly to monitor threats to the safety of the United States and did not have time to obtain the search warrants.[66] The administration also believed it had the inherent authority to conduct such warrantless surveillance without interference by Congress.

Another example of executive supremacy occurred when bills were sent to the White House. President Bush often drafted a "signing statement" to accompany his signing of the bills. The statements provided his interpretation of the legislation and, to the extent that he believed the legislation interfered with his interpretation of the president's powers or violated the Constitution, he offered understandings, reservations, and even challenges indicating that he might refuse to execute or enforce some provisions of the legislation. However, the president's job is to execute the law. If he does not like the legislation, he is given the power to veto it. He is not given the power under the Constitution to refuse to enforce the law. A highly publicized example occurred in 2005, when Bush signed the McCain Amendment banning cruel, inhumane, and degrading treatment of detainees but reserved the right to ignore the ban under his power as commander in chief.

The strategy of attaching signing statements was devised by current Supreme Court justice Samuel Alito when he was deputy assistant attorney general in the Office of Legal Counsel under President Reagan.[67] However, President George W. Bush has provided more signing statements than all previous presidents combined.[68] As of January 2008, President Bush has issued 157 signing statements.[69]

Similarly, the Bush administration severely cut back on Bill Clinton's policies of open government and release of documents to the public. Attorney General John Ashcroft reversed the policy of the Clinton administration by impeding the release of information under the Freedom of Information Act. The new policy directed federal agencies that disclosure "should be made only after full and deliberate consideration of the institutional, commercial and personal privacy interests that could be implicated by disclosure of the information."[70] This policy superseded a presumption of disclosure policy established by his predecessor, Janet Reno.[71] Whereas Reno required federal agencies to justify withholding documents from the public, Ashcroft said that the DOJ would defend agency decisions not to release information unless the decisions lacked a sound legal basis. Although Ashcroft's order came within weeks after 9/11, the attacks did not prompt the new policy so much as provide a public reason for it. From the start of its term, the administration was intent on establishing a policy of withholding information from the public.

Constitutional scholars look to Justice Robert H. Jackson's concurring opinion in a 1952 Supreme Court decision, the *Youngstown Steel* case, when defining the separation of powers—and particularly the balance between the executive and Congress. In *Youngstown,* the Court ruled that President Truman did not have the authority to seize steel mills during the Korean War to avoid what the president believed would have been a crippling union strike with a major impact on defense contractors and the economy.[72] In his concurring opinion, Justice Jackson, one of the wisest justices to sit on the bench and the lead prosecutor at the Nuremberg trials after World War II, identified three distinct categories to illustrate the executive's powers vis-à-vis those held by Congress.

Jackson recognized that the president's powers are at their zenith when the president acts with the express or implied authorization of Congress. In that situation, the president acts with all the powers he possesses in his own right plus what Congress delegates. The middle ground occurs where Congress has been silent on an issue. In that situation, the president relies on his own independent powers, although there is a "zone of twilight" where Congress and the president may have concurrent authority or where the power is uncertain. The president is at his nadir when he acts inconsistently with the wishes of Congress. In those circumstances, the president can only rely upon his own powers minus any powers that Congress has.

Since the president shares war powers with Congress, courts and constitutional scholars have long held that the president does not have the authority to ignore congressional acts that address actions in wartime. Thus, according to Justice Jackson's analysis and contrary to John Yoo's memos, when Congress passes a law that the military cannot torture, the president cannot disregard the law and direct the military to torture. The president is not above the Constitution. The president can neither disregard a law that interferes with his powers nor interpret the law as he wishes. In writing a legal opinion for his superiors, John Yoo had an obligation to inform his superiors of how his views and analysis differed from those of Justice Jackson as well as those of other judges and even of constitutional scholars.

In both the August 1 and the March 14 memos, Yoo writes as if his analysis is effortless and without doubt. This kind of writing is effective in an advocacy brief to a court, but it is not appropriate in an objective advisory memorandum to his superiors, his clients. To make intelligent decisions, the client must be correctly informed of the law. To the extent that there is a conflict, tension, or divergence in the law, the lawyer must advise the client of the circumstances and inform the client of alternative positions. John Yoo did not inform his client that courts and constitutional scholars have disagreed with his interpretation; he presented the law as if his were the only acceptable interpretation. He owed his superiors a more reasoned and balanced opinion. And in the case where the government is the client, one can argue that the advisor has a heightened responsibility to be as accurate as possible, so that the government always acts lawfully, ethically, and pursuant to the Constitution.

The question is why Yoo presented such extreme views as if they were the norm. As a graduate of Yale Law School and a professor of law at the University of California, Berkeley, a highly prestigious school, Yoo must have known that his views were singular and many people disagreed with them. In an interview Yoo gave after the March 14 memo was released to the public, he indicated that he wanted to avoid being "vague." His justification for taking a one-dimensional interpretation of the law on torture was that the people who had "to carry these things out" needed a clear line. He explained that "part of the job unfortunately of being a lawyer sometimes is you have to draw those lines. . . . I think I could have written it in a much more—we could have written it in a much more palatable way, but it would have been vague."[73] That is, the military and the CIA should be given clear instructions on what was lawful and what was not lawful.

However, as any law student would know, an advisor should not provide "clear" guidelines when the law is "vague" or, very likely, in opposition to the advisor's interpretation. Instead, the advisor should clearly articulate and inform the client of contrary authorities and address the conflicts. Even when a client asks a lawyer to justify an illegal action, as likely occurred here, the lawyer is ethically obligated to explain to the client the current state of the law and why the requested behavior is unlawful. By not providing a reasoned opinion accurately identifying the state of the law, Yoo supplied the administration with what it needed: an appearance and, essentially, a certification of legality. Yoo's advice made it easy for the highly regarded OLC to immunize CIA agents and the military.[74]

In response to being roundly criticized for providing such a severe definition of torture and giving the commander in chief absolute dominion in times of war, including the authority to torture with impunity, Yoo replied that "just because the statute says—that doesn't mean you have to do it. [T]here's still the moral question—after you've answered the legal question—whether you should do it at all."[75] In other words, Yoo is saying that he just did his job as a lawyer. It was up to the military and the CIA to decide what to do with his interpretation of the law. He was not making policy, he asserted. He only prepared the legal basis for the policy.

Unfortunately, it is not that simple. His statements reflect the same attitude one hears from the personnel and even the top brass at Guantanamo and anywhere else in the military: "I am just doing my job. Someone else makes the policy." Similar words were spoken during the Nuremberg trials by the Nazi lawyers who provided the legal bases for Nazi war crimes and by the military brass who fought on behalf of the Nazis. These times are not equivalent to World War II, when over six million people were killed. But fewer numbers do not excuse the response, "I am only doing my job." That language should never be the excuse of a thoughtful person.

John Yoo's speaking style is similar to his writing. He uses simple, uncomplicated terms that appear seductively reasonable. His smooth, even tone draws the audience into accepting his surface premises. He can make the unconscionable seem reasonable. It is only when one delves deeper into what he is saying or one is familiar with the law he is ostensibly interpreting that his errors in legal reasoning and judgment become apparent.[76]

Perhaps inadvertently, Yoo included a revealing statement in his March 14, 2003, memo. For some time, there had been indications that Michael Chertoff, subsequently the secretary of the Department of Homeland Security (DHS), was involved in the drafting or review of the torture memos and in reviewing the legality of harsh interrogation techniques used in Guantanamo. At his hearing to become secretary of Homeland Security in February 2005, Chertoff denied any awareness of the techniques. He told the committee that he was not aware of meetings between the FBI and the DOJ's Criminal Division that occurred when he was the head of the Criminal Division—even though the meetings were attended by Chertoff's top deputy, his counsel, and two other senior Criminal Division officials. At these meetings, the FBI raised questions about the harsh interrogation techniques at Guantanamo. In addition to denying knowledge of the meetings, Chertoff claimed that he was not informed of any torture practices at Guantanamo, and that he was unaware that the interrogation techniques were anything other than "kind of plain vanilla."[77]

Yoo's memo undermines Chertoff's testimony. In writing that the criminal statutes of assault, maiming, and interstate stalking, as well as torture statutes, did not apply to the conduct of the military and the executive in times of war, Yoo wrote that the Criminal Division of the DOJ concurred in his analysis. The person in charge at the time was Michael Chertoff. Three months after this torture memo was signed and dated, the Senate approved him for a seat on the Court of Appeals for the Third Circuit. He resigned from the court on February 15, 2005, to become the director of DHS. John Yoo left the government in 2003 and rejoined the faculty at UC Berkeley School of Law as a tenured professor. Jay Bybee was confirmed as a judge on the Ninth Circuit Court of Appeals in March 2003. He remains relatively unscathed by the release of the memos.

On June 30, 2004, Jack Goldsmith, the new head of the Office of Legal Counsel, withdrew the memoranda. In a book he wrote after leaving the OLC, Goldsmith condemned the "extreme conclusion" taken in the August 2002 memo regarding the powers of the commander in chief, a conclusion that had "no foundation in prior OLC opinions, or in judicial decisions, or in any other source of law."[78] He further wrote that the memo "rested on cursory and one-sided legal arguments that failed to consider Congress's competing wartime constitutional authorities, or the many Supreme Court decisions potentially in tension with the conclusion." He added, "When one concludes that Congress is disabled from controlling the President, and especially when one concludes this in secret, respect for separation of powers demands a full consideration of competing congressional and judicial prerogatives, which was lacking in the interrogation opinions."

On January 4, 2008, the Human Rights Clinic at Yale Law School, along with San Francisco counsel, filed a lawsuit in San Francisco federal court on behalf of Jose Padilla and his mother against John Yoo. (The media were quick to point out that Yoo was a graduate of Yale Law School.) The complaint alleged that Yoo's torture memos provided much of the legal bases, justifications, and authorizations for the government's violation of Padilla's constitutional and statutory rights, including physical and mental abuse, prolonged sensory deprivation, and torture that Padilla suffered while in the naval brig.[79]

PART TWO

LAWLESS DETENTIONS IN AMERICA

TWO AMERICAN CITIZENS, Yaser Hamdi and Jose Padilla, and one American resident, Ali al Marri, were held in the naval brig in Charleston, South Carolina, without charges and without access to lawyers and their families. They were denied their guaranteed rights to due process and the rule of law provided by the Constitution. They were kept in isolation, tortured, and deprived of sensory stimulation.

Terrorist Timothy McVeigh, who blew up the Oklahoma Federal Building in April 1995, was provided all his due process rights as soon as he was captured. Unlike McVeigh, who was personally responsible for the bomb that killed 168 people, Padilla, Hamdi, and al Marri were only tangentially, if at all, connected to the deaths of the 9/11 victims. Yet the administration designated Padilla, Hamdi, and al Marri enemy combatants and denied them the constitutional rights guaranteed to every citizen and legal resident living in the United States. In this part, I tell the story of these three men.

This part also recounts how America seized over 1,500 Arab and Muslim men, most but not all immigrants, solely because of their ethnicity. They were placed in preventive detention without due process protections, some for months, while the government investigated whether they had ties to terrorism. None was ever convicted of any crime associated with terrorism.

YASER HAMDI, AMERICAN CITIZEN

Yaser Hamdi was an American citizen born in Baton Rouge, Louisiana, on September 26, 1980, of Saudi parents. His father was a chemical engineer working for a Saudi oil company. When Hamdi was three, he returned with his parents to Jubayl, Saudi Arabia. In Saudi Arabia, Hamdi, the eldest of five children, was a high school honor student.[1] When he was a sophomore in college, he left home, apparently without telling his family or friends. He later sent word through his uncle that he was in Pakistan doing aid work.[2] Soon after, he must have crossed the border into Afghanistan. According to the U.S. government, he joined the Taliban in July or August 2001 to fight the Northern Alliance, which controlled a small section of northeast Afghanistan.[3]

Hamdi was captured by the Northern Alliance in December 2001, along with John Walker Lindh.[4] They had spent seven days and nights holed up with four hundred other Taliban soldiers in a fortress controlled by the Northern Alliance, which had allied itself with the United States after 9/11. Of the four hundred soldiers in the fortress, only eighty walked out after the week passed. The rest died after the Northern Alliance dropped grenades and burning diesel fuel into the basement and then flooded it with freezing water.

American interrogators interviewed Hamdi while he was in Afghanistan. He identified himself as a Saudi citizen who had been born in the United States.[5] Hamdi was sent to the detention center at Guantanamo Bay in February 2002. In April, the military transported him to a naval brig in Norfolk, Virginia, where he became the first American citizen to be declared an enemy combatant. Eighteen months later, the government transferred Hamdi to a naval brig in South Carolina. In both brigs, he was held incommunicado. He had no access to a lawyer or to his family. No charges were filed against him.

Frank Dunham, the federal public defender who represented Hamdi, noted that when the military first flew Hamdi from Guantanamo, his plane landed at Dulles Airport in Virginia. Dunham believed that the administration initially intended to bring criminal charges against Hamdi, as it brought charges against John Walker Lindh. However, after sitting on the tarmac for an hour, Hamdi's plane took off with him still aboard and headed for the naval brig in Virginia.[6] At that moment, the government classified Hamdi as an enemy combatant. Someone in the administration had apparently changed his or her mind about bringing charges. Perhaps the Department of Justice realized that it lacked sufficient evidence to prosecute Hamdi and decided to hold him in isolation and incommunicado, interrogating him at its pleasure.

Dunham was a lawyer in northern Virginia and a former prosecutor when he was named the first federal public defender in Alexandria, Virginia, in 2001. Edward B. MacMahon, Jr., his co-counsel, recalled that Dunham learned from a news account that Hamdi had been detained without charges and said, "That's just wrong—you can't do that to an American citizen."[7] Dunham then sought to represent Hamdi.

Dunham believed that the government either did not have enough evidence to prosecute Hamdi successfully or did not want to reveal its sources. He assumed that some of the evidence might have been brutally obtained from al Qaeda figures who were being held in other parts of the world through the government's extraordinary rendition program. Under this program, the administration seizes people overseas and, without any lawful process, whisks them off to countries known to torture prisoners. In other situations, the CIA transports the captives to secret CIA detention centers located outside U.S. sovereign territory. It has never been clear whether American agents stand by while the detainees are tortured in the foreign countries, or whether the agents are only recipients of the information obtained through torture.[8]

There were also murmurings among members of the legal community that Hamdi himself might have been tortured.[9] It was easier for the government to place Hamdi in isolation, without charges, holding him for as long as necessary as an enemy combatant, rather than provide him with a trial where his treatment, as well as that of some detainees held in foreign countries under our extraordinary rendition program, would be exposed. However, one of Hamdi's attorneys believes that although Hamdi was mistreated, he was not treated as badly or subjected to as extreme sensory deprivation as that imposed on Padilla and al Marri.[10] The military and the administration did not consider Hamdi the same kind of threat.

Nevertheless, e-mails between military officials responsible for supervising, guarding, and observing Hamdi indicated that he was very stressed and could break. One e-mail, written when Hamdi had been in the brig less than a year, read: "As you have indicated before, know we want to stay consistent with the privileges afforded the detainees at Camp Delta [in Guantanamo], but I have little else to offer this individual and I continue to be ever vigilant of his mental state. I would like to have some form of an incentive program in place to reward him for his continued good behavior, but more so, to keep him from Whacking out on me."[11]

A second e-mail, sent six months later, was more explicit in describing Hamdi's deteriorating and fragile mental state:

> The last thing that I wanted to have happen was to send him anywhere from here as a "Basket Case," of use to no one, to include himself. . . .
> He indicated he would continue to endure, but he did not leave me with a good impression that he is capable of going on much longer. . . . I fear the rubber band is nearing its breaking point here and not totally confident I can keep his head in the game much longer. I will continue to monitor his behavior and get [blacked out] onboard, but fear that once this individual decides to go south, there will be little if anything, I can do to bring him back around.[12]

In an e-mail sent in spring 2002, a prison official speaking about Hamdi reflects the common response of soldiers that has been pervasive throughout the War on Terror: "Best to not discuss his status at all with him. Realize that's tough on human level but realize anything you say becomes statement of US govt, at least potentially. Safest and honest answer is 'I don't know, sorry.'"[13]

Frank Dunham argued the case through the District Court for the Eastern District of Virginia and the Court of Appeals for the Fourth Circuit. The case bounced between these courts several times, and each time the higher court agreed with the administration's position that, as an enemy combatant, Hamdi could be held indefinitely. The fact that the term *enemy combatant* did not seem to have any meaning in the law apparently did not give the court much pause; this very conservative judicial body accepted the administration's position without question.

With extraordinary persistence, dedication, and a passion one does not often see in representation, Dunham managed to bring Hamdi's plight before the Supreme Court. There his persistence and dedication paid off. He convinced the Court that even someone like Yaser Hamdi, who had been caught on the battlefield, has the right to a fair and meaningful hearing to determine whether the government was justified in holding him for as long as it chose.

The Court was divided in its opinions, disagreeing on what rights Hamdi had and how the case should be resolved. However, Justice Sandra Day O'Connor represented a majority of the justices when she wrote that Hamdi was entitled to a meaningful due process hearing to challenge his detention and his designation as an enemy combatant. The hearing was to include notice of the factual basis for his classification and an opportunity to rebut the government's assertions before a neutral decision maker.[14] In summation, Justice O'Connor wrote what is undoubtedly one of the most memorable lines in all Supreme Court literature: "A state of war is not a blank check for the President."[15]

Unfortunately, O'Connor did not question the legitimacy of the government's definition of the term *enemy combatant* as it applied to Hamdi.[16] Perhaps she was hesitant to take on too much at this time—especially if she wanted the justices to join in her decision. But cases that were decided in the following years similarly did not question the legal authority and validity of the term *enemy combatant*.

Yaser Hamdi had also asked the Court to rule that the Fourth Circuit erred in denying him immediate access to counsel upon his detention.[17] However, after the Court agreed to take the case and before the parties argued the case before the Supreme Court, the government provided Hamdi with access to his lawyer, thereby mooting the issue.

Regrettably, the *Hamdi* case might be read as allowing the government to hold persons incommunicado, in isolation, and without access to counsel for an extended period. The only comment Justice O'Connor made on this issue was that if the War on Terror continued indefinitely, the Court would have to reconsider whether the government could hold a detainee for his entire life.

Within four months after the Supreme Court issued its opinion requiring the government to provide Hamdi with a hearing to challenge his status, the government released Hamdi and sent him back to Saudi Arabia. Pursuant to his plea agreement, he renounced his American citizenship.

Under the plea agreement, Hamdi consented to never travel to Afghanistan, Iraq, Israel, Pakistan, Syria, the West Bank of Palestine, or Gaza.[18] He was also banned from traveling to the United States for ten years. For fifteen years, he must inform the United States embassy in Saudi Arabia of any plans to travel outside Saudi Arabia. Since his return to Saudi Arabia in fall 2004, little has been written about him.[19]

Hamdi has since married and has a daughter. In late summer 2007, he was in school, studying business, including economics and finance. Although before his trip to Afghanistan Hamdi had thought of becoming a religious scholar, on the advice of his father, he has taken a more conventional path.[20] Hamdi hopes to write a book someday.

One of Hamdi's lawyers, Geremy Kamens, described him as having a "fantastic disposition" and being a "funny guy." Hamdi "laughed easily and was very friendly—and a great sense of humor in which he was often self-deprecating. He never seemed bitter about what happened—only extremely interested in returning home and getting on with his life. . . . He spoke English well but often laced with slang that he'd learned from the guards."[21] Kamens recounts that "one of the first things he ever said to me was that he 'really wanted to get out of here because he was just chilling.' . . . He was just a nice young kid who knew that Frank and I were trying to help him."[22]

The government's public explanation for holding Hamdi as an enemy combatant was to prevent him from returning to the battlefield before hostilities ceased. However, a Pentagon representative said after the government released him, "Hamdi was no longer considered a threat to the United States and did not possess any further intelligence value."[23] More likely, Hamdi was never much of a threat to begin with. He was just one of many foot soldiers with no intelligence value captured after the United States attacked Afghanistan.

Had the administration agreed to provide Hamdi with the hearing that Justice O'Conner required, the government would have had to reveal the circumstances of Hamdi's capture and the brutal treatment he received in the brig. The prosecution would also have had to reveal the sources of its evidence against Hamdi. It was a lot cleaner to send Hamdi on his way and forget about him.

One could argue that Yaser Hamdi was more fortunate than John Walker Lindh, who was captured with him in Afghanistan. Lindh is still in federal prison, serving a twenty-year sentence. Unless a president pardons him, Lindh will continue serving time until at least 2018, assuming his sentence is reduced by three years for good behavior. However, in his plea agreement Hamdi agreed to give up his U.S. citizenship. It is very unlikely that Lindh would have been equally willing to give up his citizenship. American citizenship means a lot more to Lindh; unlike Hamdi, he is not a citizen of any other country.

Frank Dunham died of brain cancer in November 2006. As Edward B. MacMahon, Jr., Dunham's co-counsel, put it, "The Hamdi case was, in my judgment, one of the greatest accomplishments ever by an American attorney."

JOSE PADILLA, AMERICAN CITIZEN

Jose Padilla, the other American citizen who was held in isolation for nearly three years in a naval brig in South Carolina, was not captured on the battlefield as Hamdi had been. American officials arrested Padilla at Chicago's O'Hare International Airport as he disembarked from a flight from Zurich.

Jose Padilla was born in Brooklyn on October 18, 1970. His mother, Estela Ortega Lebron, is Puerto Rican and lives in Florida. His father, also Puerto Rican, died when he was four, after which the family moved to Chicago.[24] As an adolescent, Padilla joined a local street gang, the Latin Kings. When he was fourteen, he and friends attacked and robbed two Mexican immigrants who may have been members of a rival gang. Padilla's friend stabbed and killed one of the immigrants. Padilla, who had kicked the victim, was sent to a juvenile detention center until he was nineteen.[25]

Soon after his release, Padilla's girlfriend gave birth to his first son, Joshua. Padilla moved to South Florida, where his mother had relocated. In 1991, Padilla met Cherie Maria Shultz, a Jamaican immigrant. Several months after they met, Padilla was involved in a traffic incident in which he fired a gun in the air. A few months later, while in detention, he assaulted a guard. He pleaded guilty to both charges and spent ten months in jail. While in jail, Padilla told Shultz that he wanted to clean up his life. He took an interest in religion, mentioning to Shultz that he had had an out-of-body experience accompanied by visions: "In one, he saw a man in a turban surrounded by the dust of the desert. In the other, he saw a beautiful woman in a dark corridor at the end of which was a door with a 'crystal loving light' peeking out from beneath."[26] According to Shultz, these visions changed his life.

When he was released from jail, Padilla got a job at a local Taco Bell where Shultz worked. The manager at the fast-food restaurant was Muhammed Javed, a Pakistani American and cofounder of the Broward School of Islamic Studies. Shultz became interested in Islamic studies, and Javed invited her to take scripture classes taught by his wife at their home. Occasionally, Padilla accompanied Shultz to class. On one such occasion, Javed's wife suggested that Padilla visit the mosque with other Muslim men. According to Shultz, when Padilla saw the men in turbans at the mosque, he remembered his vision from jail and felt that this was "where he belonged."[27] Both Padilla and Shultz accepted Islam and entered into serious study of the faith. Padilla studied Arabic and scripture at the Darul Uloom Mosque in Pembroke Pines and then at Masjid Al-Iman in downtown Fort Lauderdale. In 1994, Padilla changed his name to Ibrahim. Later, when he was in the Middle East, Padilla took the name Abdullah al Muhajir.

In 1996, Padilla and Shultz were married in Broward County, Florida. Two years later, Padilla said that he wanted to immerse himself more fully in Arabic language and Islam, and Mr. Awad, the imam at Masjid Al-Iman, took up a collection at the mosque to pay for Padilla to go to Egypt for study. Padilla told his former boss that he was leaving to teach English in Cairo. In Egypt, Padilla maintained minimal contact with his wife and his mother. A year later, he entered into an arranged marriage with Shamia'a, the daughter of a villager. Shultz learned of Padilla's plans to marry and filed for divorce. Padilla and Shamia'a moved to Cairo, where he taught English. There she gave birth to their first son, Hussein. In 2000, he traveled to Saudi Arabia on pilgrimage. When he returned, he told his wife that he had obtained a job teaching English in Yemen and planned to move there. Shamia'a returned to her native village, where she gave birth to a second son, Hassan.

The administration has a different version of what Padilla did while in the Middle East. Padilla is said to have met several times with Abu Zubaydah, Bin Laden's chief lieutenant (whose full name is Zayn Al Abidin Muhammad Husayn) and Khalid Shaikh Mohammed, the man described as the mastermind of the 9/11 attacks.[28] In these meetings, he discussed plans to construct a dirty bomb and to blow up apartment buildings using natural gas. While in Pakistan, Padilla received training in wiring explosives. Padilla traveled to Afghanistan at least twice. Under interrogation, he admitted completing a training camp application entitled "Mujahideen Identification Form/New Applicant Form." For three months in fall 2000, Padilla guarded a Taliban outpost north of Kabul. He also met 9/11 co-conspirator Ramzi Bin al-Shibh, who trained Padilla in telephone call security and e-mail protocol.

Padilla was arrested in May 2002 with $10,526 in his possession.[29] The government alleged that he was planning to detonate a radio-active dirty bomb. The government held Padilla on a material witness warrant and placed him in federal criminal custody in New York. On June 9, President Bush declared Padilla an enemy combatant. The government whisked Padilla out of federal prison in New York and delivered him to the naval brig in Charleston, South Carolina. His lawyer, Donna R. Newman, found out about the move the following day, when the prosecutor phoned her to say that the government had declared Padilla an enemy combatant.

"A what?" Newman said. "Look up *Quirin*," he replied, referring to the 1942 Supreme Court decision about Nazi saboteurs in *Ex Parte Quirin,* which was used to support the use of the term *enemy combatant.*[30] (In fact, the *Quirin* case does not breathe life into the term *enemy combatant.* There was no attempt to give legal meaning to the term *enemy combatant* in *Quirin.* In the Court's opinion, the term only appeared once and was used either generically, to represent any combatant who fights for the other side, or as a synonym for the legally recognized term *unlawful combatant.* But the fact that the *Quirin* decision did not support the administration's position did not really seem to matter to the prosecutors. The administration was intent on declaring Padilla an enemy combatant, regardless of whether *enemy combatant* was a legitimately recognized term of law.)[31]

Chief Judge Michael B. Mukasey of the Federal District Court for the Southern District of New York appointed Donna R. Newman to represent Padilla on May 15, 2002, the day after he was brought to New

York from Chicago. Like Padilla, Newman was born in Brooklyn. She came to the law late, having raised two children and worked as a speech pathologist before applying to law school at the age of thirty-five. She was on a panel of attorneys available to represent criminal defendants in federal court in situations where the federal public defender was unable to take the case, either because of a conflict of interest or because the public defender's

office could not add another case to its workload. Newman did not know why the judge appointed her instead of assigning the case to a public defender.[32]

Andrew Patel, also a member of the panel, was appointed as co-counsel on June 12, 2002, three days after Padilla was designated an enemy combatant. Years earlier, he had represented El Sayyid Nosair, allegedly the mastermind behind the 1993 World Trade Center bombing. After a U.S. Supreme Court decision in June 2004 declaring that after Padilla was moved to the brig in South Carolina his lawyers were required to refile his case in the federal court in South Carolina, Patel and Newman's appointments were terminated. However, they continued to represent Padilla, now on a pro bono basis. After he was transferred to Florida, Patel was again appointed to work with the federal public defenders and was paid for his work.[33] Newman ceased to represent Padilla.

The government confined Padilla to the naval brig in South Carolina for three and a half years. For the first twenty-one months, he was held in total isolation under extremely harsh conditions. Padilla's attorneys claim that the sensory deprivation was so severe that he is now insane.

According to Andrew Patel, the guards and security personnel at the brig, and perhaps even his interrogators, had requested from the "powers above," presumably high-level members of the administration and military, that Padilla be allowed to socialize and have meals with enemy combatants in the brig.[34] The only other enemy combatants in

Donna Newman. Courtesy Donna Newman.

the brig, as far as we know, were Yaser Hamdi and later Ali al Marri. The interrogators denied that request.

Patel also indicates in his declaration that Padilla was given a "truth serum" that made him feel drugged. Patel believes that the serum may have been lysergic acid diethylamide (LSD) or phencyclidine (PCP).[35] The brig's technical director testified that it was only a flu shot.[36]

During the first twenty-one months Padilla spent in the brig, his lawyers tried without success to obtain access to him. In his declaration, Vice Admiral Lowell E. Jacoby, director of the Defense Intelligence Agency, described the reasons behind the government's policy of denying access. According to Jacoby, the Defense Intelligence Agency's "approach to interrogation is largely dependent upon creating an atmosphere of dependency and trust between the subject and interrogator."[37] To that end, any "insertion of counsel" "can undo months of work and may permanently shut down the interrogation process."[38] "Only after such time as Padilla has perceived that help is not on the way can the United States reasonably expect to obtain all possible intelligence information from Padilla."[39] Consistent with Jacoby's statement that the government intended to create an atmosphere of trust and dependency with Padilla, Donna Newman believes that the government likely told Padilla during his interrogations that Ms. Newman, his attorney in New York, "has abandoned you."[40] Since the interrogators kept all news media, as well as his lawyers, from Padilla, he had no knowledge of what his attorneys were doing on his behalf.

In the early stages of the Padilla litigation, the team had a significant victory. Thanks in large part to Stanford professor Jenny Martinez, who wrote much of the brief, the Federal Court of Appeals for the Second Circuit ruled in December 2003 that the president did not have the power to detain Padilla, an American citizen seized on American soil, as an enemy combatant. The court further concluded that congressional authorization was required for detention of American citizens on American soil, and Congress had not given such authorization. Although Congress had passed an Authorization for Use of Military Force (AUMF) Joint Resolution immediately after 2001, the court ruled that this did not confer the power to seize Padilla. The appeals court instructed the federal district court to issue a writ of habeas corpus directing Secretary of Defense Rumsfeld to release Padilla from military custody in thirty days, at which time the government could bring criminal charges against him. The court added that Padilla was entitled to the constitutional protections provided all American citizens.

Professor Jenny Martinez had worked for the United Nations War Crimes Tribunal in The Hague and understood the complex issues surrounding combatant status and the law of war. While working on the Padilla case, she was employed at Jenner and Block, a law firm in Washington, D.C. However, she was about to leave the practice to go into academia. The firm generously allowed her to work pro bono on the Padilla brief for much of her final six months there. Because they were working alone, Newman and Patel needed her expertise in developing the appeal to the Second Circuit.

This win in the Second Circuit would prove important in setting the stage for the appeal to the U.S. Supreme Court. Martinez believes that because the prestigious Second Circuit had adopted her argument, the Supreme Court was inclined to give credence to her position that the president did not have an all-inclusive power to designate someone an enemy combatant and hold him indefinitely without a hearing.[41]

The government appealed the Second Circuit decision to the U.S. Supreme Court. The Supreme Court agreed to hear both the Hamdi and Padilla cases in spring 2004.

Padilla did not meet his lawyers until March 2004, after the Supreme Court agreed to hear his case. The government allowed him access to his lawyers for the same reason that it allowed Yaser Hamdi access: to moot the issue of the right to an attorney. The government taped the initial meetings between Padilla and his lawyers, and government personnel were present. For this reason, the attorneys did not discuss Padilla's case with him, other than to inform him of their court filings on his behalf. The attorneys "acted like newscasters" and told Padilla only about matters that were public record. They advised him to say as little as possible.[42]

Although Padilla's case reached the Supreme Court at the same time as Hamdi's, the Court deferred ruling on the merits of Padilla's case. Instead, in a 5–4 ruling, the Supreme Court decided that Padilla's lawyers had filed the case in the wrong lower court. The Supreme Court held that once Padilla had been declared to be an enemy combatant and transferred to the brig in South Carolina, all subsequent filings should have been filed in that district. Padilla's lawyers had initially filed their petitions in the Federal District of the Southern District of New York—perhaps thinking that the New York court would look more kindly and sympathetically on his plight, and then appealed to the Second Circuit Court of Appeals, which hears cases from New York. The lawyers had to start all over again, refiling all their petitions in federal district court in South Carolina, where the brig was located.[43] Justice delayed was justice denied.

In 2005, the district court ruled that the government was holding Padilla unlawfully in the brig, as his lawyers had argued.[44] The court ordered that he be released within forty-five days. The government appealed, and the U.S. Court of Appeals for the Fourth Circuit agreed with the government's position that Padilla could continue to be held in the brig, just as it had in the Hamdi case.[45] Over three years had passed since Padilla was first brought to the brig. His case was set for a second appeal to the U.S. Supreme Court. Meanwhile, in August 2005, the brig officials, perhaps deciding that Padilla was not of much use to them anymore and no longer needed to be in complete isolation, permitted Padilla's mother to visit him, providing it was "done quietly," without media attention.[46]

On November 20, 2005, soon after the U.S. Supreme Court agreed to hear arguments regarding Padilla's petition, the administration saw the writing on the wall. It feared, based on the earlier Hamdi decision, that the Supreme Court would likely decide that Padilla also had the right to a due process hearing, and that the Court might rule that Padilla's right to a due process hearing was even broader in scope, with more due process protections than those provided to Yaser Hamdi. After all, Padilla had been captured on American territory, whereas Hamdi had been captured on the battlefield in Afghanistan. To head off such a decision, President Bush retracted Padilla's designation as an enemy combatant.

When the government declared that Padilla was no longer an enemy combatant, Judge Luttig, who wrote the opinion in the Court of Appeals Fourth Circuit decision supporting the administration's position that Padilla was an enemy combatant and could be held in the brig indefinitely, was outraged. Luttig, a conservative jurist, fumed that he had stuck out his neck on behalf of the government's position that Padilla was a dangerous person who must be held in the brig, and then three months later the government turns around and declares that Padilla is not that much of a threat after all. Luttig was convinced that the administration had misled him as to the seriousness of the danger.

Luttig gave voice to his anger. He refused to allow the government to go forward with its designation of Padilla as a criminal defendant. Luttig ordered the government to justify Padilla's move into the criminal justice system "in light of the different facts that were alleged by the President to warrant Padilla's military detention and held by this court to justify that detention, on the one hand, and the alleged facts on which Padilla has now been indicted, on the other."[47] In response, the administration filed a brief with the Supreme Court arguing that the president had the authority to transfer Padilla and that Luttig could not interfere. The Court agreed. After the Supreme Court approved Padilla's transfer, Luttig (who had been thought to be on a short list of candidates for an appointment to the Supreme Court) resigned from the Fourth Circuit and accepted a position as general counsel and senior vice president for Boeing.

Padilla's attorneys would not quit, however. They requested that the Supreme Court still agree to hear Padilla's petition. The lawyers argued that the government should not be able to avoid an important constitutional issue by moving Padilla. However, the Supreme Court refused to hear the case. In his opinion, Justice Anthony Kennedy wrote, "Even if the Court were to rule in Padilla's favor, his present custody status would be unaffected" because he was now charged in a civilian court.[48] However, Kennedy made it clear that should the government reverse its course and reclassify Padilla as an enemy combatant, the district court "would be in a position to rule quickly on any responsive filings submitted by Padilla."[49] Kennedy also noted that Padilla retained the right to seek habeas in the Supreme Court.

Commentators and scholars had hoped that the Court would hear Padilla's case.[50] They feared that until the Supreme Court ruled on the issues, the government still had the power to classify an American citizen as an enemy combatant and hold him or her for an indefinite period in isolation.[51] Transferring Padilla to the criminal justice system did not moot the issue, they argued. Justice Ruth Bader Ginsburg agreed with Padilla's attorneys in her opinion, dissenting from the Court's refusal to hear the case. She wrote, "Nothing the Government has yet done purports to retract the assertion of Executive power Padilla protests. Although the Government has recently lodged charges against Padilla in a civilian court, nothing prevents the Executive from returning to the road it earlier constructed."[52] The Supreme Court had deferred the issue to another day.[53]

The government charged Padilla with conspiracy in the Federal District Court for the Southern District of Florida, alleging that he was part of a North American cell that supported jihad causes overseas.[54] He was not charged with the crimes that the federal government had earlier alleged—planning to detonate a dirty bomb and using natural gas lines to blow up apartment buildings—because the government's evidence had been obtained through "harsh questioning of two senior members of Al Qaeda," Abu Zubaydah and Khalid Shaikh Mohammed.[55] The evidence from these two detainees would likely not have been admissible in court and would have exposed classified information, including evidence that Zubaydah and Mohammed had been waterboarded.[56]

In addition, a declaration by Michael Mobbs, a Pentagon official called in support of the government's petition, indicated in a footnote that the sources for the information regarding Padilla may not have been "completely candid." Mobbs stated that although much of the information had been corroborated, some had not, and in one case a source had recanted some of what he had said. That source was likely Zubaydah. During his interrogation, Zubaydah, who had been shot in the groin and severely wounded when he was captured, required "various types of drugs to treat medical conditions."[57] The administration withheld medications and painkillers depending upon Zubaydah's responses in interrogation.[58] Zubaydah was also held in a "dog box," designed so that he could not stand, to reduce him to a state of "learned helplessness."[59] The approach toward detainees such as Zubaydah was to break them down "'through isolation, white noise, completely take away their ability to predict the future, create dependence on interrogators.' As explained by CIA interrogators, they were going to become Zubaydah's 'God.'"[60]

The government decided to go with the conspiracy charges. On October 4, 2006, Padilla's attorneys filed a "Motion to Dismiss for Outrageous Government Conduct" in the federal district court in Florida, describing how the government had held Padilla in "complete sensory deprivation" while he was in isolation in the South Carolina naval brig.[61] The government's brief responded that regardless of the allegations of torture, the law did not permit dismissal of the indictment.[62]

During one meeting that Patel had with Padilla in the Florida federal prison, Patel asked a simple question concerning an event prior to his arrest. Patel writes in his declaration that Padilla "began to blink his eyes and he appeared to have goose bumps on his arms and neck." Patel then makes an odd comparison: "Mr. Padilla's reaction to my innocuous question was the same reaction that I would have expected if he had been stuck by a cattle prod." Later in the declaration, Patel writes that Padilla "retains the belief that he will be returned to the Brig if he discusses events that have occurred there."[63] Patel comments that he has represented Mr. Padilla for over four years. He has shown Padilla numerous legal documents filed in federal court naming himself as Padilla's counsel, as well as transcripts of arguments that he made on Padilla's behalf. His client has seen him argue on his behalf, and has spoken with his mother about the work that his attorneys were doing on his behalf. "Nevertheless," Patel writes, "Mr. Padilla remains unsure if I and the other attorneys working on his case are actually his attorney or another component of the government's interrogation scheme." Padilla was forever terrified of being seen as "crazy, fearing that he could be sent back to the brig or worse."[64]

According to Donna Newman, "There came a point when he didn't trust us." Padilla never said it, but she sensed it from his behavior. As Newman saw it, Padilla feared that if he opened up, the government would return him to the brig. "Why chance it?" she added.[65] According to Newman, Padilla understood that there was no real value in assisting in his defense. The government had made it clear to him, she believes, that if he won they would redesignate him as an enemy combatant and return him to the brig. Vice Admiral Jacoby had succeeded in creating a bond between the government interrogators and Jose Padilla.

In December 2006, Padilla's attorneys filed a reply to the government's response.[66] The reply included affidavits from Padilla, two psychiatrists, and one of Padilla's attorneys. Exhibit E in the reply brief consisted of the still frames from the unclassified video of Padilla being transported from his cell to the dentist.

The trial judge, Marcia Cooke, first decided to hear the defense argument that Padilla was incompetent to stand trial. The defense used the tape of Padilla in prison and evidence from its expert psychiatrists and psychologists to argue that Padilla was not able to assist in his trial. They argued that Padilla met the full diagnosis of post-traumatic stress disorder, having suffered severely traumatic events while in the naval brig. The government argued in response that Padilla could not be incompetent because he had told his lawyers about his treatment and had assisted the attorneys with other descriptions of his experiences in the brig. Craig S. Noble, a psychologist at the brig, testified at Padilla's competency hearing. He recounted how he had conducted a "cell front visit" with Padilla, speaking to Padilla through the bean hole. Noble found no new indication of "distress or lethality."[67] Noble added that Padilla "was responsive to me" and "smiled."[68] Rodolfo Buigas, the Bureau of Prisons psychologist, testified that Padilla suffered from anxiety and personality disorders but was competent to stand trial. "I saw this individual happy. I saw this individual joking," Buigas testified.[69]

In the end, Judge Cooke ruled that Padilla was competent to stand trial.[70] She said that Padilla "clearly has the capacity to assist his attorneys."[71] She noted that Padilla had paid attention during court hearings, discussed issues with the doctors who had examined him, and provided his attorneys with some information about his detention in the brig.[72] "He had to communicate something to his lawyers in order for counsel to file that motion," she said.[73]

Patel was not surprised.[74] The threshold for finding a defendant competent to stand trial in federal court is very low. Padilla may be passive and unhinged. Perhaps he is nothing more than a "piece of furniture," as members of the staff at the brig had described him. However, under the law, the court must find that the defendant is "suffering from a mental disease or defect rendering him mentally incompetent to the extent that he is unable to understand the nature and consequences of the proceedings against him or to assist properly in his defense."[75] Judge Cooke chose not to make this finding.

It may have been a close call for the judge, but one can imagine the political ramifications of a ruling declaring Padilla incompetent, especially if his mental disease was caused by official mistreatment. The judge never reconsidered her ruling.

On April 10, 2007, Judge Cooke issued a decision denying Padilla's motion to dismiss the indictment based on the government's outrageous conduct. The judge ruled that if the government had mistreated Padilla in the brig, any evidence derived from that mistreatment would be excluded. She believed that excluding the evidence was more appropriate than dismissing the criminal charges outright. Padilla was going to trial. Of course, to avoid public disclosure of Padilla's treatment in the brig, the government did not intend to introduce any evidence derived from interrogating Padilla.

Punishing the government for illegal treatment of a detainee by barring the tainted evidence from his trial is not a sufficient deterrent when the government is more interested in the information than in prosecution. As Patel explained, under this limited deterrent theory, "we can do anything we want to an American citizen, but as long as we don't use what we extract from him, it doesn't matter."[76]

On August 16, 2007, a Florida jury convicted Padilla on three counts: conspiracy to commit illegal violent acts outside the United States, conspiracy to provide material support to terrorist organizations, and providing material support to terrorist organizations.[77] A key piece of evidence against him was the form he had filled out in 2000 while attending an al Qaeda training camp in Afghanistan. On January 22, 2008, Padilla was sentenced to seventeen years and four months in prison, with credit for time served in the military brig. The administration had sought the maximum penalty of life imprisonment.[78] In sentencing Padilla, Judge Cooke "noted that the government had all the evidence necessary to try Padilla in criminal court at the time he was arrested in May 2002 at Chicago's O'Hare International Airport."[79] She also indicated that "the conditions of his confinement defied the standards for pre-trial detention." Essentially, she was saying that the cruel and inhumane treatment of Padilla in the military brig never should have happened.

One must ask whether the government ever had any justification for holding Jose Padilla for three and a half years as an enemy combatant. Padilla was nothing more than a low-level functionary. As Judge Cooke indicated, the government could have successfully prosecuted Padilla in the criminal justice system when he was first captured. If he had been prosecuted immediately and given the constitutional rights due any defendant, we would likely never have heard of him. And we would never have had to witness an American citizen lose his mind because of the merciless way his government treated him.

Today Padilla is serving his time at the Supermax, a federal maximum security prison in Florence, Colorado.

ALI SALEH KALAH AL MARRI, AMERICAN RESIDENT

Ali Saleh Kalah al Marri, a dual national of Saudi Arabia and Qatar, entered this country with his wife and five children on September 10, 2001.[80] He had arrived in Peoria, Illinois, to enroll, as a legal resident, in a computer science master's program at Bradley University, having previously obtained a B.A. in business administration from Bradley. Not much is known about his life between attending Bradley for his B.A. and enrolling in the M.A. program, although the government claims that he trained at an al Qaeda camp in Afghanistan between 1996 and 1998, learning the use of poisons and toxic chemicals.

When he was arrested, al Marri's laptop included lectures in Arabic by Osama bin Laden and others on the importance of jihad and martyrdom, files labeled "Jihad arena" and "martyrs," and information on industrial chemical distributor websites, including information on potassium and sodium cyanide. There was also information on computer programs used by hackers. Like Jose Padilla, al Marri was first arrested on a material witness warrant in December 2001. In the following months, the government charged him with counterfeiting, credit card fraud, making false statements on bank applications, and making false statements to the FBI. His trial was scheduled for July 2003. However, on June 23, 2003, President Bush declared al Marri an enemy combatant. Attorney General John Ashcroft was quoted as saying that when al Marri refused to plead guilty in federal court prior to his trial, the government classified him as an enemy combatant. The administration removed al Marri from his cell in Peoria, where he was awaiting trial, and placed him in solitary confinement in the same Charleston, South Carolina, naval brig that held Hamdi and Padilla. By moving him to the brig, the government could now interrogate al Marri without any interference from his lawyers.

Prosecutors accused al Marri of meeting with Khalid Shaikh Mohammed. They also alleged that Mohammed communicated with al Marri's brother, Jaralla Salah Mohammed Kahla al Marri, who is being held as an enemy combatant in Guantanamo. The administration contended that because al Marri is not a citizen, he does not have the same rights that Hamdi and Padilla have as citizens. Federal district court judge Henry Floyd agreed.[81]

On August 8, 2005, al Marri's lawyers filed a thirty-page complaint challenging that the conditions under which the administration confined al Marri at the naval brig violated this country's "most basic laws and fundamental norms," including the U.S. Constitution, federal laws, and international treaties.[82] According to Jon Hafetz, al Marri's lead attorney, al Marri was treated at least as badly as Padilla. The complaint and a subsequent document[83] filed in March 2008 alleged that while held in isolation in his nine-by-six-foot cell, al Marri had no contact with anyone other than the guards, who just gave him orders. During his solitary confinement, the military lowered the air temperature and refused to provide additional clothes or even socks, causing him to shiver constantly. He spent over twenty days in bed because the floor was too cold. For more than two years, he was denied a mattress and had to sleep on a hard and jagged metal surface. His blanket was a tear-resistant "suicide blanket," designed to thwart construction of nooses. His interrogators denied him access to a clock, mirror, toothbrush, toothpaste, soap, and even toilet paper. He wore leg irons and handcuffs when he showered. He was also denied a dictionary, because access to dictionaries "will permit them greater understanding of the English language, and enhance their ability to gather intelligence . . . of brig operations/related INTELL stuff."[84]

On several occasions, interrogators stuffed al Marri's mouth with cloth and covered it with heavy duct tape. Once, when he managed to loosen the tape, interrogators retaped his mouth even more tightly. Al Marri started to choke until a panicked agent from the FBI or Defense Intelligence Agency removed the tape.[85]

Sometimes, the military cut off the water supply to his sink and toilet for as long as twenty days. The window in his cell was covered to block out all sunlight, and the window in the door was covered in black so he could not see into the brig. The interrogators placed an industrial fan by his door, which operated around the clock. The guards adjusted the fan speed depending on whether al Marri was "compliant." Like Padilla, he claimed that noxious odors were introduced into his cell. Al Marri stuffed his vents with food to block the smell. He was under constant video surveillance, even when taking a shower or using the bathroom. When he finally met with his attorney, he told his counsel that was losing his mind and spoke of possible imminent death.

Because the government denied him all social contact and he had almost nothing to distract him, al Marri became preoccupied with his pain and degradation. His interrogators told him that they would send him to Egypt or Saudi Arabia, where he would be tortured and sodomized and his wife would be raped in front of him. The interrogators also told him that his brothers and father had been jailed because of him.

According to the complaint, al Marri suffered numbness, problems with vision, constant headaches, back pain, dizziness, uncontrollable tremors, inexplicable arching of his body, and ringing in his ears. In addition, he experienced hypersensitivity to external stimuli, manic behavior, difficulty concentrating and thinking, obsessional thinking, difficulties with impulse control, difficulty sleeping, difficulty keeping track of time, and agitation.

As in Guantanamo, at the end of each lawyer-client meeting, the guards remove all notes taken by Hafetz and the other members of the team of lawyers and send them to Washington for review. Although he cannot be certain, Hafetz suspects the government listens in on his meetings with al Marri.[86]

In November 2006, the government filed a motion in federal court to dismiss al Marri's habeas case for lack of jurisdiction. The government argued that the Military Commissions Act of 2006 removed federal court jurisdiction over al Marri's habeas action because he was a detained foreign national and an enemy combatant.[87] Since al Marri had never been determined to be an enemy combatant by a Combatant

Status Review Tribunal (CSRT), as detainees in Guantanamo were, the government argued that al Marri was "awaiting" such determination. The government added that the Department of Defense had ordered that al Marri be provided such a hearing upon dismissal of his habeas petition.[88]

Unlike Guantanamo detainees, al Marri had been arrested on American soil and was a legal resident. The Military Commissions Act denied foreign nationals, but not American citizens, the right to file habeas petitions. Thus this provision affected millions of Americans who were lawful residents legally entitled to be living in the country. The Military Commissions Act makes no mention of legal residents or people captured and detained in the United States.

One month later, al Marri's lead counsel, Jonathan Hafetz, filed a response to the government's motion to dismiss. Hafetz has impressive credentials. He is an attorney in the ACLU's National Security Project and formerly directed litigation for the Liberty and National Security Project of the Brennan Center for Justice at New York University Law School. He is a graduate of Yale Law School, holds a master's degree in history from Oxford University, and is a Fulbright scholar. He also represents detainees in Guantanamo, including al Marri's brother, and two American citizens detained in Iraq.

Hafetz and his colleagues argued in their response that the MCA did not repeal jurisdiction over habeas petitions filed by resident aliens[89] and that there was no valid suspension of the writ as required by the Constitution.[90] In addition, they argued that a review by the D.C. Circuit of CSRT designation of enemy combatant status was not an adequate substitute for habeas corpus.[91]

In June 2007, the very conservative Fourth Circuit Court of Appeals, which had ruled against Hamdi and Padilla in earlier cases, perhaps sensed the changing mood of the country regarding the administration's approach to the War on Terror. The three-judge panel agreed with al Marri's lawyers and instructed the federal district court to issue a writ of habeas corpus directing the secretary of defense to release al Marri from military custody within a reasonable time.[92] The court indicated that the government could transfer al Marri to civilian authorities to face criminal charges (like Padilla), initiate deportation proceedings against him, hold him as a material witness for some period, or detain him for a limited time under the Patriot Act. "But military detention of al-Marri must cease," the court concluded.[93]

The court based its decision on the fact that the government had never alleged that al Marri was a member of any nation's armed forces, fought alongside any nation's armed forces, or had borne arms against the United States (as was alleged against Jose Padilla). Consequently, the president did not have the authority to seize al Marri, hold him as an enemy combatant, and subject him to indefinite military detention. In addition, the court noted that the Military Commissions Act of 2006, which purported to strip federal courts of jurisdiction over enemy combatants in habeas matters, did not apply to al Marri, because he was a civilian captured and detained on American soil. Moreover, al Marri was neither determined by the United States to have been properly detained as an enemy combatant nor awaiting such determination, as required by the statute.

The United States petitioned for an en banc hearing to review the three-judge panel's decision. On August 22, 2007, a majority of the judges of the Fourth Circuit voted to grant en banc review of the decision, thus vacating the three-judge decision.[94]

In the meantime, al Marri's lawyers filed a document in spring 2008 requesting interim relief from the prolonged isolation al Marri had endured for nearly five years. The petition argued that the improvement in al Marri's conditions since he began visiting with his lawyers had been uneven and that he had "exhibited marked signs of psychological deterioration." They added that his "ability to tolerate this confinement is clearly eroding severely."[95] The lawyers noted that al Marri's only contact with the outside world was with his lawyers and with representatives of the International Committee of the Red Cross.

An expert on the psychiatric effects of confinement, Dr. Stuart Grassian declared that he had "only very uncommonly encountered an individual whose confinement was as onerous as Mr. Almarri's, except for individuals who had been incarcerated brutally in some third-world countries." Grassian commented that al Marri had become "increasingly obsessional" and "has become increasingly fixated on mundane aspects of his surroundings, from the humming noise of a fluorescent light to the preparation of his food."[96] In a footnote to the petition, the attorneys wrote that "there are cabinets full of recordings documenting his interrogation and other treatment in the Brig," but the government had refused to provide the tapes and other evidence.[97]

A week after the attorneys filed the motion for interim relief from prolonged isolation, they filed to preserve the video and audio recordings arising from al Marri's detention and interrogations. The court papers noted that "the government acknowledged the existence of approximately fifty recordings documenting interrogations of Mr. Almarri and Jose Padilla at the Brig," and that the government had admitted destroying many recordings of al Marri's interrogations.[98] The attorneys do not have copies of any of the tapes, nor have any attorneys seen any of the tapes. Hafetz did not know who made the films but assumed that they were taken at the brig and that some were from the period before the lawyers had access to him in October 2004. Hafetz asserted that "al Marri's treatment in various respects was close, if not tantamount, to torture, and those interrogations were illegal." He added that "his abusive interrogation underscores the illegality of his detention as an 'enemy combatant.'"[99]

On July 15, 2008, more than eight months after the oral arguments, the Fourth Circuit Court of Appeals issued a very fractured opinion.[100] There were seven separate opinions over 216 pages. Judge William B. Traxler provided the vote to constitute the majority in two rulings, one favoring the administration, the other favoring the defendant. The vote was 5–4 on both. Unfortunately for al Marri and for people who do not believe the president has the power to detain those seized in the United States, the decision favoring the administration overturned the 2007 district court decision.

The court, based on Judge Traxler's opinion, held that the Authorization for Use of Military Force resolution provided President Bush with the required authority "to detain enemy combatants in the war against al Qaeda, including belligerents who enter our country for the purpose of committing hostile and war-like acts such as those carried out by the al Qaeda operatives on 9/11."[101] Thus, if the government's allegations about al Marri are true, the government may hold him as an enemy combatant. However, also according to Judge Traxler, the government has not afforded al Marri sufficient due process to challenge his designation as an enemy combatant. Consequently, al Marri may pursue more procedural safeguards than earlier provided him. The federal district court must hold further hearings on whether there is sufficient evidence to hold him. Traxler stated that al Marri should be given the opportunity to demand that the government submit more reliable evidence than merely a declaration, which is hearsay, to hold him.

As Traxler and the majority of the court saw it, due process safeguards were even more important and required a somewhat higher standard when the detainee had been captured in the United States, as al Marri was, as opposed to someone like Yaser Hamdi, who was captured on the battlefield in Afghanistan. Thus the standard of review that is acceptable for someone like Yaser Hamdi—a standard that allows for hearsay—would not necessarily be sufficient for someone like al Marri, who was captured in the United States, without further demonstration by the government that it was absolutely necessary to rely exclusively on hearsay. Al Marri's lawyers have asked the Supreme Court to review the case.

Meanwhile, al Marri continues to remain in isolation in the naval brig in Charleston, South Carolina. He has not seen his wife and five children since he was designated an enemy combatant in June 2003. Beginning in 2008, he is now permitted two calls per year to his family.[102] Letters can take over seven months to review before he receives them.[103] His only face-to-face communications are with his attorneys and, occasionally, with members of the Red Cross. As Hafetz explains it, "Everything is a privilege."[104]

PREVENTIVE DETENTION

Immigrants in Detention

Shakir Baloch, a native of Pakistan, immigrated to Canada in 1989, becoming a Canadian citizen in 1994.[105] While living in Canada, he entered the United States seeking work and was residing in the United States on September 11. On September 19, while conducting an investigation of his roommate, federal agents interrogated Baloch about the attacks. He denied any involvement but disclosed that he had previously been deported from the United States and had obtained false identification documents and passports. Baloch was arrested under a program known as PENTTBOM, an acronym for Pentagon/Twin Towers Bombings. The FBI initiated PENTTBOM immediately after September 11[106] to seize illegal immigrants, investigate whether they had any ties to terrorism, and hold them "until cleared." He was taken to the Metropolitan Detention Center (MDC) in Brooklyn, New York.

PENTTBOM's focus was on prevention of future attacks rather than prosecution. The FBI seized individuals who had "been identified as persons who participate in, or lend support to, terrorist activities."[107] The FBI tracked down suspects through cell-phone logs of the hijackers, searches of the hijackers' cars and personal effects, tips by "members of the public suspicious of Muslim and Arab neighbors who kept odd schedules," and interviews with hijackers' neighbors.[108] Federal and local enforcement agencies also created "watch lists" designed to identify potential hijackers and terrorists.[109] Friends and acquaintances of the suspects, and people who just happened to be in the area when the investigators arrived, were also interrogated. The detentions gave the FBI time to investigate whether the aliens were connected to terrorist activities.

An estimated 1,500–2,000 people were detained without charges while the government investigated them.[110] The exact number of persons held in the program was never officially revealed. The Office of the Inspector General reported that over 1,200 people were questioned following 9/11.[111] After November 3, 2001, when the number was at 1,147, the government stopped releasing figures.[112] Between September 11, 2001, and August 6, 2002, 738 were arrested. The detainees were held until they were cleared.

Nearly all the people detained were men of either Muslim or Middle Eastern descent. The largest number, approximately 33 percent, came from Pakistan—more than double the number from any other country. The second-largest group was from Egypt. Sixty-three percent of the detainees were between twenty-six and forty, although many were older. The detainees spent an average of eighty days locked up without charges. More than a quarter of detainee clearance investigations took over three months. Baloch was held for nearly seven months. One detainee was held for 244 days.[113] Another man was held for more than twenty-six months.[114] A third man was held for eight months in solitary confinement before he was brought before a judge or assigned a lawyer.[115] Although the detainees did not suffer the extensive harm and prolonged sensory deprivation experienced by Jose Padilla, Yaser Hamdi, and Ali al Marri, the number of people detained in the PENTTBOM program and denied their due process rights was five hundred times the number held at the naval brig in Charleston, South Carolina.

Under the Fifth Amendment of the Constitution, people living in the United States are entitled to due process. The amendment does not distinguish between citizens and noncitizens. As Justice Stephen Breyer reiterated in a Supreme Court case decided in 2001, "The Due Process Clause applies to all 'persons' within the United States, including aliens, whether their presence here is lawful, unlawful, temporary, or permanent."[116]

The vast majority of immigrants were held on such minor violations as extending a stay past the expiration date, entering the country without inspection, or entering the country with invalid immigration documents. Prior to 9/11, although the INS had the authority to arrest and detain foreign nationals who had violated the terms of their entry into the country, violations would have been resolved through paperwork.[117] The FBI detained all individuals who were "of interest" or whose status was uncertain. There were no clear criteria for determining who was of interest. Under a "hold until cleared" policy, the INS was instructed not to release any detainees, even on bond, until cleared by the FBI. In the New York City area, anyone picked up on a PENTTBOM lead was automatically deemed "of interest" for purposes of the hold until cleared policy. Once cleared by the FBI, the individuals still had to be processed by the Immigration and Naturalization Service. Even those the FBI determined to be of "no interest" were affected by the bureaucracy and subject to release delays.[118] After aliens had been ordered deported or had voluntarily agreed to go home, the DOJ continued to block their departure to investigate whether they had ties to terrorism.[119] More than five hundred detainees were deported. None have been charged as terrorists.[120]

Under this government policy, only noncitizens were subjected to scrutiny. American citizens were not affected and could go on with their lives. The choice to detain only foreign nationals may have seemed reasonable in those early, fiercely patriotic days following 9/11, where all nineteen hijackers were foreign nationals of Arab descent. However, it is certainly true that America's safety is not ensured by investigating only foreign nationals. Timothy McVeigh was a citizen. So was the Unabomber. The Lackawanna Six, an accused al Qaeda sleeper cell composed of Middle Eastern men, were all citizens. However, by excluding citizens from the PENTTBOM roundup, the administration found it easier to deny due process rights without raising a public outcry.

The government's rationale for holding immigrants in violation of their visas was based on the "mosaic" theory of terrorism. FBI agents in local field offices were not in a position to determine whether a single piece of information or a single person was of significance in a larger mosaic picture. However, FBI headquarters, as the central repository of all the various bits of information and evidence, would be in a position to determine whether a particular alien was "of interest." Thus detainees would be held until the FBI's central office cleared them. However, the FBI's centralized clearance process was slow and understaffed, resulting in long waits for investigations and clearances.[121]

Ten days after the attacks, chief immigration judge Michael Creppy ordered that the immigration cases not appear on the public docket and not be discussed outside the immigration court. He further instructed that the hearings be closed to the press, visitors, and even family members. In addition, judges were not permitted to confirm or deny whether a particular case was on the docket or scheduled for a hearing. It was, essentially, a complete blackout both on substantive and procedural grounds.[122] The only exception was that a detainee's attorney was provided a record of the proceeding, provided that the file did not contain classified information. However, many detainees did not have access to their attorneys in the early days of their incarceration. Attorneys had difficulty discovering where their clients were detained. The DOJ blocked names and locations of detainees, stymieing attorneys and rights groups, such as the ACLU, in their efforts to ensure representation.[123]

The immigrants detained in PENTTBOM were housed in prisons throughout the country. Aliens of "high interest" were detained at the MDC, where conditions were substantially harsher than at other facilities. The MDC was locked down twenty-three hours a day. Initially, detainees were not allowed to make legal phone calls and were not informed of their legal right to engage pro bono services. After the initial incommunicado period, when detainees were permitted to make one telephone call per week to their attorneys, MDC personnel would dial incorrect numbers and tell the detainee that the number was busy or no one answered. An unanswered call counted for their one call per week. Calls answered by voicemail also counted.[124]

Under federal law, a detainee must be notified of the proceedings against him.[125] Under PENTTBOM, it took an average of fifteen days for immigration officials to notify detainees held at the MDC of the charges.[126] The detainee must also be provided with a list of free legal services providers and allowed to be represented by an attorney or other representative. Under the law, immigrants are not entitled to court-appointed attorneys provided by the government in deportation hearings unless they are charged with a crime. They are permitted to hire their own counsel, if they can afford an attorney, or they may be able to find an attorney willing to handle their case for free. Initially, detainees were not allowed attorney visits. The first recorded visit occurred on September 29, nearly two weeks after detention.[127] Detainees were also not allowed visitation privileges and were limited in their ability to contact their consulates.

Shortly after arriving at the MDC, Baloch requested to speak with an attorney. Although Baloch had the right to seek legal assistance, it was not until November 7, six weeks after his arrival at the MDC, that he was allowed to make his first phone call to the Legal Aid Society (which had agreed to represent detainees). He met with an attorney two weeks later. His meetings with his attorneys were both audio- and video-recorded. Knowing that the conversations were recorded induced him to censor his conversations with his attorney.

In addition, although the law required that INS officials notify the immigrants that they had a right to contact and speak with consular officials of their country, when Canadian officials inquired about Baloch they were not told that he was being held at the MDC.[128] He did not meet a Canadian consular official until December 13. On April 16, 2002, more than six months after he had been picked up, Baloch was put on a plane to Toronto without any personal identification or money.

Detainees at the facilities alleged that they had been physically and verbally abused, pushed into walls and doors, denied access to the bathroom for twenty-four hours, subjected to arbitrary strip searches, short-shackled, and deprived of sleep by guards banging on their cell doors. They were also provided inadequate medical care and recreation, deprived of their religious practices, and held incommunicado during the first few weeks of their detentions.[129] Family members and friends who inquired about the detainee were frequently falsely informed that the person was not at the MDC.[130]

Shakir Baloch and others sued Attorney General Ashcroft and other officials for violating their rights in holding them on minor violations to provide time for the agents to investigate whether they were terrorists. A federal district court in New York denied their claim.[131] The court wrote that it was permissible for the government to have an ulterior motive in arresting the men for immigration violations. As long as the arrests were legal, "the government may use its authority to detain illegal aliens pending deportation even if its real interest is building criminal cases against them."[132]

Baloch and other plaintiffs also filed a second claim, alleging that their due process rights and other constitutional rights were violated while they were imprisoned at the MDC. Baloch identified one instance where five guards threw him from corner to corner of the cell and called him a "fucking Muslim terrorist," saying, "You did this to us. We're going to kill you." The judge allowed the plaintiffs to go forward on the due process and constitutional law claims. The case was appealed. However, a case raising similar issues was accepted by the Supreme Court in June 2008.[133]

Other challenges to various aspects of the PENTTBOM program were rejected by the courts. In one case, the Center for National Security Studies sued under the Freedom of Information Act (FOIA) to obtain the names of the people detained, their citizenship status, their attorneys, dates of arrest and release, locations of arrest and detention, any charges filed against them, and reasons for the detentions. The court of appeals in the District of Columbia ruled against the FOIA request on the basis of a law enforcement exemption in the act.[134] The exemption provides that records or information compiled for law enforcement purposes, where the production of the law enforcement records or information could reasonably expect to interfere with enforcement proceedings, can be withheld from the public.

The court of appeals asserted that releasing the information would assist al Qaeda in mapping the course of the investigation and provide the terrorist organization with a composite picture of the investigation and information as to which of their members had been compromised. In addition, the court believed that releasing the information could deter cooperation by the detainees.[135] The court trusted the government's statement that many detainees might have links to terrorism.

In another case, this one in response to the closed-door immigration hearings ordered by chief immigration judge Michael Creppy, several media organizations sued for access to the hearings on First Amendment grounds. Similar to the decision in the Center for National Security case, the Third Circuit Court of Appeals also agreed with the government. The court noted that the newspapers did not have a First Amendment right of access to deportation hearings, as they would have to criminal proceedings, where there is an "unbroken, uncontradicted history" that establishes the right.[136] The court accepted the government's arguments that releasing the names of detainees would allow terrorist groups to intimidate them and create false information; that the detainees have a privacy interest in their names because release of their names associated with 9/11 attacks would injure their reputations and possibly endanger their safety; and that releasing the information could compromise the ongoing investigations.

However, the underlying reason for the hesitation of both appeals courts to overrule the federal government is that courts traditionally defer to the executive on national security issues. Since the executive has far more access to intelligence than judges do, judges are reluctant to second-guess the executive on these matters. Consequently, even though the Third Circuit recognized "the dangers presented by deference to the executive branch when constitutional liberties are at stake, especially in times of national crisis, when those liberties are likely in greatest jeopardy," it concluded, "On balance, however, we are unable to conclude that openness plays a positive role in special interest deportation hearings at a time when our nation is faced with threats of such profound and unknown dimension."[137]

This deference to the executive was not untypical during that early period following the attacks on September 11. Although disclosing public information is essential in a free society (the policy of access to information is implicit in the FOIA), in times of war the law is often silent. The judiciary is hesitant to second-guess the executive in matters of national security. Deferring to the executive seems like a reasonable approach, since the executive has superior knowledge on security. However, a policy of deference trusts that the executive is acting with integrity. As documented throughout this book, integrity hardly seemed like a controlling tenet in the Bush administration. The administration repeatedly ignored the Geneva Conventions, the U.S. Constitution, and the rule of law in pursuing its War on Terror.

Perhaps the most passionate and memorable words on whether courts should defer to the executive on matters of national security were spoken by Judge Tatel in dissenting from the majority opinion in the Center for National Security Studies case. Judge Tatel is one of a handful of judges who stood up to the executive in those early days following 9/11 by speaking compellingly for a balance between national security and liberty. This balance requires that courts not reflexively defer to the executive but rather thoughtfully consider all the evidence in the circumstances presented. Pointing to congressional testimony, human rights reports, and articles about alleged governmental abuse, Judge Tatel believed that there was sufficient evidence to justify an investigation into the government's conduct.[138]

In recognizing the compelling governmental interest in responding to the September 11 attacks, Judge Tatel wrote that there is an equally important interest in the case that the court overlooks:

> Knowing whether the government, in responding to the attacks, is violating the constitutional rights of the hundreds of persons whom it has detained in connection with its terrorism investigation—by, as the plaintiffs allege, detaining them mainly because of their religion or ethnicity, holding them in custody for extended periods without charge, or preventing them from seeking or communicating with legal counsel. . . . Just as the government has a compelling interest in ensuring citizens'

safety, so do citizens have a compelling interest in ensuring that their government does not, in discharging its duties, abuse one of its most awesome powers, the power to arrest and jail.[139]

In addition to deference to the executive, there may have been another motivation underlying the support of both appeals courts for the executive. Judges sometimes refuse to rule against the executive for fear of the consequences. What if a judge releases the defendant, and the defendant then commits a terrorist act? No judge wants to be held responsible for making that mistake. Better to defer to the executive and let the Supreme Court make these weighty decisions, judges think. Unfortunately, in this situation, the U.S. Supreme Court refused to review the Center for National Security decision when it was appealed.

As years have passed and the memories of 9/11 partially faded, courts have become more willing to confront the executive.[140] This sea change began when the Supreme Court issued its rulings against the executive's unlimited claim of power in June 2004 in *Hamdi v. Rumsfeld* and *Rasul v. Bush*.

Material Witnesses in Detention

The administration also detained approximately seventy mostly Arab or Muslim men, without charges, as "material witnesses."[141] Because criminal law depends on witnesses' testimony at criminal proceedings, individuals who can provide material and relevant testimony in a proceeding are sometimes held as material witnesses to ensure that their testimony will be available. Material witnesses are, by definition, distinct from criminal defendants. However, after September 11, 2001, the administration manipulated the law by creating a new policy that would allow it to hold suspicious people as material witnesses while they were investigated. The government was not as interested in holding the people as "witnesses" as it was in holding them as suspects. Like detaining immigrant visa violators, holding material witnesses was a form of preventive detention.

Under the statute that provides for holding material witnesses, a person may be arrested and held to secure his testimony at a criminal proceeding.[142] However, if the testimony of the person can be secured by deposition (a statement taken under cross-examination) or if it is otherwise certain that the person will appear at the criminal proceeding, the government is not permitted to detain him. Nevertheless, after

9/11, the government misused the statute, detaining mostly Muslim and Arab men as material witnesses. The administration held these men, often under maximum security conditions, for as long as necessary to investigate whether they were a threat to the nation. The men were not charged with a crime at the time of the arrest. In twenty of thirty-three cases, the material witnesses were never brought before a grand jury.[143]

In one case, investigators who searched the car of two hijackers immediately after 9/11 discovered a phone number that led to a San Diego address. A man named Osama Awadallah had lived there eighteen months earlier. FBI agents picked him up. They did not advise him of his right to counsel or against self-incrimination. During the interview, Awadallah admitted knowing one of the hijackers, although he had not seen him for over a year. The FBI wanted Awadallah to testify at a grand jury hearing on the terrorist attacks. The agency filed an affidavit stating that Awadallah was a flight risk with family ties in Jordan and that he needed to be detained until he testified. The FBI did not mention that Awadallah had three brothers in San Diego, one of whom was a citizen.

He was flown to New York, kept in solitary confinement, shackled, and denied phone calls to family members and friends. Twenty days after his arrest, Awadallah testified before a grand jury in New York, admitting that he knew one of the hijackers. A few days later, he testified for a second time. Finding inconsistent testimony, the U.S. Attorney arrested him for making false statements during his grand jury testimony. He was released on bail on November 27, 2001, having spent eighty-three days in prison.

Awadallah challenged the indictment on the grounds that a grand jury hearing is not a legal "criminal proceeding" as required by the statute. The federal district court agreed and dismissed the indictment. The court also noted that because the material witness statute did not apply to grand jury witnesses, his arrest and detention were unlawful. The court of appeals reversed that decision. The appeals court acknowledged that it would be improper for the government to employ the statute as a pretext to detain persons for criminal activities for which the government has not yet established probable cause, the requirement for an arrest. Since the burden to establish probable cause is much heavier than the burden to hold a material witness—a material witness can be held with only a statement from an FBI or other law enforcement agent saying that the person is a flight risk—the material witness warrant should not be taken lightly. Nevertheless, the court believed that it should defer to the president on issues of national security—as all but one court did in the immigration detention cases. This appeals court found a reasonable balance between the liberty infringement in holding someone as a material witness and the government's "countervailing interests" of national security. In Awadallah's situation, the court accepted on trust the facts in the government's affidavit that Awadallah "may well have incentive to leave," and "there is no way to prevent him from leaving, no effective way, unless he is detained."[144]

Hold first, charge later was the administration's approach. In more than twenty-four of seventy cases, the detainee had no hearing for three or more days. In ten cases, a hearing was never provided to contest the detention. One man was held for seven days before appearing in court, and his court proceeding lasted less than five minutes. Another man did not appear before a judge for fifty-seven days following his arrest. He was interviewed at least six times without counsel and not provided an attorney, although he had requested one. The government failed to inform witnesses that they had a guaranteed right to counsel and discouraged them or otherwise delayed providing counsel. In violation of basic due process rights, the DOJ also failed to inform thirty-six men of the reasons for their detention.[145]

At least forty-four people were held as material witnesses from September 11, 2001, to November 24, 2002.[146] More than half those held as material witnesses in connection with the September 11 attacks were held for a month or longer, and several were held for ninety days.[147] At least one man was detained for over a year. Seventeen were American citizens. Twenty-four of the men were deported, and two of them (Padilla and al Marri) were designated as enemy combatants. The government has apologized to thirteen of the men for wrongfully detaining them.[148]

PART THREE

LAWLESS DETENTIONS
IN GUANTANAMO

I

GUANTANAMO AND THE ROAD TO THE SUPREME COURT, 2002–2004

The previous part looked at three men—two American citizens, Jose Padilla and Yaser Hamdi, and Ali al Marri, an American resident, who were tortured and held in isolation and incommunicado, without charges, without due process protections, and without access to lawyers—and the more than 1,500 men who were held in preventive detention in American cells. This part looks at the belly of the beast, Guantanamo Bay, where over a period of seven years the United States held more than eight hundred men in detention. The men were frequently kept in isolation, cruelly treated, and even tortured. They were held without charges and without due process protections or access to lawyers for years. The difference between the men in part 2 and the men in this part is that the Guantanamo detainees were foreign nationals with no ties to the United States.

Yet, in Guantanamo too, the United States could have detained the captured combatants to protect our nation and still have treated them humanely and with dignity. Guantanamo would not have been a blot on our nation's history if we had followed the rule of law as articulated by the Geneva Conventions. If we had adhered to the GC and treated the prisoners as lawful combatants or prisoners of war, or even as unlawful combatants, we could have held them lawfully for the duration of the conflict but held them with dignity. We could have prosecuted those Taliban and al Qaeda detainees who committed war crimes pursuant to the law of war and our Constitution. Instead, we designated all captives held in Guantanamo as enemy combatants to circumvent the rule of law and provide cover to mistreat and torture them. We could have done better.

WHY GUANTANAMO?

After the United States attacked Afghanistan in November 2002, the military needed to find a secure detention center for captured Taliban and al Qaeda combatants. The administration decided on the naval base in Guantanamo Bay, Cuba, a tropical forty-five square miles of land and water along the southeast coast of Cuba.

The United States entered Guantanamo Bay in 1898, during the Spanish-American War. It never left. In 1901, Congress passed the Platt Amendment, which demanded that Cuba "sell or lease to the United States lands necessary for coaling or naval stations at certain specified points to be agreed upon by the President of the United States."[1] The Cuban constitutional convention ratified the Platt Amendment later that same year.

Two years later, with the Spanish-American War over, the United States entered into a lease with Cuba that guaranteed that "the United States shall exercise complete jurisdiction and control over and within" Guantanamo Bay.[2] A treaty in 1934 seemingly gave Cuban sovereignty over Guantanamo Bay but required that both parties agree to termination of the lease.[3] Cuba has tried to terminate the lease year after year, even refusing to accept the annual rent of "two thousand dollars in gold coin."[4] The United States has never agreed.

The administration selected Guantanamo Naval Base as the best location to house Taliban and al Qaeda captives for one noteworthy reason. American officials believed that because Guantanamo was not on American territory, prisoners would not have the constitutional right to file habeas corpus petitions in federal court. Habeas hearings provide for a due process hearing before a neutral decision maker. The government hoped to rely on *Johnson v. Eisentrager,* a U.S. Supreme Court ruling that detainees held outside U.S. jurisdiction could not bring habeas petitions in American courts.[5] Thus, as the administration saw it, the captured combatants would be held in limbo, with no access to the courts or lawyers and entirely at the mercy of the military and the interrogators.

John Yoo, who was the deputy assistant attorney general in the Department of Justice's Office of Legal Counsel at the time of the attacks on 9/11,[6] mirrored the thinking of the administration when he wrote, "No location was perfect," but Guantanamo "seemed to fit the bill." He added, "The federal courts probably wouldn't consider Gitmo as falling within their habeas jurisdiction."[7]

The first group of prisoners, dressed in orange jumpsuits and wearing earmuffs or noise-blocking headphones and goggles or hoods, arrived from Afghanistan and Pakistan on January 11, 2002. Their feet were manacled and their hands short-shackled to chains on their belts. They were taken to an outdoor detention center called Camp X-ray.

The detainees were relentlessly exposed to the burning tropical sun with little or no shade. There were no bathrooms in the eight-by-eight cells; buckets were used instead. Metal pipes for urinating were added later. Detainees were also given drinking water in buckets. To an outsider, the cells looked a lot like dog kennels. The military rushed to build more secure and protected indoor housing, as well as structures to isolate the highest-risk prisoners. But until the indoor housing was built, prisoners lived in the cages.

The military held the detainees in strict isolation and subjected them to nearly constant interrogation. Before each session, the detainees were strapped to stretchers for their safety as well as the safety of the soldiers transporting them, according to the administration. Prisoners were not informed of the charges, if any, against them. Nor were they allowed to meet with their families or counsel.

When the first twenty captives arrived in Guantanamo, Richard B. Myers, chair of the Joint Chiefs of Staff, contributed to the administration's attempt to dehumanize the enemy by stating that the detainees "would gnaw hydraulic lines in the back of a C-17 to bring it down."[8] In 2002, Secretary of Defense Donald Rumsfeld described the captives in Guantanamo as "the worst of the worst."[9]

At the beginning, however, the administration did not know what kinds of people it had captured. The administration had hoped that among these captives were high-level operatives who would provide critical information when interrogated. However, over time it became apparent that not one of the initial three hundred captives, known as enemy combatants, was anything more than a low- to mid-level participant.[10] A study published in 2006 that relied exclusively on government records and documents concluded that 55 percent of the detainees had not committed any hostile acts at all against the United States or its allies.[11] Only 8 percent were characterized as al Qaeda fighters. No more than 5 percent of the detainees had been captured by U.S. forces; 86 percent had been arrested by either Pakistan or the Northern Alliance and turned over to the United States. Lieutenant Colonel Berg, one of the people assigned to facilitate prosecutions in Guantanamo, echoed the findings of the report when he said, "In many cases, we had simply gotten the slowest guys on the battlefield. We literally found guys who had been shot in the butt."[12]

A significant number of the Guantanamo detainees arrested by Pakistan or Northern Alliance forces were not captured on the battlefield at all; they were seized in their homes, in the fields, and on the streets and

په هغه اندازه پانګه وګټی چه د تاسی خوب کی هم نه وی راغلی. د طالبانو
ضد قوا سره مرسته وکړی چه قاتلا ن او داره ماران د افغانستان څخه وشړی.

Leaflets dropped in Afghanistan offering monetary rewards for Taliban and al Qaeda fighters.
Courtesy of Herbert A. Friedman.

sold for the bounties offered by the United States.[13] It was an extremely
lucrative business, and many people took advantage of the opportunity.
Tribes living in the Pakistani and Afghani regions sold members of
enemy tribes to the United States. Other Afghanis and Pakistanis seized
Arab expatriates living in Afghanistan and sold them. The ransoms
ranged from $5,000 to $20,000 or more.[14]

Airplanes dropped flyers and leaflets written in Pashto or Dari,
two local languages, announcing the payments. The leaflets included
pictures of American twenty-dollar bills and said such things as "The
reward, about $4,285, would be paid to any citizen who aided in the
capture of Taliban or al Qaida fighters," "Get wealth and power beyond
your dreams—help the anti-Taliban force to rid Afghanistan of murderers and terrorists," and "You can receive millions of dollars for helping
the anti-Taliban force catch al Qaida and Taliban murderers. This is
enough money to take care of your family, your village, your tribe for
the rest of your life—pay for livestock and doctors and school books
and housing for all your people."[15]

From the time the first prisoners arrived in Guantanamo, habeas
lawyers had tried to meet with them and represent them in their habeas
hearings. For over two years, however, the administration did not
permit a detainee to meet a lawyer. They believed that the prisoners
would be more likely to reveal confidences and intelligence in the interrogations if they were isolated from outside contact. It was not until
June 2004, when the Supreme Court ruled in *Rasul v. Bush*, that the
administration acknowledged the detainees' legal right to consult with

a lawyer. And even then, it took up to six months for lawyers to meet with their clients, since each lawyer had to be cleared for access to classified intelligence.

For years, the military did not release the names of the prisoners, so families and lawyers had no way of knowing for sure who was held there. During those years, the military embarked on a fierce interrogation policy that involved cruel, inhumane, and degrading treatment, as well as torture.

MARTIN LUTHER KING WEEKEND, JANUARY 2002

The first case on behalf of the detainees was filed in January 2002, over Martin Luther King weekend. A spirited Southern California lawyer, Steve Yagman, and one of the most revered constitutional law professors in America, Erwin Chemerinsky, had read that the military was transporting men from Afghanistan to Guantanamo Bay, Cuba. These two men dropped their other work and swiftly drew up court papers to file an emergency matter. As they saw it, everyone must be afforded due process and access to a neutral magistrate to determine whether that person is being lawfully held. The detainees transported from Afghanistan to Guantanamo were no different from any other captives when it came to due process rights.

They called their case *Coalition of Clergy v. Bush*.[16] It was the first case on behalf of the Guantanamo detainees. The lawyers filed on January 20, 2002, nine days after the first detainees arrived. The coalition consisted of concerned clergy, journalists, lawyers, and law professors who feared that the men sent to Guantanamo were likely

not to have representation or access to the court system and believed
someone had to assist them. Yagman and Chemerinsky, along with
the coalition, filed their habeas corpus petitions as "next friends" on
behalf of the men in Guantanamo. *Next friend*s is a legal term used
when litigants are unable to represent themselves.

Yagman, a former Harlem schoolteacher, was known in the local
legal community as a man with strong convictions and a "street fighter." To some, he was a champion of civil rights, to others, an aggressive
and eccentric advocate. He had filed more than five hundred lawsuits
against the City of Los Angeles and the Los Angeles Police Department,
alleging civil rights violations as a result of police misconduct.[17]

Erwin Chemerinsky is a frequent commentator on television and
radio, and his articles appear regularly in newspapers and magazines.
He participates in countless panel discussions, symposia, and lawyers'
and judges' forums. He has argued numerous appellate cases before the
U.S. Supreme Court and other appellate courts and has testified before
congressional committees. He is the author of five books, including a
constitutional law treatise and a constitutional law casebook, has written over one hundred law review articles, and writes regular columns
on the Supreme Court for three periodicals. At the time Chemerinsky
filed suit in this case, he was a distinguished professor at the University
of Southern California School of Law in Los Angeles. He is presently
the inaugural dean of a new law school at the University of California,
Irvine, in Orange County.

In an e-mail, Chemerinsky described the origins of the lawsuit. It is
a fascinating account not only of the rushed emergency filing on behalf
of the detainees, but also of how the attorneys were personally driven
to file and advance this litigation in spite of their hectic lives and their
many other commitments.

> On the Sunday of Martin Luther King Day weekend in 2002, Stephen
> Yagman called me. We had worked together on many cases over
> many years. We talked about the reports of men being brought to
> Guantanamo in handcuffs, blindfolded, and drugged The reports,
> I think, were that they would be housed in 8 foot by 8 foot cages
> (though that might have come later). He thought that a lawsuit should
> be brought. We discussed a habeas petition and the ability to use [a
> federal statute] 28 U.S.C. 2242, which allows a habeas petition to be
> filed by a person being held or "on behalf" of a person being held.
> We discussed *Johnson v. Eisentrager*. We discussed who the plaintiffs
> might be.
>
> Yagman then recruited some clergy, journalists, and professors to

be plaintiffs. He quickly wrote a complaint. I agreed to be co-counsel with him. I was flying on Monday (MLK Day) to speak in New York on Tuesday and Thursday/Friday, but was returning to L.A. in between to teach my classes on Wednesday. As a result, I don't recall even getting to see the complaint before it was filed (but I might have). The case was titled *Coalition of Clergy v. Bush.*

I landed in New York on Monday and had about twenty-five calls from reporters who had seen the complaint. Every network morning show wanted me to appear. Yagman said he did not want to do this and asked me not to do this. I said that I would handle it however he wanted. In hindsight, I think we made a mistake in not getting out the message quickly about why the government's actions were unacceptable.

I was quoted in *USA Today* and a few other newspapers. The result was unlike anything I'd ever seen. When I turned on my computer on Wednesday morning, I had over two hundred new messages. About 195 of them were incredibly nasty and hateful. Many wished me and my family dead. I recall mentioning this to a *Daily Journal* reporter and he asked me to send them to him. He then wrote a column about it. The hate e-mail, mail, and phone calls continued all week. A secretary at USC felt threatened by the messages she was receiving and called campus security. They came to investigate me.

I was responsible for writing all of our briefs in the case. The government moved to dismiss and I wrote our opposition. The case was assigned to Judge Howard Matz. He scheduled a hearing in February. Yagman and I agreed that I would argue it. It turns out that Yagman got caught in a snowstorm in Aspen and never made it to the hearing.

The hearing was strange. Paul Clement, then the deputy solicitor general, came from D.C. to argue for the government. He and a bunch of lawyers from the U.S. Attorneys office were at one table. I was by myself at the other. I asked Bob Berger, who was one of the plaintiffs, to come up and sit with me. Bob used to be the op-ed page editor at the *L.A. Times.* He now is a professor in the Journalism School at USC. Judge Matz came out and said that he had drafted an opinion. He would give copies to counsel, but no one else could see it. We could have fifteen minutes to read it and then we'd have oral arguments. It was a twenty-five-page opinion and it ruled against us on everything.

True to his word, we then had oral argument. It was lengthy. My task was to persuade Matz that he change his mind. The low point for me was during a discussion of third-party standing. Matz said to me at one point, "Professor, you know the cases better than I do, but you're not persuading me."

I had little doubt as to the outcome. There were three issues: standing [under the legal term *standing,* the person filing the lawsuit must have a particularized and actual or imminent connection to the litigation and be in danger of sustaining a direct injury or harm from the action that is challenged; a court will dismiss a case where no party has standing], venue [whether the case was filed correctly in federal court Los Angeles and not in Washington, D.C.], and whether those in Guantanamo could have access to habeas in light of *Johnson v. Eisentrager*. Matz ruled against us on all three issues, though he said that standing was a close question. I recall the opinion coming out the day after the hearing on Friday. As expected, Matz ordered dismissal of the case.

We then filed an appeal and asked for expedited review. Again, I wrote the briefs. The oral argument again was strange. Judge Noonan was not present. He was listening in on a speaker. He did not ask a question. He coughed occasionally so we knew he was there. Paul Clement argued for the government and again he did a superb job. I remember most that there were a lot of questions about whether we could show that the Guantanamo detainees did not otherwise have access to the courts. I recall being very frustrated in my rebuttal and saying, "There have been virtually no suits by or on behalf of Guantanamo detainees. There are two possibilities here. One is that they like being held in cages at Guantanamo and just don't object. The other is that their families don't know where they are and don't have resources to file lawsuits for them. The latter is much more plausible, isn't it?"

The decision came down on a Monday in November. One of my frustrations since the outset has been that the courts seem in no hurry to decide these cases. These cases involve the imprisonment of human beings. Almost a year had gone by to that point.

I remember being upset as I spoke that night and making reference in my introduction to losing the Guantanamo case in the Ninth Circuit and the Supreme Court granting cert in another case that I had won. I did not discuss the merits of the Ninth Circuit opinion, but I recall expressing sadness at the court's failure to provide protection. A couple of years later, I was on a panel with Marsha Berzon [one of the panel members in the Ninth Circuit decision] at another conference and she raised her opinion in *Coalition of Clergy* and defended it. I remember being surprised, but saying little.

Around this time, a man in San Diego contacted Yagman and said that his brother (Salim Gherebi) was in Guantanamo. He asked Yagman to provide representation. Yagman agreed and *Gherebi v. Bush* was filed. Yagman asked Matz to consider it on the earlier briefs. Matz agreed to do this and immediately granted the government's motion to dismiss. We appealed. The Ninth Circuit granted expedited review and also agreed to consider it based on the earlier briefs. The case was argued in August 2003. I recall I had a conflict that day that could not be rearranged. Yagman said that he'd argue.

In December 2003, the Ninth Circuit ruled in our favor. It held that *Johnson v. Eisentrager* was distinguishable.

In June 2004, the S.Ct. in *Rasul* came to the same conclusion as the Ninth Circuit. It also remanded *Gherebi* based on a footnote in its Padilla decision about venue needing to be where the person is being held or, if the person is outside the U.S., where the responsible military officials are being held. The case was transferred to D.C.

The case then got transferred to Judge Green and was put together with all of the other Guantanamo cases. You know the rest.

That is the story. To me, it really is one of the justice system failing those who needed it the most.[18]

Erwin Chemerinsky has continued to represent Salim Gherebi. As of October 2008, Gherebi was still in Guantanamo.

THE ROAD TO THE SUPREME COURT

In spring 2002, an American woman contacted Washington, D.C., attorney Thomas Wilner on behalf of a lawyer in Kuwait. The lawyer was concerned about twelve young Kuwaitis who were missing after traveling to Afghanistan in 2001. According to the lawyer, the young men had gone to Afghanistan as charitable workers. They were on a mission of good works providing humanitarian aid in Afghanistan and Pakistan. Their parents were very worried.

The Kuwaiti lawyer had contacted several well-known and well-connected Washington attorneys before contacting Wilner, but the other attorneys were unwilling to assist. Wilner was a graduate of Yale University and the University of Pennsylvania Law School, and now a managing partner of the International Trade and Government Relations Practice in a leading Washington law firm, Shearman and Sterling. He agreed to take the case but reserved the right to withdraw if any of the young men turned out to be terrorists.

Wilner sought to use his connections with insiders in the Department of Justice and the Department of State to locate the men, but no one would reveal the Kuwaitis' whereabouts. He then flew to Kuwait to meet the families. While there, he learned that the men were being held at the naval base in Guantanamo, Cuba. The International Red Cross and the U.S. government had informed the Kuwaiti government, and the government passed the information to the parents, who informed Wilner. After Wilner agreed to represent the detainees, he discovered that the Kuwaitis had been seized by local villagers and sold to the U.S. military for bounties.

When Wilner returned home from Kuwait, he informed his firm that he would represent the young men. There was resistance from some of the firm's partners, one partner saying that, as a "patriot," he would not represent a detainee. But the courageous Tom Wilner could not be dissuaded. Other partners feared that the firm could lose business. The younger partners were more concerned than were the older partners.

It was not clear whether the younger law partners were of a more conservative generation or whether they were worried that if Wilner's actions caused clients to leave, they faced greater financial consequences. Wilner offered to resign and take the cases with him but the partners, to their credit, asked him to stay.

The Kuwaitis insisted on paying Wilner. The firm, however, preferred not to "make money off the terrorists." Wilner decided to donate the money to charity. At first, the firm sent all fees to a 9/11 charity. After two years, the firm reassigned the fees to the firm's charitable giving program. The families paid for the first couple of years, with the state of Kuwait assuming the costs thereafter. The families together spent about $2 million on the cases. Wilner suffered financially as a result of this arrangement, but he considers it to be entirely worth it.

Although some of the attorneys worried about the firm's finances, Wilner's international and domestic clients respected his choice to defend the detainees. They felt that if he was willing to stand up for the detainees, he would represent them just as vigorously.

Initially, the firm's partners asked Wilner not to publicize his work on behalf of the detainees. He refused, arguing that since the government was trying the detainees in the media, he needed to respond in the media. His work in the media was part of his legal obligation in serving his clients, he said. For a second time, he offered to resign. Again, the firm pulled back. However, in those early years, the firm rarely mentioned that one of its partners was representing Guantanamo detainees.

Like other attorneys who had courageously agreed to represent detainees shortly after 9/11, Wilner received hate mail. Many of his friends had counseled him not to represent the detainees. One surprising exception was Robert Mueller, the director of the FBI. At a dinner

Thomas Wilner. Courtesy Shearman & Sterling LLP.

party in December 2002, Mueller toasted Wilner, saying, "This is what a lawyer should do." Mueller believed that although the detainees were bad people, our system required that they be granted a hearing to challenge the legality of their detentions. The father of a detainee said to Wilner that he had always "looked up to the United States" but "lost his faith" when he heard about the incarceration of his son and the others. However, after Wilner agreed to represent his son, the father told him, "Tom, you restored my faith."

WITH A LITTLE HELP FROM THE CUBAN IGUANA

Wilner filed *al Odah v. United States* on behalf of his clients in July 2002.[19] Fawzi al Odah was the lead petitioner. His father, Khalid, described his son as a twenty-five-year-old religious teacher.[20] Khalid al Odah, who had served as a colonel in the Kuwaiti Air Force during the 1991 Persian Gulf War, organized the families after the twelve Kuwaiti detainees were brought to Guantanamo.[21]

Wilner filed the case in the Washington, D.C., Federal District Court on July 8, 2002. The court dismissed the suit on July 30 on the ground that, under the 1950 Supreme Court case *Johnston v. Eisentrager,*[22] "aliens detained outside the sovereign territory of the United States"[23] may not bring a petition for habeas corpus. In the court's opinion, Guantanamo was outside U.S. jurisdiction. Thus the court did not have jurisdiction over the petitioners' habeas actions. Wilner appealed to the Federal Court of Appeals for the District of Columbia Circuit.

On March 11, 2003, the D.C. Circuit Court of Appeals affirmed the district court decision. As in the district court, the appellate judges ducked the thorny issues of America's inhumane interrogation treatment as well as due process violations of the men in Guantanamo. Instead, relying again on *Eisentrager,* the court ruled that alien military prisoners held in territory outside U.S. sovereignty had no access to the federal courts. In the court's opinion, Cuba's "sovereignty" trumped U.S. jurisdiction and control in Guantanamo. Accordingly, the court wrote that the federal district courts did not have jurisdiction to entertain habeas petitions from the Kuwaitis or from any other Guantanamo detainees.

In his briefs to the district and appeal courts, as well as in his petition to the U.S. Supreme Court, Wilner asked for only modest relief. He requested that his clients be informed of the charges against them, that they be permitted to visit with their families and with counsel, and that they be afforded access to a hearing before an impartial tribunal to consider whether there was any lawful basis to their detention. That is, he requested the fundamental due process rights afforded all defendants. He acknowledged that the rights he was requesting on behalf of his clients were subject to any restrictions reasonably necessary to protect national security.

The federal district court consolidated the *al Odah* case in the federal district with a case filed on behalf of British and Australian citizens who were also held in Guantanamo, *Rasul v. Bush*. The cases remained consolidated all the way up to the Supreme Court.

Joseph Margulies, the lead attorney in *Rasul*, had become involved early in representing Guantanamo detainees when an attorney for David Hicks, an Australian detainee in Guantanamo, contacted him. Hicks had trained in an al Qaeda camp and served with the Taliban until the Northern Alliance captured him and handed him over to the United States. Hicks would become known as "Australia's own Taliban." An attorney in London who represented Shafiq Rasul and Asif Iqbal also contacted Margulies. Margulies had a long history of representing people on death row and people who had accused police officers of brutality

According to Margulies, Shafiq Rasul and Asif Iqbal had been boyhood friends in the town of Tipton, in Britain's west Midlands.[24] In early September 2001, they traveled to Pakistan, where Iqbal was to enter into an arranged marriage. In October, they crossed over the border to Afghanistan to provide humanitarian aid. When the United States bombed Afghanistan, they joined a group of refugees from Kunduz, but soon the Afghan warlord Rashid Dostum surrounded them. Dostum's men transported them to his prison at Shebargan. In December, they were handed over to the Americans and held at the U.S. military base in Kandahar until January 2002, when were shipped to Guantanamo. In his book, Margulies provides powerful descriptions of the harsh treatment endured by these two men while in Guantanamo.

The team of attorneys joining Margulies included Clive Stafford Smith and the Center for Constitutional Rights (CCR). CCR has been instrumental in Guantanamo litigation, becoming the clearinghouse for habeas attorneys. In spring 2002, Michael Ratner was its president. Ratner and the center received three hundred pieces of hate mail in February 2002, when they filed their first case.[25]

Clive Stafford Smith was born in England but at the age of eighteen moved to the United States. A graduate of Columbia Law School, he had been living in New Orleans and was a prominent death penalty lawyer when he joined the *Rasul* team.[26] In any gathering, Stafford Smith is always one of the most engaging and spirited people in the room.

The consolidated cases of *al Odah* and *Rasul* had lost in the federal trial court and the Federal Appeals Court for the District of Columbia Circuit.[27] Losing cases in those early days of litigation following September 11 was common, as Yagman, Chemerinsky, and other attorneys can testify. Judges were hesitant to decide in favor of the detainees. They preferred to trust the administration, believing that government officials had access to privileged information showing how dangerous the detainees were. Besides, what judge wanted to be branded as the judge who released a terrorist? For the habeas attorneys, it was frustrating to be on the losing end of the decisions because the courts were afraid to oppose the government.

The writ of habeas corpus (known as the Great Writ) protects a person from being held in custody or otherwise deprived of liberty without an effective and speedy judicial inquiry into the legality of the detention. The question before the judge is not whether the detainee is innocent or guilty—that is decided at trial. Rather, the question is the legality of the detention. Habeas has a long history, with roots deep in early English law, going back as far as the Magna Carta in 1215, five centuries before we became a nation. Habeas corpus (literally, "present the body") was designed to protect individuals from being imprisoned by an English monarch without recourse to law and a fair and just hearing. A person who believed that the Crown was holding him in violation of the laws would file a habeas petition. Alexander Hamilton, one of our nation's founders, wrote, "The practice of arbitrary imprisonments have been, in all ages, the favorite and most formidable instruments of tyranny." Habeas is the "remedy for this fatal evil."[28]

When the United States won its independence, we adopted English common law as a fundamental piece of our heritage, and the right to habeas corpus was an integral part of the English common law. In drafting the Constitution, the founders included this clause: "The privilege of the Writ of Habeas Corpus shall not be suspended, unless when in Cases of Rebellion or Invasion the public Safety may require it."[29] After the states formed a nation, Congress enacted a statute giving the federal trial courts the power to hear habeas corpus applications in "all cases where any person may be restrained of his or her liberty in violation of the constitution, or of any treaty or law of the United States."[30]

And this is where the issue comes to the forefront for the Supreme Court to resolve. To what extent was the statutory right to habeas, as created by Congress, applicable to the Guantanamo detainees, and how much additional protection was available to the detainees under the constitutional right to habeas? This was not an academic question. If Congress has the power to provide habeas protection, does it not also have the power to take away that right? But if the right extends beyond the statute to the Constitution and our heritage through English common law, Congress's removal of the statutory right does not eliminate the underlying right under constitutional and common law. Under the Constitution, Congress cannot restrict constitutional habeas rights, except in times of rebellion or invasion. The *Rasul* court and later cases reviewing Guantanamo detainees' concerns had to consider whether the detainees had a right to habeas (either statutory or constitutional). There is also an argument that the U.S. Supreme Court has the power in its own right to hear habeas cases, and that Congress cannot take away that right. This issue was raised in 2007.[31]

After the D.C. Court of Appeals ruled against their clients, Wilner, Margulies, and the other attorneys for al Odah and Rasul petitioned the U.S. Supreme Court to hear their cases. Except in very limited circumstances, the Supreme Court is not required to accept cases presented to the Court. Instead, the justices rely on their discretion in selecting cases to hear. Cases that raise issues with wide implications are attractive to the justices. On the other hand, the justices, who are often conservative by nature and careful to maintain their credibility in the public arena, are hesitant to step into problems they may not be able to resolve wisely. All courts, from the Supreme Court on down, expect their decisions to be followed and, if necessary, enforced. However, unlike the executive, courts do not have armies at their disposal to enforce their decisions. Consequently, they may decline to rule on issues that could cause them to clash with another branch of government, particularly the executive branch in times of war. The executive branch had asked the Court to defer in detainee matters, arguing that the rights and treatment of detainees are matters exclusively for the executive in times of war. Wilner needed to persuade the Supreme Court justices that it was in their interest to take his case, and that the Court would find a resolution that was reasonable, legally sound, just, and welcomed by the public.

Wilner's brief was a model of elegance. His petition presented three arguments to the Court. First, he argued that under the Constitution and the principle of separation of powers, the courts have a critical role in striking a balance between protecting national security and conserving the fundamental legal principles in our Constitution. It is true, Wilner argued, that the executive must guard our security. Our security is essential to our survival as a nation. However, the courts must act as impartial arbiters to examine the executive's actions. The executive's power does not exclude the judiciary's responsibility to oversee its actions. If the judiciary defers to the executive, the executive has no need to explain the necessity of its actions. At the least, the Court should require the executive to justify its actions. Wilner added that by permitting the administration to pursue its actions without judicial inquiry, the Court would be granting the administration license to imprison foreign nationals arbitrarily outside its jurisdiction, at any time and for any period. Without judicial inquiry, the administration was also at liberty to mistreat prisoners. Wilner pointed out that the prisoners were not asking for immediate release. His clients were only requesting that they be given the right to visit with their families and consult with counsel. The petitioners were also asking that an impartial tribunal determine whether there was cause to detain them.

Secondly, Wilner argued that the administration's mistreatment of the detainees and the denial of their rights and protections under the Geneva Conventions had become an international embarrassment. Here was an opportunity for the Supreme Court to make it right and redress the harmful image that the United States had been projecting to the world.

Finally, Wilner responded to the government's position that Guantanamo was not within U.S. jurisdiction and, consequently, the detainees did not have the right to file habeas corpus petitions. As both Tom Wilner and Joe Margulies pointed out, the government's military base in Cuba was entirely self-sufficient. It had its own water plant, schools, transportation services, and entertainment facilities. The United States exercised full criminal jurisdiction over everyone in Guantanamo, whether U.S. citizens or foreign nationals. Cuba's laws had no effect in Guantanamo. Moreover, since the term of the lease was infinite, the United States was not about to abandon the base.

Then Wilner added a twist to his Guantanamo argument. When the Cuban iguana crosses the border from Cuba into Guantanamo, it is protected under U.S. law, specifically the Endangered Species Act.[32] "Even animals on Guantanamo are protected by U.S. laws and regulations," Wilner wrote. However, "human beings held prisoner at Guantanamo are not entitled to the same protection as a Cuban iguana." The terrible

Iguana crossing. Photograph by the author.

irony was that if the Court did not agree to review Wilner's case, the Cuban iguana would be safeguarded while the human beings held at the base could look to no American or international laws to guarantee their safety and humane treatment.

After Wilner submitted his petition to the Supreme Court, Linda Greenhouse, the highly respected *New York Times* Supreme Court reporter (until she left in 2008 to join Yale Law School), phoned him. Greenhouse and Nina Totenberg at National Public Radio were the queens of Supreme Court reviewers. Greenhouse read nearly all the petitions and briefs that the parties submitted to the Court. Over her thirty-plus years of writing on the Supreme Court, she had developed an intuitive sense of the kinds of cases the Court would hear. Greenhouse told Wilner that, initially, she had not expected that the Supreme Court would hear his case. It was fraught with conflict and interference with the power of the commander in chief in time of war. However, after reading his petition, she changed her mind. Wilner had convinced her that the justices could not ignore the profoundly important issues raised, particularly that of the power of the executive in times of war. She was right. The Supreme Court agreed to hear the case.

After the Supreme Court took on the case, the military released Rasul and Iqbal. The case continued with the twelve Kuwaiti citizens, including Fawzi al Odah, all represented by Wilner, and the two Australians, David Hicks and Mamdouh Habib, represented by Margulies and his associates.

A HISTORIC SUPREME COURT DECISION:
RASUL V. BUSH

On June 28, 2004, eighty-four-year-old Justice John Paul Stevens proudly announced the Court's decision upholding the rule of law in Guantanamo Bay, Cuba, in the consolidated cases of *Rasul v. Bush* and *al Odah v. United States.* In a 6–3 decision, the Court ruled that the detainees had the right to file habeas corpus petitions in federal district court challenging their detentions.

As the justice with the most seniority among those who joined the majority opinion, Stevens had the job of deciding who would write the opinion. Stevens, whose views on the importance of habeas review and judicial oversight of executive power took form while he clerked in 1947 for Justice Wiley Rutledge (appointed by FDR), chose himself.

According to a former law clerk, Stevens in 2004 was still as sharp and as much an old-style Republican pragmatist as when President Gerald Ford appointed him thirty years earlier. Stevens is the only justice on the Court who always writes the first draft of his opinions; other justices typically ask their clerks to do the work. First drafts are circulated among the justices for comments, as they construct an opinion on which the majority can agree.

The Supreme Court directly addressed Wilner and Margulies's major concerns. Stevens agreed that the Court had the jurisdiction to hear the case and to decide for itself how far the executive can go in denying detainees habeas rights in times of war. Stevens pointed out that the petitioners in this case differed from the German prisoners in *Eisentrager* in "important respects." He noted that the Guantanamo petitioners were not nationals of countries at war with the United States; they had not been afforded access to counsel, charged, tried, and lawfully convicted of wrongdoing, as had the detainees in *Eisentrager.* Another difference, although one that Stevens did not include in his comparison of the two cases, was that six of the detainees in *Eisentrager* had been tried and acquitted. The military had provided the detainees in *Eisentrager* the due process of law guaranteed under the Constitution, a right that was not made available to the Guantanamo detainees. In addition, as Stevens made clear, the Guantanamo detainees were imprisoned in territory over which the United States exercised exclusive jurisdiction and control.

Stevens affirmed that the detainees had a statutory right to habeas as set out by congressional law.[33] Because he decided the case on the statutory right to habeas, he did not need to address whether the detainees also had a constitutional right to habeas (*Eisentrager* was concerned with the constitutional right). However, Stevens added that the right to habeas was fundamental, suggesting that the detainees might also have a right to habeas under the Constitution and the common law. He noted that the right to habeas preceded any congressional statute and that common law habeas extended not only to persons "within [the] sovereign territory of the realm" but in "all other dominions under the sovereign's control."[34] A person reading this opinion could interpret it as meaning that detainees held in U.S. custody overseas could also file habeas petitions in federal district courts.

Stevens gave little deference to the government's position that Guantanamo was on Cuban soil. He pointed out that the "United States exercises complete jurisdiction and control over the Guantanamo Base, and may continue to permanently if it chooses."[35] He added, "Considering that the statute draws no distinction between Americans and aliens held in federal custody, there is little reason to think the Congress intended the geographical coverage of the statute to vary depending on the detainee's citizenship. Aliens held at the base, no less than American citizens, are entitled to invoke the federal courts' authority under the habeas statute as the basis for the decision."[36] Justice Anthony Kennedy wrote in a concurring opinion, "Guantanamo Bay is in every practical respect a United States territory."[37]

Stevens never mentioned the Cuban iguana in his opinion. However, if you looked carefully, you could see it proudly peeking out from behind the pages of the decision.

It was an incredible victory for Wilner, Margulies, and their colleagues. They had won one of the most important human rights cases in modern history. Although the decision was based on a statute, that statute rested on a fundamental principle in our Constitution, a principle integral to America's spirit and essence—the right to file a petition for a habeas corpus, due process hearing.

It was also an extraordinary day in American constitutional law. That same day, the Court had ruled, in *Hamdi v. Rumsfeld,*[38] that an

American citizen who is designated an enemy combatant has the constitutional right to a meaningful hearing.

With the *Rasul* decision in their pockets, the lawyers made plans to visit the detainees. Until then, the government had denied habeas attorneys the right to meet with their clients. However, even after *Rasul*, the lawyers could not immediately board a plane to Guantanamo. Each lawyer had to obtain a security clearance, and clearances could take up to six months. While planning their trips, the attorneys rushed to file their habeas cases.

Beginning in July 2004, the world of Guantanamo litigation dramatically changed. What had started in winter and early spring 2002 as a few courageous lawyers standing up to defend the Constitution when it was not fashionable now became a flood. According to one estimate, as many as five hundred lawyers were extricating themselves from their busy lives and volunteering to contribute their skills to future cases.[39] These new lawyers brought much-needed legal assistance to the hundreds of detainees who required representation.

However, the Supreme Court victory, although sweet, was short-lived. The administration was not ready to concede. The administration challenged every detainee's habeas petition and sought congressional legislation foreclosing habeas for all detainees. Habeas lawyers had to return to the Supreme Court in 2006 and again in 2008, each time to reassert the fundamental right to a due process hearing that they thought they had won in June 2004.

—

II

INHUMANE TREATMENT OF
DETAINEES AT GUANTANAMO

An entire book could be written on the administration's inhumane treatment of the Guantanamo detainees. This is not that book. However, it
is important to provide a snapshot of the kinds of human rights abuses
that the detainees have suffered over their years in Guantanamo. The
treatment of the detainees falls into two categories: confinement without charges or a hearing, that is, the lack of due process and absence
of fundamental fairness; and mental and physical abuse suffered by the
detainees while in the detention centers.[1]

INTERROGATION LOG OF A GUANTANAMO DETAINEE

The abuse of Mohammed al-Qahtani, a Saudi, is well documented.
The administration believed that al-Qahtani was intended to be the
fifth terrorist on United 93, the flight that crashed into a Pennsylvania
field when passengers tried to take over the controls. Al-Qahtani had
tried to enter the United States on August 4. Mohammed Atta, a leader
of the 9/11 attacks, had planned to meet him in the airport parking lot
in Orlando, Florida. Al-Qahtani had no credit cards, carried $2,800
in cash, and had booked no return flight.[2] An immigration agent,
believing that al-Qahtani was attempting to stay permanently, did not
approve his entrance into the United States and returned him to Dubai.
In December 2001, he was captured fleeing Tora Bora in Afghanistan.
The military sent him to Guantanamo two months later. In July 2002,
the government realized that he had been deported from Orlando in
August 2001 and conducted more severe interrogations.

Time obtained an eighty-four-page interrogation log for al-Qahtani.[3]
The log begins in November 23, 2002, and continues for nearly two
months, until January 11, 2003. Although it is not necessarily a complete account of all that occurred in the interrogations, the log does
include descriptions of cruel, inhumane, and degrading treatment and
torture.

When al-Qahtani refused to provide information, the officials asked for permission to use "counter resistance strategies." In November 2002, William J. Haynes, the general counsel of the Department of Defense, had recommended that Defense Secretary Rumsfeld approve these techniques. The Haynes memo identified three categories: Category 1 consisted of yelling and deception. Category 2 included twelve techniques, including stress positions for up to four hours, thirty days of isolation, hooding during interrogation, twenty-hour interrogations, removal of clothing, and use of detainees' phobias, such as fear of dogs.[4] Category 3 techniques were only to be used on the most resistant detainees and included waterboarding. Haynes recommended blanket approval of fifteen of the eighteen techniques. His recommendations included all of categories 1 and 2, but only "grabbing, poking in the chest with the finger, and light pushing" of the four strategies proposed in category 3.

On December 2, Secretary Rumsfeld approved the techniques that Haynes recommended. After he signed the memo, Rumsfeld wrote, "I stand for 8–10 hours a day. Why is standing limited to 4 hours?"[5] The strategies recommended by Haynes and approved by Rumsfeld were then applied to al-Qahtani beginning on December 2, 2002.[6]

Al-Qahtani endured months of isolation and sleep deprivation. He was deprived of sleep for up to twenty hours a day for days at a time. At one point, when his heart rate dropped precipitously, he was hospitalized for twenty-four hours. However, even then, the guards played loud music by such artists as Christina Aguilera to keep him awake and disturb his prayer and chanting sessions. He was not permitted to pray except to a shrine dedicated to Osama bin Laden and was made to wear a sign reading, "I am going to hell because I am full of hate."

At one point, he was taken to a new interrogation room decorated with photos of 9/11 victims, the U.S. flag, and flags of coalition forces. They shaved his beard and head and, to add to this cultural disgrace, photographed him after the shaving. Women interrogators stood or sat very close to him with their foreheads touching his. He found it unbearable to have a woman in his personal space. Another time, a woman interrogator straddled him on the floor. They required him to look repeatedly at women in bikinis. He was forced to stand while the national anthem was played. They poured water over his head to keep him awake or when he refused to drink. They placed a mask with a smiley face on him and taped a picture of a three-year-old victim over his heart. Another time, they placed a hood over his head. The interrogators required him to write letters to victims of 9/11 expressing condolences.

Al-Qahtani was told that his status was lower than a dog and that he needed to elevate his status to that of a dog. They instructed him to bark happy for victims of 9/11 and to growl at pictures of al Qaeda terrorists. They placed a towel over his head in imitation of a burka, and interrogators instructed him to dance with the interrogator. Another time, after he went to the latrine, they stripped and searched him. The interrogators turned up the air conditioner and removed his blankets when he refused to talk. Medical personnel were present throughout the interrogations to make sure he did not die. When he refused to eat or drink, they attached him to an IV or threatened force-feeding.

A letter by an FBI agent that covers September and October 2002, before the period of the log, says that a dog was used "in an aggressive manner to intimidate" al-Qahtani. The letter also specifies that al-Qahtani had been "subjected to intense isolation for over three months" and "was evidencing behavior consistent with extreme psychological trauma (talking to non-existent people, reporting hearing voices, crouching in a corner of the cell covered with a sheet for hours on end)."[7]

Gitanjali Gutierrez, a litigator with the Center for Constitutional Rights (CCR), represents al-Qahtani. Gutierrez was the first habeas attorney to meet with a detainee in Guantanamo. When she first met al-Qahtani in December 2005, Gutierrez wore a hejab, the head covering worn by Muslim women, as a sign of respect for his religion and to let him know that she was on his side and not another government interrogator.[8] Gutierrez and other female lawyers and paralegals often cover their hair and neck with a hejab when meeting their clients, depending on the conservatism of the detainee.[9]

Gutierrez drafted a declaration describing her impressions after six meetings with al-Qahtani, from December 2005 through September 2006. The declaration was used "in support of CCR's request in Berlin Germany, for the prosecutor to conduct a war crimes investigation under Germany's universal jurisdiction laws ('the Rumsfeld case')."[10] The Center for Constitutional Rights had filed a similar lawsuit in Germany against Rumsfeld and other administration officials in 2004, but the case was dismissed in February 2005, presumably because of U.S. pressure. This second complaint was filed immediately after Rumsfeld resigned.[11]

The second suit accused the defendants of ordering, aiding, or failing to prevent war crimes. Eleven of the twelve plaintiffs were Iraqi citizens tortured at Abu Ghraib. The twelfth was Mohammed al-Qahtani.

Under German law, the 2002 Code of Crimes against International Law, the German federal prosecutor has the power to prosecute war criminals, regardless of where the crime was committed or the nationality of the accused.[12] Defendants included, in addition to Rumsfeld, former CIA director George Tenet and the authors of the "torture memos," John Yoo and Jay Bybee.[13] In April 2007, the German federal prosecutor said she would not proceed with the investigation. The parties appealed in November 2007.[14]

In her declaration, Gutierrez writes that she had to meet with al-Qahtani in the same type of cell in which he was held in isolation and subjected to other abuses. She notes that he could not yet discuss some of the methods used on him because they were secret and classified. He had no memory of other interrogation methods used on him or events that occurred in Guantanamo. His weight had fallen from 160 pounds to 100, and during their meetings, he exhibited signs of post-traumatic stress disorder and other traumatic conditions.[15]

The military had planned to prosecute al-Qahtani for murder, giving him a military commission hearing. However, on May 13, 2008, the convening authority, Susan J. Crawford, who supervises the commission hearings, released a statement that she had dismissed the charges against al-Qahtani.[16] Because evidence against him had been obtained by torture, the coerced confessions would have caused problems for the prosecution in presenting its case. Although the military dismissed the charges against al-Qahtani, it retained the option to prosecute him at some later date.

A Note on Waterboarding in Guantanamo

Waterboarding received an enormous amount of media attention in 2007 and 2008. Although many people assume that the military waterboarded detainees in Guantanamo, at the time of this writing, fall 2008, there are no documented cases of waterboarding in Guantanamo. That is not to say that people were not waterboarded in Guantanamo; there are several indications that they were. However, I could not find any written confirmation.

Brent Mickum, a habeas lawyer and partner at Spriggs Hollingsworth, a Washington, D.C., law firm, indicated that he had heard from two people who should know that waterboarding did occur at Guantanamo. One of his sources was a soldier from North Carolina who had been among the first guards assigned to Guantanamo in 2002. The soldier contacted him after Mickum appeared on C-Span on April 3, 2007. The soldier was not familiar with the term *waterboarding*, but when Mickum described the procedure, the soldier said, "We use that all the time. We called it drown-proofing."[17]

In researching the term *drown-proofing*, I could not confirm that the term was commonly used as a synonym for waterboarding. The closest connection between drown-proofing and waterboarding seemed to be in the training of Navy SEALS, who endure something called drown-proofing when they go through SERE training. They are placed in deep water, and their hands and feet are tied while they must accomplish certain tasks.[18] This procedure may be associated with waterboarding among some military personnel.

In 2005 and several times thereafter, Mickum spoke with a civilian contractor who had been in Guantanamo in 2003.[19] The contractor informed Mickum that when he was Guantanamo in 2003, the operation was in chaos and the interrogators were continually asking for direction. Although he did not participate in waterboarding the prisoners, the contractor knew all about waterboarding and told Mickum that he had overheard interrogators talking about seeing the procedure in Guantanamo.

It is possible that official documentation showing that waterboarding did indeed happen in Guantanamo will eventually surface. Mickum noted that CIA interrogators work in their own trailer at Guantanamo, and no one else knows what happens in these trailers. However, at the time of this writing, administration officials have only admitted to three instances of waterboarding, all at other venues. As part of the dirty process known as extraordinary rendition, the CIA kidnapped suspected high-level detainees and flew them to CIA black sites or prisons in other countries to be harshly interrogated and tortured. In some cases, these detainees were waterboarded. After the CIA had finished with them, they were packed up and flown to Guantanamo.

FBI REPORT: JULY 29, 2004

Over the years, the FBI has compiled an extensive volume of abuses that agents observed while in Guantanamo. One of the most prominent observations was recorded on July 29, 2004:

> On a couple of occasions, I entered interview rooms to find a detainee chained hand and foot in a fetal position to the floor, with no chair, food or water. Most times they had urinated or defecated on themselves, and

had been left there for 18–24 hours or more. On one occasion, the air conditioning had been turned down so far and the temperature was so cold in the room, that the barefooted detainee was shaking with cold. When I asked the MPs what was going on, I was told that interrogators from the day prior had ordered this treatment, and the detainee was not to be moved. On another occasion, the A/C had been turned off, making the temperature in the unventilated room probably well over 100 degrees. The detainee was almost unconscious on the floor, with a pile of hair next to him. He had apparently been literally pulling his own hair out throughout the night. On another occasion, not only was the temperature unbearably hot, but extremely loud rap music was being played in the room, and had been since the day before, with the detainee chained hand and foot in the fetal position on the tile floor.[20]

In spite of the revelations related by the FBI, the FBI apparently did little, if anything, to intercede and halt unlawful and harsh interrogation practices that the FBI agents observed at Guantanamo. Reporting the practices seems to be the extent of their intervention.

DENIAL OF TREATMENT

In some instances the problem was not what the military personnel did but what they did not do. Guantanamo officers did not actively torture Abdul Hamid Salam Al-Ghizzawi. Instead, the medics withheld treatment for life-threatening illnesses as he withered away.[21]

Al-Ghizzawi is a citizen of Libya. He lived in Afghanistan for ten years, marrying an Afghani woman. He and his wife have a daughter, born in 2001. Although he had trained as a meteorologist in Libya, he and his wife ran a small bakery that also sold honey and spices. In fall 2001, when the United States began bombing Afghanistan, Al-Ghizzawi and his family fled to a rural area where his in-laws lived. Not long after he arrived, armed men came to his home and told the family to turn over "the Arab." To avoid any harm to his family, Al-Ghizzawi cooperated. The armed men sold him for bounty to the United States. He has been in Guantanamo since spring 2002.

The panel at Al-Ghizzawi's first administrative CSRT hearing in Guantanamo found him not to be an enemy combatant, one of the very few decisions in favor of the detainee. With that decision, the military should have released him. Instead, the Department of Defense ordered a second hearing. At the second hearing, a different panel in Washington, D.C., found him to be an enemy combatant.[22]

Al-Ghizzawi suffers from hepatitis B and tuberculosis. Yet according to his lawyer, Candace Gorman, and despite Al-Ghizzawi's and Gorman's repeated requests, military medics have not treated him for his illnesses. Over the six years he has spent in Guantanamo, he has become seriously debilitated. His symptoms include weight loss; severe pain in his abdomen, left side, and back; constant pain that travels down his legs; a bloated stomach area, causing digestive problems such as vomiting and diarrhea; and a noticeably jaundiced complexion. In addition, his eyesight has deteriorated to the point where he can no longer read, he is always exhausted, and he finds it difficult to walk even a short distance before fatigue sets in. He is often confused and disoriented, and has difficulty concentrating.

When Gorman saw him in summer 2007, he was shivering and his teeth were clenched. His cell is always cold. The military provides him and most other detainees with cold, smelly plastic sheets rather than blankets. The guards removed his thermal undershirt as punishment after catching him with toilet paper on the way to the shower, a violation of detention rules. In another shower-related incident, the guards came to Al-Ghizzawi's room to ask him whether he wanted to take a shower. He responded, "Wait a minute," because he wanted to finish what he was doing. The guards returned with the brutal Emergency Response Force (ERF) which "ERFed" him, knocking out a tooth.[23]

When Gorman visited him in July 2007, he told her that because he had been in isolation for an extended period, he had begun to talk to himself. He was distraught over his condition. Even though he is proficient in English, he was having trouble understanding her. He was near tears when he talked about his family.

In September 2007, two people came to see him: a military doctor and a government official from Washington, D.C. The official asked whether he was a member of al Qaeda or the Taliban. Al-Ghizzawi responded, "No, you already let go all the Taliban and al Qaeda." The official laughed and left. Gorman thought that perhaps the visit portended a review prior to releasing him. However, nothing further came from the visit. The military doctor then informed Al-Ghizzawi that he had a liver infection. The doctor wanted to do a liver biopsy but told him that it was a dangerous procedure with possible "irreversible damage." Al-Ghizzawi declined the procedure and consequently has had no treatment. Gorman spoke to a civilian doctor who explained that the condition can be treated without a biopsy.[24]

When Gorman visited Al-Ghizzawi in late fall 2007, she almost did not recognize him. Her client was "doubled over in pain, and coughing and gagging on his own phlegm."[25] She wrote, "Mr Al-Ghizzawi is dying a slow and painful death," and he "assumes he will die soon (and it appears that way to counsel as well)." She concluded, "After a day and a half of meetings, Mr. Al-Ghizzawi was too exhausted and ill to continue, he apologized to counsel for having to end the meeting early and asked to be taken to an isolation cell so that he could lay down." During the second visit, he told her that his brain was not "working right" and that "he had been trying to keep his mind active by singing songs and talking to himself." He was working on his will. He had been in solitary confinement for more than a year.

Another round of medical muddle and uncertainty occurred in January 2008. Gorman revealed on her blog that a medical doctor at Guantanamo had informed her client that he had AIDS. She filed for access to his medical records and to mandate medical treatment.[26] The government, in opposing access to the medical records, replied that Al-Ghizzawi did not have AIDS and that he had never been so informed. The response intimated that Al-Ghizzawi had made this accusation on his own.[27] The captain of the Medical Corps said that Al-Ghizzawi had been tested four times for the HIV virus, and each time Al-Ghizzawi was informed that the results were negative.

It has never been made clear why the military will not treat him for hepatitis B and tuberculosis. Perhaps they do not want to admit that they have an infectious, or even just ill, detainee at the base. The clinic had no patients in May 2007, I was told when visiting the base, because no one was sick. In reading Gorman's reply to the government's response, one senses her growing frustration and rage.[28] In one of her briefs, she wonders whether the government is subjecting her dying client to "some kind of psychological torture."[29]

On April 8, 2008, the district court judge rejected her motions for medical treatment and access to Al-Ghizzawi's medical records.[30] Noting the reluctance of courts to second-guess the medical treatment provided by government officials, the court decided that, at most, the parties have a difference of opinion. Trusting the government's briefs and not feeling the need to review the medical records on his own, the judge decided that Al-Ghizzawi was being offered adequate medical care. "To be candid," the judge wrote, "if Al-Ghizzawi is currently suffering any harm from his medical condition, it is largely self-inflicted."[31] The judge pointed out that Al-Ghizzawi had declined to have his blood tested or to have an ultrasound of his liver taken and had complained about the temperature of the water when given medication. Deferring

Candace Gorman. Courtesy Mike Kelly Photography.

to the military in times of war was clearly on the judge's mind when he concluded his opinion by noting that it would "not be in the public interest to permit a wartime detainee such as petitioner to leverage that lack of cooperation into a claim for Court intervention into the medical care provided detainees at Guantanamo."[32]

When Gorman visited Al-Ghizzawi on July 15, 2008, she noted that he had been in solitary confinement in a windowless cell for over nineteen months, had threatened to kill himself by drinking his skin medication unless he received medical treatment, and "now spends his days talking to himself and washing and rewashing his clothes in his toilet bowl."[33] Candace Gorman continues to fear that the Guantanamo medics will let him die and then describe his death as an "apparent suicide," "like they did with the last death."[34] As his spirited and indomitable advocate, she wrote nearly one year ago, "Mr. Al-Ghizzawi's death will not be as quiet. . . . I promise."[35]

Gorman is, unfortunately, not the first person to believe that the military might prefer a patient to die in Guantanamo than be released. If he dies in Guantanamo, people will soon forget. If he is released, he is free to talk about his case again and again. Of course, if Al-Ghizzawi is released before his death, he will be no more than the shell of the man that he once was.

SUICIDES AT THE BASE

Candace Gorman was aware, as all habeas attorneys and members of the media were, of the four detainees who had actually committed suicide. Three killed themselves in 2006, and one in 2007. The three in 2006 had collaborated to hang themselves within a few minutes of each other, using torn sheets and clothing to fashion their nooses.[36] Immediately following the suicides, the military sought to collect all legal documents held by detainees throughout the prison, even though lawyer-client privilege should have shielded the documents from the military personnel. The military's purpose was to investigate whether the documents somehow assisted the men in coordinating their suicides. The military believed that notes might have been written on the documents and passed to other inmates.[37]

Since the suicides, the military has issued thick green rubber blankets that cannot be torn into strips for prisoners the military believes may be suicidal. The lone suicide in 2007 was a hunger striker who weighed 88.5 pounds at one point. The military would not provide further details as to how he died.[38] These suicides have been an embarrassment to the military, since they speak against the stated policy of making "sure everyone is safe," a message that reporters are repeatedly told while touring Guantanamo.

The military explains the suicides as acts of politics and military tactics rather than desperation. The former commander of the base, navy rear admiral Harry Harris, described the hangings as "asymmetric warfare," a term that has been defined at times as not "fighting fair."[39]

THE EMERGENCY RESPONSE FORCE

Like Al-Ghizzawi, some detainees have accused the military of sending in a team of soldiers who use excessive force in response to minor infractions. This response team has been called by several names, including Emergency Response Force (ERF), Extreme Reaction Force, and Internal Reaction Force (IRF). Australian detainee David Hicks described an incident involving the force in an affidavit he filed on August 5, 2004. He referred to it as the Internal Reaction Force. Hicks wrote, "I have witnessed the activities of the Internal Reaction Force, which consists of a squad of soldiers that enter a detainee's cell and brutalize him with the aid of an attack dog. The IRF invasions were so common that the term to be 'IRF'ed' became part of the language of the detainees. I have seen detainees suffer serious injuries as a result of being IRF'ed. I have seen detainees IRF'ed while they were praying, or for refusing medication."[40]

Shafiq Rasul, the lead petitioner in the *Rasul* case, said that to be ERFed meant being slammed on the floor, pinned to the ground, and assaulted by a soldier wielding a riot shield.[41] Another former detainee described an experience of being pinned down while the squad poked fingers in his eyes, then forced his head into the toilet and flushed.[42] In still another instance, an IRF team cuffed a prisoner's wrists to his ankles and jumped on his back, immobilizing him. The prisoner, Abdul Zahir, required back surgery afterward.[43]

In January 2003, Specialist Sean Baker, a member of the Military Police Company of the Kentucky National Guard, volunteered to play the role of an uncooperative detainee for an ERF training exercise. He was told to wear the orange jumpsuit worn by detainees instead of his uniform. The four other military police in the training session thought Baker was actually a detainee. When they found him under the bunk, they pushed his face down on the floor, beat and choked him, and slammed his head against the floor several times. He called out that he was a soldier, but apparently they did not hear him or did not believe him. He suffered brain seizures and was subsequently given a medical discharge.[44]

ERF actions are routinely videotaped so that they can be reviewed by senior officers.[45] Baker's tape is missing.[46]

HUNGER STRIKERS AND FORCE-FEEDING

Claiming that they prefer death to the interminable and suffering days at Guantanamo, detainees have refused to eat by going on hunger strikes. The military has responded by describing the hunger strikes as "voluntary fasts."[47] Explaining that it is saving lives, the military force-feeds the detainees. Detainees argue that it is their choice whether to live or die, not the American government's decision.[48] The number of hunger strikers has fluctuated over the past seven years. In September 2005, as many as 131 detainees were on hunger strike.[49]

The director of the clinic detailed for me the procedure the military follows when dealing with people on hunger strikes and the policy behind the procedure.[50] If a detainee refuses to eat for nine consecutive meals, he is sent to the medical facility for observation. The military considers a detainee's intent to commit suicide a "mental health issue." The detainee meets with a psychologist, who determines why the detainee is not eating. According to the clinic director, the reason could be physical or mental. Since hunger strikers gain standing and respect from other detainees, there are all kinds of pressures on them to participate in a hunger strike, he explained.

If the detainee continues to refuse to eat after meeting with the psychologist, the medics restrain him in a "feeding chair," where his head and his body are strapped forcefully in place while he is force-fed. The restraint chairs are for the safety of the nurses, according to the clinic director. A feeding tube three to four millimeters thick and twenty-seven centimeters long is threaded through the detainee's nostril and into his stomach. Sometimes the tube goes down the pipe into the lungs, and the prisoner chokes. A fortified supplement, such as Ensure, is poured into the tube. The detainee is fed twice a day, one nostril each time. Habeas lawyers have claimed that the tube is often yanked out and bloodied. The director informed me that the principle behind the force-feeding is "preserving life." The medics keep the detainee at the facility for an hour after he is force-fed, to keep him from vomiting. Habeas lawyers have said that if a detainee vomits, defecates, or urinates on himself, the medics require him to sit in it. According to the clinic director, detainees who are fed through a nasal tube are at normal weight for their height and age. The director revealed that two detainees had been on strike for over six hundred days when I was at Guantanamo in May 2007.

Attorney Tom Wilner interviewed his client, Fawzi al Odah, about the feedings for a BBC report. In the interview, al Odah explains his attitude in participating in the hunger strikes and the military's response. Like other media services, the BBC has no direct access to the detainees. Media are permitted to visit the detention centers and observe the detainees, but they cannot speak to incarcerated detainees. Only habeas lawyers can talk to detainees

Someone at the BBC had the original idea of asking Wilner whether he would be willing to do an interview on their behalf, asking questions they had prepared. Wilner agreed, conducting the interview on February 1, 2006, at Camp Echo. Wilner sent the interview to the Department of Defense in Washington before forwarding it to the BBC five weeks later. Wilner also had cleared the BBC interview with a Kuwaiti press person who, according to Wilner, enthusiastically encouraged him to do the interview. The BBC then hired two actors to reenact the interview for broadcast:

Q: Fawzi, I am surprised. There are no more tubes in you. I'm glad to see you're no longer on hunger strike.

A: You know what they did?

Q: No. What?

A: They tortured us to make us stop.

Q: What happened?

A: After your trip in December they made a decision: no more hunger strikes. They told me: if you continue the hunger strike, you will be punished. First, they took my comfort items away from me one by one. You know, my blanket, my towel, my long pants, then my shoes. They also stopped giving me cough drops to ease the pain from the tubes. Then they put us in isolation, me and the others on hunger strike. I was put in isolation for ten days. I didn't care.

Then, on January 9—I remember the day, because it was the day before our holiday, Eid al Adha—an officer came in and read me an order from General Hood [army brigadier general Jay W. Hood, commander of the Joint Task Force at Guantanamo at the time]. It said if you refuse to eat, we will put you on the chair—these are special, new metal chairs they have brought to Guantanamo—that you will be strapped up and down very tightly in the chair and that Ensure would be forced into me using a thicker tube with a metal edge. The tube would no longer be left in all the time, but would be forced in and pulled out at each feeding, and that this would happen three times a day. I told him, "This is torture." He said to me: "Call it whatever you like; this is the way it's going to be; we're going to break this hunger strike."

On the next day, January 10, they started this force-feeding in the chair. The person in the next cell over had this done to him. I couldn't see him. But I could hear his screams of pain when they pushed the tube into him and pulled it out. He screamed to stop or at least be more careful. I heard the doctor say: "I have to do it this way. I'm supposed to cause you pain."

After they stopped, this guy called over to me: "Stop your strike. Don't go through this. It's not worth it; it's too painful." They then came to me. They said, "Eat or we are putting you in the chair and forcing you." I thought about why I was on this strike. I thought: I'm brave, but I'm not stupid. There is no purpose in undergoing this metal chair treatment. On the chair, I'll be restrained and unable to resist. They are determined to torture me. One way or another they'll make me stop this strike. This is not why I went on hunger strike. So I told them I would eat, and I did.

Q: Oh Fawzi, I'm so sorry.

A: A lot people did still refuse to eat voluntarily. But then they treated them even worse. Not only did they push the tubes in and pull them out for each feeding, they would force three or four bags of Ensure mixed with other ingredients in a short period of time, like half an hour. This would make the prisoners urinate and defecate all over themselves and throw up. They didn't even change their clothes. They would just leave them there in their chairs for a long time, for hours. Everyone knows this is what happened. Ask anyone.

Q: What did others on strike say?

A: One guy, a Saudi, told me that he had once been tortured in Saudi Arabia and that this metal chair treatment was worse than any torture he had ever endured or could imagine. One guy who suffers from hemorrhoids was kept on the chair for four or five hours, strapped in tightly, and he went to the bathroom all over himself and was left there. Made to just sit there that way for hours. They gave these formulas on purpose to make them defecate and urinate and throw up on themselves. The whole purpose was to break the hunger strike. And they did that. There are now only about three or four people on strike, and I don't know how they continue, how they have endured this treatment.

Q: Fawzi, do you mind if I ask you some more specific questions about yourself for a BBC radio interview?

A: No, go ahead.

Q: Obviously, no one from the outside world can see you, so describe your physical appearance now.

A: I am much lighter than I was. I am now about 120 pounds, down from about 150 pounds when I came here. I have become an old man here. I'm only twenty-nine, but I have been here four years in isolation and have gotten old and much weaker.

Q: How's your health?

A: I'm always tired; I have pain in my kidneys; I have trouble breathing; I have pain in my heart and am short of breath. I have trouble urinating and having bowel movements.

Q: How would you describe your mental health?

A: I have given up. They took away the one thing I had control over— whether to eat. The one way I could protest that I'm innocent. I am hopeless. I don't care about anything anymore. I just want to be released. My health doesn't matter. Death in this situation is better than being alive and staying here without hope. Dying would be better if it helped end this situation.

Q: And now you are eating voluntarily?

A: I don't think it is voluntary. I am now eating and drinking because they force me to by giving us no choice and torturing anyone who refused to eat. I refused any food or water for over five months, until they forced us to stop by torturing us.

Q: Was this the first hunger strike?

A: No. This was the fourth hunger strike but the longest. The first one was three days, then ten days, then two weeks, and then this. And I would still be on this strike if I had any choice. Death is better than continuing life like this.

Q: Have you achieved anything—any concessions—through the previous hunger strikes?

A: The problem is that we achieved only temporary changes. Things got better for a few weeks and then went back to being bad.

Q: Did those in charge at Guantanamo agree to negotiate with detainees or hold any discussions in any way?

A: For a while they did. And there were some changes in conditions, but then it went back.

   You must understand that the real problem here is not the horrible conditions—the lousy food, no reading materials, bad medical care, being in isolation. The real problem is being here without reason, without hope, without a hearing. I am an innocent person who has done nothing wrong, and I have had no opportunity to show that. That is the real problem.

   General Hood sent messengers to me and asked to talk to me himself about ending my hunger strike. I refused. I told the messengers to tell him that the problem was not you—you are irrelevant. The issue is not the food or the conditions. My issue is with the people in Washington. They are making the decisions. We need to be released or have the opportunity to show that we are innocent. You are holding innocent people without charge or any chance to get out. That is wrong.

Q: When did you start your last hunger strike?

A: I started on August 8. I was forced to stop it on January 10, so it was over five months.

Q: Do you want to die?

A: Of course I don't want to die. It's much better to eat and live than to starve and die. But death is better than continuing to live this way in indefinite detention, with no reason. I am innocent and have done absolutely nothing wrong, and I don't even get a chance to show that. Death would be much better than living like this, especially if it would help my other brothers here who are also innocent.

Q: How long have you been here now, Fawzi?

A: I have been here four years, more than four years, stuck for almost every moment of that time alone in this tiny cell eating every meal in it, in my bathroom.

Q: Have things gotten better or worse?

A: Nothing has really changed. The immediate reaction by the guards if you refuse to do anything right away is to punish you. Even the physical abuse has really not gotten better. The guards will beat you up quickly if you give any problem at all.

Q: They say in Washington that they have rules against physical abuse.

A: I don't know. But it doesn't matter what the rules are. They probably say they have rules against torture, but look what they just did to end the hunger strike. The biggest problem is that everyone is told that we are terrorists. We can't even explain to them who we are, that I am a teacher who wants to help people and never did anything wrong. That's not what they are told. They are very young people. They think we are terrorists and they treat us that way. They hate us. They think we are responsible for everything bad. If anything bad happens to the United States anywhere in the world, they immediately react to us and treat us badly, like animals. It's understandable they would treat us that way. And maybe if we were terrorists they should treat us that way. But we're not. The real problem is that they are holding innocent people here as if they are terrorists. And they don't give us any chance to prove that we are not.

Q: You now have access to lawyers; in the past you didn't. Is this not an improvement?

A: I mean no disrespect, Tom. I know you have been trying your hardest. But the U.S. court system is a joke. After four years, nothing has changed. We are innocent, yet we are still here, locked up like animals. We have still never had a hearing and we are still being abused. Look at these conditions. Even if we were convicted criminals, do you think we should be treated this way—kept in isolation in a tiny cell? With almost no exercise and no chance to see the sun. And the fact is we're not convicted. We haven't even been charged, and we are totally innocent.

Q: In Washington they say you are being treated humanely.

A: Those who say that either don't know or are lying. I wish that people who say that would come down here and see for themselves and actually talk to us to try to learn the truth.

Q: Some congressmen have come down here and said that Guantanamo is like a Caribbean resort and that you are eating great food.

A: To me, this is unbelievable. How can they say that without actually coming down here and talking with us and seeing what's happening. As I told you before, that is one of the reasons I stopped eating. They said I was eating great food down here, which is a lie. If I continued to eat, I accepted the lie, I condoned it.

Q: Have you been tortured?

A: I have told you all this before, and I don't want to repeat it again. No details here. But I was tortured badly in Kandahar. I was tortured here too, I was beaten up badly at first when I was brought here. Also, when I first started on this last hunger strike, they abused us badly. They pulled the tubes in and out force-feeding me, which caused a lot of pain. And if I resisted or tried to take the tubes out, they would strap me down, hold my head back and force the tubes in and out causing a lot more pain. It was useless to resist.

I was also told I would be tortured, "put in the chair," unless I stopped the strike. I stopped without undergoing that, but all the others who continued were tortured.

Q: The American authorities say you are being held because you are a dangerous enemy combatant. What do you say to that?

A: It is rubbish. Why don't they charge me, then, if they really think this is true. It's absolutely untrue. And I have never had a fair hearing. I left my home to teach and work for needy people on my official leave. I was caught out of the country and couldn't get back. I have never supported terrorism. I hate it. I have never done anything against the United States. I was simply sold by a Pakistani for money to the United States. It is wrong that they would hold an innocent person like me all these years with no chance and no hope. Why are they afraid of giving me a hearing? I was simply unlucky. I was out of the country and couldn't get back home. Everything else is simply rubbish.

Q: What do you say to their allegations against you? They allege that you admitted traveling through Afghanistan with Taliban members, that you admitted firing an AK-47 rifle at a training camp near Kandahar, that you admitted staying at a guest house with fighters armed with AK-47s, that you engaged in hostilities against the U.S. or its coalition partners, that you carried an AK-47 through the Tora Bora mountains for ten to eleven days during the U.S. air campaign in that region, and that you were captured with five other men by the Pakistani border. How do you react to those allegations?

A: We have discussed each of these before, you and me, in preparing for a hearing I may hopefully get one day. I don't think it is right to discuss these details on radio; I should discuss them at a hearing in court.
As you know, they are stupid. I was out of my country and couldn't get back. I found myself in an area that suddenly became incredibly dangerous, with everyone carrying guns around and hunting Arabs. I was in this place at the wrong time and couldn't get home. And I still can't get home.

Q: Are you prepared to face a court to answer any allegations against you?

A: Absolutely. That is all I have been asking for. For four years, that is what I have asked for. A fair court with fair procedures is what I have been asking for. That is all I have asked for from the beginning, so that the truth can be known.

Q: Have you been charged with any offense?

A: No. I have not ever been charged with an offense, not here or at home in Kuwait.

Q: What is your message now to your family?

A: They should be patient. I have a fair and just cause. I never did anything wrong. I always followed my family and religious teaching, and I never did anything wrong. My whole life has been devoted to trying to help people and trying to work for peace and for the truth. I will always do that, no matter what.

Q: The U.S. authorities won't allow the media to conduct one-to-one interviews with you. They say this is partly for your protection. What do you say to this?

A: That is also rubbish. I'd love to talk to a fair person, to a reporter who could learn the truth and report it to the world.

Q: Before all this happened, what was your view of America?

A: I loved America. It freed my country from Saddam Hussein. My father fought with America against Saddam. I respected America because of its belief in human rights and fairness. It stood for human rights and fairness around the world. America was the country we all looked up to.

Q: What is your view now?

A: I am disappointed in the American government. Very disappointed. It has abandoned all of its own traditions and beliefs, which were the

cause of my respect for it. As someone who lived in the U.S., I cannot
believe the American people know what is happening down here. This
is wrong.

Q: Thank you very much, Fawzi. I will continue to do everything I can to
try to get justice for you.

A: Thank you, Tom. Thank you for trying.[51]

After the BBC aired the show, the administration threatened to ban
Wilner from Guantanamo. But since Wilner had not violated any rules,
the administration backed down. Wilner agreed to inform officials of
any future interviews. However, the incident did not end there. Kuwaiti
consultants to the families demanded that Wilner be fired for acting
"out of control." Since the Kuwaitis were paying the bills, Wilner was
terminated

Another firm replaced Wilner. The other firms involved in the Guantanamo litigation appointed Wilner as lead counsel in the ongoing *al
Odah* litigation. Wilner continues to be involved in representing Guantanamo detainees but now takes cases pro bono. Of the twelve detainees that Wilner represented, eight have been sent home. Four, including
al Odah, remain at Guantanamo, although Wilner is optimistic that at
least two of the four will be released by 2009.[52]

III

THE ADMINSTRATION UNDER SIEGE, 2004–2006

June 28, 2004, was a day of rejoicing. The historic U.S. Supreme Court decision in *Rasul v. Bush* had established due process rights for all detainees. This was a human rights victory. The rights and protections embedded in our Constitution and our belief in fundamental fairness had prevailed. The Supreme Court had turned back the executive's claim to unlimited powers as commander in chief in times of war.

Or so we all thought. As it turned out, the elation was short-lived. The administration was hardly ready to concede defeat or even to admit that any substantive changes had occurred. As far as the administration was concerned, it was business as usual. But in maintaining business as usual, the administration was acting from a position of being under siege. The detainees may have been literally caged in, but because of *Rasul,* the administration was also caged in, albeit figuratively. And rather than acknowledging the winds of change brought about by the Supreme Court and providing due process to the detainees, the administration hunkered down and put on blinders. It was determined to stay the course.

As they battled back in response to *Rasul,* the administration flailed out from the Pentagon and White House compounds with four different lines of attack. First, it created special administrative hearings, called Combatant Status Review Tribunals (CSRT), which would establish enemy combatant status for each detainee. The administration intended these hearings to substitute for, and thereby derail, due process habeas hearings in federal courts. Second, it interfered with the attorney-client relationship between the habeas attorneys and their clients. The administration was concerned that the habeas lawyers might consult with the detainees, and then the detainees would no longer talk to military and CIA interrogators. Third, it challenged the breadth of the *Rasul* decision by arguing that even if the detainees had the right to file habeas petitions, the federal courts had no power to act on them. Essentially, the administration was contending that the detainees had a right without a remedy. Fourth, it convinced Congress to enact a law to eliminate all habeas actions and filings by the detainees. There were approximately 595 detainees in Guantanamo at the time that *Rasul* was decided.[1]

COMBATANT STATUS REVIEW TRIBUNALS

In response to the *Hamdi* and *Rasul* decisions requiring due process hearings to determine whether the detainees were lawfully held and pursuant to the order of July 7, 2004, the administration created the Combatant Status Review Tribunals (CSRTs). The first CSRT hearing was held August 2, 2004. Most of the initial hearings were completed that fall. CSRTs may sound impressively legal, but they hardly served justice. The presumed purpose of the CSRT panels was to establish whether the detainees at Guantanamo Bay continued to be enemy combatants.[2] DOD officials had already determined that the detainees were enemy combatants before these hearings were held, and in nearly every case, the CSRT panels did nothing more than rubber-stamp the earlier determinations.

When one hears the word *tribunal,* one usually thinks of a court where an advocate argues on behalf of each party. But CSRTs were not courts; they were administrative hearings. Administrative hearings often lack the protections provided in a court session, although they still must provide minimum due process protections. In CSRTs, where no lawyers represented the detainees, those protections were severely lacking.

A detainee at a CSRT hearing was not permitted to have a lawyer represent him or argue on his behalf. Instead of a lawyer, the military provided him with a personal representative. The representative was not a lawyer and had no personal loyalty to the detainee.[3] When a detainee revealed confidences, the representative nearly always disclosed those confidences to the CSRT panel members and other military personnel. The panel members were appointed by the Department of Defense.

The CSRT hearings allowed unreliable and hearsay evidence, as well as secret or classified information, often from anonymous sources. There was a presumption that the classified evidence was reliable and accurate. Because the detainee was not permitted access to the classified evidence, he could not rebut it. Information obtained by torture was admissible.[4] For example, the government used the statements that Mamdouh Habib made when he was tortured in Egypt, under the

CIA's extraordinary rendition program and before he was transported to Guantanamo, in making its determination that he was an enemy combatant.[5]

The military permitted the detainees to call witnesses. However, the only witnesses that detainees were effectively able to call were other detainees, who were also designated as enemy combatants. No witnesses from outside the base ever appeared.[6] Detainees were only able to submit evidence on their behalf if the evidence was "reasonably available," which it never seemed to be.[7] In the majority of cases, the only testimonial evidence the detainees could submit was their own. Letters from family and friends were the only documentary evidence detainees could tender to the court.

In 78 percent of the cases, the personal representative met only once with the detainee. Meetings were sometimes as short as ten minutes, including time for translation.[8] And, as noted earlier, since the personal representatives were not lawyers and they revealed client confidences to the panel, they offered little, if any, assistance. In many cases, because of their allegiance to the panels, personal representatives were more harmful to the detainees than if they had not been involved in the hearing process at all.

Two examples illustrate how difficult it was for detainees to present evidence in these hearings. In 1999, Abdul Razzaq Hekmati was regarded as a war hero by the Afghanis for organizing a daring prison break from the Taliban's top-security prison in Kandahar for three high-profile men opposed to the Taliban. However, Hekmati was later falsely accused of being a Taliban commander and serving on the security detail for Osama bin Laden. His accusers included a provincial governor Hekmati had earlier accused of corruption and Hekmati's distant cousin, who was involved in a long-running family feud.

At his CSRT hearing in October 2004, Hekmati requested that two of the men he had assisted in escaping be permitted to testify on his behalf. Both men had become high officials in Hamid Karzai's Afghani government, one the minister of energy, the other a general in the border guards. Although both men were well known to American authorities in Afghanistan and had spoken out on Hekmati's behalf, neither man was contacted, and the president of Hekmati's CSRT ruled that the men were "not reasonably available."[9]

On December 30, 2007, Abdul Razzaq Hekmati died of cancer in Guantanamo after being held for five years. When the naval base was accused of allowing him to die, a spokesman for the Joint Task Force said, "We make every attempt to preserve life here at Guantanamo and we regret any loss of life."[10]

Another example of the absurdity and misery at CSRT hearings concerned detainees who had been captured wearing Casio watches, model F-91. This particular Casio watch was a "common watch used by al Qaida operatives to detonate improvised explosive devices," according to the evidence presented by the military at Guantanamo hearings.[11] One Kuwaiti detainee who had been wearing a Casio when captured testified in his defense that many Kuwaiti citizens wear the same watch "because it has a compass by which a person can locate Mecca, and an alarm that can be set to ring at daily Muslim prayer times."[12] However, his testimony was deemed insufficient, and he was declared an enemy combatant.

The administration initially hoped that the CSRT hearings would satisfy Article 5 of the Third Geneva Convention (GC3), which specifies that competent tribunals must determine a combatant's status.[13] However, Article 5 also specifies that the combatant must enjoy prisoner of war status until the tribunal makes a decision and that the tribunal must determine whether the combatant is a lawful or unlawful combatant. And it requires that a "competent tribunal" determine the combatant's status. CSRT hearings did not meet any of these Article 5 standards. They did not determine whether someone was a lawful or unlawful combatant; they only decided whether the detainee was an enemy combatant, a term not recognized by the GC. They did not accept that the combatant was presumptively a lawful combatant, or prisoner of war, until determined otherwise. In fact, the panel began the proceedings assuming that the detainee was an enemy combatant. In addition, because CSRT hearings lacked substantial due process procedures, they could not qualify as "competent" tribunals as required under Article 5.

In making its determination that a detainee was to be considered an enemy combatant even before the CSRT panel heard the case, the DOD established an elaborate process: First, officers in the field made an initial determination as to whether someone was an enemy combatant. Second, a screening team of government officials, including military lawyers, intelligence officers, and federal law enforcement officials, reviewed the determinations and decided whether to send the person to Guantanamo. Third, a general officer designated by the combatant commander added a further assessment. Fourth, Department of Defense officials evaluated that assessment. Fifth, the secretary of defense or his designee reviewed the detainee's status. Consequently, the CSRT panels provided "a layer of review in addition to the other layers of review already in place for enemy combatants detained at GTMO."[14]

The CSRT tribunals made their decisions on the same day in 81 percent of the cases. The decision was nearly always unanimous. In the records that law professor Mark Denbeaux and his son Joshua Denbeaux—both habeas attorneys—were permitted to examine, the panels always found the detainees to be enemy combatants.[15] The government claimed that 38 of 558 detainees who had hearings were found not to be enemy combatants. However, the two Denbeaux could not find this result in the records they examined, perhaps because the 38 detainees were subjected to "do-over" hearings in Washington, D.C., that reversed the decisions.

Case Study: Majid Khan

Majid Khan emigrated with his family from Pakistan in 1996, when he was sixteen. The family was granted asylum in the United States. Khan graduated from a high school outside Baltimore and worked for the State of Maryland and Electronic Data Systems.[16] In February 2002, Khan traveled to Pakistan to marry. According to his lawyer, Gitanjali Gutierrez, Pakistani police seized him on March 5, 2003, and turned him over to the CIA.[17] Family members and released detainees interviewed by Gutierrez before October 2007 indicate that he was flown to Islamabad at the end of March 2003 and then to a secret CIA detention center, where he was likely tortured. Gutierrez believes, based on those interviews, that Khan was at the CIA-directed Salt Pit facility in Afghanistan, a detention center used by the CIA in its extraordinary rendition program.[18] There is still no official explanation as to where the military held Khan and how it treated him between March 2003 and September 2006. On September 6, 2006, President Bush announced that fourteen high-value detainees, including Khan, were at Guantanamo. On August 9, 2007, the DOD announced that it had classified the fourteen high-value detainees, including Khan, as enemy combatants.

On April 15, 2007, the guards brought detainee Majid Khan from his cell to a nondescript gray module nestled inside the detention centers at Guantanamo. They escorted him into a rectangular room with tables and chairs. Khan was directed to sit in a black felt-lined chair against

Majid Khan on the day of his graduation from Owings Mills High School, Baltimore, Maryland. Courtesy Center for Constitutional Rights.

one of the two longer walls. Two gray plastic chairs flanked him, one on either side. It was 8:48 A.M.

An interpreter on the military payroll sat in one of the plastic chairs. Khan's personal representative, a major in the U.S. Air Force, sat in the other chair. Three military officers, sitting in high-backed leather chairs behind a long, brown, polished table set with microphones, faced Khan. An American flag covered the wall behind the officers. The members of the panel were a colonel in the U.S. Air Force serving as the president, a commander in the U.S. Navy, and a lieutenant in the U.S. Air Force. A sergeant first class was the reporter. A major in the U.S. Air Force acted as the recorder. A lieutenant colonel was the judge advocate (military attorney) for the tribunal. Majid Khan, the detainee, was about to have a Combatant Status Review Tribunal hearing to determine whether his status as an enemy combatant should be continued.

PRESIDENT: This hearing will come to order. You may be seated. Good morning.

DETAINEE [MAJID KHAN]: Good morning. How are you guys doing?

PRESIDENT: Very good, fine, thank you. . . . This Tribunal will determine whether you meet the criteria to be designated as an enemy combatant against the United States or its coalition partners or otherwise meet the criteria to be designated as an enemy combatant. . . .

PRESIDENT: Do you have any questions concerning the tribunal process?

DETAINEE: Ah, I personally am not satisfied with the process itself. But I don't have questions. So far, from what I understood. But I'm not satisfied with the course ah—the tribunal process. I would—I would rather have fair trial rather than have a tribunal process, but I, so far, what I understood, I understood how it goes. But the personal representative told me, ah—but I'm not satisfied with it at all.

PRESIDENT: Very well. This is an administrative process and we will continue through it, and if you have any questions about what we are doing at any time, please feel free to ask.

DETAINEE: The same goes for you too.

PRESIDENT: Certainly.[19]

Khan's understanding of English was significantly better than the other Guantanamo detainees. Nevertheless, his limited education and work experience hardly qualified him to argue alone, without the assistance of counsel, before a military panel that would determine whether he was to remain incarcerated at Guantanamo.

The president of Khan's panel began the CSRT hearing by asking the recorder to read the unclassified summary of the evidence against Khan. The recorder began, "The following facts support the determination that the Detainee is an enemy combatant." He then recited facts, lettered from *a* to *i*. One item recounted that "a computer harddrive [*sic*] seized from a residence where munitions were discovered contained linkages to media seized from the Detainee's residence." Kahn was concerned about this fact, as his testimony would show. The facts also included statements from Kahn's brother and father and from two other men, Iyman Faris and Uzair Paracha, who had been convicted of providing material support to al Qaeda. The gist of their statements was that Majid Khan was involved with a group that he believed to be al Qaeda, and that he might have expressed a desire to become a martyr for al Qaeda. Khan's father allegedly believed that his son had "begun to be influenced by anti-American thoughts and became extremely religious in his behavior."[20]

After completing the recitation of facts, the recorder requested that there be a "closed Tribunal session," without Majid Khan's presence, for the recorder to present classified evidence. Khan, like other detainees, was not permitted to see the classified evidence and consequently had no opportunity to refute it—although it could be used against him. The president granted the request, indicating that the closed session would occur at a later time.

The president allowed Khan's personal representative to identify the evidence that Khan wished to present to the tribunal. The evidence included Khan's statements of having been tortured while in Guantanamo and before he arrived, and written statements and testimony from Iyman Faris, Saifullah Paracha (Uzair Paracha's father), and Khan's father. Khan intended to present his own statements in response to the accusations against him, along with written questions for his witnesses. Khan also wanted to include in his defense a photo of his young daughter.

The president then stated that Uzair Paracha "volunteered not to participate," adding that "because this process cannot compel the testimony of non-U.S. witnesses, the witness is not reasonably available." Before the hearing, the attorney for one of Khan's brothers stated that written testimony the president determined to be relevant would be provided. The testimony was never submitted, though, and the president explained, "Again, because this process cannot compel the testimony of non-U.S. military personnel, this witness testimony is not reasonably available."[21] Khan's personal representative read statements into the record in which Paracha, Faris, and Khan's father denied the incriminating statements that they had allegedly made about Khan and his connection to al Qaeda.

The hearing moved to Khan's presentation of his own testimony. He began by intelligently and methodically identifying the flaws in the evidence and the testimony against him, including the testimony of the various witnesses. He addressed each piece of testimony individually. However, having no lawyer to assist him, he could not think of a way to refute the testimony regarding the alleged computer, hard drive, and media evidence. The best he could argue was that he never owned a computer or a hard drive while living in Pakistan or the United States, and that everyone in the family shared the computers in the household. A lawyer, with the assistance of an expert, might have been able to trace the computers to people other than Khan.

Near the end of the session, an especially poignant, even heartrending, dialogue took place between Khan and the president of the panel. It spoke volumes as to what these often uneducated men faced when they were brought before these panels of American military officers. Kahn at least had the advantage of knowing English and being familiar with our constitutional form of government. Yet even he could not take on this overpowering process, in which the detainee is presumed to be an enemy combatant. In closing his presentation, Khan tried as best he could, in the absence of counsel and with his limited oratorical and persuasive skills, to convince the panel that he was not a member of al Qaeda. He approached the issue by asking the president of the panel what he would do if someone had accused him of being a member of al Qaeda:

> DETAINEE [MAJID KHAN]: Last—last question is . . . and ah—when I
> talk about I've never been to Afghanistan and I never met
> UBL [Usama bin Laden], I cannot possible be member of al
> Qaida. I admit I can't prove I am not al Qaida. It is very dif-
> ficult to prove that someone is not al Qaida. Now there was
> few more sentence in which me and PR [personal representa-
> tive] decided may not be very appropriate to ask, but this is
> a very important question I need to ask you. Let's say just
> someone claims that the Board Members are themselves al
> Qaida. And if you were—if you were in my shoes, I would
> like to know how can you prove it, that you yourself are
> not al Qaida? And if you can't, then I can't either. And if
> you can, then please let me know 'cause I will follow the
> same process to prove that I am not al Qaida. That was
> my question.
>
> PRESIDENT: Sorry, I may have lost the question in there.[22]

Gitanjali Gutierrez was not permitted to meet with her client before October 2006. For nearly a year and a half, the military had blocked a meeting between Khan and Gutierrez on the grounds that Khan had access to national security information. The classified information, as the government saw it, concerned CIA detention sites and torture techniques.

On October 16, 2007, after Gutierrez and her CCR colleague, J. Wells Dixon, obtained top-secret security clearances and agreed to additional gag orders and nondisclosure agreements imposed by the administration, the military allowed them to visit.[23] When they first saw Khan, the lawyers did not recognize him from his photos because he had lost so much weight. They thought that the military had brought them the wrong detainee, something that had happened to them in the past. The lawyers had taken over five hundred pages of notes in their first meeting—as Dixon observed, "Obviously, Khan talked a lot"—but from the five hundred pages, they produced only a one-page summary.[24] The summary revealed that Khan had been on hunger strikes to assert his right to see his lawyers and to protest his being kept in isolation. He also went on a hunger strike to get the *Washington Post*. His request for the *Post* was denied.[25]

The lawyers revealed that Khan was kept in Camp 7.[26] Until that time, no one outside Guantanamo had known about Camp 7; reporters who visited Guantanamo were led to believe that there was no camp beyond Camp 6. Dixon could not disclose the location of Camp 7. Two months after Dixon's visit, the military reported that Camp 7 had been built and readied to house the fourteen high-value detainees who had been transferred to Guantanamo from CIA black sites.[27] The Guantanamo commander said that Camp 7 was necessary to keep the high-value prisoners from retaliating against detainees in other camps who had talked to interrogators. Guantanamo military officials claimed they needed to keep the location of Camp 7 secret for fear of an attack by al Qaeda.[28]

Dixon noted that Khan's family can communicate with him through the Red Cross or by writing to a Washington, D.C., public address "where letters may or may not reach him."[29]

Khan's attorneys filed a Motion for Preservation of Torture Evidence requesting that the court require the government to preserve "all evidence concerning his torture by U.S. personnel for more than three years at secret overseas prisons operated by the Central Intelligence Agency."[30] The motion said that "Khan admitted anything his interrogators demanded of him, regardless of the truth . . . in order to end his suffering."[31] At his CSRT hearing, Khan had testified that he had repeatedly tried to kill himself by cutting and chewing his artery by his elbow,[32] and that he had written on his walls, "Stop torturing me."[33]

On December 17, 2007, Majid Khan wrote a letter to three judges on the U.S. Court of Appeals for the District of Columbia Circuit, the court that would review his CSRT hearing. The letter was attached to a motion filed by his attorneys.[34] The letter was written in his own hand, in script. The portion that the censor allowed through appears below. The grammatical and spelling errors that appear in these letters have been left uncorrected.

Dear Judges,

As you known already, I am a permanent resident of U.S.A. who used to pay 2,400 dollars every month So his government will protect his Constitutional rights. also, I have owned a house in Baltimore Maryland. My brother, nieces and nephews are American citizens. do you honestly believe that I would conspire a plot which would kill American innocent lives even possibly my American friends, teachers and family members. Even Government Sources will tell you that I've never been to Afghanistan. nor ever met "OBL." Why would I ever want to harm U.S.A., who has never done anything but to good to me and to my family.

I remember studying check & balance and Constitutional right in my high school times in States, now this the first time, I am having an opportunity to directly write to judicial branch to get justice for the crime has done against me and in name of "War on terror." I ask you to give me justice in name of "THE GOD," in name of what U.S.A. once stood for, and in name of what Thomas Jefferson fought for. They made a big mistake by torturing me, they didn't have any option but to make me something, which I was not to coverup on the mistake they made. I ask you not to allow them to destroy any evidence and allow me to have a chance to prove that I am innocent.

But actually, I am writing this letter about the "motion to rule Act were torture." I ask you, for only a few minutes while you reading this, just think of me as human being. don't think as if I am a terrorist. don't buy the government propaganda, just think of me a guy who went to Baltimore High School and at age 23 got married left 2 month pregnant wife and all sudden I'm kidnapped by a group of people who are capable of doing any think, even execute me.

I ask you again think of me as a human being . . . not a terrorist. and this human being is a practically an American . . . just for few minutes. [Approximately a half page is redacted.]

please, pay attention to this! I ask you for the last time . . . please close your eyes and just imagine for a Second these things are happening to a person . . . and that very person is happen to be your own Son and or a nephew . . . would you still Say this was not tortured?

He also wrote a second letter to the same judges, dated December 21, 2007:

Respected Judges,

This is my Second letter to you. In this letter, with Gods will (InshAllha) I am going to prove that I am a victim of "War on Terror." English is my second language So please forgive my English grammar and spelling mistakes. [A little over a page of text is redacted.] The only Conclusion I Came up with was that, U.S.A government made a big mistake by torturing a permanent resident of U.S.A. They had no option but to make me Top Secret detainee to do coverup on their mistake. Not only that I was resident of U.S.A. but I officially Spoke [illegible] English and if I had gone to media to show the world what they did to me than at [illegible] puts lots of people in Washington in bad spot, possibly for long time in prison. That is the very reason they made me Enemy Combatant, taking away all my rights. that is the very reason they made me Top Secret. So the public won't know what I got to Say about the crime that Bush Administration committed in name of Good American people or in name of So Called "War on Terror."
    For God Sake! I am a victim of "War on Terror."
    please give me justice. don't let them get away with this, don't let them do Coverup on that. The future of Constitutional rights are on your hands . . . please don't be affraid to do the right thing!

"Do-overs" and Colonel Stephen Abraham

In the rare situations when a CSRT panel ruled that the detainee was not an enemy combatant, the military held a second hearing, or "do-over."[35] In nearly every second hearing, the panel found the detainee to be an enemy combatant, even when the DOD submitted no new evidence. In the rare instances when the DOD lost the second hearing, the military conducted a third hearing.[36]

One courageous man finally shined a light on the sham CSRT hearings. Lieutenant Colonel Stephen Abraham was a reserve military intelligence officer and an attorney who acted as a liaison between the Office for Administrative Review of the Detention of Enemy Combatants and various intelligence organizations. He was assigned as a panel member on one CSRT hearing. On June 15, 2007, Abraham filed a declaration with the U.S. Supreme Court alleging that the CSRT process failed to rise to even minimum due process standards.[37] That declaration made history.

Three months earlier, the Court had declined to hear *Boumediene v. Bush*, which challenged the administration's denial of habeas for Guantanamo detainees. After reading Abraham's affidavit, the Court reversed itself, deciding to hear *Boumediene.* It had been decades since the U.S. Supreme Court had reversed itself in the granting of certiorari petitions; Stephen Abraham had changed the course of Guantanamo litigation. A month later, he testified before the House Armed Services Committee, shining further light on the CSRT hearing process.

Abraham's affidavit and his later House testimony painted a dismal picture of the Guantanamo CSRT hearing process. As a liaison, Abraham found that the process of collecting information was haphazard and lacked quality control. He stated that when he attempted to collect exculpatory evidence, the military denied him access to the evidence.

As a panel member, he found that the military applied pressure on CSRT members to classify a detainee as an enemy combatant. In the few instances where the hearings found a detainee "not an enemy combatant," "the focus of inquiry on the part of the leadership was 'what went wrong.'"[38] In the one panel hearing on which Abraham sat, he and his fellow panel members determined that the detainee was not an enemy combatant, finding that the government's evidence "lacked even the most fundamental earmarks of objectively credible evidence. Statements allegedly made by percipient witnesses lacked detail. Reports presented generalized indirect statements in the passive voice without stating the source of the information or providing a basis for establishing the reliability or the credibility of the source."[39] Yet he discovered that, "when we found no evidence to support an enemy combatant determination, we were told to leave the hearings open. When we unanimously held the detainee not to be an enemy combatant, we were told to reconsider. And ultimately, when we did not alter our course—did not change our determination, did not go back and question the very foundation by which we had reached our decision, a new panel was selected that reached a different result."[40]

Abraham was shocked at the disregard for due process in these hearings. "What I expected to see was a fundamentally fair process in which we were charged to seek the truth, free from command influence. In reality, command influence determined not only the lightning fast pace of the 500-plus proceedings, but in large part, the outcome."[41] He testified that "I knew of no authority for holding a second CSRT, or what has been referred to as a re-do." Not only was he "shocked" to learn of the do-over, but he was "surprised as to its results. . . . Because [of] the information that we were given . . . there was no way that our

Board could reach any other conclusion. . . . It simply didn't even rise to the level of evidence."[42]

All of Abraham's outrage was rolled up into his statement before the House committee: "I am here as a person charged by my oath as a commissioned officer and as an officer of the court to uphold and defend the Constitution of the United States. What I witnessed while assigned to ARDEC respected neither oath."[43]

When she read Abraham's testimony and affidavit, habeas lawyer Candace Gorman was stunned. She realized that Abraham had sat on the panel that judged her client, Abdul Hamid Salam Al-Ghizzawi—who had been diagnosed with both hepatitis B and tuberculosis—not an enemy combatant.[44] The do-over panel with different members had reversed that decision.

A CSRT Definition of *Enemy Combatant*

With the creation of the CSRTs, the Department of Defense redefined the term *enemy combatant,* which the administration had used in its briefs to the Supreme Court in the *Hamdi* case.[45] This time, the definition specifically applied to Guantanamo Bay detainees appearing before CSRT boards:

> The term "enemy combatant" shall mean an individual who was part of or supporting Taliban or al Qaeda forces, or associated forces that are engaged in hostilities against the United States or its coalition partners. This includes any person who has committed a belligerent act or has directly supported hostilities in aid of enemy armed forces. Each detainee subject to this Order has been determined to be an enemy combatant through multiple levels of review by officers of the Department of Defense.[46]

Since a "person who has committed a belligerent act" can easily include a lawful combatant under the Third Geneva Convention (GC3), the DOD's definition necessarily included both lawful and unlawful combatants. Under GC3, lawful combatants are entitled to prisoner of war status.

Equally significant is the appearance of the word *support* in the definition of *enemy combatant.* Constitutional lawyers would describe this word as both vague and overbroad. How should the CSRT decide whether a person is "supporting Taliban or al Qaeda forces" or is a person who "has directly supported hostilities in aid of enemy forces"?

Would Pakistani civilians who provide funds to help build a hospital or provide other material goods, such as blankets or children's books, to a local organization that then sends the money or goods to the Taliban fall within the definition of support?[47]

ADMINISTRATIVE REVIEW BOARDS

Once a detainee has had his CSRT hearing and is again determined to be an enemy combatant, he is given annual reviews of his status. Administrative Review Boards (ARBs), consisting of three military officers, conduct these annual reviews.[48] The detainee is not permitted to have a lawyer assist him at the hearing, nor is he permitted to see and rebut classified evidence against him. The purpose of the hearing is to determine whether his continued detention is in the interest of the United States.[49] That is, does the detainee continue to pose a threat to the United States, or is there another reason—such as "intelligence value" or "law enforcement interest"—for the United States to continue to detain him?

The first round of ARB reviews took place in 2005. Out of 463 detainees who had reviews that year, 14 were released and another 119 were transferred to the custody of their home governments, "when those governments are prepared to take the steps necessary to ensure that the person will not pose a continuing threat to the United States or its allies, including investigation or prosecution of the person by the home government."[50] Thus a detainee could be sent back to his home country, where he would be prosecuted or incarcerated. In 2006, 55 detainees were transferred, out of a total of 328 whose cases were heard by the ARBs.

Usually, other factors—such as whether the country has good relations with the United States or whether the country had exerted pressure on the United States to release its citizens—were more important than any decision by an ARB panel in determining whether a detainee was transferred back to his home country. In October 2008, only one westerner, Canadian Omar Khadr, was still incarcerated in Guantanamo. By contrast, in July 2007 Yemen had the largest number of citizens in Guantanamo (97). Fifteen months later, only one Yemeni detainee had been transferred back to his home country, compared to 40 Afghanis (of 92 held in July 2007) and 40 Saudis (of 47 held in July 2007).[51]

GOVERNMENT INTERFERENCE WITH ATTORNEYS

The Supreme Court paved the way in *Rasul* for detainees to meet with their attorneys, but the administration was not enthusiastic about hundreds of attorneys converging on Guantanamo to assist the detainees in filing habeas cases. The administration spread out in as many ways as it could to interfere with and frustrate the ability of the attorneys to access their clients.

By interfering with the attorney-detainee relationship, the administration hoped to discourage the detainees from relying on their attorneys. And in fact, it was somewhat successful. Both habeas attorneys and detainees found the lawyer-client process frustrating, and not only because of administration interference with attorney-client privilege. As detainees sometimes saw it, no matter how many times a detainee met with his attorney, nothing seemed to change; the government continued to successfully block all habeas petitions. But because the administration was feeling pressure from the attorneys' presence, the military did whatever it could to further push back as the attorneys arrived in Guantanamo.

It was not easy for habeas attorneys to visit their Guantanamo clients. The attorneys could not merely take the next plane down to Guantanamo. Habeas attorneys were not provided government records verifying the names of the detainees. The military kept the names classified, arguing that releasing detainee names would be a violation of their privacy as well as the privacy of their families. In addition, the government argued, releasing the names could expose detainees and their families to retaliation by terrorists.[52] Without the exact name of the client, the attorney often had difficulty accessing the military documents necessary to request a meeting with the appropriate detainee.[53] In April 2005, the Associated Press filed a Freedom of Information Act request to obtain the names.[54] Under a federal court order, the Pentagon released the list of names on March 3, 2006, over four years after detainees began arriving in Guantanamo and nearly two years after the *Rasul* decision.[55]

The first attorneys to fly to Guantanamo knew from other sources that their clients were in Guantanamo. The information often came from the detainee's government, since both the International Committee of the Red Cross and the United States informed countries that their nationals were imprisoned. However, not every nation released the information. And not every nation's records were complete and verifiable.

The first habeas attorney to meet with a detainee was Gitanjali

Gutierrez. She met with two British detainees, Moazzzam Begg and Feroz Abassi, on August 30, 2004, two months after the *Rasul* decision.[56] Thirty-one months and nineteen days had passed since January 11, 2002, when the first group of detainees arrived in Guantanamo.

There were other problems for habeas attorneys. Before they could board the tiny ten-seater plane in Fort Lauderdale, Florida, and take the three-and-a-half-hour flight to Guantanamo, they had to obtain security clearances. For some attorneys, the waiting period was up to six months. Once the attorneys landed in Guantanamo, the military housed them on the isolated leeward side of the island. Nearly all military personnel, restaurants, entertainment areas, and shops, as well as the detention centers, were on the windward side across the bay. One greasy spoon that closed at five o'clock served the lawyers on the leeward side. Attorneys purchased their dinners on the windward side and brought them back to their 1950s motel-style housing each evening. Each morning, the attorneys rose early to catch a ferry to visit with their clients on the other side of the island. They were always accompanied by military escorts.

An agreement between habeas lawyers and the government, known as a protective order, severely restricts the materials that the lawyers are permitted to bring into meetings with their clients as well as the materials that they are permitted to take out.[57] The protective order sets out the ground rules for visiting the naval base and a general procedure to prevent unauthorized disclosure of classified national security information. It was written after the *Rasul* decision in 2004, under the direction and supervision of a federal judge. Attorneys are not permitted to use computers—only paper and pens—when meeting with their clients. At the end of the meeting, a guard enters and collects the attorney's notes, which he seals in an envelope. The envelope is then shipped to "the privilege team" at an undisclosed "secure facility" in Washington, D.C. There, the notes are reviewed to determine whether the information is classified and at what level. After the notes have been vetted, the unclassified notes are returned to the attorney. Classified documents are kept in a secret drawer earmarked for the attorney. The attorney may see the redacted information at the secure facility but may not repeat it in any brief or document. This shocking interference with lawyer-client confidentiality is justified by "national security." Attorneys are not permitted to reveal the precise location of the secure facility. There is no name or number on the door of this facility.

Habeas attorneys have told stories of military personnel lying to them or treating them badly or with disdain. Habeas lawyers have had to wait for hours to meet with their clients and have had the military cancel meetings with their clients without reason, wasting the attorney's day or even the entire visit. In addition, the military often fails to promptly deliver correspondence from the lawyers to the detainees. In response, the military accuses the attorneys of violating agreed-upon rules.

Several examples of military stonewalling and interference affected Candace Gorman in her representation of two clients. In one situation, despite a court order granting Gorman the right to visit her client, Abdal Razak Ali, the military denied her permission to meet with him when she arrived in Guantanamo in July 2006.[58] For five days, every time she tried to arrange a visit the military challenged her client's identity. Yet the name she gave for her client was taken from the government's list of detainees and was the name the base had on record for him.

After not meeting with her client during her entire stay at the base, Gorman returned home. She then learned that the military had informed other habeas counsel that Gorman had met with her client. The military then revised its position and maintained that "counsel did not really want to see her client and instead preferred to go 'bird watching.'"[59] The government refused to set up a new visit for Gorman to see her client for reasons not explained, even after a court ordered that she be given access.

In another case, Gorman sent five letters to the government's "privilege team" in Washington, D.C., which reviews correspondence between attorneys and their clients in Guantanamo, for delivery to her client, Abdul Al-Ghizzawi.[60] Under a protective order, the privilege team was required to review legal mail for "prohibited physical contraband" within two days of receipt and then forward the mail to Guantanamo.[61] The first letter was sent on August 15, two on August 16, and two more later in the month. On September 11, she received a message from Al-Ghizzawi that he had not received any letters since her visit in July. In his letter, Al-Ghizzawi said it appeared that she must no longer want to represent him.[62] On her way to meet with Al-Ghizzawi on September 25, 2007, her escort handed her an envelope. The envelope contained some of the mail she had sent to her client.[63]

In July 2007, the military informed Gorman of a "new rule" that she could no longer bring legal mail in Arabic without first receiving a stamp of approval.[64] To obtain the stamp of approval, Gorman had to permit an Arabic translator at the base to read the legal mail. This new rule was an arbitrary procedure created ad hoc by the military. There was no such requirement in the protective order.[65]

I personally observed the contemptuous attitude of the military toward Gorman, an attitude that was reflective of the military's generally hostile attitude toward habeas lawyers and perhaps particularly toward women. While I was about to visit one of the detention centers, I noticed Gorman in the waiting area outside the center. The military was arranging for her to go inside and meet her client. She smiled at me in greeting and I smiled back. I mentioned to the officer escorting me that I wondered why she was waiting there for such a long time. Although it was obvious to the officer that I knew who she was, the officer replied, "Who knows who she is. She could be a cleaning woman."

The correspondence between habeas attorney Clive Stafford Smith and the military is revelatory of the military's attitude toward habeas attorneys. Stafford Smith was one of the first attorneys to offer his services to the Guantanamo detainees and was part of the *Rasul* habeas team. In 2005, officials accused Stafford Smith of precipitating the hunger strikes. In 2007, they accused him of sneaking underwear in to his clients. Stafford Smith wrote the following letter in response to accusations that he had precipitated the hunger strikes.

August 16th, 2005

Andrew I. Warden
Trial Attorney
U.S. Department of Justice

Dear Andrew:

I do not want to make a federal case out of this, and I feel sure that if I bring it to the attention of your office there will be no repetition of the matter. However, I am compelled to complain about the absolutely unacceptable intimidation that took place on my most recent trip to Guantanamo.

On the first day I arrived at Camp Echo with the Wilmer team on August 5th, I was very surprised when Lt. Cdr. Delaconte refused to shake my hand, though Captain Brown was (as usual) polite. At 08:40, Delaconte insisted that I go alone to talk with him and Brown in Echo 008, which is the kitchen. We spoke for twenty minutes.

Delaconte handed me a copy of Exhibit A to the Amended Protective Order (APO) and said, in a very hostile tone, "I expect you to abide by the order in your conversations with your clients." I replied that of course I would and I did not understand what he meant by bringing this up. He said, again in a very aggressive tone, "I believe you have already violated the order." I replied that of course this was not true, and asked him to tell me what he was talking about.

He began by saying that I was forbidden from talking about the
London Bombings, because this was a current political event. I had
not talked to any of my clients since the bombings, since they happened
on July 7, the day after I last left the island. However, as I said to him,
such an issue would clearly be directly relevant to some of my clients for
any number of reasons—some, for example, must assess the probability
of a successful application for asylum in Britain versus seeking an alternative country for their return.

He then alleged that I was the one who had "planned" the hunger
strike. He said that 239 (who is Shaker Aamer) had told the command-
ing officer this. I pointed out that I had not even been able to see 239 on
my last visit there. I had been scheduled to see him on July 7th, and was
evacuated the day before.

Third, Delaconte said that I had taken documents in to my clients
during meetings, in violation of the order. He did not elaborate on this
accusation, which is simply false—utterly false.

He went on to say that in his opinion I had violated the order and
that if I did not obey his instructions I was subject to the revocation
of my security clearance, contempt of court and prosecution for this.
He demanded that I agree in advance of my meetings what I would
and would not discuss with my clients.

I believe Captain Brown will corroborate that I did my best to be con-
ciliatory, but I told him that I had violated none of the rules and did not
appreciate his allegations. Neither did I appreciate the fact that none of
my clients were brought over that day so the entire day was wasted.

Let me say, first, that Lt. Cdr. Delaconte was extremely polite for
the rest of my visit. I do not hold any of this personally against Lt. Cdr.
Delaconte (who was doubtless just the messenger from whoever con-
cocted this) or Captain Brown (who was consistently polite throughout). But I do not take kindly to being threatened. I recognize that
advocates take different views of the issues, but most of us are not
in the habit of threatening people.

If there ever is any perceived problem, there is a perfectly civilized
process for dealing with any issue. This generally begins with the presumption that a particular individual has not committed any crime and
(as with the letters your office has previously sent to Baher Azmy and
Brent Mickum) proceeds with a sensible exchange of views to seek a
satisfactory understanding.

I have no desire to bring this to the attention of the court as I feel certain that it will not be repeated. Neither do I require a reply from your
team. I simply want to make my objection a matter of record. I do not
expect it to happen again.

I remain,

Yours sincerely,
Clive A. Stafford Smith

cc. Gitmo Petitioners' Team[66]

Another exchange between Stafford Smith and the DOD arose when the DOD accused him of providing "contraband" underwear to his clients.

Department Of Defense
Headquarters, Joint Task Force Guantanamo

August 12, 2007

Mr. Clive Stafford-Smith

Re: Discovery of Contraband Clothing in the Cases of Shaker A Amer, Detainee ISN 239, and Muhammed Hamid al-Qareni, Detainee ISN 269

Dear Mr. Stafford Smith,

Your client Shaker A Amer, detainee ISN 239, was recently discovered to be wearing Under Armor briefs and a Speedo bathing suit. Neither item was issued to the detainee by JTF-Guantanamo personnel, nor did they enter the camp through regular mail. Coincidentally, Muhammed Hamid al-Qareni, detainee ISN 269, who is represented by Mr. Katznelson of Reprieve, was also recently discovered to be wearing Under Armor briefs. As with detainee ISN 239, the briefs were not issued by JTF-Guantanamo personnel, nor did they enter the camp through regular mail.

We are investigating this matter to determine the origins of the above contraband and ensure that parties who may have been involved understand the seriousness of this transgression. As I am sure you understand, we cannot tolerate contraband being surreptitiously brought into the camp. Such activities threaten the safety of the JTF-Guantanamo staff, the detainees, and visiting counsel.

In furtherance of our investigation, we would like to know whether the contraband material, or any portion thereof, was provided by you, anyone else on your legal team, or anyone associated with Reprieve. We are compelled to ask these questions in light of the coincidence that two detainees represented by counsel associated with Reprieve were found wearing the same contraband underwear.

Thank you as always for your cooperation and assistance,

Sincerely,
Commander, JAGC, U.S. Navy
Staff Judge Advocate

Clive Stafford Smith's response follows:

29th August, 2007

Commander XXXXXXXXXXXXXX
Staff Judge Advocate
Headquarters, Joint Task Force Guantanamo

Re: The Issue of Underwear
("Discovery of 'Contraband Clothing' in the Cases of Shaker Aamer (ISN 239)
and Mohammed al Gharani (ISN 269)")

Dear Cmdr. XXXXXXXXXXX:

Thank you very much for your letter dated August 12, 2007, which
I received yesterday. In it, you discuss the fact that Mr. Aamer was
apparently wearing "Under Armor briefs" and some Speedo swimming
trunks and that, by coincidence, Mr. el Gharani was also sporting
"Under Armor briefs."

I will confess that I have never received such an extraordinary letter
in my entire career. Knowing you as I do, I hope you understand that I
do not attribute this allegation to you personally. Obviously, however,
I take accusations that I may have committed a criminal act very seriously. In this case, I hope you understand how patently absurd it is, and
how easily it could be disproven by the records in your possession. I also
hope you understand my frustration at yet another unfounded accusation against lawyers who are simply trying to do their job—a job that
involves legal briefs, not the other sort.

Let me briefly respond: First, neither I, nor Mr. Katznelson, nor
anyone else associated with us has had anything to do with smuggling
"unmentionables" in to these men, nor would we ever do so.

Second, the idea that we *could* smuggle in underwear is farfetched.
As you know, anything we take in is searched and there is a camera in
the room when we visit the client. Does someone seriously suggest that
Mr. Katznelson or I have been stripping off to deliver underpants to our
clients?

Third, your own records prove that nobody associated with my
office has seen Mr. Aamer for a full year. Thus, it is physically impossible for us to have delivered anything to him that recently surfaced on
his person. Surely you do not suggest that in your maximum security
prison, where Mr. Aamer has been held in solitary confinement almost
continuously since September 24, 2005, and where he has been more
closely monitored than virtually any prisoner on the Base, your staff
have missed the fact that he has been wearing *both* Speedos *and* "Under
Armor" for 12 months?

Since your records independently establish that neither I nor Mr. Katznelson could have been the one who delivered such undergarments to
Mr. Aamer, this eliminates any "coincidence" in the parallel underwear
sported by Mr. el Gharani. Your letter implies, however, that Mr. Katz-

nelson might have something to do with Mr. el Gharani's underthings. Mr. Katznelson has not seen Mr. el Gharani for four months. As you know, Mr. el Gharani has been forced to strip naked in front of a number of military personnel on more than one occasion, and presumably someone would have noticed his apparel then.

Without bringing this up with me, it was therefore patently clear that my office had nothing to do with this question of lingerie. However, I am unwilling to allow the issue of underwear to drop there: It seems obvious that the same people delivered these items to both men, and it does not take Sherlock Holmes to figure out that members of your staff (either the military or the interrogators) did it. Getting to the bottom of this would help ensure that in future there is no shadow of suspicion cast on the lawyers who are simply trying to do their job, so I have done a little research to help you in your investigations.

I had never heard of "Under Armor briefs" until you mentioned them, and my internet research has advanced my knowledge in two ways— first, *Under Armour* apparently sports a "U" in its name, which is significant only because it helps with the research.

Second, and rather more important, this line of underpants is very popular among the military. One article referred to the fact that "*A specialty clothing maker is winning over soldiers and cashing in on war.*". . . .

This stuff is obviously good for the men and women stationed in the sweaty climate of Guantanamo, as we could all attest.

It would be worth checking whether this lingerie was purchased from the NEX there in GTMO, since the internet again leads one to suspect that the NEX would be purveyors of *Under Armour:*

> Tom Byrne, Under Armour's director of new business development, told *Army Times* that "The product has done very well in PXes across the country." . . .

There must be other clues as to the provenance of these underpants. Perhaps you might check the label to see whether these are "tactical" underwear, as this is apparently something *Under Armour* has created specially for the military. . . . Indeed, I feel sure that your staff would be able to give you better information on this than I could (though I have done my best) as this *Under Armour* stuff apparently provokes rave reviews from your colleagues. . . .

On the issue of Speedo swimming trunks, my research really does not help very much. I cannot imagine who would want to give my client Speedos, or why. Mr. Aamer is hardly in a position to go swimming, since the only available water is the toilet in his cell.

I should say that your letter brought to mind a sign in the changing room of a local swimming pool, which showed someone diving into a lavatory, with the caption, "We don't swim in your toilet, so please don't pee in our pool." I presume that nobody thinks that Mr. Aamer wears Speedos while paddling in his privy.

Please assure me that you are satisfied that neither I nor my colleagues had anything to do with this. In light of the fact that you felt it necessary to question whether we had violated the rules, I look forward to hearing the conclusion of your investigation.

All the best,

Yours sincerely,
Clive A. Stafford Smith[67]

Smith never received an official response to his letter. He believes that the investigation is closed.[68]

The military undermined the trust that habeas attorneys needed to establish with their clients in strange ways. For example, in several documented incidents, the military informed detainees that their lawyers were Jewish and that Jewish lawyers would not faithfully represent their interests. According to attorney declarations filed with the court, in February 2005, an interrogator named "Megan" asked a detainee, "Did you know your lawyers are Jewish?"[69] She also told Fayiz Al Kandari, one of Tom Wilner's clients, not to trust his lawyers.

Another of Wilner's clients, Fouad Mahmoud Al Rabiah, asked him during a visit, "By the way, may I ask what religion you are?"

"Jewish," Wilner answered.

Apparently, the interrogators had told Al Rabiah not to trust his lawyers because they were Jewish, and that if he signed the form to be represented by Wilner he "would be kept here forever." Al Rabiah also reported that his interrogators had told him, "Your lawyers are Jews. How could you trust Jews? Throughout history, Jews have betrayed Muslims. Don't you think your lawyers, who are Jews, will betray you?" Another time they said, "Don't ever believe that a Jew will help a Muslim unless he gets more out of it than he gives." And, "What will other Arabs and Muslims think of you Kuwaitis when they know the only help you can get is from Jews?"

On another occasion, an interrogator said to a client of Wilner's, "Your lawyers are Jews. They are from one of the world's biggest law firms, which is Jewish and represents the Government of Israel." In actuality, Wilner's firm, Shearman and Sterling, had represented the State of Israel in a small trade dispute fifteen years before; Israel had not been a client since.

Tom Wilner, along with other lawyers in his firm, filed a motion to enjoin the government interrogators from "spouting vile religious slurs and other deprecating remarks" designed to "abrogate trust and confidence between the Kuwaiti Detainees and their counsel."[70] Specifically, the lawyers wanted to end the government's interfering with or otherwise burdening the attorney-client relationship. The military then moved on to other forms of harassment.

The military monitors attorney-detainee visits with closed-circuit cameras but is not permitted to record sound.[71] However, although the protective order requires that oral communications between counsel and detainee not be monitored, Candace Gorman, Wells Dixon, and other attorneys have had their doubts. Gorman wrote, "I don't believe that it is off but that is what the protective order requires."[72] Dixon said that "neither lawyers nor detainees believe for a second that the government does not listen in on conversations. . . . Everyone operates on the assumption that everything is recorded and reviewed."[73] In addition, habeas attorneys believe that their conversations are monitored in their offices and even in their homes.

In June 2007, the Center for Constitutional Rights sued the National Security Agency and the Department of Justice on behalf of Thomas Wilner, Jonathan Hafetz, Gitanjali Gutierrez, Wells Dixon, Candace Gorman, and other attorneys representing detainees in Guantanamo. The lawsuit contended that security personnel in Guantanamo had monitored electronic or telephonic communications with their clients as well as with released detainees, family members, and others affiliated with the detainees outside the United States.[74] In a filing in May 2008, these lawyers expanded their lawsuit with more specific complaints, arguing that the government's eavesdropping was significantly more intrusive than the monitoring of conversations with Guantanamo clients.

Candace Gorman, who was a sole practitioner, felt that the monitoring was so pervasive that she had to discontinue her practice. In an affidavit filed with the court, she wrote, "I stopped taking on new cases because I could no longer ensure that communications with my clients and others were confidential."[75] She added, "If my communications are not confidential then I cannot practice law until I can figure out a way to make those communications confidential. It really is as simple as that."[76] Gorman settled her last two cases in fall 2007. In January 2008, she left her home in Chicago with her husband and youngest daughter for the International Criminal Court (ICC) in The Hague.

She received a three-month appointment with the court in the spring and is working on the issues of reparations, pro bono counsel, and victims of war crimes.[77]

Wells Dixon, an attorney with the Center for Constitutional Rights in New York, said in his declaration that not only were his communications with clients and their families compromised, but "my personal privacy and the privacy of my wife have also been directly impacted by the likelihood that our telephone, fax and email communications are subject to warrantless surveillance," because he and his wife had used their personal accounts during the course of representing Guantanamo detainees.[78]

Tom Wilner's declaration was even more frightening in its accusations of government intrusion. Wilner claimed that government officials warned him that he was being monitored: "I have been informed on two occasions by government officials, on the condition that I not disclose their names, that I am probably the subject of government surveillance and should be careful in my electronic communications with others."[79] He added, "I believe certain government officials continue to believe it would further national security to monitor my communications and that, in the absence of court supervision preventing it, they would do so."[80] Wilner further notes that his belief that his communications are monitored has made it difficult for him to carry out his obligations as a lawyer.

The plaintiffs requested, under the Freedom of Information Act, the production of records that the two defendant agencies had allegedly compiled and retained. In response, Justice Department officials said that they could "neither confirm nor deny the existence of documents" requested by the plaintiffs.[81] The government argued that revealing the information would "severely undermine surveillance activities" and cause "exceptionally grave harm to the national security of the United States."[82]

The government defends its refusal to reveal the information on several grounds: the information could "easily alert targets to the vulnerability of their communications"; "reveal NSA's organization, functions and activities by revealing the success or failure of NSA's activities"; and reveal the "sources and methods by which NSA collects foreign intelligence information."[83] To the government, national security trumps lawyer-client privilege.

Consequently, habeas lawyers, people designated as enemy combatants, and others who play no role in the War on Terror, including

American citizens, now must be concerned that their privileged communications will be monitored without warrants and without judicial approval, in violation of the Fourth Amendment. Such circumstances will not only chill the actions of habeas lawyers and their detainee clients but possibly also chill the actions of their other clients. Commercial and private clients having no connections with the War on Terror who hire attorneys who have represented detainees may find their conversations subject to government monitoring. The fact that the government may listen in on all kinds of private conversations without notifying the subjects and without warrants will inevitably make it difficult for the detainees and others to reveal to their lawyers information that would assist in their defense. The Fourth Amendment right to a warrant or judicial approval before the government may search or seize information from a defendant has become another casualty in the War on Terror.

The military's willingness to listen in on conversations became a personal matter for me. When I visited Guantanamo in May 2007 as an author, in preparation for writing this book, a military official confronted me on my second day there. He asked me whether I was a "habeas lawyer." That seemed like an odd question, since I had clearly indicated on my application that I was a law professor and did not represent clients. He added that the military had made a mistake and should never have permitted me to visit.

Since the military in Guantanamo had vetted me before my arrival and had seen my background—I had even sent them a copy of my article on how the term *enemy combatant* had been manipulated by the administration to circumvent the Geneva Conventions, providing cover for the torture of detainees—I could not understand why the military had suddenly become concerned about me. The only possible explanation was that the military must have been overhearing the conversations I was having with two other visiting reporters. At our nightly dinners, I explained the legal implications of what we had seen that day and corrected the misinformation that the military had given us on our guided tours. Naively, I had not suspected that the military at Guantanamo might be eavesdropping on our conversations.

In an article that appeared May 5, 2007, it emerged that many detainees were no longer cooperating with their lawyers out of frustration with their long detentions and their belief that nothing was changing.[84]

The detainees had declined to meet with the lawyers, declined mail from their lawyers, and refused to provide information to their lawyers. Some detainees were suspicious that the lawyers were working for the government. The article quoted a client writing to his attorney: "Your role is to polish Bush's shoes and make the picture look good."

The lawyers accused the government of fueling the suspicions and frustrations of the detainees. Professor Mark Denbeaux, who represented two detainees, said that one client had asked him to bring toothpaste. When he brought it with him, the military confiscated it before he could meet with his client. His client took that as proof that Denbeaux was powerless.

When I met Candace Gorman on the plane to Guantanamo two days after the article was published, she assured me that the article was overstated. She believed that most of the detainees trusted their attorneys and continued to cooperate with them. However, it was clear that the detainees were frustrated and wary, especially as their fragile mental states continued to decline. Gorman's client, Al-Ghizzawi, whose mental and physical states had been seriously deteriorating, began to believe that she was abandoning him after not receiving any letters from her in nearly two months.[85]

THE ADMINISTRATION'S LEGAL POSITION FALTERS

The administration dug in and tried to pretend that nothing had changed after the *Rasul* decision. In spite of the Supreme Court's ruling that each detainee was entitled to a due process hearing and had the right to file a habeas petition in federal court, the administration held to the same hard-line position in response to all habeas filings, arguing the bewildering position that even if the Supreme Court permitted the detainees to file habeas actions, the federal courts should nevertheless refuse to entertain the petitions or to grant relief because the detainees were aliens held outside the sovereign territory of the United States. That is, the government renewed its argument that Guantanamo was outside U.S. sovereignty and that the *Eisentrager* case still applied—precisely the argument that habeas lawyers believed the government had lost in *Rasul*.

To the government's good fortune, one federal district court judge accepted the government's position.[86] However, another federal judge allowed the detainees to file their petitions, ruling that Guantanamo was under U.S. jurisdiction, as Justice Stevens had indicated in his opinion in *Rasul*.[87] But as the parties continued to argue over the breadth of the *Rasul* ruling, with litigation and counterlitigation, appeals and more appeals, the government succeeded in manipulating the legal system, thereby blocking the courts from acting on the habeas petitions. There is a saying in the law that you can "paper someone to death." The federal government with its incredible resources—and with many judges still fearful of issuing a decision that would release a "terrorist"—was able to paper the detainee attorneys to keep them from moving forward with their habeas petitions.

At the same time, the administration called on Congress to enact legislation that would put an end to habeas filings for good. At the urging of the administration and fearing it would be accused of being labeled "weak on terrorism" if lawmakers did not vote for the legislation, Congress enacted the Detainee Treatment Act (DTA).[88] The president signed the law on December 30, 2005.

One section of the act was engineered by Senator John McCain, a Vietnam vet who had been captured and tortured in Vietnam. The McCain Amendment, as it was called, placed restrictions on the interrogation of the detainees in response to reports that detainees had been tortured.[89] The amendment prohibited the military from engaging in cruel, inhuman, and degrading treatment of detainees, including those in Guantanamo.

The president, however, succeeded in obtaining protections for military and CIA agents accused of mistreating the detainees. The law permitted an agent to use the defense that he did not know the practice was unlawful and had relied on the advice of counsel, particularly legal documents issued by John Yoo and the Office of Legal Counsel that narrowly defined torture.[90] In addition, the president added a signing statement reserving the power to disregard the ban under his constitutional authority to supervise the executive branch and as commander in chief.[91]

The major thrust of the legislation, however, was designed to strip the federal district courts of jurisdiction to hear habeas appeals by the Guantanamo detainees.[92] In the place of habeas actions, the legislation provided for exclusive review of CSRT decisions by the Court of Appeals for the District of Columbia Circuit.[93]

The DTA also limited the extent to which the court could examine CSRT hearings. The act did not permit the court to carefully examine whether the CSRT hearings provided a fair due process hearing. The act mandated that the court, when reviewing CSRT hearings, only consider whether the CSRT panel properly followed specified DOD procedures, limiting the review to whether CSRT determinations were "consistent with the standards and procedures specified by the Secretary of Defense" and whether the use of the secretary's standards and procedures were "consistent with the Constitution and the laws of the United States" to the extent that the Constitution and laws were applicable. In addition, even if the court ruled in favor of the detainee, the DTA did not authorize the circuit court to order his release. Instead, the court would likely only order another CSRT hearing.

In a 1977 Supreme Court case, the justices had allowed Congress to eliminate habeas hearings if it provided a substitute remedy that was commensurate with habeas corpus relief. The standard that the Court proposed was that the relief must be neither inadequate nor ineffective in challenging the legality of a detention.[94] Habeas lawyers were convinced that the DTA did not meet this Supreme Court standard. But in forcing the habeas lawyers to litigate whether the DTA was an adequate substitute, the government was again able to delay the detainees' due process habeas hearings.

Not only did the DTA divest federal courts of jurisdiction to hear habeas challenges, but the legislation also barred "any other action against the United States or its agents relating to any aspect" of the detainees' detention. The administration hoped that this provision would put a halt to any lawsuits detainees might bring to challenge their treatment or living conditions in Guantanamo.[95]

In addition, the DTA ordered that the U.S. Court of Appeals for the District of Columbia review all military commission decisions and sentences. However, as with the review of CSRT hearings, the act restricted the court's ability to fully inquire into the commission hearing process. The review process was limited to whether the commission applied standards consistent with the president's order in creating the commissions, and whether those standards were consistent with the Constitution and laws of the United States, to the extent applicable.

Nevertheless, the appeals court had some wiggle room in reviewing both CSRT hearings and military commissions. In executing its charge, the court could read the term "to the extent applicable" narrowly or broadly. With the passing of time, and sensing that the courts needed to take a more active role in reviewing the administration's "harsh" and "enhanced" interrogations in Guantanamo and elsewhere, the appeals court expanded its review. The court first defined the breadth of its charge in summer 2007.

As tough as the administration was playing, its unyielding positions were beginning to lose their luster, if not crumble. Neither the habeas lawyers nor the U.S. Supreme Court—which was about to enter the fray again—intended to let up. The pressure was on the administration. Due process and the rule of law were demanding validation. The winds of change were blowing ever more forcefully.

IV

WINDS OF CHANGE, 2006–2008

A SECOND HISTORIC SUPREME COURT DECISION:
HAMDAN V. RUMSFELD

Justice John Paul Stevens, now at the age of eighty-six, must have smiled at the providence of life. Here he was in his ninth decade and authoring his second historic decision on the rights of Guantanamo detainees. It was June 29, 2006, two years and one day after Stevens had issued his *Rasul* decision.

Writing for a 5–3 majority, Stevens ruled in *Hamdan v. Rumsfeld* that the Detainee Treatment Act (DTA) Congress had enacted in 2005 at the behest of the administration—which aimed to deny habeas actions filed by the Guantanamo detainees—did not apply to cases that were pending at the time of the legislation.[1] Habeas attorneys could pursue their habeas cases. Again, Stevens, pragmatist that he was, avoided a constitutional battle over whether Congress could deny the detainees the right to file habeas. Instead, he said that the legislation did not clearly state its intention to block habeas actions that had already been filed.

Then Stevens again pushed back against the president. Stevens ruled that the president did not have the authority to establish the military commissions he had created in November 2001. Military commissions, also known as military tribunals, are creatures of exigency. They are not favored in the law because they do not provide the same due process protections that are available to criminal defendants in civil courts or even in military courts-martial. However, in times of war, when the civil courts or the military courts-martial are not available or not easily accessible because of military operations, the military may have no choice but to try a defendant in a military commission. Stevens explained that this was not such a time. Guantanamo was not an active battlefield. Moreover, the president never obtained congressional approval for commissions, which he would need to establish them in Guantanamo.

The military had planned to prosecute Salim Hamdan, the lead petitioner in the case, in a military commission. Hamdan was born in Yemen and had been Osama bin Laden's bodyguard and chauffeur. When he was captured in Afghanistan in November 2001, he was turned over to the United States for a bounty.[2] Hamdan played no leadership role in al Qaeda, nor did he have command responsibilities. He did not participate in planning any activity. At most, he was a mid-level detainee, although his lawyers argued that he was simply a low-level foot soldier. The U.S. military accused him of transporting shoulder-fired missiles used by al Qaeda members and receiving weapons training. On June 7, 2004, a CSRT panel determined that he was an enemy combatant.

On July 14, 2004, the military charged Hamdan with conspiracy to commit an offense triable by military commissions. The conspiracy count was for attacks on civilians, murder by a belligerent, and terrorism. Prosecutors often prefer to pursue conspiracy charges rather than the underlying substantive charges, because conspiracy is much easier to prove. In this case, rather than proving that Hamdan attacked civilians or committed murder, the government only needed to prove that Hamdan conspired to commit these offenses. To prove conspiracy, a prosecutor is only required to show an agreement between two or more persons to commit a crime, and that one of the persons had knowingly committed an overt act in furtherance of the agreement or conspiracy. The overt act does not have to be much more than, for example, buying the weapon to be used in the criminal act or scouting the location where the crime is to be committed.

Stevens also believed that the military commissions lacked the power to proceed because the commission procedures violated the Uniform Code of Military Justice (UCMJ). The UCMJ had set out the due process rules and procedures for military commissions. Stevens explained that significant due process rights were missing from the military commissions in Guantanamo. For example, the military could exclude the accused from ever hearing the evidence against him. Even when the defendant's military lawyer had access to the evidence, the commission's presiding officer could bar the lawyer from revealing the information to his client. In addition, evidence obtained through coercion or torture was admissible. Witnesses did not have to be sworn in. Stevens also pointed to the inadequacy of an appeals process in which a three-member review panel made recommendations to the secretary of defense, who forwarded the record to the president for a final decision.

Stevens further questioned whether the conspiracy offense with which Hamdan was charged was an offense against the law of war that a military commission could try. Stevens thought not. However, Justice Kennedy opted out of that part of the opinion, leaving only four justices in agreement on this point. Five justices are needed for a binding decision.

Perhaps the most striking part of Stevens's decision came near the end. He ruled that Common Article 3 (CA3) of the Geneva Conventions applied to Hamdan and other al Qaeda members.[3] The administration had argued that CA3 did not apply to al Qaeda because the conflict with al Qaeda was "international in scope" and consequently did not qualify as a "conflict not of an international character," as specified in CA3.[4] Stevens explained that "not of an international character" should be read in "contradistinction to a conflict between nations." That is, where one of the parties to a conflict is not a nation, such as al Qaeda, CA3 will apply if al Qaeda is in the territory of a party to the convention. Since Afghanistan was a party to the convention, members of al Qaeda—including Hamdan, who was captured in Afghanistan—were at least minimally covered by the Geneva Conventions through CA3. Stevens concluded that since CA3 applied, Hamdan could only "be tried by a 'regularly constituted' court affording all the judicial guarantees which are recognized as indispensable by civilized peoples."[5] Emphasizing his concerns, Stevens noted that a regularly constituted court would include ordinary military courts and would specifically exclude special tribunals, such as these military commissions. Due process protections are guaranteed in ordinary military courts.

The Court's application of CA3 was huge. Here was a declaration to the world that we live in an international community and we must recognize our obligations to, and our respect for, the global community. From the beginning of the War on Terror, the administration had disregarded the GC by illegitimately designating all detainees as enemy combatants. Stevens's message was loud and clear: we are part of the international community and must abide by the international treaties we sign and ratify. Some habeas attorneys were disappointed that Stevens did not apply the Third Geneva Convention (GC3) and declare Hamdan a lawful combatant and prisoner of war. But his decision was the first step in recognizing that the Geneva Conventions applied, at least in part, to the detainees held at the naval base in Guantanamo. It was a start, and an enormous one at that.

Not only did the Supreme Court apply international law in reaching its decision, but it sent a firm message to Congress and the president: the new commissions had to comply with the international law requirements of CA3, specifically the creation of a "regularly constituted court affording all the judicial guarantees which are recognized as indispensable by civilized peoples." Unfortunately, the Bush administration did not respond by actively creating a meaningful hearing process. The administration and the habeas lawyers continued to disagree on the standards for a regularly constituted court and what judicial guarantees were recognized as indispensable by civilized peoples. Nevertheless, for the second time in two years, the Supreme Court directed the administration and the military to abide by the rule of law and provide due process protections.

Two weeks after the *Hamdan* decision, the navy promotion board denied Hamdan's military-assigned lawyer, Lieutenant Commander Charles Swift, a promotion. Because of the military's "up or out" system, the navy had sent Swift a clear message. After giving twenty loyal and dedicated years to the military, Smith's career was terminated. The navy wanted nothing more to do with him. In fall 2007, Swift became a visiting clinical professor at Emory School of Law. However, as a civilian attorney, he continues to represent Hamdan.

THE MILITARY COMMISSIONS ACT

When Justice Stevens issued his decision in *Hamdan,* habeas attorneys were elated, as they had been immediately after the *Rasul* decision. Finally, they thought, they could pursue their habeas cases on behalf of their clients in Guantanamo. However, the administration was still in battle mode. It immediately returned to Congress and urged it to enact legislation to absolutely foreclose habeas filings by Guantanamo detainees.

Again, Congress did the administration's bidding. On October 17, 2006, Congress enacted the Military Commissions Act (MCA).[6] The administration thought that this time it had gotten it right: the MCA would unequivocally strip the federal district courts of all habeas actions filed by Guantanamo detainees and other aliens held as enemy combatants anywhere else in the world. The text of the act applied "to all cases, without exception, pending on or after the date of the enactment . . . which relate to any aspect of the detention."[7]

Like the Detainee Treatment Act (DTA), the MCA authorized the

Federal Court of Appeals in the District of Columbia Circuit to hear
all CSRT appeals. The same court was also authorized to review military commission hearings, although detainees were required to file
their appeal of a commission decision first with the Court of Military
Commission Review.[8]

The administration asked Congress to write one other provision into
the MCA. After the Supreme Court ruled in *Hamdan* that Common
Article 3 applied to the treatment of detainees,[9] government officials
were concerned that they could now be prosecuted under the federal
War Crimes Act for violating CA3. The War Crimes Act of 1996 prohibited war crimes committed by a member of the U.S. armed forces
or a U.S. civilian, such as an official who directs or authorizes the commission of a war crime.[10] War crimes included a grave breach of the
Geneva Conventions, including Common Article 3.[11] Punishment for a
war crime under the act included the death penalty.[12]

The new legislation restricted the crimes that violated CA3 and also
created a more restrictive standard for cruel, inhuman, or degrading
treatment from that used in CA3.[13] The administration intended the
new provisions to protect American officials from prosecution under
the War Crimes Act. In addition, the new legislation was made retroactive to 1996, when the legislation was first enacted. Thus government
officials were protected from prosecution for acts committed any time
after 9/11 that would have been crimes under the earlier version of the
War Crimes Act.

The administration believed that now that Congress had authorized
the military commissions, the Supreme Court would have a more difficult time finding them unconstitutional. When Congress and the president work together, the courts are more inclined to defer to them.[14]

Habeas lawyers returned to court. They argued the familiar theme:
by stripping away all rights to habeas in the MCA legislation, Congress
had violated the Constitution. Congress can suspend habeas only in
times of rebellion and insurrection.[15] Since there was no congressional
finding or statement that there had been a rebellion or insurrection,
the lawyers argued that Congress could not remove the constitutional
right to habeas. Consequently, the habeas attorneys argued that even
if Congress had validly removed statutory habeas rights, the constitutional right to habeas still existed.

Moreover, they contended, the DTA's statutory procedure, where
the Circuit Court of Appeals of the District of Columbia Circuit hears
all appeals from the CSRT hearings, did not constitute an adequate

and commensurate substitute for habeas. The DTA legislation severely restricted the appeals court in its review of the CSRT hearings in ways not found in a habeas hearing. In a DTA hearing, a defendant is not provided the opportunity to present witnesses and otherwise broadly challenge the evidence against him; a defendant does not have access or the ability to present all exculpatory evidence; the government has a rebuttable presumption in its favor, unlike criminal proceedings, where the government has the burden to prove its case; and the court does not have express power to release the defendant. In addition, because this appeals court was not the usual forum for these kinds of evidentiary review hearings, the detainees' cases, with their many procedural issues, were likely to take significantly longer to resolve than habeas cases heard in the federal trial courts.

In February 2007, the Court of Appeals for the District of Columbia Circuit rejected the habeas lawyers' arguments and ruled that the detainees did not have any constitutional rights to habeas. The court held that Congress, in passing the Military Commissions Act of 2006, clearly intended to terminate the detainees' rights to file habeas petitions in federal court. In holding that the detainees had no constitutional right to habeas, the court returned to the administration's single-minded position that Guantanamo was outside U.S. territory, contradictory to Stevens's opinion in *Rasul*. The appeals court, in its unswerving devotion to the administration's position, said that it could not find any precedent for the right of noncitizens to file habeas when outside the territory of the United States.[16] Because of its ruling that no constitutional rights existed for the detainees, the court did not need to consider whether the DTA provided the detainees with an adequate substitute to challenge their detentions.

In deciding *Rasul,* Justice Stevens had indicated that the Constitution would apply along with the federal statute in providing habeas rights to the detainees. However, the court of appeals dismissed Stevens's statement regarding the Constitution as "dicta," that is, language outside the precedent that the court was required to follow. The court also ignored the Supreme Court's statement in *Rasul* that Guantanamo was within the territorial control of the United States.

The lawyers for the detainees filed a petition for certiorari in the Supreme Court, requesting the Court to act quickly in the case, known as *Boumediene v. Bush.* Lakhdar Boumediene, the lead petitioner, was born in Algeria in 1966. He left for Yemen in 1990 and moved to Albania in 1995, where he was employed by the Red Crescent Society of the United Arab Emirates until 1997, when he relocated with his family to Bosnia. In 2001, he was arrested by Bosnian authorities for allegedly planning an attack on the American embassy. The federal chief prosecutor, with the approval of the Bosnian Supreme Court, recommended that Boumediene and the other Bosnians who had been arrested with him be released for lack of evidence. Nevertheless, on the day they were to be released they were handed over to the U.S. military, which sent them to Guantanamo. All of the petitioners in this case had been captured in Bosnia, except a French citizen who had been captured in Pakistan.[17] In fall 2008, the administration withdrew the allegation that the detainees had planned to attack the embassy, and instead alleged that the detainees had planned to travel to Afghanistan in late 2001 to take up arms against U.S. forces.[18]

THE THIRD GUANTANAMO CASE:
BOUMEDIENE V. BUSH

On April 2, 2007, the Supreme Court refused to hear *Boumediene v. Bush.* Justice Breyer, joined by Justices Souter and Ginsburg, would have granted certiorari, pointing out that the administration had been holding detainees for over five years and that the habeas issue was not going away. In addition, Breyer recognized that that the D.C. court opinion may have been inconsistent with the Supreme Court's decision in *Rasul.* He also pointed out that many of the detainees were "citizens of friendly nations including Australia, Canada, Kuwait, Turkey and the United Kingdom,"[19] and not citizens of a country that was at war with the United States. In addition, many of the detainees "were seized outside of any theater of hostility, in places like Pakistan, Thailand, and Zambia."[20] However, these three justices were one short of the required four votes to grant cert.

Justices Stevens and Kennedy wrote a separate opinion, reasoning that the Supreme Court should defer until after the D.C. court of appeals reviewed actual CSRT detainee hearings. At that time, the Supreme Court could determine whether the remedy provided by the DTA was speedy and adequate. However, the two justices added that should petitioners later indicate that the administration had unreasonably delayed the proceedings under the DTA or otherwise injured or prejudiced the detainees' position, the Supreme Court might reconsider granting cert.

Supreme Court observers believed that Stevens would have preferred to have joined the Breyer opinion and granted cert. However, he joined Kennedy's opinion in a political ploy that has come to be known as a "defensive deny." The pro habeas bloc, consisting of Stevens, Souter, Ginsburg, and Breyer, needed Kennedy as the fifth vote if they were to prevail in a final decision in favor of the habeas rights of the detainees. If Kennedy was not ready to decide in their favor, it would be risky to grant cert on the case, which only required four votes, and take the chance that Kennedy would join the opposing four justices in the Court's decision of the case.

For three months, it appeared that the administration had finally succeeded in blocking the habeas cases. Perhaps the winds of change were not really blowing all that fiercely after all. But, in fact, the winds were gathering their strength for the next gale. On June 15, habeas attorneys submitted Lieutenant Colonel Stephen Abraham's courageous declaration challenging the integrity and reliability of the CSRT hearings. Two weeks later, on June 30, 2007, the last day of the Supreme Court term, the Supreme Court reversed itself and agreed to review the D.C. Circuit Court's *Boumediene* decision. The Court needed five votes for the new decision. Such reversals are extraordinary, and it had been decades since a similar reversal had occurred.[21] Although no one outside the Court knew for sure what prompted the justices to reverse their earlier denial of certiorari, speculation necessarily focused on the Abraham declaration.

Since five members of the Court had decided to hear the case, the habeas lawyers believed that they had a strong chance to prevail on the merits. It was time to remind the Court once again how important it was for the justices to rule on the side of due process and the Constitution. In their multiple briefs to the Supreme Court, the habeas lawyers pointedly wrote that if the administration prevailed in this case, this and future administrations would be free to disregard all constitutional restraints on their actions by simply choosing to detain foreign nationals outside U.S. sovereign territory, including territory such as Guantanamo, where the United States exercises complete jurisdiction. One brief described the situation as creating "offshore prison camps far removed from any battlefield that are totally outside the law."[22] The fundamental cornerstone of American criminal jurisprudence—the right to meaningful notice of the basis for detention and an opportunity to be heard before a neutral, independent decision maker—might begin to wither and, over time, disappear in other circumstances as well. The briefs also suggested that the military could hold prisoners for their entire lives, even torturing the detainees without their having any recourse.

The government responded, as it had in the past, that these detainees were provided more procedural protections than would have been available to them as foreign nationals detained outside U.S. sovereign territory under the Constitution; that these detainees had more protections than any other captured combatants in the history of warfare; and that the DTA system provided more protection than the Geneva Conventions do for prisoners of war. The government also argued that the system was best served if the Court allowed the review process to function as Congress had determined through the DTA appeals process.

SUPREME COURT ORAL ARGUMENTS

On the morning of December 5, 2007, like every morning before oral argument, Justice Stevens left his office sometime after 9:00 A.M. and settled into an overstuffed chair on the side of the downstairs clerks' office that is closest to his end of the chambers. His clerks joined him, making small talk, often about pro tennis or the Chicago Cubs. Then they briefly reviewed the key issues in the upcoming case that morning. On this day, there was only one case to review. Just before 10:00 A.M., they walked over to the chambers. Meanwhile, demonstrators wearing orange jumpsuits and black hoods stood outside the courthouse protesting the unlawful detentions in Guantanamo as snowflakes fell.

As the justices entered the packed courtroom, they knew that every seat would be filled. Unlike most Supreme Court arguments, reservations had been necessary to guarantee a seat. The *Boumediene* case was expected to be the most important case the judges had heard since 9/11. This time, the justices would decide on whether the detainees had a constitutional right to habeas. Specifically, the case focused on whether the detainees retained constitutional rights to habeas after Congress enacted legislation withdrawing the statutory right to habeas. The arguments considered the related and esoteric issues of exactly what constitutional right to habeas existed under English law at the time we became a nation and adopted English common law, as well as what right to habeas existed in 1789 (when Congress created the federal courts and authorized the district courts to issue the writ of habeas). The justices struggled over what rights the detainees had, whether the hearings in the District of Columbia Court of Appeals were an adequate substitute for habeas hearings, and whether the court of appeals should make the initial determination as to adequacy of rights.

Justice Scalia pursued the issue of whether a constitutional right to habeas was ever provided in England, or in America, to foreign nationals who were in a territory that was not under the sovereign control of either country. The fact that the earlier *Rasul* decision recognized that Guantanamo was in the exclusive jurisdiction and control of the United States and in every practicable respect a U.S. territory did not seem to end the issue as far as Scalia was concerned.

Justice Steven Breyer, in a dialogue with the solicitor general (the attorney for the government), noted that a detainee cannot make the argument, in a CSRT hearing or in a DTA review by the court of appeals, that he should be charged with a crime or released, but he can make this argument in a habeas hearing. The solicitor general, Paul Clement, seemed to agree but argued that the detainee is nevertheless provided sufficient protection under the DTA process.

The audience was most concerned with Justice Kennedy's questions, since lawyers believed that he would be the deciding vote in a likely 5–4 decision. Kennedy kept his thoughts close to the vest but seemed to indicate that the court of appeals could first decide on the adequacy of the DTA appeals process, and the Supreme Court could review the appeals process later on.

At the end of the hearing, Tom Wilner expressed his concern, after hearing the argument, especially Kennedy's comments, that the Court could decide to send the case back to the court of appeals and allow that court to go forward and review CSRT petitions. Since the appeals court would likely work very slowly in addressing the procedural issues raised by the DTA legislation, taking its time in reviewing all the evidence and methodically deciding each case, the court was likely to review only a few cases at a time. In Wilner's thinking, several more years might pass before the detainees, some of whom had been there since 2002, would have their day in court. A decision along those lines would have been incredibly disheartening for the habeas attorneys and their clients.

It was snowing, dark, and cold outside the Supreme Court that day. Some people thought the weather was appropriate. The inclement weather certainly did not deter the people dressed in orange jumpsuits and black hoods from protesting the government's treatment of the detainees. Nor did it hinder the media from setting up their cameras and microphones to allow habeas lawyers to make statements in support of the rule of law and due process. The weather also did not stop Stephen Abraham from posing for a photo with Seth Waxman, the lawyer who argued the case on behalf of the detainees, at the foot of the steps to the Supreme Court.

A PARALLEL CASE ON REVIEWING CSRT HEARINGS

Meanwhile the D.C. Circuit Court of Appeals considered whether to go forward with its own review of the CSRT hearings as provided by the DTA and MCA legislation. In July 2007, the court of appeals ruled against the government, holding that the court, in reviewing the CSRT hearings, must have all the information that the CSRTs are authorized to consider and not only the information forwarded to the hearings. Specifically, the court held that the government must provide all evidence "reasonably available" to the government bearing on the issue of whether the detainee meets the criteria of being an enemy combatant.[23]

Further, to be sure of engaging in "meaningful review," the court adopted a presumption that attorneys for the detainees have a "need to know" the classified information relating to their clients' cases. The only exception recognized by the court was that the government might withhold from counsel, but not from the court, certain highly sensitive information. Consequently, the administration was required to provide the court with all the information it had against a detainee, even classified information.

The government moved for a rehearing, arguing through affidavits that releasing the information would compromise CIA, military, and FBI investigations and sources of information. The government also indicated that it had not preserved all the evidence but had only retained the evidence that was forwarded to the CSRT hearings.

On October 3, 2007, the court denied the government's request for a new hearing. The court wrote that if the government had not preserved the entire body of information with respect to a detainee, it would have to reassemble the information it did collect or convene a new CSRT hearing, taking care to retain all the information this time.[24] The court also considered the government's argument that the disclosure of the evidence could "seriously disrupt the Nation's intelligence gathering programs" and that the burden of reviewing all the information would be so great that it would divert limited resources and sidetrack the intelligence community from performing critical national security duties.

Seth Waxman (left) and Stephen Abraham on the steps of the Supreme Court. Courtesy Stephen Abraham.

The court was not persuaded, noting that the government could meet its concerns while providing the necessary evidence.

The government had argued that because so much information might be classified and the burden of reviewing it enormous, none of the information should be turned over to the defense counsel. But the court said that it would review as much classified evidence as necessary to determine what should be released to counsel.

The administration would not yield. It then asked the court of appeals to hear the case "en banc," meaning that ten members of the court would review the July three-panel decision. In February 2008, with the court splitting 5–5, with several separate opinions filed, the court denied the rehearing.[25] The government, still relentless in its attempt to limit the evidence available to the court and defense counsel, then petitioned the U.S. Supreme Court to hear the case. The petitions were placed on hold while the Supreme Court considered the *Boumediene* case.[26]

THE RETURN TO WAR CRIME PROSECUTIONS:
HICKS, KHADR, AND HAMDAN

Meanwhile, military prosecutors were moving forward, or at least trying to move forward, in prosecuting alleged war criminals in the newly created military commissions at Guantanamo. Under the new provisions, statements obtained by torture were not admissible, "but statements 'in which the degree of coercion is disputed' [might] be admitted if reliable, probative, and the admission would serve the interests of justice."[27] That is, even if the information was obtained coercively or through harsh treatment, the statements might nevertheless be admissible. However, for statements obtained after December 30, 2005 (the date the DTA was enacted), the "methods used to obtain those statements must comply" with the DTA. The DTA forbids cruel, inhuman, and degrading treatment of the detainees, which would include torture.[28] The first candidate for trial by military commission was David Hicks.

David Hicks

David Hicks has been described as "Australia's own Taliban," a term similar to the label "American Taliban," which was pinned on John Walker Lindh. In the government's series of detainees, Lindh was number 001 and Hicks 002.[29] However, their young lives were very different. Hicks was expelled from school at fourteen, played Australian football (he stood five feet five inches and weighed 115 pounds), and worked as a kangaroo skinner in the Australian outback. At seventeen, he began a relationship with an Aborigine woman, Jodie Sparrow. He had two children with her in three years before going off to train horses in Japan. From Japan, he joined the Kosovo Liberation Army in Bosnia.

After Bosnia, Hicks returned to Australia. He sought to enlist in the army but was rejected. After trying Bible classes in an Evangelical Christian church, he converted to Islam and left for Pakistan. Hicks took the name Muhammed Dawood and wore Islamic robes. He wrote a letter to his family saying he wanted to travel the Silk Road on horseback. He joined a Pakistani guerrilla group and patrolled the Kashmir border in territory claimed by both Pakistan and India. In his travels, he met the "lovely" Osama bin Laden. He went to Afghanistan, trained in an al Qaeda camp, and joined the Taliban forces.[30] The Northern

Alliance captured Hicks on December 9, 2001, and sold him for bounty to the U.S. military. The military charged Hicks with war crimes on June 10, 2004.

The U.S. military had planned to prosecute Hicks along with Salim Hamdan and a third defendant, Omar Khadr, in 2004. When Hamdan's lawyers challenged the military commission process, the military put the three prosecutions on hold pending the Supreme Court decision. However, during that time, Hicks's military-appointed attorney, Marine Corps major Michael D. Mori, was advocating on his behalf throughout Australia.

Initially, Australia wanted nothing to do with Hicks. The Australian government was closely aligned with the Americans in the War on Terror, and the Australian government saw no reason to question the American detention of Hicks. Unlike other countries, such as Britain, which inquired into the status of their nationals in Guantanamo and negotiated for their release, Australia shut its eyes to Hicks's circumstances.

Mori knew that he had to raise Hicks's visibility and educate the Australian people. He wanted the people to understand that Hicks was not a dangerous terrorist and that he was being denied fundamental due process rights. Mori figured that if he succeeded in publicizing Hicks's humanity and the unfairness of his continuing detention, the Australian people would eventually pressure their government to act on his behalf. Mori visited Australia six times to publicize his client's plight, pointing to Hicks's claims that he had been tortured when he was captured in Afghanistan and during his years of confinement in Guantanamo.[31]

Major Mori's tireless advocacy and his multiple trips to Australia on behalf of his client paid off. The conservative Australian government reversed its position and leaned on the American administration. The American military consented to enter into a plea agreement with Hicks. Hicks was anxious to plead to anything to get himself out of Guantanamo. Five years of abuse was enough. He was desperate to go home.

While Hicks's military commission trial was in its initial stage, the parties worked out a plea agreement that would release Hicks but save face for the U.S. government.[32] To satisfy the administration, Hicks pleaded guilty to providing material support for terrorism. However, this crime did not exist at the time he was captured. Although it appeared in the *Manual for Military Commissions (MMC)*—which specifies offenses triable before military commissions—this crime first appeared in the Military Commissions Act of October 2006 (MCA), and was incorporated into the new *MMC* in January 2007.[33] The *MMC* did not exist in 2001, when Hicks was arrested.

The MCA, to justify the addition of what appeared to be an ex post facto offense, included an introductory clause that stated that the act was codifying offenses that "have traditionally been triable by military commissions."[34] The clause added that the act "does not establish new crimes that did not exist before its enactment, but rather codifies those crimes for trial by military commission."[35] Congress could only hope that a court reviewing the challenges to crimes as ex post facto would accept this shaky explanation.

Major Michael Mori's public stance on behalf of Hicks had enraged the American military prosecution team.[36] On the eve of Hicks's trial, before the prosecution and defense attorneys agreed to the plea bargain, the chief prosecutor in the military commissions, Colonel Morris (Mo) Davis, issued a statement that Mori might have violated military policy and military ethics rules in traveling to Australia and issuing public statements about his client.

The habeas lawyers immediately interpreted Davis's behavior as mean-spirited. They believed that Davis intended to create a conflict of interest for Mori and force him to withdraw from his representation of Hicks just when the trial was to begin. The implication was that, if Hicks were convicted, the military might be less inclined to pursue its charges against Mori, but if Hicks walked away with an acquittal, the military would be more inclined to pursue charges.

The following day, Hicks pled guilty to providing material support for terrorism. The matter with Mori ended. Mori was subsequently reassigned away from Guantanamo to serve as staff judge advocate (legal advisor) to the commanders of the Marine Corps Air Station Miramar in San Diego, California.[37] The Australian Lawyers' Alliance honored Mori for his work on behalf of Hicks and his ability to "engage the Australian public in what was really about fairness and justice and the rule of law."[38] As a friend said, if she ever needed a lawyer, she would hire Michael Mori.

Six months after Hicks pled, Davis seemed to take a 180-degree turn. On October 6, 2007, he abruptly resigned as chief prosecutor in Guantanamo, implying that the process was unjust. Davis later claimed that his supervisor wanted more of a role in the prosecution and was interfering with his handling of the cases. In addition, he asserted that the trials had become highly politicized. He indicated that he had been pressured to pursue "sexy" and "high-interest" cases in the run-up to the 2008 elections.[39]

But Davis's anger at the system did not stop there. In February 2008, still in uniform as a senior legal official for the air force, he moved even farther to the edge. The man who only eight months earlier had written about the "fair and transparent nature of the military commissions"[40] agreed to testify, at Salim Hamdan's war crimes trial, that the hearings might indeed be rigged. Davis said that his testimony would address the "potential for rigged outcomes," explaining that he had "significant doubts about whether [the commission system] would deliver full, fair and open hearings."[41]

Hicks was sentenced to nine additional months of incarceration and in May 2007 was relocated to Yatala Prison in Adelaide, South Australia, to serve the remaining portion of his sentence.[42] The plea bargain Hicks signed required him to state that the U.S. government had never illegally mistreated him and specified that he would never file suit against the Americans over the treatment that he had received. Hicks was released on December 29, 2007.[43] He was the first person to be tried in a military tribunal since World War II.

Omar Khadr

Omar Khadr's military commission case had also been put on hold until after the Supreme Court ruled on the *Hamdan* case. In June 2007, the military renewed its prosecution of Khadr.

Omar Khadr's case attracted international attention. A Canadian citizen, Khadr was fifteen, a juvenile under both international and American law, when he was captured in Afghanistan.[44] He was born September 19, 1986, in Toronto, Canada, but spent a significant portion of his childhood in Afghanistan and Pakistan with his family. He and his three brothers and sister were strongly influenced by his father, Ahmad Said Khadr, a senior deputy to Osama bin Laden.

Ahmad had taken the family to Pakistan and Afghanistan to run a charity organization that allegedly had ties to al Qaeda. In late 1994, Ahmad was arrested by Pakistani authorities for providing money to support the bombing of the Egyptian embassy in Pakistan. While he was imprisoned, the children moved back to Canada to live with their grandparents in Toronto, attending public school. However, Omar returned to Pakistan the following year. In 1996, the Khadr family moved from Pakistan to Jalalabad, Afghanistan. From 1996 to 2001, the family traveled throughout Pakistan and Afghanistan, at times apparently staying at or near Osama bin Laden's compound. Omar and his brothers and sister all received military training as children. Omar's training was in small arms, AK-47s, and land mines.[45]

The daughter, Zaynab, and the eldest son, Abdullah, allegedly ran an al Qaeda training camp in the 1990s.[46] Another brother, Abdurahman, was arrested as a suspected member of al Qaeda in November 2001, but he claimed to have been sent to Guantanamo to act as an informant in 2003 at the request of the CIA. He left Guantanamo several months later and, on behalf of the CIA, went to Bosnia. Abdurahman also stated that he was on the CIA payroll after his capture.[47]

Ahmad Said Khadr, the father, was killed in a shootout with Pakistani forces in 2003.[48] The youngest son, Abdul, was with his father when he was killed. Abdul was fourteen at the time and was paralyzed in the shootout. He and his mother, Maha Elsamnah, returned to Canada and are living in Toronto.[49]

On July 27, 2002, Omar Khadr and other al Qaeda operatives were in a compound near Khost, Afghanistan. American forces surrounded the compound, and a firefight ensued. Khadr was accused of throwing a grenade that killed Sergeant First Class Christopher Speer, who led the attack. In a criminal investigation task force report, an American fighter told his military interviewer that when he entered the compound, he saw Khadr sitting up facing away from him leaning against brush.[50] The American fighter "fired two rounds both of which struck KHADR in the back."[51]

Just before shooting Khadr, the American fighter had shot another man in the head and killed him. The man was lying on the ground with an AK-47 beside him.[52] Because of dust and the angle of the walls, the American fighter could not say for certain who threw the grenade. However, from the circumstances, he believed that the grenade was thrown by someone other than the man who had been firing the rifle. According to the report, the American fighter "believe[d] that KHADR threw the grenade."[53] The American fighter stated that after the shooting, when medics came to treat Sergeant Speer and Khadr, the boy "was able to move his arms and was repeating 'kill me' in English."[54]

However, it appeared that the report was corrupted. In March 2008, a secret report was inadvertently released that indicated that the military commander who wrote the report of the firefight had altered his statement two months later to cast blame on Khadr. The initial

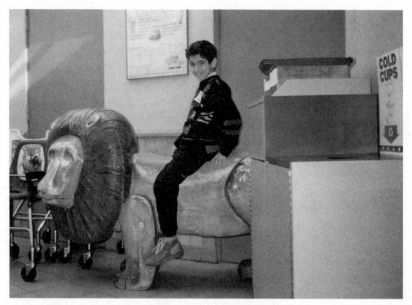

Omar Khadr at the zoo in Toronto, 1993. Courtesy Zaynab Khadr.

battlefield report of the firefight said that the person who threw the grenade that killed Sergeant Speer also died in the firefight. However, the report written by the same commander two months later said that the attacker was "engaged" by U.S. forces. This revised report implied that Khadr could have been the person who threw the grenade.[55]

After the firefight, Khadr was taken to Bagram Air Base in Afghanistan. According to his attorney, Dennis Edney, Khadr was denied medication while being interrogated in the hospital, his head was used as a "mop" to clean the floor, he was hung by his wrists, and soldiers "flagellated" his face, while other soldiers, nurses, and doctors looked on. Because bathrooms can be "security risks," Khadr was not fed for three days and was provided only sips of water for one and half days before he was flown from Bagram to Guantanamo. At Guantanamo he was tossed off the plane and onto a truck "as so much human baggage."[56] Edney said that he has never represented someone who has been treated so badly. He believes that we are all damaged by Guantanamo.

Khadr cannot see with one eye and sees dots with the other eye. Edney was unable to obtain glasses that would protect Khadr's eyes from the glare of the fluorescent lights in his cell. Ultimately, he was able to convince the authorities to turn off the lights at night, except for one over Omar's bed. In one meeting, Khadr asked Edney to bring him crayons. The military denied the request. Edney has never seen Khadr unchained. When Khadr leaves the military court, he is required to wear earmuffs and blackened goggles.

On April 5, 2007, the government charged Khadr with five crimes: murder in violation of the law of war, attempted murder in violation of the law of war, conspiracy, providing material support for terrorism, and spying.[57]

In 2008, Edney traveled, at his own expense, around the United States and Canada to speak on behalf of Khadr. His travels remind me of the work of Michael Mori, the military attorney for David Hicks. Edney is looking for a similar political victory. He does not believe that Khadr will obtain justice in a military commission trial held in Guantanamo. Edney hopes that Canada will request that Khadr be sent home and believes that the United States, if asked, would comply.

Because Khadr had been involved in an armed conflict with U.S. forces in Afghanistan, his lawyers have argued that the law of war protected him. A lawful combatant under the Geneva Conventions has the right to kill during armed conflict. Khadr's lawyers also argued that the Optional Protocol to the Convention on the Involvement of Children in Armed Conflict, ratified by Congress in 2002, prohibits the recruitment of children into armed conflict and also places obligations on nations that take child soldiers into custody.[58] The Optional Protocol defines a child as someone below the age of eighteen, unless the child attains majority earlier under specific law applicable to the child.[59] Article 7 of the Optional Protocol requires the state party to cooperate "in the rehabilitation and social reintegration of persons who are victims of acts contrary [to the protocol]."[60] Prosecuting Khadr as a war criminal would be inconsistent with this provision. Khadr's lawyers added that "if jurisdiction is exercised over Mr. Khadr, the military judge will be the first in western history to preside over the trial of alleged war crimes committed by a child."[61] In addition, the lawyers argued that Congress never intended to abrogate or limit its obligations under the Optional Protocol when it passed the Military Commissions Act.[62] The government lawyers responded that Congress was aware of Khadr's case when it enacted the MCA and also pointed to the imprisonment of Hitler Youth after World War II as a precedent for exercising jurisdiction over juveniles.[63] However, the Optional Protocol did not exist during World War II.

There is no international treaty or convention that specifically says that a country cannot bring war crime charges against a juvenile who is fifteen. The Convention on the Rights of the Child, which was signed by the U.S. government but not ratified, similarly defines a child as someone below the age of eighteen.[64] In language akin to the Optional Protocol,[65] it directs that children under the age of fifteen not take direct part in hostilities.[66]

The Convention on the Rights of the Child, although not binding on the United States, is instructive in its minimum protections of juveniles and in setting out basic principles that should be applied to all children held in detention. One section provides that children not be subjected to torture or other cruel, inhuman, or degrading punishment.[67] Another provides that the arrest and imprisonment of a child should be a measure of last resort and the child should be held for the shortest appropriate period of time.[68] In addition, children must be separated from adults while in detention unless it is in the child's best interests not to be separated.[69] Khadr has been held in an adult detention facility in Guantanamo since 2002. He has been interrogated while in Guantanamo not only by American officials but also by Canadian security agents.[70]

The convention also requires, as does the Optional Protocol mentioned above, that children combatants be socially reintegrated into society. Specifically, it provides that nations "shall take all appropriate measures to promote physical and psychological recovery and social reintegration of a child victim of: any form of neglect, exploitation, or abuse; torture or any other form of cruel, inhuman or degrading treatment or punishment; or armed conflicts. Such recovery and reintegration shall take place in an environment which fosters the health, self-respect and dignity of the child."[71]

The International Committee of the Red Cross considers juveniles to be under eighteen years of age. In its 2004 annual statement, it expressed concern for the possible psychological impact that detention at Guantanamo might have during this important stage of a young person's development.[72] Relying on information obtained from British prisoners released from Guantanamo, Omar Khadr's lawyers state that Khadr's physical and mental health has deteriorated. They write that he has lost the use of one eye and has a punctured lung. The lawyers add that Khadr may still have shrapnel in his eye and that he was denied medical treatment on instruction from U.S. interrogators.[73]

On June 4, 2007, as Omar Khadr's military commission trial was to begin, the military judge at Guantanamo ruled that they did not have the authority to pursue a military commission trial of Khadr.[74] He ruled that under the MCA, military commissions were designed to prosecute "unlawful enemy combatants."[75] However, Khadr had been found by his CSRT hearing only to be an "enemy combatant." The judge explained that the terms *enemy combatant* and *unlawful enemy combatant* were not the same, since someone could also be a lawful enemy combatant under the MCA.

The military appealed to the newly created Court of Military Commission Review. In September 2007, the reviewing court agreed with the government's argument that the trial judge had the authority to make a fact-finding decision as to whether a designated enemy combatant was also an unlawful enemy combatant.[76] The trial judge made the determination that Khadr was an unlawful enemy combatant.

According to documents released in July 2008, Omar Khadr was visited at Guantanamo by Canadian officials in February 2003.[77] Immediately prior to the visit, Khadr was subjected to the "frequent flyer program," in which he was moved from cell to cell every three hours to disrupt his sleep patterns and soften him up for the interrogations. In the Canadian interrogations, which lasted over four days and which appear on five DVDs released by Khadr's attorneys, the Canadian official identifies Khadr as Umar rather than Omar. The official describes Khadr as a "Mama's little boy" who "has probably found pseudo-parents among the other detainees."[78] The interrogator also notes the obvious, that "Umar does really not understand the gravity of his situation." He adds that Khadr "believed that Canada could have him brought home 'if we wanted.'"[79] Near the end of the report, he concludes, "Finally, as an amateur observer of the human condition, Mr. Gould would describe Umar as a thoroughly 'screwed up' young man. All those persons who have been in positions of authority over him have abused him and his trust, for their own purposes. In this group can be included his parents and grand-parents."[80]

The final paragraph begins, "He does, however, have some feelings," and then describes how he urinated on a photo of his family, although later on, when he presumably thought that no one was watching, "Umar laid his head down on the table beside the picture in what was seen as an affectionate manner."[81] In tapes of the interview, Khadr is seen crying several times, and also saying to the Canadian interrogator, "Promise you'll protect me from the Americans."[82] At one point, the interrogator states that Canada cannot do anything for him. Khadr replies that he was tortured by the Americans in Baghram and is afraid of torture by the United States.

As of October 30, 2008, Canada has not requested that the United States release Khadr to Canada for further action or even prosecution. Khadr's military commission trial has been set for January 26, 2009.[83]

Omar Khadr was not the only child seized by the United States. Reprieve, a legal rights group located in London, issued a document identifying at least twenty-seven boys who were under eighteen when they were captured in the early years of the War on Terror.[84] The study by Clive Stafford Smith, legal director of Reprieve, revealed that fourteen juveniles were still being held at Guantanamo in spring 2006. It noted that the U.S. military defines juveniles as under sixteen rather than eighteen.[85] However, there appears to be no formal U.S. document or policy statement indicating that the United States defines juveniles as those under sixteen. The best source is a Pentagon news release from 2004, which indicates that medical tests determined that three juveniles being released that day were under the age of sixteen. This news release also states that "age is not a determining factor in detention. We detain enemy combatants who engaged in armed conflict against our forces or provided support to those fighting against us."

Mohammed Jawad, who was either sixteen or seventeen at the time he was captured—he does not know his exact birth date—and Mohammed el Gharani, who was fifteen when captured, have also received media attention. Jawad faces war crimes accusations before a military commission for allegedly tossing a grenade into a U.S. Army vehicle in Afghanistan, injuring two soldiers. His lawyer argues that he was forced to fight with the Taliban. Both young men have tried to commit suicide while in custody. El Gharani slit his wrists, ran into the walls of his cell, and tried to hang himself. Jawad tried to hang himself and banged his head on metal structures in his cell.[86] Like Khadr, both men were subjected to the frequent flyer program.[87] According to prison records, Jawad was moved 112 times in a two-week period in May 2004.[88]

The United States has admitted capturing three Afghani boys aged ten, twelve, and thirteen on April 21, 2003. The young prisoners were placed in Camp Iguana, a facility designed for the juveniles and, according to the Pentagon news release, provided the opportunity to learn math, reading, and writing in their native language. The three Afghani boys were released the following year, on January 29, 2004.[89]

Salim Hamdan

The military intended to begin the trial of Salim Hamdan in June 2007, at the same time as Omar Khadr's trial. However, the military judge presiding over Hamdan's prosecution, Captain Keith J. Allred, took his lead from the judge in Khadr's case and similarly ruled that the prosecution could not go forward until it was determined that Hamdan was an unlawful enemy combatant and not merely an enemy combatant.[90] Although the Pentagon did not appeal Judge Allred's Hamdan ruling, it was overturned after the Court of Military Commission Review ruled on the same issue in Khadr's case and overturned the military commission decision.[91]

But the challenges to Hamdan's status did not end there. Hamdan's attorneys then asked Judge Allred to hold a hearing under Article 5 of the Third Geneva Convention to determine whether Hamdan qualified for POW status.[92] Article 5 states that should any doubt arise as to whether the person is a lawful combatant or POW, his or her status must be determined by a competent tribunal. Where Article 5 hearings are held, the prisoner enjoys the protection of a lawful combatant until the tribunal determines his status. Hamden, however, never enjoyed the protections provided POWs while waiting for his Article 5 hearing.

After the hearing, Judge Allred concluded that Hamdan was not a POW, but rather was an unlawful enemy combatant who could be tried for war crimes by the military commission.[93] Had the judge determined that Hamdan was a POW, Hamdan could only have been tried for war crimes and not merely belligerent acts on the battlefield. In addition, if he were tried for war crimes, he would be entitled to the same kind of trial before the same courts and with the same procedures that an American soldier would receive in a criminal trial.[94] Such a trial could not be held by a military commission but would have to be by courts-martial, which provide significantly more constitutional protections. However, there is another side to the issue of being classified as a POW. If Hamdan had been declared a POW, the government could have decided not to bring any charges against him, but instead could hold him without charge until the cessation of hostilities, as permitted by the Third Geneva Convention.

Perhaps the most significant aspect of Judge Allred's rulings is that he agreed to hold an Article 5 hearing for Hamdan. In granting the hearing, Judge Allred acknowledged that at least some of the combatants captured in Afghanistan, including Taliban members and al Qaeda members supporting the Taliban (such as Salim Hamdan), were entitled to Article 5 hearings to determine whether they were lawful combatants.

In February 2008, Hamdan's attorneys raised two additional issues. They argued that their client could not assist in preparing for his upcoming trial later in the spring because he was breaking down mentally after being confined in his cell nearly around the clock for six years.[95] The defense attorneys asked that the commission be postponed until Hamdan's condition improved. Dr. Daryl Matthews wrote a declaration on March 31, 2004, on Hamdan's behalf, noting that he had experienced frustration, rage, loneliness, despair, depression, anxiety, and emotional outbursts while being held in solitary confinement. Hamdan apparently told Matthews that he had "considered confessing falsely to ameliorate his situation."[96]

Hamdan's lawyers asked to interview Khalid Shaikh Mohammed and six other high-value detainees in support of their claim that Hamdan was not involved in the conspiracy to attack Americans. The military judge agreed to this request but only allowed them to provide written questions.[97] The lawyers were not permitted face-to-face meetings with the detainees, although this would have been preferable to assess their credibility as potential witnesses.[98] In February 2008, the former chief prosecutor at Guantanamo, Morris Davis, agreed to testify on behalf of Hamdan that the military commission hearings might be rigged.[99] In his testimony, Davis stated that military officials had interfered with his decision-making process as to which cases to prosecute. He stated that the officials wanted the trials to go forward as quickly as possible to give them legitimacy before the 2008 elections.[100] In addition, he noted that William J. Haynes, general counsel of the Department of Defense, said to him, "We can't have acquittals. We've been holding these guys for years. How can we explain acquittals? We have to have convictions."[101]

Hamdan was charged with two crimes: conspiracy and providing material support for terrorism.[102] However, when his case was first heard by the Supreme Court in 2006, four justices questioned whether the conspiracy offense for which Hamdan was first charged was an offense against the law of war that the military commission could try. As for providing material support for terrorism, that crime did not exist as a war crime at the time Hamdan was captured, as in the case of David Hicks, who pled guilty to this crime.

On August 6, 2008, a six-member jury acquitted Hamdan on the conspiracy charge but convicted him of providing material support for terrorism. Although the prosecution requested a sentence of thirty years to life, the jury decided on sixty-six months. The judge gave Hamdan credit for time served, leaving him only five months of imprisonment.[103] He could be released in January 2009. The prosecution requested that the trial judge order a new sentencing hearing, arguing that Hamdam should not have received credit for time served because he was in prison as an enemy combatant and not for the crimes for which he was charged.[104] The judge refused to reconsider the sentence.[105]

Military Commission Trials Grind On

On February 11, 2008, prosecutors filed charges against six detainees accused of the most serious war crimes against the United States. They included Khalid Shaikh Mohammed, the supposed mastermind of 9/11, and Mohammed al-Qahtani (the charge sheet spelled his name al Kahtani), considered to be the twentieth hijacker. The other four were Ramzi bin al-Shibh, an al Qaeda operative who had lived with three of the hijackers and assisted them in financial transactions; Ali Abdul al-Aziz Ali, a lieutenant to Mohammed who wired money to the hijackers; Mustafa Ahmed al-Hawsawi, who assisted the hijackers with money and credit cards; and Walid Muhammad Salih bin Attash, who assisted in training two of the hijackers.[106] The prosecutors intended to seek the death penalty on charges of murder, attacking civilians, terrorism, conspiracy, and several other crimes.[107]

On May 13, 2008, the convening authority, Susan J. Crawford, who supervises the commission hearings, dismissed the charges against al-Qahtani.[108] Since the evidence against al-Qahtani had been obtained by torture, his coerced confessions would have caused problems for the prosecution. However, the military retained the option to prosecute him at a later date.

At the hearings of the other five men, the defense attorneys intend to challenge evidence that was obtained from the detainees, arguing that the military and CIA harshly treated and tortured the men while they were in custody. However, the administration plans to argue in response that the evidence it will submit against these men was obtained in non-coercive settings, when the men were reinterrogated under "clean" conditions. Consequently, regardless of what the men revealed when tortured, a new group of military and FBI interrogators have questioned the prisoners by using "rapport-building techniques."

These new "good cop" interrogators, who called themselves the "Clean Team," provided the detainees with food and Starbucks coffee during the questionings. The prisoners were read rights similar to Miranda warnings and were told that their statements would be considered voluntary.[109] However, unlike criminal defendants in the civil justice system, the detainees were not permitted to have attorneys present during the interrogations. Unlike the other five detainees, al-Qahtani never revealed anything at these "clean" sessions.

There are serious questions as to whether evidence obtained when the government first tortures someone and then interrogates him in a "rapport-building" environment is admissible in court. Is the new evidence tainted by the former interrogation? Also, did the new interrogators have access to the earlier coerced testimony? If so, the defense could argue that the military never would have known what to ask without seeing the earlier testimony.

Under the Military Commissions Act, statements obtained prior to December 30, 2005, the date of the enactment of the Detainee Treatment Act, are admissible if the judge finds that the statements are reliable, sufficiently probative, and in the interests of justice.[110] Statements made after that date are admissible if the statements meet the earlier standards and the interrogation methods used to obtain the statements did not amount to cruel, inhuman, and degrading treatment.[111] Consequently, evidence obtained prior to December 30, 2005, through prolonged isolation, prolonged sleep deprivation, painful stress positions, prolonged standing, and sexual humiliation may be admissible. Evidence of CIA techniques in obtaining information is withheld from the trials on the ground that the information is classified and protected by national security concerns.

At their trials, the detainees have the right to be represented by attorneys, called judge advocate generals, assigned by the military. The prisoners are also permitted to enlist the aid of civilian attorneys, although the government does not pay for them. Civilian attorneys require security clearances. Classified evidence is only available to defense attorneys with security clearances. The attorneys are not permitted to share the classified information with their clients, since the detainees do not hold security clearances. Consequently the detainees, who have no access to the information against them, can take only a limited role in their defense. Defense attorneys may not be permitted to share classified information with attorneys representing other detainees, since attorney clearances are often limited to information regarding their clients.

The military intends to file war crime charges against as many as eighty other detainees in the future.

VICTORY: *BOUMEDIENE V. BUSH*

When *Boumediene v. Bush* was argued in December 2007 before the U.S. Supreme Court, everyone in the courtroom had their eyes and ears focused on Justice Anthony Kennedy.[112] He was the swing vote. Unless he agreed with the arguments in favor of habeas rights for the detainees in Guantanamo, it was unlikely that the Court would rule in their favor.

On June 12, 2008, Justice Kennedy rose to the occasion. In this third case on Guantanamo, the most important of the three, Kennedy wrote a powerful decision championing the constitutional right to habeas corpus for Guantanamo detainees. Justice Stevens, as the justice in the majority with the most seniority and the author of the two previous decisions, *Rasul* and *Hamdan,* upholding the statutory rights of Guantanamo detainees to habeas, could have assigned the opinion to himself. But in a savvy move, he offered it to Kennedy—thinking that if he could bring Kennedy on board by giving him authorship of this major constitutional decision, he would have his five-member majority for the habeas decision he wanted. Stevens was not going to let authorship get in the way of making history.

The 5–4 decision was a major rejection of the Bush administration's cynical position that by holding the detainees at the naval base in Guantanamo, it could put them beyond the reach of American law. The fact that the administration designated them as enemy combatants or held them outside the continental United States during wartime did not bar the detainees from enjoying their constitutional right to habeas.

In his opinion, Kennedy made it abundantly clear that the Supreme Court and not the executive was the final arbiter of the Constitution. He recognized the importance of the separation of powers among the three branches of government: executive, legislative, and judiciary. But he maintained that although the president and Congress may make the laws, it is the domain of the courts to ultimately decide matters of the Constitution. In what will likely be one of the most frequently quoted passages from his opinion, Kennedy wrote, "The Constitution grants Congress and the President the power to acquire, dispose of, and govern territory, not the power to decide when and where its terms apply. To hold that the political branches may switch the Constitution on or off at will would lead to a regime in which they, not this Court, say 'what the law is.'"[113]

In December 2007, at the oral arguments to the *Boumediene* case, habeas attorney Tom Wilner had worried that Kennedy might decide to send the case back to the lower court to consider the issue of whether, by withdrawing the right to habeas, the MCA was an unconstitutional suspension of the writ of habeas. The government had argued that the DTA review process in the U.S. court of appeals was an adequate substitute. Kennedy acknowledged that the court usually sends an undecided issue back for the lower court to consider before the Supreme Court will review it. (The court of appeals had not decided whether the DTA was an adequate substitute because the court believed that the detainees, as foreign nationals housed in Guantanamo, had absolutely no right to habeas.) However, Kennedy made clear that six years without the right of habeas was enough. If the case were returned to the lower court, the detainees would have had their lives on hold for many more years. The Supreme Court would decide the issue by itself.

Ruling that the DTA review process in the court of appeals was not an adequate substitute for habeas, the Court declared that Section 7 of the MCA—the provision that had stripped habeas jurisdiction from the district courts—operated as an unconstitutional suspension of the writ of habeas.[114] Kennedy explained that the DTA procedure in the court of appeals was not an adequate substitute for habeas because it had not allowed the detainees to challenge the president's claimed authority to hold them indefinitely, to contest CSRT findings of fact, to supplement the record on review with exculpatory evidence, or to request release.

Kennedy also questioned the CSRT hearings, which, he wrote, "fall well short of the procedures and adversarial mechanisms that would eliminate the need for habeas corpus review."[115] He pointed out that the detainee has limited ability to rebut the evidence and the testimony against him, that he does not have the assistance of counsel, and that he is likely not aware of the critical allegations against him because so much of the evidence is classified. He added, "And given that the consequence of error may be detention for the duration of hostilities that may last a generation or more, the risk is too significant to ignore."[116] Throughout his opinion, Kennedy was well aware of the elephant in the room: some of the detainees had been imprisoned in Guantanamo for over six years and counting, without any access to due process hearings.

The decision, however, did not ignore the realities of wartime. Underlining the importance of practical considerations and reasonable procedures in times of war, Kennedy stated that habeas is not an automatic right available to a detainee as soon as he is captured. He noted that the president must be given authority to protect the nation against terrorists and to apprehend and detain those who impose a danger. That is, the executive must be permitted a window of time when the courts do not intercede while the military reasonably screens and properly holds combatants captured and detained abroad. Kennedy also agreed that the Department of Defense may hold a CSRT hearing to review the detainee's status before the detainee is permitted to file a habeas petition. Of course, in the end, a federal district court may not grant the detainee the relief he seeks in his petition. In that situation, the detainee could possibly be held in detention for the duration of hostilities, however defined.

As elated as the habeas attorneys were with this decision, they understood that it was not over yet. The Supreme Court did not release any detainees. Nor did the Court resolve other important questions and concerns. These include: Who qualifies as an enemy combatant? How long and under what authority can the president hold an enemy combatant? How broad are the due process protections available to detainees? What limitations exist on the administration's physical and mental treatment of the detainees, and can the detainees sue the government for their mistreatment?[117] Another knotty question has arisen as a result of the decision. Kennedy struck down Section 7 of the MCA, which denied federal courts jurisdiction to hear habeas actions by the detainees, declaring that the section was an unconstitutional suspension of the writ of habeas. As a result, detainee lawyers now argue that the statutory right has been resurrected along with the Court's establishment of the constitutional right. The lawyers believe that statutory habeas provides rights in addition to those available under the Constitution, and have sought to file their habeas actions under both the Constitution and the habeas statute.

The district courts, in reviewing the habeas petitions, will consider these issues, and the cases are all likely to be appealed. At the time of this writing, it is unclear what will happen to those prisoners who are entitled to release. It is clear that many will not be accepted by their home countries. Others will be tortured if sent back home.

Finally, there is talk that the Guantanamo facility will close, and the remaining detainees, along with newly captured prisoners, will be moved to either the continental United States or new detention centers at the Bagram Air Base in Afghanistan. If they are transported to the continental United States, the detainees would continue to have the right to file habeas actions. However, if they are sent to Bagram or another military base overseas, the issue arises as to whether they continue to have the right to file habeas petitions in federal court. Since the *Boumediene* decision concerned only detainees in Guantanamo, there are questions as to what rights prisoners held in Afghanistan, currently a war zone, would have. Justice Kennedy hinted at the differences between Guantanamo and a war zone by writing that "if the detention facility were located in an active theater of war, arguments that issuing the writ would be 'impracticable or anomalous' would have more weight."[118] However, an important motivation behind the *Boumediene* decision was that the prisoners had been held for over six years without a meaningful due process hearing. That would not change for many of the prisoners.

Forgotten in all the excitement of the decision was the man who set the *Boumediene* case in motion. If Stephen Abraham had not courageously filed his affidavit on June 15, 2007, with the U.S. Supreme Court—alleging the failure of the CSRT process to rise to even minimal due process standards—the Court would not have reversed itself and agreed to hear the *Boumediene* case. Of course, many people were involved in making this momentous decision happen, but without Abraham's affidavit, there would have been no *Boumediene* decision in 2008. After the decision, Abraham wrote, "I did no more than was compelled by the cause. We can not call ourselves members of humanity and yet deny fundamental rights of all humans. No rights are ever lost but by our consent. They are not taken but are surrendered. We must never again allow this to happen."[119]

ANOTHER BLOW TO THE ADMINISTRATION:
PARHAT V. GATES

Eight days after the *Boumediene* decision, the D.C. Court of Appeals issued its first review of a CSRT hearing under the DTA, handing the administration another startling defeat, this time in the case of *Parhat v. Gates*. Huzaifa Parhat is a Muslim Uighur (pronounced WEE-gur) from a far western Chinese province known by the Uighurs as East

Turkistan. Because of Chinese oppression of the ethnic minority, Parhat fled China for Afghanistan. After the United States bombed Afghanistan in October 2001, Parhat and fellow Uighurs fled to Pakistan. Local officials then turned them over to the U.S. military.

In reviewing his case, the circuit court ruled that the evidence the government presented against Parhat in the CSRT hearing was insufficient to categorize him as an enemy combatant.[120] The court stated that the government's assertion that Parhat was affiliated with an Uighur independence group associated with al Qaeda and the Taliban lacked sufficient foundation. In a particularly harsh rebuff to the administration, the court derisively dismissed the government's argument that its assertions were reliable because they were made in at least three intelligence documents. Alluding to Lewis Carroll's "The Hunting of the Snark," the court wrote, "Lewis Carroll notwithstanding, the fact that the government has 'said it thrice' does not make an allegation true."[121] The court continued that "many of those assertions are made in identical language, suggesting that later documents may merely be citing earlier ones, and hence that all may ultimately derive from a single source." That common source, Parhat's lawyers suggested and the court found credible, "is the Chinese government, which may be less than objective."[122] The court further ridiculed the government's argument that the statements made in the intelligence documents were reliable because the government would not have put them in the documents if that were not the case. "This comes perilously close to suggesting that whatever the government says must be treated as true, thus rendering superfluous both the role of the Tribunal and the role that Congress assigned to the court."[123]

The judges directed the government to release Parhat, transfer him to another country, or expeditiously convene a new CSRT hearing. The court also made it clear that it would not permit the military to continue a series of "endless 'do-overs.'" Relying on the *Boumediene* decision, Parhat could also file a habeas writ in federal district court. Unfortunately, the problems for Parhat will continue even if the district court releases him and the other Uighurs still at Guantanamo. The Uighurs cannot return to China, where they would be tortured and likely killed. Under U.S. pressure, Albania accepted six Uighur detainees in 2006. The Uighurs are miserable in their new home.[124] No other country has been willing to accept Uighur detainees since then. According to J. Wells Dixon, attorney for the Center for Constitutional Rights (CCR), which has represented the Uighurs since 2003, Albania would not accept any other Chinese detainees. An official in Albania told him, "China threatened our national interests in Kosovo and Albania and we are a small country."[125]

Four months after the *Parhat* decision, on October 1, 2008, the United States dropped the enemy combatant designation for the Uighurs. Six days later, a federal district court judge ordered that the seventeen remaining Uighurs be released into the United States while their habeas hearings were heard.[126] However, the government appealed, arguing that even though they are no longer enemy combatants, they are still a danger if released into the United States and that the executive alone has the authority to decide when and where to release them. The court of appeals blocked the transfer until at least November 24, when a hearing before the court will be held.[127] In the meantime, the Uighurs remain in Guantanamo, Camp 4.

The wheels of justice grind slowly, and as of October 31, 2008, more than four months after the *Boumediene* decision, there still have not been any habeas hearings in federal court and no detainee has been released by judicial order. Nevertheless, as of June 12, 2006, following the *Boumediene* decision, Americans can finally say that the Cuban iguana is no longer the only protected species in Guantanamo.

PART FOUR

FOREIGN PRISONS
AND CIA BLACK SITES

THE EVOLUTION OF EXTRAORDINARY RENDITION

"We don't kick the [expletive] out of them. We send them to
other countries so they can kick the [expletive] out of them."
Unnamed official
(quoted in Priest and Gellman, "U.S. Decries Abuse")

Extraordinary rendition is another term for international vigilan-
tism. The term is understood today to refer to kidnapping suspects
worldwide and transporting them to other nations to be tortured or
killed. The practice originated in 1986, when the Reagan administration began kidnapping terrorist suspects in other countries and transporting them to the United States for trial.[1] The program escalated
dramatically in 1995 under President Clinton. The CIA proposed a
deal with Egypt in which the CIA would seize suspected Egyptian
and other Muslim terrorists—some of them convicted in absentia—
around the globe and transport them to other countries, particularly
Egypt, for "interrogation." Because Egypt considered these terrorist suspects a threat to the regime, the country welcomed the CIA
program.[2] Many of the people sent to Egypt were never heard from
again.[3]

President George W. Bush took the concept of extraordinary rendition a giant leap forward. He increased tenfold the people seized by CIA
agents and transported them to any number of countries. Beginning
after the attacks of 9/11, CIA agents wearing black shirts, black pants,
and black hoods or masks seized the suspects, cut off their clothes with
knives and scissors, stuffed tranquilizers and enemas up their anuses,
diapered them, manacled their hands and feet, loaded them onto a
CIA-controlled aircraft (often a Gulfstream jet), and transported them
to another country or to a CIA-controlled "black site" to be tortured
and perhaps killed.

The suspected terrorists caught up in the CIA's web were known as
"ghost detainees." They were meant to disappear. There was no official

record of them in the countries to which they were taken. The prisons and ghost prisoners were concealed from the International Committee of the Red Cross, which under international law is afforded access to prisoners to verify that they are treated humanely.

According to several sources, over one hundred people have been rendered,[4] and perhaps as many as 150 since 9/11.[5] However, one commentator believes that the number of renditions is closer to six hundred and may even have reached one thousand.[6]

At least four countries that receive detainees have been accused by the U.S. State Department of committing human rights violations and practicing torture: Egypt, Syria, Jordan, and Morocco. In addition to these four countries, prisoners have been sent to detention centers in Diego Garcia, an atoll in the Indian Ocean,[7] Uzbekistan, Afghanistan, Pakistan, and Thailand, as well as Guantanamo. Poland and Romania have given the CIA use of their airports for rendition flights. There are also indications that Poland and Romania permitted the CIA to erect detention sites in their territories.[8] As many as fourteen European nations in addition to Poland and Romania have assisted the CIA, actively or passively, by permitting suspects to be picked up and rendered to detention facilities.[9]

The term *extraordinary rendition* applies to transporting suspects to other countries as well as transporting them to secret CIA detention centers. The current program of operating covert CIA black sites began when President Bush issued a secret directive on September 17, 2001, authorizing the CIA to detain terrorists in facilities outside the United States.[10] The office in charge had been given the fitting name "Rendition Group" and is within the CIA's Counterterrorist Center (CTC).

Much to the exasperation of the CIA and the administration, "plane spotters"—airport personnel, hobbyists, and other enthusiasts who enjoy observing arrivals and departures of aircraft—have been instrumental in disclosing the existence and frequency of extraordinary rendition flights. Plane spotters view, photograph, record, and catalog aircraft. Spotters are present at all airports, whether huge international airfields or tiny local airstrips in faraway countries. They track registration numbers painted on the tail of each plane and report their findings to other spotters through the Internet. They notice any unusual takeoffs and landings at odd hours, as well as unusual and isolated locations of planes, such as those parked at the periphery of the airport or hidden behind large hangars. The Gulfstream jets parked at the corners of airfields became natural curiosities for the plane spotters. Thus, one spotter identifies a particular Gulfstream jet take off from an airfield in Poland and posts identifying information on the spotters' website. Another spotter sees the same plane land hours later at a remote airfield in Afghanistan and posts that information. By posting information on their sightings at various outposts around the world, the plane spotters accidentally uncovered the CIA's extraordinary rendition program.

The spotters access the Federal Aviation Administration (FAA) registry of American-owned planes, with their logs and flight plans, on the Internet to determine the identity of the planes and their ownership.[11] The plane spotters' discoveries have revealed that many, although not all, of the CIA aircraft are Gulfstream V executive jets.[12] The CIA owns or leases these Gulfstreams and other aircraft through dummy corporations with nonexistent officials and owners.[13]

Responding to criticism of its extraordinary rendition program, the United States has denied that it renders captives to other countries for the purpose of torturing them. President Bush and administration officials have repeatedly stated that before they transfer a captive to any country, they seek assurances from that country that it will not torture the prisoner.[14] However, America's request for information and the country's assurances that it will not torture are made through diplomatic channels and are not publicly disclosed.[15] Consequently, the American people cannot confirm that these promises are honored, or for that matter that the United States actually officially requests such assurances in the first place.

In September 2006, President Bush revealed that fourteen "high-level" detainees were transported from secret CIA black sites to Guantanamo,[16] and that the CIA had used "an alternative set of procedures" to obtain information from these high-level detainees. He added that "I cannot describe the specific methods used—I think you understand why—if I did, it would help the terrorists learn how to resist questioning, and to keep information from us that we need to prevent new attacks on our country. But I can say the procedures were tough, and they were safe, and lawful, and necessary."[17] Khalid Shaikh Mohammed, accused of being the mastermind behind 9/11, was one of these fourteen detainees. He was captured in Pakistan on March 1, 2003, and taken to secret CIA locations abroad, including black sites in Afghanistan and Poland, where he was tortured and underwent waterboarding.[18]

According to Mike McConnell, the director of National Intelligence, "You can do waterboarding lots of different ways."[19] He described it this way: "You lay somebody on this table, or put them in an inclined position, and put a washcloth over their face, and you just drip water right here," pointing to his nostrils. He continued, "Try it! What happens is, water will go up your nose. And so you get the sensation of potentially drowning." Another source described the process differently: "The prisoner is bound by an inclined board, feet raised and head slightly below the feet. Cellophane is wrapped over the prisoner's face and water is poured over him. Unavoidably, the gag reflex kicks in and a terrifying fear of drowning leads to almost instant pleas to bring the treatment to a halt."[20]

In testimony before a House subcommittee, Steven G. Bradbury, acting chief of the Office of Legal Counsel at the Department of Justice, said that waterboarding was not like the "water torture" used during the Spanish Inquisition and by autocratic governments into the twentieth century, but was subject to "strict time limits, safeguards, restrictions." "The only thing in common is, I think, the use of water."[21] He indicated that no water entered the prisoners' lungs, implying that a cloth or cellophane was used.

Over the centuries, there have been several variations on "water cure" tortures.[22] In the Inquisition procedure, a hose was forced into the prisoner's mouth and water was pumped into his stomach, causing his organs to distend. A similar method was adopted in 1900 by the U.S. military in the Philippines: "Lay them on their backs, a man standing on each hand and each foot, then put a round stick in the mouth and pour a pail of water in the mouth and nose, and if they don't give up pour in another pail. They swell up like toads."[23] A second method, illustrated in the movie *Battle of Algiers,* was sticking the prisoner's head into a barrel of water, making the chest swell and leaving the prisoner near asphyxiation. At that point, someone often stomps on the prisoner's stomach. A third method is generally called waterboarding. A person is attached to a board, and the board is dipped into water. Nazi interrogators frequently used this method. The fourth method was apparently invented by the Dutch in the sixteenth century. The person is tied down, and a cloth, or more recently, cellophane, is placed over his mouth. The prisoner chokes as water alternates with a vacuum in the mouth, sinuses, throat, and ultimately the respiratory tract. Presumably, Bradbury was suggesting that CIA methods resembled the third and fourth methods.

Waterboarding was adopted by Americans in the Philippines early in the twentieth century. A major in the U.S. forces used it during the

Spanish-American War. The water cure was used in Vietnam in 1968 on a captured North Vietnamese soldier. In 1983, a Texas state sheriff and his deputies used it on prisoners.[24]

McConnell admitted that in waterboarding someone, "I assume you can get to the point that a person is actually drowning."[25] That would certainly be torture, he added. However, he then went on to relate, perhaps inadvertently, that if waterboarding "ever is determined to be torture, there will be a huge penalty to be paid for anyone engaging in it."[26] Soon after he made this statement, CIA director Michael Hayden confirmed that, in addition to Mohammed, two other detainees, Abu Zubaydah and Abd al Rahim al Nashiri, who had been connected to the bombing of the USS *Cole* in Yemen, had also been subjected to waterboarding.[27]

According to CIA sources, "Khalid Sheik Mohammed won the admiration of interrogators when he was able to last between two and two-and-a-half minutes before begging to confess." Apparently, the average is "fourteen seconds before caving in."[28] A former CIA agent said that Zubaydah "was able to withstand the water boarding for quite some time. And by that I mean probably thirty, thirty-five seconds."[29] The agent added, "And a short time afterwards, in the next day or so, he told his interrogator that Allah had visit[ed] him in his cell during the night and told him to cooperate."[30] The agent believed that waterboarding broke Zubaydah.

In January 2008, after Alberto Gonzales resigned and Michael Mukasey was appointed attorney general, Mukasey wrote a letter to Senator Patrick Leahy, chair of the Senate Judiciary Committee, in which he said that waterboarding was not authorized in the current CIA interrogation program. However, he did not bar the process. He indicated that it could be authorized at a later date through a government procedure. As to the legality of waterboarding, Mukasey wrote that "reasonable minds can and do differ, in the absence of concrete facts and circumstances," as to whether waterboarding is lawful. Consequently, as attorney general, he "should not provide answers absent a set of circumstances that call for those answers."[31] When Mukasey appeared before Leahy's committee the following day, Senator Edward Kennedy asked Mukasey, "Would waterboarding be torture if it were done to you?" Mukasey replied, "I would feel that it was." But Mukasey would not specify whether waterboarding was torture if done to others, or whether waterboarding was illegal.[32]

One week later, a White House spokesman announced that waterboarding was legal and that President Bush could authorize the CIA to waterboard prisoners "under certain circumstances," such as where there was a "belief that an attack might be imminent."[33] The president had vetoed a bill that explicitly prohibited the CIA from waterboarding prisoners.[34]

No doubt, many people will agree with the administration that Khalid Shaikh Mohammed deserved his fate and that interrogating him under torture was the only way to discover critical information needed to prevent another attack. Six human rights groups have reported that Mohammed's two sons were also detained and interrogated by the CIA. The two sons, aged six and eight at the time, were allegedly used as leverage to force Mohammed to cooperate.[35] Under torture, Mohammed apparently revealed the identities of Jose Padilla and Ali al Marri. However, it is still unclear today whether either man posed a serious threat to our nation's security.

Abu Zubayah, accused of being bin Laden's chief lieutenant,[36] was another al Qaeda operative who was captured in Pakistan and held in Thailand, Diego Garcia, Poland, North Africa, and possibly other CIA black sites before being shipped to Guantanamo.[37] He too revealed the identity of Jose Padilla under torture.

Although President Bush announced in August 2006 that there were no longer any detainees in the CIA detention centers after the fourteen high-level detainees were transferred to Guantanamo, seven months later the administration admitted that the CIA sites had been reopened. In fact, they were reopened within three months of his announcement.[38] Abd al Hadi al Iraqi, described as a high-ranking al Qaeda operative, was held in a CIA black site after August 2006. He was later sent to Guantanamo.[39]

CASE STUDY: KHALID EL-MASRI

Khaled El-Masri is a German citizen of Lebanese descent.[40] He was born in Kuwait in 1963 and raised in Lebanon. After fleeing the civil war in Lebanon in 1985, he settled in Germany and became a citizen in 1995. Married with five children, he worked as a truck driver and car salesman.

On December 31, 2003, El-Masri boarded a bus in Ulm, Germany, and headed to Macedonia. Ulm, on the Danube River, had been known as a center of Islamic activity for years, hence German and American officials presumably maintained surveillance over the local community.

When El-Masri reached Macedonia, local officials detained and questioned him. He had no idea why, and no one explained the reason. After several hours of interrogation, the officials transferred him to a hotel in Skopje. El-Masri was detained in the hotel for twenty-three days. The curtains were drawn. He was not permitted to leave the room. He was continually interrogated in English, although his English was limited. During his twenty-three days of confinement in the hotel room, he was not allowed to contact a lawyer, a translator, consular officials, or his wife.

Much of the interrogation focused on what he knew about his mosque in Ulm and the people who attended it. The interrogators continually pressed him about a meeting in Jalalabad, Afghanistan, that he supposedly had with an Egyptian. El-Masri had never been to Jalalabad and could not explain the meeting. On the tenth day of his detention, an unidentified interrogator proposed to El-Masri that if he confessed to involvement with al Qaeda, he would be permitted to return home. El-Masri refused, again denying that he had any connection to al Qaeda or any other terrorist organization.

On January 23, 2004, several Macedonian agents recorded a fifteen-minute video of El-Masri. They instructed him to say that he had been treated well and that he would soon be returning to Germany. The agents then handcuffed and blindfolded him and drove him to a building near the local airport. Inside the building, El-Masri's clothes were cut off with scissors and knives, and he was beaten. Pictures were taken of him. He was then thrown to the floor and, according to his recollection, a firm object was shoved into his anus.

El-Masri was then dragged to a corner of the room and his blindfold removed. Several men dressed in black pants and shirts and wearing black ski masks appeared before him. One man put a diaper on El-Masri. They dressed him in a track suit and attached a belt with chains to his wrists and ankles. They covered his ears with earmuffs, put eye pads over his eyes, and slipped a hood over his head. He was packed onto an airplane, apparently a Boeing 737 jet operated by Aero Contractors and owned by Premier Executive Transport Services, both CIA-controlled dummy corporations.[41] Once on the plane, El-Masri was thrown to the floor, positioned spread-eagled, and his arms and legs secured to the plane. After being given two injections, he passed out.

The plane landed in Afghanistan. He was taken to a small, dirty concrete cell. There was no bed. A dirty blanket and some old, torn clothes that he could use as a pillow were on the floor. A bottle of putrid water stood in the corner. El-Masri's lawyers from the American Civil Liberties Union (ACLU) believe that El-Masri was in a CIA black site facility known as the "Salt Pit," an abandoned brick factory north of the Kabul business district.

That night, El-Masri was taken to an interrogation room, stripped naked, photographed, and medically examined. On the following nights, El-Masri was again interrogated about a trip allegedly taken to Jalalabad, about attending Palestinian training camps, and about whether he knew 9/11 conspirators Mohammed Atta and Ramzi bin al-Shibh. Two interrogators identified themselves as Americans. When El-Masri asked to meet with a German representative, his requests were refused. The interrogatories continued. When El-Masri went on a hunger strike to protest the mistreatment, a feeding tube was forced through his nose into his stomach.

On May 28, El-Masri was blindfolded and handcuffed, placed in a shipping container, and taken from his room. A plane arrived at the airport near the Salt Pit, and El-Masri was told to change back into the clothes he had worn in Macedonia. He was blindfolded, ear-muffed, and chained to the seat of the plane. Upon landing, he was transferred to the back of a vehicle, still blindfolded. Six hours later, his blindfold was removed, his passport was returned, and he was told to exit the vehicle. He found himself on a deserted road in the hills of Albania. It was night. Soon after, El-Masri was picked up by Albanian officials, who took him to Mother Teresa Airport in Tirana and arranged for him to fly to Frankfurt, Germany. From Frankfurt, El-Masri made his way to his home in Ulm. His wife and children were gone. They had relocated to Lebanon when he failed to return from Macedonia. Having not heard from him in months, they assumed that he had abandoned the family. They have since returned to Germany.

What happened? Why did the CIA return El-Masri to civilization without any explanation after six months? Apparently, in April 2004, three months into the abduction, the CIA realized that it had seized the wrong man. The CIA agents in black had mistaken him for a key al Qaeda operative with a similar name.[42] George Tenet, then director of the CIA, and Condoleezza Rice, the president's national security advisor at that time, were both advised that the CIA had the wrong man. Nevertheless, rather than releasing him immediately and admitting the error, the CIA and the administration held El-Marsi at the Salt Pit in Afghanistan for an additional two months. That El-Masri's seizure was a mistake should not be the central theme of this story, however. Our use of extraordinary rendition, no matter who the victim, reduces us to the level of our enemies.

After El-Masri's story surfaced, the American Civil Liberties Union filed suit on his behalf. The suit was brought against George Tenet, unnamed employees of the CIA, CIA contractors, and the corporate defendants who provided the aircraft and crew to transport El-Masri to Afghanistan. It alleged that the defendants violated the due process clause of the U.S. Constitution by subjecting El-Masri to treatment that "shocks the conscience," and deprived him of his liberty in the absence of legal process. The ACLU also sued on the grounds that the defendants had violated international laws and legal norms that prohibit prolonged arbitrary detention and cruel, inhuman, and degrading treatment. The federal trial court dismissed the ACLU's complaint, ruling—based on the state secrets doctrine—that there was an unreasonable risk that privileged state secrets would be disclosed if the lawsuit proceeded further, especially if the case went to a full trial. The ACLU appealed to the Fourth Circuit Court of Appeals. The higher court agreed with the trial court.[43]

The state secrets doctrine was established in a 1953 Supreme Court case.[44] Essentially, the rule allows the United States to prevent the disclosure of information in a judicial proceeding if "there is a reasonable danger that such disclosure will expose military matters which, in the interest of national security, should not be divulged."[45] Although some of the evidence concerning El-Masri had been made public, the federal court of appeals wrote that how the CIA organizes its personnel and supervises its most sensitive intelligence operations, and how the director participates in such operations, are state secrets. In addition, if the case were to succeed at trial, El-Masri would need to demonstrate and reveal facts that would expose the existence, details, and implementation of CIA espionage contracts. The court went on to say that even if El-Masri were able to make his case without revealing state secrets, the defendants themselves would not be able to properly defend themselves without revealing privileged evidence that would disclose the means and methods of CIA operations. Consequently, the case was barred. The Supreme Court refused to hear the case.[46] Senator Patrick Leahy, chair of the Senate Judiciary Committee, commenting on the state secrets defense, said in February 2008 that the administration "has taken a legal doctrine that was intended to protect sensitive national-security information and seems to be using it to evade accountability for its own misdeeds."[47]

In January 2007, a German court issued an arrest warrant for thirteen people involved in El-Masri's kidnapping and rendition. A Spanish paramilitary police agency provided the names, since the CIA agents had brazenly spent significant amounts of American taxpayer money to enjoy rest and relaxation time at the Spanish island of Palma de Mallorca before rendering El-Masri to the black site in Kabul.[48] German Justice Ministry officials dropped the matter in September 2007, after the U.S. government refused to cooperate with the German request.[49]

El-Masri's lawyer has described him as a "psychological wreck." In May 2007, El-Masri was arrested for allegedly setting fire to a supermarket following an argument over a defective MP3 player that he had purchased.[50]

CASE STUDY: MAHER ARAR

Maher Arar, a Syrian-born Canadian citizen, was picked up at New York's Kennedy International Airport on September 26, 2002, on his way back to Montreal, Canada, from a trip to Tunisia.[51] Arar and his wife had been under surveillance for a year by Canadian intelligence authorities after he was observed with Abdullah Almaki, who had been under investigation for possible connections to al Qaeda.[52] While passing through immigration, Arar was pulled out of line, taken to an interview room, questioned by the FBI, fingerprinted, photographed, and his luggage searched. Arar requested a lawyer but was informed that only U.S. citizens were entitled to lawyers.

He was chained and shackled and moved to the Metropolitan Detention Center in Brooklyn, New York. At the detention center, he was stripped, given an orange jumpsuit, and put in solitary confinement. Arar was repeatedly questioned about his relationship to Abdullah Almalki.[53] An official of the Canadian consular office in New York was permitted to visit him on October 3. Two days later, a New York lawyer visited Arar. However, their limited visits did not protect Arar's rights. At his meeting with Immigration and Naturalization on October 6, where Arar explained that he feared torture if he was sent to Syria, Arar was told that his lawyer did not choose to attend the session.[54]

On October 6, the FBI falsely informed Canadian authorities that Arar would likely be deported to Canada. On October 8, when the Canadian consul requested that Arar's wife be permitted to speak to her husband, the consul was informed that he had been removed from the detention center.[55] Arar had been loaded onto a CIA Gulfstream V jet and flown to Jordan by the CIA's Special Removals Unit that same day. From Jordan, he was driven across the border to a tiny, rat-infested underground prison in Syria.[56]

Arar's cell, which lacked all sanitary facilities, was located within the Palestine Branch of Syrian Military Intelligence. Once in the Syrian prison, his captors repeatedly beat him with their fists and with two-inch-thick electrical cables. For the first twelve days, Arar was interrogated for eighteen hours a day. He was told that if he did not confess, he would be placed in a "spine-breaking 'chair,'" hung upside down in a 'tire' for beatings and subjected to electric shocks."[57] To ease the torture, Arar falsely confessed to having trained with terrorists in Afghanistan. In fact, he had never been to Afghanistan and had not been involved in any terrorist activities.

Beginning on October 23, 2002, Canadian consular authorities visited Arar eight times. Members of the Canadian parliament visited him on April 22, 2003. When the consul visited him on August 14, 2003, Arar yelled out that he had been tortured and was being kept in a grave. But it took nearly two months longer for his cries to be heard. After being kept at Sednaya Prison, also in Syria, for six weeks, Arar was released on October 5, 2003.

After Arar was released, he alleged in court documents that U.S. officials had coordinated and planned the interrogations and had provided the Syrians with a dossier of specific questions. He further claimed that Syrian officials shared the information they obtained from Arar with the United States. Barbara Olshansky, who had been working with the Center for Constitutional Rights, filed suit on behalf of Arar against the U.S. government, alleging violations of Arar's rights both under American constitutional law and international law and asking for monetary damages. However, that lawsuit was foreclosed, like El-Masri's, on the grounds of protecting America's state secrets. Arar appealed, and the Court of Appeals for the Second Circuit affirmed the dismissal of his lawsuit. Although acknowledging the needs of national security policies and our relations with foreign countries, the court did not dismiss on state secret grounds. Instead, the court ruled that Arar did not have a lawful federal claim or cause of action or a legal remedy for damages against Ashcroft and other government officials, or against the United States.[58] The court concluded by tossing the issue back to Congress, writing, "We do not doubt that if Congress were so inclined" it could "authorize a cause of action for money damages to redress the type of claims asserted by Arar." Surprisingly, and without a request from either party, the full circuit court announced it would rehear the case en banc in December 2008.

Meanwhile, Canada officially apologized to Arar and offered him $8.9 million in compensation.[59] Arar and his wife and children remain on the U.S. watch list and are banned from flying to the United States.[60]

CASE STUDY: ABU OMAR

Another well-known rendition began on the streets of Milan, Italy, in 2003. Egyptian-born cleric Hassan Mustafa Osama Nasr, known as Abu Omar, was on his way to mosque for noon prayers in February 2003. He was confronted by several men and forced into a white van. Abu Omar was taken to a military air base, where he was stripped and diapered, and his head wrapped in duct tape. He was then hauled onto a plane and flown to Egypt.[61]

When he surfaced fourteen months later, Abu Omar claimed he had been brutally battered in an Egyptian prison. He had been tortured with electric shocks, hung upside down, and sexually abused. Because his statements received a great amount of publicity in Italy, the Italian government investigated the abduction. Italian prosecutors subsequently issued warrants for the arrest of the American CIA agents who committed the extraordinary rendition of Abu Omar with the assistance of Italian military intelligence agents.[62]

However, President Bush refused Italy's request that he return the CIA agents to Italy so they could be arrested (all the agents had summarily vanished from Italy after Abu Omar was transported to Egypt).[63] Italy planned to try the CIA agents in absentia, along with some Italian intelligence officers, including the former commander, Niccolo' Pollari, and deputy commander, Marco Mancini, of the Italian military intelligence agency, SISMI.[64] The trial judge initially suspended the trial in June 2007, intending to wait until Italy's highest court, the Constitutional Court, ruled on whether the Italian prosecutors had violated state secrecy rules in preparing their case. However, in March 2008, the trial judge reversed course and decided to go forward with the trial.[65]

The ACLU filed a federal lawsuit on behalf of foreign nationals who were kidnapped and transported in the CIA's extraordinary rendition program against Jeppesen Dataplan, the company that supplied aircraft, flight crews, and flight and logistical support to the CIA for transporting the men. Through subsidiary corporations, Jeppesen is a wholly owned subsidiary of Boeing Company. In October 2006, a senior Jeppesen official admitted, "We do all of the extraordinary rendition flights—you know, the torture flights."[66]

The federal court permitted the United States to intervene in the lawsuit, then dismissed the lawsuit on the same bases as were used to foreclose Arar's and El-Masri's lawsuits against the government. The court wrote that the "core of the Plaintiffs' case against Defendant Jeppesen are 'allegations' of covert U.S. military or CIA operations in foreign countries against foreign nationals—clearly a subject matter which is a state secret."[67] By convincing the judges to defer to these "national security" issues, the administration, in its state secrets defense, had created a powerful wall to block inquiries into its unlawful actions.

VIOLATING HUMAN RIGHTS LAWS

These extraordinary renditions violate international laws and norms designed to protect the most fundamental rights of all peoples. Though interrogations of dangerous criminals and terrorists can be vital to national security, no American wants to be a party to torture. President Bush has repeatedly asserted that we do not torture. But when it comes to "harsh treatment," however defined, administration officials parse the issue.

International treaties and resolutions protect individuals against torture or extraordinary renditions like those that ensnared El-Masri, Arar, and Omar. Nearly every country, including the United States, has signed the international treaty known as the Convention against Torture (CAT).[68] The treaty bans torture in a nation's territories and by its peoples. CAT defines torture as "any act by which severe pain or suffering, whether physical or mental, is intentionally inflicted on a person for such purposes as obtaining from him or a third person information or a confession, punishing him for an act he or a third person has committed or is suspected of having committed, or intimidating or coercing him or a third person."[69] The treaty requires that no "exceptional circumstances whatsoever," including a state of war or any other public emergency, may be invoked as a justification of torture.[70] The treaty also requires that no country "expel, return or extradite a person to another State where there are substantial grounds for believing that he would be in danger of being subjected to torture."[71] The United States circumvents this requirement by stipulating that as long as the receiving country either declares that it does not torture or guarantees that it will not torture the particular detainee sent by the United States, the U.S. administration is not in violation of the treaty. The administration professes that it always seeks assurances from any country to which it transfers prisoners that the country will not torture.

In addition, when ratifying the Convention against Torture, the United States added a "reservation." The purpose of a reservation is to modify the sense of the treaty as it applies to the United States. This particular reservation provided that transporting people to other countries to be tortured would only be a violation of CAT where it was "more likely than not" that the person would be tortured.[72] Thus, by seeking assurances from another country that the person would not be tortured, the administration would have met the "more likely than not" standard. The letter of the law is thus arguably followed, although the spirit of the law is broken.

CAT also requires a nation "to prevent in any territory under its jurisdiction other acts of cruel, inhuman or degrading treatment or punishment."[73] However, as the language from the treaty indicates, this provision against cruel, inhuman, and degrading treatment is limited to acts within the nation's jurisdiction. Consequently, as the United States sees it, nothing in the treaty prevents us from sending a prisoner to another country where he or she will be subject to harsh treatment, including treatment that is cruel, inhumane, and degrading, as long as the treatment is not torture.

In a further nuanced analysis, the United States has also argued that other international human rights laws and treaties—particularly the International Covenant on Civil and Political Rights (ICCPR), which provides human rights protections to all persons—do not apply to extraordinary renditions.[74] Since 9/11, the international community has persistently tried to put an end to extraordinary rendition. The United States has, in response, been successful in eluding any international responsibility.

On December 6, 2006, the United Nations General Assembly adopted the International Convention for the Protection of All Persons from Enforced Disappearance. Twenty states were necessary to ratify the treaty. When the treaty was opened for signature on February 6, 2007, fifty-seven nations signed it immediately. The United States was not one of them.[75] Regarding the United States' refusal to sign this treaty, a State Department spokesman has said that the convention "was not one that met our needs and expectations."[76]

There are additional treaties, international declarations, and human rights norms that should also apply to the treatment of suspects caught in the web of extraordinary rendition. But the United States has maneuvered its way out of these norms too. [77] For example, the United Nations General Assembly adopted certain fundamental freedoms and human rights in its Universal Declaration of Human Rights (UDHR). This resolution prohibits cruel, inhuman, and degrading treatment and torture, as well as arbitrary arrest and detention. However, since UDHR is not a binding treaty, the United States can ignore it—although many of its provisions are deemed to be customary law, meaning that they should apply as legal norms to all peoples in the international community.

Finally, there is the international concept of *jus cogens*. Jus cogens recognizes that there are universally accepted legal norms for the global community. One commentator describes them as "overriding principles of international law. . . . They are rules of customary law which cannot be set aside by treaty or acquiescence but only by the formation of a subsequent customary rule of contrary effect."[78] Examples of norms that are acknowledged by the international community are the prohibition of use of force, the right to self-determination, racial nondiscrimination, the crime of genocide, and crimes against humanity.[79] Another "customary international law of human rights" is the prohibition of "torture or other cruel, inhuman, or degrading treatment or punishment."[80]

One hopes the day will arrive when customary international laws and norms of human rights will be valued and honored by our government.

PART FIVE

DETENTIONS IN AMERICA
WITH DUE PROCESS

EVEN IN TIMES OF WAR, our nation can and should provide due process rights to alleged terrorists. The criminal defendants described in this part were all alleged to be connected to the War on Terror, the Taliban, al Qaeda, or the 9/11 plot. Yet, unlike Jose Padilla, Yaser Hamdi, and Ali al Marri, who were held incommunicado, deprived of all sensory stimulation, and denied access to lawyers and to fair hearings before neutral decision makers to challenge their detentions, the men described in this part were prosecuted, convicted, and sentenced in the criminal justice system. There were problems in some of these prosecutions, and pressures were placed on the defendants that interfered with their due process rights. The prosecutions were certainly not perfect. For example, John Walker Lindh was cruelly mistreated and tortured by the U.S. military for fifty-four days before the administration allowed him contact with his lawyer. Nevertheless, the fact that these men were provided with access to their attorneys and the due process protections necessary for meaningful hearings demonstrates that the administration could have done it right for all detainees. In fact, there were times, which are not recorded here, when the government lost cases it brought against suspected terrorists. Had the administration chosen the due process course of law that speaks to America's heritage and reflects the vision of our founders, we would not today be witnessing the derogation of the rule of law and its terrible human consequences.

JOHN WALKER LINDH

John Lindh was sixteen in 1997, when he converted to Islam at a mosque in Marin County, California, one of the wealthiest counties in the nation, located across the Golden Gate Bridge from San Francisco. He did not tell his parents at the time. They learned of it when the imam at the mosque phoned John at his home. John says seeing the film *Malcolm X* at the age of twelve first drew him to Islam. He was moved by the pilgrimage scene—the hajj—because it "seemed very natural" to him and "made sense."[1] A few years later, Frank Lindh remarked to his son, "You have always been a Muslim, you just needed to find out."[2]

Frank Lindh and his former wife, Marilyn Walker, were raised as Roman Catholics. Frank is still a practicing Catholic. John, his older brother Connell, and his younger sister Naomi were raised Catholic. The family first lived in Washington, D.C., where Frank worked for the federal government and attended Georgetown Law School at night. They moved to the Bay Area when John was ten. Frank was employed with a law firm and later worked as a lawyer for Pacific Gas and Electric Company in San Francisco. Seven years later, Frank and Marilyn separated and later divorced.

At the age of seventeen, John, who was named after both the nineteenth-century Supreme Court justice John Marshall and the Beatle John Lennon, left home to study Islam. With his parents' blessing, he traveled to Yemen to immerse himself in the study of Islam and the Arabic language.[3] He adopted the name Sulayman, Arabic for Solomon. (Later on in his journeys, Lindh took another name, Abdul Hamid, after a Muslim religious leader of times past.) When John's visa expired nine months later, he returned home. It was May 1999. Back in California, John Lindh wore Muslim clothing when he went out, an oddity even in freethinking California. When John and his father visited Ireland, John wore Muslim dress. He was unhappy at home, though, and yearned to return to Yemen. "There's nothing for me here," he said to his father at the end of the year.[4] In February 2000, John Lindh returned to Yemen. This time he did not return when his visa expired.

Instead, in November 2000, Lindh left Yemen for Pakistan, writing to his parents that he intended to continue his studies there. In April 2001, he wrote that he planned to go up into the mountains of Pakistan for a few months to escape the summer heat. Unbeknownst to his parents, he found his way to a military training camp run by Harakat ul-Mujahideen (HUM). In its charges against Lindh, the U.S. government characterized HUM as a terrorist organization. In early June, Lindh crossed into Afghanistan, without his parents' knowledge, to join the Taliban army. The Taliban had been described to him as practicing the purest form of Islam. As a convert, he probably found the idea of purity of religion appealing.

Lindh volunteered to serve in the Taliban military to fight its political and religious enemy, the Northern Alliance, which controlled the northeastern corner of the country. Serving the Taliban army against the heathen was part of his religious duties in becoming a true Muslim.

John Walker Lindh in Ireland, 1998. Courtesy Frank Lindh.

Since he spoke only Arabic and no local Afghani languages, Lindh trained at al Farooq, an infantry camp set up for non-Taliban volunteers. The volunteers were part of a foreign brigade unit known as Al Ansar, meaning helpers or supporters. Bin Laden partly funded these camps. At the camp, Lindh heard Osama bin Laden lecture on two occasions. At one of these lectures, Lindh dozed off. Another time, he personally met bin Laden.[5] Upon completion of Lindh's infantry training, the Taliban handed him a rifle and two grenades. About a week before September 11, 2001, Lindh arrived at the front line in the northeastern Takhar province to serve as a guard.

Lindh heard about 9/11 while stationed at Takhar. When asked why he did not desert after hearing of the attacks, he replied to an interviewer that he was "scared for his life."[6] He feared that he would not be able to find safe passage out of the Taliban-controlled area into Pakistan, especially since he was American and did not speak the local languages. John's unit remained at its station until the United States began bombing the country.

The United States bombed the Takhar region on November 5. By November 10, John and his unit had fled. They reached the town of Kanduz, where their commander negotiated a deal to pay the warlord and chief of the Northern Alliance, General Rashid Dostum, five hundred thousand dollars for safe passage to Kabul or Pakistan.[7]

Dostum took the money but then reneged on the deal. He herded the Taliban prisoners to a nineteenth-century fortress the size of several football fields, Qala-i-Jhanga, on the outskirts of Mazar-i-Sharif in Afghanistan.

As the prisoners arrived, Dostum's men searched them for weapons. One of the prisoners pulled out a grenade and blew it up, killing Dostum's chief of police. Fearing for their safety, Dostum's men ended the searches. Later that evening, after several other prisoners had blown themselves up with grenades, Dostum's guards directed the prisoners into the basement of a pink classroom building in the fortress. It became known as the Pink House. The next morning, Sunday, November 25, the guards ordered the prisoners to go to a horse pasture near the Pink House for interrogations. The four hundred or so prisoners were seated side by side, their arms tied behind their backs.

Two American CIA agents, who had been sent to Afghanistan to link up with Dostum after 9/11, interviewed the prisoners. In a video recording made at the time and later shown on British television, the CIA agents are shown interviewing Lindh, who is kneeling before them.[8] One man, Johnny Michael Spann (known as Mike), is dressed in jeans and a black shirt, the other, Dave, in Afghani attire. Both carry rifles and pistols. Dave carries a video camera, Spann a small still camera. No American troops are present.

In looking at the videotape, one is inclined to wonder why these two CIA agents would stand among hundreds of Taliban fighters, tied up or not, to interview them without more American cover. It is hard to imagine that the agents would have trusted the corrupt warlord Dostum and his men to protect American personnel if a riot broke out. Johnny Spann, Mike's father, believes that the CIA had never properly trained its agents for this kind of situation. He holds the U.S. government responsible for what happened next.[9] Perhaps the agents were so poorly trained that they never expected anything to happen, even after the grenade incidents of the previous day. Unfortunately, the two CIA agents had grossly misjudged the desperation of at least some of the captives.

In the horse-pasture interview with John Lindh, the CIA agents ask him whether he is from Ireland. "Irish, Ireland?" Spann asks. "Who brought you here? You believe in what you are doing here that much, you're willing to be killed here?"[10] Lindh refuses to answer. Months later, Lindh explained that he was afraid that the two men were mercenaries on Dostum's payroll and would kill him if they discovered that he was American.[11] The two agents never revealed that they were agents of the CIA or even that they were working for the U.S. government.

When John refuses to talk, Dave says to Spann for Lindh to over-hear, "The problem is, he's got to decide if he wants to live or die, and die here. We're going to leave him, and he's going to fucking sit in prison the rest of his short life. It's his decision, man. We can only help the guys who want to talk to us. We can only get the Red Cross to help so many guys." Obtaining no response from Lindh, they return him to the group of prisoners sitting in the pasture. Moments later, one of the prisoners, believed to be an Uzbek, tosses a grenade. More than any of the other ethnic groups, the Uzbek prisoners feared Dostum. Dostum himself was Uzbek, and the word was that he brutally tortured and then killed any Uzbeks who opposed him. The Uzbeks believed they had to act first to save their lives.

Chaos ensues. Prisoners who have succeeded in loosening their bonds attack the guards and race toward the Americans. Some Taliban run the other way, into the basement of the Pink House. Dostum's guards fire on the prisoners in the pasture. It is unclear exactly what happened next. One version is that Spann started firing his gun, and when he ran out of ammunition, the prisoners killed him.[12] Another version is that after Spann was down, somehow his own gun killed him.[13]

Johnny Spann, Mike's father, traveled to Afghanistan and met with two Afghani doctors who were with Mike Spann when he died. The doctors initially told him much the same version that he had heard from others—that Mike was attacked and killed by several prisoners.[14] However, then they added that as Mike advanced toward the Pink House and started shooting, Taliban in the yard jumped up and rushed him. One of the doctors added that as the prisoners attacked Mike, his AK-47 ran out of bullets. Mike pulled out his handgun to continue shooting, but "there were too many of them and they were taking him to the ground." Johnny Spann was dubious about this version, which seemed too pat, almost like an old western movie. He wondered whether "Dostrom [had] gotten them together and told them this is what we got to tell."

Mike Spann is remembered as the first American who died in combat in the war in Afghanistan.[15]

The videotape shows Dave, the other CIA agent, running to a nearby house immediately after the grenade explodes. Inside the house, he asks a German journalist to use his satellite phone. Frantically, Dave calls the

American base in Tashkent for military support. Next we see Dostum's men running toward the side of the fortress, around spindly pine and alder trees and down the surrounding hills. In pursuit are Taliban soldiers who have garnered rifles and artillery from the stockade at the fortress. Other Taliban fighters head for the safety of the basement. Dostum's men return, and a primitive battle is engaged. The camera sweeps over men who appear to be from another time, as they clamber over the mud walls and slide down the hills at the perimeter of the field. Some run this way and hide behind trees and stones. Others halt behind a squiggly tree or low brush and shoot at random targets. This is not a twenty-first-century war. It is not twentieth-century either.

The American military support that Dave called for arrives with missile air strikes that destroy houses and kill Taliban fighters. However, the next day's bombing is what people remember most. The video shows the guards in retreat as a B-52 prepares to drop a bomb on the Taliban fighters. Instead, amid the shouting of Dostum's men at the planes above, the bomb misses its mark and drops on a gatehouse in which the men are sequestered. Eight of Dostum's men are killed. Five Americans accompanying them are injured. The Taliban hunkering down in the basement of the Pink House are safe for the moment.

That is the end of American air strikes at the fortress, although American Special Forces remain clustered nearby. Sporadic shooting and grenade tossing continue for the next twenty-four hours. That evening, several Taliban rush out to assist Lindh, who had been shot in the leg during the melee and was lying in the pasture pretending to be dead. They carry him into the basement under cover of darkness.

It is now evening of the third day following the uprising. The remaining Taliban have regrouped in the basement of the Pink House. Dostum's soldiers returned earlier that afternoon to find bodies strewn throughout the field. They stripped the bodies of valuables, especially shoes.

The Taliban prisoners who survived the battle in the horse pasture are holed up inside the basement of the Pink House. Dostum's men, intending to kill them if they do not immediately surrender, drop grenades into the air ducts. The Taliban remain below. The Northern Alliance soldiers then pour diesel fuel into the basement and ignite the fuel. Still the men remain below. Finally, the soldiers pump cold water into the basement, forcing the prisoners to stand for hours on end in the cold water. Should they slip and fall, they risk serious illness if not death by taking in water contaminated with feces, vomit, and blood. Lindh's bullet wound festers. He must lean on a fellow comrade to stand. It is too much for the remaining men, who are suffering from dehydration, hunger, and hypothermia. Seven days have passed. The surviving eighty-six prisoners emerge, among them John Walker Lindh and Yaser Hamdi.[16] It is Saturday, December 1, 2001.

The survivors are taken to a hospital in Sherbergen, Afghanistan. At the hospital, Robert Pelton, a CNN filmmaker and contract reporter who had accompanied Dostum, sees an opportunity for a story. A huge story. He intends to interview and film the captured American, John Walker Lindh. In the video, a pained, dehydrated, and emaciated Lindh refuses to be filmed. He speaks coherently, intelligently, and rationally: "Look, you don't have my permission to film me," Lindh says. He adds, "If you're concerned about my welfare, don't film me." Pelton, wanting a story, ignores his request. Pelton offers Lindh cookies. Lindh, having not eaten for days, does not turn down the offer. The medic then administers morphine in anticipation of a blood transfusion, and Lindh's resistance withers. In the film, Pelton doggedly seeks to gain Lindh's trust. At one moment, Lindh utters that "my heart has become attached to the Taliban." He adds that "the goal of every Muslim" is to be a "shahid" or martyr. Pelton seizes on those words. He has his story.

Frank Lindh's cousin was the first in the family to see a news story on the Internet about a young American captured at the Qala-i-Jhangi fortress. He immediately e-mailed Frank and Marilyn to ask whether the unnamed American could be John. At that point, John had been missing for more than seven months. It was Saturday evening. Early the next morning, Frank telephoned the law office of a prominent San Francisco attorney, Jim Brosnahan. Brosnahan returned the call Sunday afternoon, saying that he had seen the story on television and would meet Frank Monday morning. Frank and his family stayed with friends because of media harassment.

Frank had met Brosnahan once before, when they were on opposite sides of a case. Frank had been impressed with Brosnahan's legal skills and integrity. A partner in Morrison and Foerster, he had a reputation of representing clients that other attorneys might pass over as society's outcasts. Brosnahan loved the challenge. "I am a fighter," he said to Lindh.[17]

According to Frank Lindh, the American Civil Liberties Union (ACLU) declined to take Lindh's case or provide any assistance to the family. As Frank Lindh said, "You knew you were in trouble when the ACLU would not take the case."[18] However, the ACLU normally does not defend clients in criminal actions; it engages in impact litigation, in an attempt to force policy changes. In fact, the ACLU had been instrumental in obtaining sensitive documents after 9/11 concerning treatment of the detainees.

In the meantime, the media was ablaze with news of the American from California, with the politicians all taking potshots. New York senator Hillary Clinton, without much inquiry and within days of his capture, described John Lindh as a traitor. California senator Barbara Boxer said that it looked like treason to her. Other public figures, including Attorney General John Ashcroft, Secretary of State Colin Powell, and Vice President Dick Cheney, also publicly denounced Lindh. Frank Lindh said it felt like a "lynch mob" to him.[19]

On Monday, December 3, 2001, Brosnahan wrote a letter to Attorney General John Ashcroft and other high-level Bush administration officials informing them that he had been hired to represent Lindh. There had been some serious grumbling from members of Brosnahan's firm, especially partners in New York. In response, Brosnahan and his team of lawyers removed Lindh's case from the firm's catalog of cases and defended him in their own names. Brosnahan received hate mail and veiled threats. Someone phoned word of a bomb threat into the firm's Washington, D.C., office.

John Lindh had asked for a lawyer soon after the Americans seized him. The military and FBI officials who were guarding and interrogating Lindh in Afghanistan never informed him that his parents had hired Brosnahan. The Department of Justice's Professional Responsibility Advisory Office, the ethics arm of the agency, informed the FBI in Afghanistan that Frank Lindh had hired legal counsel for John and that they should cease interrogating him without counsel. But the prosecutorial office and the FBI ignored the opinion, even when the ethics group warned the agents that whatever statements they obtained from Lindh would be inadmissible in court. Apparently, the prosecutors and the FBI were more concerned with obtaining information that might assist them in their search for al Qaeda and Taliban leaders, as well as in possibly discovering future plots. To the agents, Lindh could be a valuable and immediate pipeline. The possibility of Lindh's statement being suppressed in a criminal trial was not nearly as compelling at the moment as was gathering intelligence.

In addition, a Supreme Court case decided in 1986 had determined that police interrogating a defendant were not obligated to notify him that his relatives had hired counsel on his behalf.[20] The Court ruled that the defendant should hire his own counsel. Lindh had not chosen his lawyer at that time, the government argued. The fact that there was no opportunity for Lindh to do so did not seem to affect the government's reasoning.

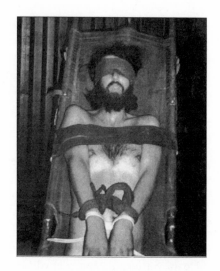

After the Pelton interview, Lindh was transported to General Dostum's compound and interrogated by a Special Forces interrogator. The next day, his hands and feet were bound and a hood was placed over his head as he was taken to the "Turkish School House" in Mazar-i-Sharif. The Turkish School House was an actual school building used as a headquarters by the U.S. Special Forces.[21] Here, too, he was questioned by military interrogators. Lindh was at the Turkish School House for six days.

Immediately before he was to be flown to Camp Rhino, a temporary marine base in the high desert seventy miles south of Kandahar, some of his guards wrote "shithead" on his blindfold—or on duct tape attached to his blindfold, according to other testimony—and posed for photos of themselves standing next to him. The photo session was considered "barracks humor," and soldiers indicated that they believed Lindh was "unaware" of the photo session.[22] A document that describes the military investigation of the photo session also states that several soldiers generously "gave up their own food, cots, heaters and sleeping gear to Mr. Lindh in order to sustain him and support his recovery."[23]

At Camp Rhino, soldiers stripped off all of John Lindh's clothing. Wearing only a blindfold, Lindh was duct-taped to a stretcher and put in a metal shipping container about fifteen feet long, seven feet wide, and eight feet high. Military personnel photographed him as he lay on his back fully exposed, hands and feet restrained to the stretcher and shivering in the freezing Afghan winter night. There was no light, heat

John Walker Lindh at Camp Rhino, 2001. Courtesy U.S. government.

source, or insulation inside the container. Light and air came through two small holes in the container's sides. When he wanted to urinate, guards propped him up on the stretcher into a vertical position. At some point, he was given a thin blanket.[24]

At Camp Rhino Lindh was interrogated by an FBI agent who read him his Miranda rights. However, the agent then added, "Of course, there are no lawyers here." Lindh, believing he had no choice, agreed to speak to the agent. According to Lindh's lawyer, he waived his right to have a lawyer present and agreed to answer questions because he believed that he would never "get out of that metal box" unless he agreed to talk.[25] Lindh was still restrained when he signed a statement that would become the focus of an intense legal battle.

On December 14, a week after arriving at Camp Rhino, Lindh was transferred to the USS *Peleliu*, a navy ship cruising in the Indian Ocean. Suffering from dehydration and hypothermia, he was given intravenous fluids, and the bullet in his leg was finally removed. He was allowed to receive letters from his parents and family for the first time on January 6, 2002.

On his flight to America nearly two months after he was captured, Lindh was beaten. His face appears puffy in his mug shots.[26] Lindh was delivered to federal prosecutors in Alexandria, Virginia, and held in the Alexandria city jail. The next morning, the administration allowed him to speak to his parents and meet Jim Brosnahan, George Harris, and Tony West, his team of distinguished lawyers from the prestigious firm of Morrison & Foerster. The military had held John Lindh for fifty-four days without access to counsel.

The government charged Lindh with ten counts connected to joining the Taliban. The most serious was the charge of conspiracy to murder Mike Spann, the CIA agent who interviewed him at the fortress. In two nationally televised press conferences, Attorney General Ashcroft accused Lindh of training with al Qaeda in Afghanistan and serving under the direction of Osama bin Laden.[27] Lindh faced the possibility of multiple life sentences plus an additional ninety years in prison. The judge set the trial for August 2002, to continue through the first anniversary of the 9/11 attacks.

Lindh's lawyers filed motions to suppress the statements Lindh had made to the FBI agent in Afghanistan, arguing that the agent had coerced Lindh and that he was under duress when he made the statements. The lawyers also argued that the FBI agent misled Lindh as to the availability of an attorney. Finally, the lawyers stated that government agents had harshly treated, if not tortured, Lindh during those fifty-four days before he reached America's shores. Based on the defense arguments, government prosecutors feared that they might lose the suppression hearing. On the other side, Lindh's lawyers worried that even though they believed the law favored their position in the suppression hearing, they could nevertheless lose because the judge was known to favor the prosecution.

Serious negotiations began in late afternoon on Friday, July 12, 2002, when the prosecutors approached the defense after a hearing on a motion to quash a subpoena.[28] The initial offer required Lindh to plead guilty to providing material assistance to al Qaeda. Lindh refused, saying that he could never agree to it because it was not true. He had not provided assistance to al Qaeda, but rather was a soldier in the Taliban army. The government's initial offer also required that Lindh agree never to travel outside the United States. Lindh refused that provision too, because one of the "five pillars of Islam" requires that he participate in a pilgrimage to Mecca.[29] Over the weekend, the government returned with another offer. Each government proposal was an "exploding offer," meaning that it would evaporate at the moment the suppression hearing began.

Early Monday morning, around 2:00 A.M., the government prosecutors and Lindh's attorneys struck a deal.[30] The government agreed to drop nine of the ten charges. Lindh agreed to plead guilty to violating the economic sanctions imposed on the Taliban in a 1999 Clinton executive order. He also agreed to a weapons charge that he had carried a rifle and two grenades while serving as a soldier in the Taliban military. The government agreed to drop the other counts in the indictment, including the charge of conspiracy to commit murder. Lindh was given two consecutive ten-year terms.

The defense had hoped to obtain a lesser sentence in the plea bargain, but the prosecutors informed them that the White House had issued the requirement of twenty years, and "we can't negotiate that."[31] There is no parole in the federal system, although prisoners may have up to 15 percent of their sentence discharged for good behavior. Consequently, Lindh would serve a minimum of seventeen years, and thus, with good behavior, the earliest possible release would be at the age of thirty-seven.

Looking back, one wonders whether Lindh could have negotiated a better deal. Several facts suggest that Lindh's lawyers acted too quickly in accepting the government's offer and should have demanded a better offer or continued to trial. It was not at all certain that the judge, though conservative, would have admitted the confession into evidence. As explained above, there were serious questions as to whether Lindh's confession met due process requirements. If the confession were admissible, the government would have had to reveal confidential sources to explain the circumstances of the interrogation that led to the confession, intelligence information that the government would not necessarily want to reveal. In addition, Lindh's defense team could have argued that Lindh had been tortured by U.S. military personnel while held in Afghanistan. If any evidence of torture was admitted, the evidence would certainly discredit the government's position. Lindh's lawyers could also have filed numerous legal motions in an attempt to forestall the start of the trial, waiting for potential jurors' passions to cool over time.

On the other hand, there were powerful reasons for Lindh's team to accept the government's offer, given the circumstances. The judge was intent on moving forward with the trial and would not allow defense motions to interfere with the start date within weeks of September 11, 2002, the first anniversary of the attacks. Even without the confession, the government had the advantage of bringing the case against Lindh in Virginia, a conservative region, with a likely conservative jury. The trial would be held in a courtroom near the Pentagon, which had been attacked. The 9/11 attacks were still in the minds of all Americans, many of whom feared further attacks. Moreover, if the jury found Lindh guilty, he would be sentenced to a minimum of thirty years on the charges and could have been sentenced to multiple life imprisonments plus ninety years. And finally, the government had its ace card: the DOJ indicated that if they did not like the result of a trial, or even if they did not want to pursue a trial at all, they could, at any time, refuse to release Lindh and instead declare him an enemy combatant. As an enemy combatant, Lindh would have been detained in the naval brig in Charleston, South Carolina, along with two other American citizens, Jose Padilla and Yaser Hamdi. In fact, Lindh's lawyers believe that at any time, perhaps even after he is released from federal prison, the administration may still classify him as an enemy combatant.[32]

At the time the American forces first seized Lindh, Mike Spann's father, Johnny Spann, suggested that Lindh knew of the uprising. Johnny

Spann believed that the prisoners planned the uprising in the basement the night before, and since Lindh was among them, he had to have heard some mention of the planned uprising. Spann added that even if Lindh did not actually participate in the death of his son, he could have prevented it by informing the two CIA agents that an uprising was about to occur.[33] Lindh claimed that he had no advance knowledge. Even if the Uzbek prisoners did foment plans that night, Lindh would not have known because he did not speak their language.[34] Johnny Spann attended all of Lindh's court appearances.

At John Lindh's sentencing, the judge permitted Johnny Spann to address the court. He conveyed his deep concerns about the plea agreement. Believing that Lindh was involved in his son's death, he said that the sentence was too lenient. Judge Ellis, who presided over the plea negotiation and the sentencing, replied, "Let me be clear about that. The government has no evidence of that." Judge Ellis added that Mike Spann fought for what we believe in America, and one of those beliefs is that "we don't convict people in the absence of proof beyond a reasonable doubt."[35]

I sometimes think someone should write a book about the two fathers, Frank Lindh and Johnny Spann, and their two young sons, who came from opposite poles in America. Mike Spann grew up in Winfield, Alabama, a small town three hours from Birmingham. John Lindh grew up in Marin County, one of the wealthiest counties in the country. Both fathers are good men who are devoted to their sons. Both sons believed in their causes. America's War on Terror had captured these two fathers in a flicker of time. They are forever bound in torment. Both fathers, perhaps unwittingly, perhaps necessarily, now live their lives for their sons.

In 2004, soon after the administration released Yaser Hamdi, attorney Jim Brosnahan filed a request with President Bush to commute Lindh's sentence. In his request, Brosnahan noted that Hamdi had been released and that his path was very similar to John Lindh's. Both were U.S. citizens who had joined the Taliban army, receiving training before 9/11. Both fought in northwestern Afghanistan against the Northern Alliance. Both were members of the Taliban army that Dostum seized and held at the fortress at Qala-i-Jhanga, outside Mazar-i-Sharif. Both men survived the seven-day ordeal in the Pink House. Moreover, the military transported both men to the United States.

Hamdi was designated an enemy combatant but then was released in summer 2004, after only three years in custody. John Lindh was never designated an enemy combatant and began his twenty-year prison term in a medium-security federal prison in Victorville in Southern California. (Lindh's team of lawyers had requested that he serve his time in California so that his parents and family could visit him easily. The government agreed.) However, today Yaser Hamdi no longer has American citizenship, and John Lindh does.

In February 2007, the Bureau of Prisons moved Lindh from the medium-security prison in California to a maximum-security prison in Florence, Colorado, one hundred miles south of Denver. No reason was given for the move. The Bureau of Prisons has the authority to make such moves without challenge. The official name of this prison is the United States Penitentiary—Administrative Maximum, but it is known as the Florence Supermax or the ADX Supermax. The Supermax is considered the "crown jewel" of the prison system by guards who work there, and has been described as "a clean version of hell" by its former warden, Robert Hood.[36] The facility is small, with fewer than five hundred prisoners. It is home to many of America's most violent and notorious criminals, including Ted Kaczynski (the Unabomber) and Terry Nichols, who was convicted along with Timothy McVeigh in the 1995 bombing of the Oklahoma City federal building.. The Supermax also houses convicted terrorists Zacarias Moussaoui and Richard Reid. Jose Padilla was transferred there after his Florida conviction.

At the Supermax, Lindh was held in solitary confinement, spending twenty-four hours a day in "'lockdown' conditions."[37] He was permitted no more than one hour of exercise daily, alone in a cage, and exercise was not provided on a regular basis. The guards served his meals through a slot in his door. He ate alone and spoke to no one in the prison, neither other prisoners nor guards. The prison bureau permitted him to read a few books, but no magazines or newspapers. He did not have access to a radio or an iPod or other musical source. From the window in his cell, he could see the sky but not the earth. His father was permitted to talk to him about the "beautiful countryside" surrounding the prison but was not allowed to describe the terrain to him. The only time John saw the terrain was on his way into the prison.

When John Lindh met with visitors, he sat on one side of an enclosed booth. His visitor sat on the other side, separated by a glass panel. They spoke through a phone. Visits were permitted for up to five hours. A prison official sat two doors away listening to the conversations. The guards escorted Lindh into his half of the visiting booth with his feet manacled and his hands cuffed and shackled to a belly chain. He would bend down and stick his hands through a slot in the door to have his handcuffs unlocked so that he could lift the receiver to talk to his visitor. In his former prison, inmates met their families and friends in a room with large tables and no separators. Lindh could hug his parents. Frank Lindh wrote in late April 2007 that since his son was transferred to the Supermax, his "ability to visit John is very constrained."[38] The FBI vets and approves all visitors. It took Frank Lindh nearly six months to obtain approval.

A *Newsweek* article suggests that the government intended for Lindh to be a witness against certain Guantanamo detainees at upcoming military commission trials and that the government wanted to "ensure his security,"[39] hence the move to the Supermax. He was expected to testify at the trial of David Hicks, who had also served with Taliban forces and trained in an al Qaeda camp. After pleading guilty to a reduced charge, Hicks received an additional nine months and was released from prison in December 2007. In April 2007, Jim Brosnahan again requested that the president commute or, at minimum, reduce Lindh's sentence, comparing his sentence to that given David Hicks. Brosnahan argued that the two men were captured in similar circumstances, but unlike Lindh, Hicks was now a free man. The president never acted on Brosnahan's petition.

Frank Lindh is not convinced the government relocated Lindh to the Supermax for security reasons. A month after an article sympathetic to John Lindh appeared in *Esquire*,[40] the officials at his medium-security prison moved Lindh from his cell to a restrictive Special Housing Unit. Soon after, officials transferred Lindh to the Supermax. Frank Lindh believes that no prison system wants a "sympathetic character."[41] Prison officials want only faceless inmates, so that the officials can control the population. When an inmate receives publicity or notoriety, prison officials take the inmate out of circulation. Frank Lindh believes that the *Esquire* article was too supportive of Lindh, and consequently, the prison administration needed to cut off his son from the system. Besides, if Lindh is isolated from other prisoners, no prisoners will have any information to reveal to the media after their release.

There is also the possibility that certain people in the administration were not pleased by Brosnahan's petitions, especially to the extent that they shone light on Lindh's situation. Perhaps moving John Lindh to the Supermax was the administration's warning to Brosnahan to abandon the petitions and the favorable publicity he was obtaining for Lindh.

Frank Lindh acknowledged that the government may have moved his son for his own protection; however, he does not think it likely, since he knew of no incident that occurred around that time. Nor was he aware of any threats, although, of course, he might not have been privy to security information. Nevertheless, Frank Lindh noticed one positive change when visiting his son at the Supermax. Frank observed that John seemed less jittery than when Frank visited him at the medium-security prison. Frank believed that his son felt safer at the Supermax because he was completely isolated. Frank described him as being in "good spirits," and commented that the life of a monk suited him.[42] He is "in good psychological health today," Frank Lindh reported in September 2007.[43]

In November 2007, Frank Lindh e-mailed to say that "John was moved a month ago to a federal prison in the Midwest. He is being housed in a special unit (in what until recently was Death Row, before it was moved to a new penitentiary across the road). There are only forty or so other inmates in his unit, most of them Muslims. It's his best situation yet."[44]

The penitentiary that is currently housing Lindh was "established to house inmates who, due to their current offense of conviction, offense conduct, or other verified information, require increased monitoring of communication between inmates and persons in the community in order to protect the safety, security, and orderly operation of Bureau facilities, and protect the public."[45] Apparently, it was designed to house Muslim and Middle Eastern prisoners.[46] Five of the "Lackawanna Six," American citizens convicted of providing material support for terrorism, are housed at the facility.[47]

The detainees are permitted to interact during the day. They may leave their cells and share meals and recreational activities, a significant improvement over the Supermax. However, visiting hours, phone calls, and mail are severely restricted. John is only permitted visitors for a total of four hours a month, and only on weekdays. There is only one visiting booth in the facility.[48] He can receive mail only from his family and his lawyers. As at the Supermax, the visits at the prison in the Midwest take place in partitioned rooms separated by a glass pane. Conversations are through a telephone receiver and are monitored.[49]

In January 2008, Frank wrote to say that he and his daughter visited

John, "and he continues to thrive despite everything."[50] The communal setting and the fact that many of the inmates, including John, pray and hold prayer meetings remind Frank of a Catholic seminary. Frank has three uncles who were priests at one time. John listens to the radio, and he and the other inmates may speak Arabic to each other. John is not shackled during visits, as he was at the Supermax.

In all three prisons, John Lindh has been under severe restrictions, known as Special Administrative Measures (SAMs). Initially, under these administrative regulations, the administration permitted him to meet only with his lawyers and his immediate family, and everyone was instructed not to reveal their conversations. Although regulations now permit him to meet with some people besides immediate family and lawyers, no one else has visited him.

The administration has maintained its injunction against Lindh's speaking to the media. The rationale appears to be that if John Lindh had conversations with the media and the conversations were made public, Lindh would be able to communicate with Taliban and al Qaeda members outside the prison. It seems odd to think that there is any information John Lindh still has that he could communicate to others, assuming he ever had security information. Nevertheless, the administration has renewed the SAMs each year.

Until John arrived at the prison in the Midwest, he was prohibited from speaking Arabic at any time. A prisoner who was in the same medium-security prison as John in Southern California revealed that prison officials had placed Lindh in isolation because he spoke in Arabic. In one incident, John said only "Assalamu alaikum," the Arabic greeting. Another prisoner had said "Salaam" to John to bait him, and John, knowing the consequences but feeling that it was proper to return the greeting in Arabic, took the bait.[51]

On another occasion in the same prison, John was attacked and beaten outside a prison chapel by a prisoner who was a member of the Aryan Nation. Inside the chapel, a minister was presiding over a fundamentalist meeting.[52] When I asked Frank Lindh about this incident, he said that the SAMs severely restricted what he could say to me and that he could not respond to anything that I might have heard about prison life. After the incident, other Muslims in the prison bonded together to protect Lindh.

Frank Lindh describes his son as a "lightning rod" for all the grief of 9/11.[53] He describes how unimaginable it is "when the most powerful nation in the world comes down on your son."[54] Ironically, when he first learned that his son had been captured, Frank Lindh felt a great rush of relief. He thought, "Thank God he is in the hands of the Americans."[55]

RICHARD COLVIN REID

Richard Colvin Reid, the "shoe bomber," had planned to ignite an explosive device hidden in the lining of his shoe on an American Airlines flight from Paris to Miami on December 22, 2001. The passengers and crew interceded as he struck a match on his shoe. Reid was born in 1973 in London to a Jamaican father and an English mother. Reid's father spent some twenty years in jail for robbery and car theft. His parents separated when the boy was eleven. Reid was in and out of prison from the time he was seventeen. When he was in his twenties, he ran into his father, a Muslim convert, who suggested that he too convert to Islam. Reid did and worshipped for a time at the same mosque as Zacarias Moussaoui, once described as the "twentieth hijacker." In 1999 and 2000, Reid traveled to Pakistan and crossed into Afghanistan to join a terrorist training camp. While in the Middle East, he traveled to Israel and Egypt, possibly under an alias, and apparently returned to Pakistan and Afghanistan.[56]

Reid was not designated an enemy combatant, but was instead prosecuted through the criminal justice system. He pled guilty to eight counts, including attempted use of a weapon of mass destruction and attempted homicide.[57] The judge sentenced him to life imprisonment.[58] He is serving his time in the Florence Supermax.

ZACARIAS MOUSSAOUI

Zacarias Moussaoui, a French national of Moroccan descent, was arrested on immigration violations one month before 9/11, after a flight school in Eagan, Minnesota, notified the FBI that he was seeking training to fly a Jumbo 747 but was not interested in learning takeoffs or landings. Years earlier, he had visited Pakistan and Afghanistan, where he allegedly attended an al Qaeda training camp.[59]

Initially after 9/11, government agents hypothesized that Moussaoui was the twentieth hijacker. Because three of the four hijacked planes had five terrorists on each, but the plane brought down by passengers over a field in Pennsylvania had only four hijackers, the administration and the media believed that a fifth hijacker should have been on board on that flight. However, the administration subsequently came to believe that another man detained in Guantanamo Bay, Muhammed al-Qahtani, was the twentieth hijacker.[60] The government never classified Moussaoui as an enemy combatant.

Federal public defender Frank Dunham represented Zacarias Moussaoui in addition to Yaser Hamdi. Moussaoui, who was somewhat deranged, had only dismissive things to say about the American legal system and, concomitantly, mistrusted his attorneys. He refused all representation, including Dunham's. Moussaoui pled guilty to conspiracy in connection with the 9/11 attacks, protesting to the judge that Dunham and his team of federal defenders were deliberately trying to have him put him to death.

A psychologist described Moussaoui as a paranoid schizophrenic, a diagnosis supported by the fact that his father and sisters had a history of mental illness.[61] In spite of Moussaoui's irrational behavior and seeming mental illness, the judge allowed him to plead guilty and represent himself. At the penalty phase, when the jury had to choose between life imprisonment and death, Moussaoui admitted to nearly every prosecution statement about his crimes and behavior. He further claimed that he and Richard Reid, the shoe bomber, had intended to fly a plane into the White House on 9/11. Later, FBI agents admitted that it was "highly unlikely" that Reid knew of the 9/11 attacks in advance or that he had planned to participate with Moussaoui in such an operation.[62]

In spite of Moussaoui's personal and vituperative attacks, Dunham and his team persisted on his behalf. Because Dunham and his defense team were able to convince one juror to hold out for a life term, the jury sentenced Moussaoui to life imprisonment without parole in May 2006. He is now imprisoned in the Florence Supermax along with Richard Reid. Dunham and the jury proved to Moussaoui that Americans respect the individual, even if the individual does not respect us.

Although it seemed at the time that Moussaoui was afforded due process, serious questions subsequently arose as to whether the rule of law truly protected his interests. In late 2007 and early 2008, his lawyers filed several petitions with the court of appeals. They raised two distinct and troublesome issues. In one, the lawyers noted that from the beginning Moussaoui had sought, without success, interviews with certain detainees, including Abu Zubaydah and Khalid Shaikh Mohammed. Moussaoui believed that if these men were questioned, they would confirm that he was not involved in the 9/11 plot. The district court judge inquired on behalf of Moussaoui whether video or audio recordings were made of the interrogations of these and other potential witnesses. The government denied that such tapes existed.

The judge, Leonie M. Brinkema, expressed doubt that the interrogations were not being taped. Brinkema noted that local police departments routinely record confessions, "and I can't believe that it is not being done here."[63] She required that the government lawyers secure sworn declarations, under penalty of perjury, from all appropriate officials, including those working and contracting for any agency that might have been involved in interrogations, that no video or audio recordings had been made. The government supplied a statement that no such tapes existed. However, in late 2007, it became apparent that the government had misled the court and that tapes were in existence at the time of the judge's request.[64] In 2008, Judge Brinkema told a college audience, "One of the saddest realities I've had to face—in the Moussaoui case in particular—has been the reality that my government didn't always tell me the truth."[65]

Moussaoui's lawyers argued in their 2007–8 briefs that Moussaoui might not have entered his guilty plea if he had had access to these tapes or full transcripts of them.[66] The government responded that when Moussaoui pleaded guilty, he understood that he waived all legal and constitutional challenges that arose before his guilty plea, including any claims regarding access to the witnesses.[67]

On the second issue, Moussaoui's lawyers argued that Moussaoui was denied his fundamental right to an attorney under the Sixth Amendment.[68] Moussaoui had requested a Muslim lawyer, explaining that he had the financial means to hire one or he would find a Muslim lawyer to take his case pro bono. Moussaoui believed that some people who could testify on his behalf would "never, never speak to a non-Muslim." He added that a defense team without a Muslim lawyer "cannot navigate in the Muslim environment."

The district court, however, refused Moussaoui the right to choose his own counsel, saying that "in this type of case where there are national security and classified documents, you don't have totally unrestricted choice even if you have the money available to hire an attorney."[69] That is, in cases of national security, the judge believed that national security concerns and approval of counsel by the government outweighed Moussaoui's fundamental right to counsel. At one point, Moussaoui attempted to seek advice from an outside lawyer, but he was barred because the lawyer had refused to undergo the security background check. Having thus to choose among remaining with government-appointed counsel he did not trust, retaining a lawyer who had to be approved by the government, and representing himself, Moussaoui chose self-representation.

In addition, the judge forbade Moussaoui's attorneys, who had access to classified information, to reveal the information to him. At one point, his lawyers knew of specific exculpatory evidence but were restricted from revealing it to Moussaoui or even telling him that such evidence existed. On this basis, they strongly recommended to him that he not plead guilty, but they could not explain why.[70]

As of late fall 2008, there has been no decision on these matters.

THE LACKAWANNA SIX

In April 2001, six Yemeni Americans from Lackawanna, New York (near Buffalo), traveled to al Farooq, an al Qaeda training camp in the mountains outside Kandahar, Afghanistan. They agreed to tell anyone who asked that they intended to study in Pakistan with an Islamic evangelical group known as Tablighi Jamaat. The six men had been recruited by Kamal Derwish, who was born in Buffalo but spent much of his youth in Saudi Arabia. Derwish had participated in al Qaeda camps in Afghanistan and had fought in Bosnia. When he returned to the Buffalo-Lackawanna area, Derwish spoke at the local mosque, gave classes on the Koran, and recruited the men.[71]

The days at the Kandahar camp began with prayers at 4:00 A.M., followed by weapons instruction. The men were trained in handguns, M-16 rifles, grenade launchers, plastic explosives, land mines, and TNT. They met Osama bin Laden.

Several of the men did not complete the training and returned early. In spring 2002, a year after the six had traveled to al Farooq, Derwish's associate and Lackawanna recruiter, Jumma al Dosari, was captured fleeing Afghanistan. He was taken to Guantanamo, and there he revealed the recruitment operation in Lackawanna. The FBI suspected that the men were part of a sleeper cell.[72]

The men ranged in age from twenty-three to thirty. Yahya Goba had been born in the Bronx and raised for a time in Yemen. Goba had been Derwish's roommate. After Goba returned from Afghanistan, he stayed in touch with Derwish, who remained in Afghanistan.[73] Yasein Taher had been voted friendliest in his graduating class at Lackawanna High School and was soccer co-captain. He married a former cheerleader and later attended community college. Shafal Mosed was a "sports nut" and a frequent gambler at casinos across the border in Canada. He was married with a two-year-old child. Faysal Galab was a high school soccer star and part owner of a gas station in Lackawanna. He loved watching the local hockey team.

A fifth man, Mukhtar al-Bakri, had also been on the Lackawanna High soccer team. In an e-mail he sent to Goba's brother from the Middle East, where he was to be married, he wrote, "The next meal will be very huge. No one will be able to withstand it except those with faith." The FBI interpreted the message as meaning that he intended to become a suicide bomber and took him into custody on his wedding night. Al-Bakri explained that the e-mail referred to people having visions of an explosion that only those with faith could withstand. Al-Bakri revealed to the FBI the purpose of the trip to Afghanistan and the names of the others.

The sixth man, Sahim Alwan, had a job, three children, and a degree from community college. He had been president of the mosque and worked with the local job corps center. Once at the camp, Alwan panicked. The reality was far more dangerous than he had expected. He faked a leg injury, pleading with Derwish to let him go home. He was permitted to leave but was required to first meet with Osama bin Laden. Bin Laden asked him to carry videotapes of the USS *Cole* bombing to a guesthouse in Pakistan on his way home. Alwin delivered the tapes and returned home. He knew an FBI agent in Lackawanna, but he never revealed to him what he had seen and experienced in Afghanistan, or even that he had been at the camp.

About the time Alwin left the camp, the FBI received an anonymous letter stating, "Two terrorists came to Lackawanna . . . for recruiting the Yemenite youth, naming eight men." The local FBI agent reported it to his superiors, but this was before 9/11 and there was no follow-up by higher officials.

On September 13, 2002, the six were charged in criminal court with providing material support or resources to a terrorist organization or attempting or conspiring to do so.[74] Five of the men were arrested in the United States. Al-Bakri was arrested in Bahrain. All had court-appointed lawyers, except Galab, who engaged private counsel.[75] All six pleaded not guilty.

Although the prosecutors never directly threatened the defendants or their lawyers, they indicated that there were members of the administration who had "espoused the view" that the defendants should be designated as enemy combatants.[76] As Yasein Taher's lawyer explained, an assistant U.S. Attorney in the Buffalo office "described these more zealous individuals as nonlawyers who did not fully understand the law, but wanted us to at least know there were individuals in a position of power in Wash DC who took a very dim view of our clients and wanted to throw the 'book' at them."[77] He continued, "The subject did not come up again in exchanges with the gov't, but I did feel obliged to bring this conversation to the attention of Mr. Taher." Consequently, throughout the negotiations, the prosecutors intimated that they could decide to classify the defendants as enemy combatants if the defendants did not plead guilty.[78] As enemy combatants, the men would have lost their rights to due process and the rule of law, and would have been immediately incarcerated, possibly in the same naval brig in Charleston where Yaser Hamdi and Jose Padilla were held.

Five of the men pleaded guilty to providing material support to a designated foreign terrorist organization.[79] Galab, who had argued that he was innocent of providing material support to terrorists,[80] pleaded guilty to the felony of contributing funds and services to specially designated terrorists.[81] Their sentences ranged from seven to ten years. The plea agreements specified that the government could not pursue enemy combatant status against them subsequent to their pleading guilty.[82] Five of the men are in the same federal prison in the Midwest as John Lindh. The sixth, Yahya Goba, had his sentence reduced from 120 months to 108 months because he cooperated with the federal government.[83] His attorney was not able to say where Goba was presently or whether he was still in prison.[84] Faysal Galab, who had received a seven-year sentence, was released to a halfway house in May 2008.

There remain questions as to whether this band of men was, in actuality, "the most dangerous terrorist cell inside the United States."[85] More likely, they were a collection of immature and unreflective men who had no reality-based conception of what they were agreeing to and, when confronted with the harsh reality of the al Qaeda military and jihadist training camp, abandoned their incipient plans and returned home to resume their routine lives as Americans. Had they, like John Lindh, been in the wrong place at the wrong time, or did they pose a serious treat to America? Robert Mueller, FBI director, when asked whether these men were indeed a danger, replied, "Do you and the American people want us to take the chance, if we have information where we believe that a group of individuals is poised to commit a terrorist act in the United States that'll kill Americans, and we just should let it go and wait for the attack, and then after the fact, conduct our investigation? I think not."[86] The local Lackawanna area FBI agent, Ed Needham, added, "I mean, we were looking to prevent something. And we did. Obviously, nothing happened. So we all did our job."[87]

Kamal Dervish was killed on November 3, 2002, when a CIA predator drone fired a Hellfire missile at a vehicle it had been tracking in remote Yemen.[88] The intended target was an al Qaeda member involved in the bombing of the USS *Cole*. Dervish was in the vehicle.

Immediately after 9/11, the administration did the right thing: it brought charges against people the government considered dangerous. But as time progressed, the administration moved away from the rule of law, designating captives as enemy combatants and taking away due process rights that adhere to any defendant. The rule of law worked in these four cases: they were all convicted, and the country remained safe. Jose Padilla was initially in the criminal justice system before he was taken to the brig. Would it really have been worse for our nation if we had continued to prosecute him in the civil system rather than locking him up for nearly four years, much of the time in isolation, incommunicado, deprived of sensory stimulation, with no charges brought against him and no access to a lawyer?

We could have avoided all the horrors of Guantanamo and still kept the detainees incarcerated if we had adhered to the rule of law and followed the Geneva Conventions. Under the conventions, Taliban prisoners, part of the armed forces of the nation-state of Afghanistan, would be recognized as lawful combatants or prisoners of war. Al Qaeda prisoners, who were not part of a nation's armed forces, would be held as unlawful combatants. Unlawful combatants have fewer rights than lawful combatants, but if we had held both groups under the rules specified by the Geneva Conventions and not treated them cruelly, inhumanely, or degradingly—and certainly not tortured them—it would not have caused the outrage heard from the international community since spring 2002.

We moved to the "dark side," as Vice President Dick Cheney put it, when he and the rest of the administration disdained the rule of law. Yet the rule of law worked and would have continued to work had the administration trusted our magnificent Constitution and the body of law that has been with us for over two hundred years. The administration not only mistrusted the detainees, it mistrusted our nation and our faith in the rule of law. The administration refused to believe in what has made us the great nation we are. The consequences of their cynicism have been disastrous for all of us.

One must question the logic the government used in deciding whether to detain someone and prosecute him through the criminal justice system or to classify him as an enemy combatant and remove his due process protections. The administration's choice to pursue one approach or the other seems arbitrary.[89] The administration believes that it alone should decide which detainees are dangerous enemy combatants who require complete isolation and must be denied access to their families and lawyers, and which detainees are criminal defendants entitled to the protections of the U.S. Constitution.[90] With no rational standards made available to the public, how can Americans respect the government's actions and hold their government accountable?[91] If American citizens like Hamdi and Padilla, and legal residents like al Marri, can be picked up and put in isolation, deprived of sensory stimulation, and held incommunicado for over two years in a naval brig, without charges, what can stop the administration from doing the same to any of its citizens or legal residents? Our rights are only as secure as those of any other American.

Closing

Carlos Castresana, a native of Spain, has earned an unique place in the annals of international human rights law. In March 1996, he was an anticorruption prosecutor in Spain and a leader in the Union of Progressive Prosecutors. A very smart, soft-spoken, and innovative thinker, Carlos conceived the idea of initiating a complaint in Spain to prosecute Argentine generals for genocide, illegal detentions, and disappearances. Under a principle of international law known as "universal jurisdiction," any nation can prosecute perpetrators of human rights violations, genocide, crimes against humanity, and war crimes, no matter where the violation occurred.

The complaint against Argentina motivated Castresana and other progressive Spanish prosecutors to file a similar complaint in July 1996 against Chilean dictator Augusto Pinochet—the first one ever filed against him—for genocide and crimes against humanity during his murderous regime as de facto president of Chile from 1973 to 1990. Two years later, in 1998, when Pinochet traveled to England, Spain presented an extradition request to Britain based on the complaint. The incident received enormous publicity, and it looked for a time like Pinochet would be sent to Spain to stand trial after a British magistrate ruled that the requirements for extradition had been met. However, fortunately for Pinochet, in March 2000 the British home secretary decided that Pinochet was medically unfit to stand trial and rejected the extradition request. Once home, Pinochet was subjected to Chilean prosecution.

Since the incident with Pinochet, former heads of state and officials who have been accused of genocide and war crimes have been cautious in making travel plans to foreign countries, especially to European nations, in fear that they too may be prosecuted, tried, convicted, and sentenced to prison.[1]

Several years later, Castresana found a temporary home on the faculty at the University of San Francisco School of Law. His office was next door to mine, and I could not have wished for a more thoughtful and engaging colleague and neighbor. In the short time I knew him, he became a good friend. Unfortunately for the law school, in June 2006 Castresana left to accept a position with the United Nations in Mexico. He transferred to Guatemala the following year. In spring 2008, he sent me this e-mail from Guatemala.

> Your book is essential. It is a voice amid the general silence, where silence is synonymous with complicity. It is about much more than destruction of some lives. It is about destruction of the pillars of the modern state, of democracy and rule of law as it has been built since 1776. And it is not a problem of the U.S. It is our common heritage of civilization, of which Americans are not owners but just keepers, and we non-Americans are defenseless and impotent before that destruction. This is the reason your voice is so important. Everyone expected changes after the Democrats took control in January 2007, but nothing happened, Guantanamo and the Military Commissions Act are still there. Someone must record and explain it. Similar to Coetzee's statement, the former President of Spain's Constitutional Court, Francisco Tomas y Valiente (later murdered by the ETA), said: "Silence is accomplice, before and after the death of the last murdered man."[2]

I am certain that Castresana speaks for many "non-Americans" who once saw us as the nation that promoted civil society. These non-Americans have, like us, watched in horror as the Bush administration manipulated the Constitution, federal statutes, and international human rights law as it methodically dismantled the rule of law. The administration's conduct cannot be justified in a society based on the rule of law. The incalculable loss to due process and human dignity since 9/11 has caused us to lose our claim to the moral high ground in the eyes of the world. The administration's approach to the War on Terror was wholly unnecessary. We could have achieved the same results while observing the rule of law, and maintained our moral authority as well.

Writing about these times while living in the moment necessarily impedes, even denies, certain reflections that can only come with time. If I had waited to write this narrative until some years had passed, this book would be different both in tone and in context. But I could not wait. Living in these times and seeing my country lose its moral standing have done more than merely make me angry. It propelled me to the classroom to teach a course on the War on Terror beginning in January 2002. It pushed me to question the term *enemy combatant* and write a law review article challenging its legitimacy. It drove me to visit Guantanamo and see for myself what that hell looks like. It compelled me to document the administration's human rights abuses in this book. And today it is inspiring me to work on creating a truth commission for Guantanamo.

As the years pass, we will review and reassess. Circumstances that are very important to us now may fade into the background. Other events—events that we may have overlooked or that have been hidden from us—will come to the fore. Certainly, our perspectives will change and evolve. There will be a dialogue between past and present. With the passing of time, we interpret and reinterpret the meaning of events.

Writing in the moment, I do not have the advantage of historical reflection, which allows for time-honed and in-depth analysis. But by telling these stories in the moment, I can hope to reflect the rawness of the times. And in doing so, perhaps I can provide future historians who did not experience these times with a window into what we have lived through these past seven years.

When future writers study the War on Terror, they will view these incidents with less raw emotion. They will be able to draw compelling studies that we, who are caught in the midst, cannot yet accomplish to our satisfaction. However, in painting their versions of the story, future writers will not be able to call upon their own personal narratives of the events. Consequently, we who write of the moment and those who write by looking back at the times create a bond. Together we all attempt to tell the story, a story that is only beginning to emerge. I tried to tell this cautionary narrative. Others will follow with their own perspectives and narratives.

There is light at the end of the tunnel. The Bush administration may have won in the short term, but it did not win in its program to tear down the rule of law. Today, America is seeing the horror that is Guantanamo and rejecting its premises. Judges are taking stronger roles in guaranteeing that the people we have abused receive due process protections. We are beginning to acknowledge that we, as a nation, adopted a national policy of torture, a policy we are now moving to reject.

We are moving forward alongside those courageous lawyers who first stood up to challenge the administration in the days following 9/11. We are insisting that our government uphold the rule of law. We are returning to civil society.

I wrote this book for those who come after us and who must learn from us. Our children and our grandchildren will inherit our world. Perhaps the stories in this book will shed light on the dark times that we have been through. Jorge Luis Borges said it better: "Writings of light assault the darkness."

November 4, 2008
Election Day

Please see www.cubaniguana.net for updates to this book.

Addendum: Visiting Guantanamo Bay

In May 2007, I visited Guantanamo Bay as a member of the media. I was given a tour along with two other members of the media. The application process, as much a surreal experience as the visit itself, and the three-day tour are described below.

A BUMPY APPLICATION PROCESS

A fellow law professor, Mark Denbeaux, advised me when I told him I was applying to visit Guantanamo: "After they strap you in, they announce that the next bathroom stop is at Guantanamo. There are no bathrooms on the ten-seater propeller aircraft. And the bumpy flight is over three hours." The flight from Fort Lauderdale, Florida, to Guantanamo Naval Base is indeed over three hours. The island of Cuba is long and narrow, and Guantanamo is at the southern tip. Since Cuba does not permit American aircraft to fly in Cuban airspace, the plane must take a circuitous route around the island.

But applying to visit Guantanamo was even more bumpy and circuitous than the flight. The government allows two classes of people to visit Guantanamo Naval Base: members of the media and habeas lawyers. Habeas lawyers—the term is often used disparagingly by the administration—represent the detainees. Although I am an attorney, I have never been a lawyer for the detainees. Consequently, I applied to visit Guantanamo as an author representing my publisher, the University of California Press.

I asked my research assistant and law student, Jody Taliaferro, to find out how I would go about applying to visit Guantanamo. At first, she had difficulty navigating the Department of Defense maze to find the proper contact person. But finally she reached a Pentagon spokesperson who took her call. She e-mailed me that it was "a pretty intimidating path!" She added, "When I explained who I was and what I was doing on your behalf, he asked for your information (full name, university), which I could hear him typing in. He then wanted to know if you had already written anything on Guantanamo and, if so, what it was. I simply said that you had written an article that was in the publication process but I did not currently have a copy. He asked me to obtain a copy and mail it to him."

Since my article takes a stance unpopular with the administration, I was not eager to send it to a Pentagon official without going through channels. The article argued that *enemy combatant* was an illegitimate term adopted by the administration after 9/11 to circumvent the Geneva Conventions and the U.S. Constitution, thereby giving itself license to mistreat and torture detainees. My friends and colleagues were convinced that if someone at the Pentagon read the piece, they would never grant me permission to visit Guantanamo.

Jody called the spokesperson back and again asked him to outline the Pentagon's policies and procedures for allowing journalists to travel to Guantanamo. Jody suspected that either they did not have a general policy in place or they made their decisions on a case-by-case basis. She recounted, "He said that he would have to find out what your 'history, sympathies and interest were in Guantanamo.'" When she inquired as to how that was relevant, he replied, "You know exactly what I mean."

A few days later, the Pentagon spokesperson admitted to Jody that he had no official policy in place and no established procedures, but said that he would "figure something out." Apparently, he did. The next morning, another officer sent Jody an e-mail with the subject line "Greetings from Guantanamo Bay, Cuba." The e-mail read, "I can help you with your interest in visiting our operation." Three steps were required to obtain permission for visiting Guantanamo: I would review the ground rules for the visit, submit "vital information" so that the military could run a background check, and select dates of travel. The officer added that it was his "pleasure" to assist me in obtaining access and that he wanted to "change the image" of Guantanamo.

The following day, another officer at Guantanamo sent an e-mail requesting personal information, including my Social Security and passport numbers, date and place of birth, eye and hair color, height and weight, and my three most recent writings, including my article on enemy combatants. Seemingly out of the blue, this e-mail closed with two quotes from the New Testament: "No eye has seen, no ear has heard, no mind has conceived what God has prepared for those who love Him" (1 Cor. 2:9), and "Do not be deceived: God cannot be mocked. A man reaps what he sows" (Gal. 6:7). Somehow the quaint notion of separation of church and state had not filtered down to the base at Guantanamo.

Presumably to assist in filling out the form, the officer had attached a "Vital Template Table." When I opened it, I was shocked to find someone's personal information, including his Social Security and passport numbers and his date and place of birth. Jody phoned the number in the template to see whether he was a real person. The person whose name was on the template answered the phone. "How did you get my number?" he asked. Jody told him. He was a photographer who had applied to visit the base.

Although he was annoyed to have his personal data divulged, he was gracious, helpful, and quite a character. He explained that he had recently applied to visit as a photographer but that he was finding it difficult to book his flight now that he had gotten permission. He advised Jody to tell me that I should book my ticket immediately after the military granted my authorization. The seats go fast, he noted. As they were ending their conversation, he graciously offered Jody his e-mail address so that she could contact him in the future. "I already have it!" Jody replied.

The next day, a different officer at Guantanamo sent the same request for information, without the religious quotes or the attachment. This new person was very helpful in moving the process along. However, as I filled out the application form, I could not help but be concerned that someone might forward my personal information to future applicants.

A week later, we received the news: "The professor's visit to Guantanamo Bay has been approved." With trepidation, I made my final plans to take the no-bathroom-break, bumpy, and circuitous ride to that surreal place they call Guantanamo.

INSIDE GUANTANAMO

While I waited for the flight, a girl, perhaps nineteen, started chatting me up. She began by telling me that the plane was late because it was waiting for her friend to arrive. She pulled out her camera and showed me digital photos of the island, its restaurants and bars, her with her friends, and several close-ups of a friendly Cuban iguana that resides at a rocky outcropping on a particular beach. The iguana's name is Roxanne, she said. There was also a photo of her posing with Rear Admiral Harry Harris, the commander of the Joint Task Force.

"If you like to party, this place is fun," she buzzed. "But if you are not social, you feel locked in. Every Thursday is Jamaican 'barbeque all you can eat and drink' night," intimating that the liquor flows freely.

Fortunately she was a party girl, she confided. She worked as a contractor "behind the wire," meaning that she worked in the detention camps. She would have continued talking, seemingly endlessly, had the woman sitting next to me not mentioned that she was a lawyer. When the girl heard that, the conversation was over. The lawyer turned out to be Candace Gorman, who was representing Abdul Hamid Salam Al-Ghizzawi.

When it was time to board the Air Sunshine plane to Guantanamo, we passed a Gulfstream jet of the type used to transport "ghost detainees" in the CIA's extraordinary rendition program, parked fifty yards from our plane. I wondered what this particular Gulfstream jet was used for. I was thinking of photographing it but decided not to—I was not sure whether it was a good idea to have a photo of it on my camera.

When we landed on the leeward side of the island, we were met by military security. They searched our bags but not our persons; their main interest was in our electronic equipment. They checked my laptop, digital camera, digital tape recorder, and iPod. After we passed through security, the habeas lawyers went directly to their housing on the leeward side. The administrative personnel in Guantanamo have no interest in interacting with the lawyers and would prefer not to have them visit the base at all.

Karin Henriksson, a reporter for *Svenska Dagbladet,* a major daily newspaper in Sweden, her photographer Chris Malvszynski, and I were greeted and escorted to a nondescript white van. Three soldiers introduced themselves as our escorts for our three-day trip. Our guides drove us to the utility boat that was to take us to the windward side. Jamaican and Filipino contractors joined us on the boat. The workers who build the detention centers and manage most of the menial chores are all Jamaican or Filipino. They have access to areas that lawyers with security clearances cannot visit.

As we boarded the boat, one of our military escorts sang the praises of working on the base. This is like a "paid vacation," he mused. "And the fishing is great." To maintain normalcy for the soldiers who work behind the wire, the base includes an outdoor movie theater with free first-run hits, tennis courts, golf course, boats, gym, bowling alley, go carts, batting cages, Tiki Bar, McDonald's drive-thru, Subway, KFC, A&W, and a café that sells Starbucks coffee and Breyers ice cream. A Taco Bell was on the way. These were all part of the military's "MWR," or Morale, Welfare and Recreation program. There were several Naval

Exchange shops that provided the same items as any supermarket. One was entirely devoted to t-shirts, hats, and souvenirs to take back home.

"This is the Gitmo experience," cheered the escort, who preferred to be called MC2 (for mass communications, second class). "They [the military] do their best to keep us entertained," he assured us. MC2 was a naval man, a petty officer, second class. His friends called him "MC squared." MC2 was living in Hawaii when the planes attacked on 9/11. That event motivated him to join the military, though he was too old to move up the ranks. He left a wife and teenage daughter at home. MC2 hoped to be shipped to Iraq and Afghanistan to experience those outposts as well.

The soldiers on the island are called "troopers." Men outnumber women eighteen to one. The navy is in charge of the island, while the marines provide security for the base. The Joint Task Force (JTF), consisting of members of all four armed services plus the coast guard, is responsible for the security of Camp Delta, where the detention centers are located. The JTF is essentially a "tenant organization" on the island.

After stopping at the Jerk House—we were informed that it had the best food on the island—for Jamaican barbeque dinners, we checked into our townhouses. Lodging cost $15 per night for a shared double or $30 per night for a single. Our guides told us to remain within the confines of our condos at night. MC2 was housed in a condo next door.

Although secure and efficient communication is essential to the military, the Internet in our rooms did not work. We were provided dial-up as a backup. Photographers cannot e-mail photographs with dial-up. Security was tight regarding photographs. Visitors representing the media were required to use digital equipment. At the end of each day, an operations security (OP-SEC) contractor reviewed our photos, searching for what were described as security lapses. Faces of the detainees or the guards, guards' name tags, water towers, more than one guard tower in a frame, certain antennae, and pictures of the coastline were deleted. We were informed that such information could be used by al Qaeda and other terrorists in planning an offshore attack. In addition, the government wanted to protect the "privacy" of the detainees, so pictures of them were also out of bounds. Whenever an image of a secure item appeared, even in the distant background, the photo was deleted. Visiting photographers have taken as many as two thousand photos during their stay. I cannot imagine how the OP-SEC contractor reviewed these thousands of photos and maintained consistency in his decision-making. In addition, I wondered whether any photographers ever downloaded their photos into separate files on their laptops before the OP-SEC session. The entire process seemed somewhat arbitrary.

The word *arbitrary* came to mind several times on our visit, including the day we visited with the island's naval commander. While he was describing the border between Cuba and the United States, I asked him whether he would mind showing us, on the map on his wall, where the border ran in the bay. As he stood up to identify the waterline, his media assistant interrupted, "You can find the borderline and other locations in Guantanamo Bay as well as those along the coastline on Google Earth."

On Tuesday, we rose early for our first fully scripted day. It was hot and humid. MC2, our driver, stacked the van with ice-cold liters of Crystal Geyser. We were on our way to breakfast. A sign read, "You can eat as much as you want, but you cannot take any food with you." While we were eating, one of our guides commented, "This should put to rest any thoughts about the food in the military." I wondered whether he could tell that I was a food snob. Later that day, another staff person who had taken military combat photos in Iraq and Afghanistan commented that the food is even better in the war zones. "After a tough day in the field, what could be better at night than a slice of homemade cherry pie?" he said.

As we walked out of the galley, I heard "The Star Spangled Banner." An escort announced that it was reveille. "Seems pretty late for reveille," I observed. An army escort quipped, "This is a naval base."

Our next stop was a PowerPoint briefing. Our guide said that since January 2002, nearly eight hundred detainees had gone through Guantanamo. He informed us that the Taliban and al Qaeda were not "High Contracting Parties." This information was designed to explain why the detainees were not prisoners of war and accordingly not provided rights and protections under the Geneva Conventions. That night I discussed with Chris and Karin why the PowerPoint presentation was incorrect, pointing out that former secretary of state Colin Powell and international law experts had argued that the Taliban, who were the armed forces of the State of Afghanistan, were entitled to POW status. Could the military have been listening in on our nightly conversations? That thought fleetingly crossed my mind that first evening, but I immediately dismissed it as paranoia. But after being informed the next day by a high-ranking officer at Guantanamo that my visit should not have

Camp Delta. Photograph by the author.

been approved, I wondered whether the military had indeed listened in on our conversations.

The PowerPoint program included a photo of an interrogator and a detainee playing chess. "This is one way that the interrogators interview the detainees for information," the military escort explained. America does not "do detention as punishment" according to the presentation. The purpose of detaining the captives is twofold: to obtain intelligence and to prevent them from returning to the battlefield. The presenter, reading from the slide, continued that "it is unusual in modern warfare and during an on-going conflict, that we outright release enemy combatants to their home countries." "We're making history," he added, indicating that no previous nation has ever released detainees captured in a war prior to the end of the conflict.

After the briefing session, we drove to Camp Delta, the site of the detention centers. Military and media personnel entering the detention facilities must remove their badges so that detainees cannot identify us and reveal our identities to al Qaeda operatives on the outside. No one mentioned the fact that when a guard does not wear a name tag, he or she cannot be held accountable for any inappropriate behavior.

We were informed that there were six centers, numbered in the order

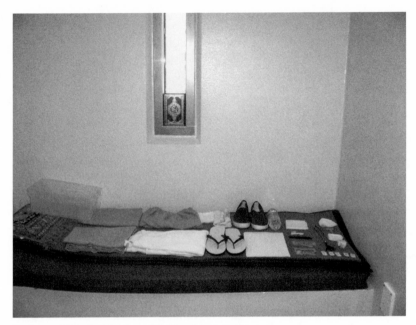

For the most compliant detainees. Photograph by the author.

For the least compliant detainees. Photograph by the author.

they were constructed. Camps 5 and 6 were the most secure facilities. However, in fall 2007, the administration revealed that there is a secret Camp 7, which houses high-value detainees. As of fall 2008, no reporter has been permitted to observe the camp or even been told its precise location. In addition to the seven numbered camps, there is Camp Echo, which is now used for meetings between habeas lawyers and their clients. Although the name likely refers to the military's phonetic alphabet, habeas lawyers are struck by the irony of the name for a place where they believe their conversations with clients are regularly monitored by the military.[1]

We began our tour with Camp 4, the home for the most "compliant" detainees. When I was there, there were forty men in the camp. The same Operations Security contractor who reviewed our photos monitored our movements through the facility. He was also involved in training the guards. We passed a wooden guard tower, a metal gate, and a ten-foot chain-link fence topped with coiled barbed wire. The cells we visited were not being used. Previous visitors had warned me to regard these empty cells as "model" prisons, rather than as genuine examples of the kind of where the detainees are housed. Each cell was eight by ten feet, and had slots in the door at the waist and ankle levels. A metal shelf bed was attached to the wall, and a squat toilet was on the floor. A black arrow pointing to Mecca is painted on the floor or beneath the bed of each cell. Traffic cones stenciled with the letter *P* are placed in front of cells during prayer.

Compliant detainees wear white uniforms and receive the most privileges. They are permitted to play soccer and can gather in common recreation areas. In addition to the sandals, toothbrush, toothpaste, and Koran that everyone receives, compliant detainees are provided a prayer rug, thermal underwear to protect them from the ice-cold air conditioning, a roll of toilet paper, tennis shoes, a plastic water bottle, and a plastic box in which to keep letters. They may also use the prison library. Those detainees who are less compliant wear tan. They have limited privileges and receive fewer extras: no soccer play or plastic box for them. The least compliant wear orange and receive only a Koran, a toothbrush, toothpaste, and sandals. They must ask for a sheet of toilet paper when needed. Toilet paper is restricted because detainees write notes on it and try to pass the notes to others. We were shown the thick green rubber blankets distributed to men suspected of being suicidal. These blankets cannot be torn into strips, thus thwarting the construction of nooses.

For suicide-prone detainees. Photograph by the author.

The recreation yards resemble chain-link dog runs. Alongside each recreation area are bulletin boards with copies of the detention rules, vetted articles from Arabic newspapers, and an Islamic calendar. In addition, copies of Common Article Three (CA3) of the Geneva Conventions are posted in all languages spoken by the detainees.

We were shown a room with eight bunk beds covered in blue plastic that once held eight compliant detainees. In May 2006, a group of detainees who lived in this room covered the window with a sheet and slicked the floor with feces, urine, and vomit. Then they started yelling. When the guards ran in to see what the problem was, they fell in a heap. The detainees then attacked them with pieces of the observation camera, lights, and the fan. It made the national news.

Many of the guards and military officers we met during camp tours described their work using the mantra "I just do my job." In addition, several military personnel told me, "I do not think about my job." No one, not even the top brass on the base, ever said anything other than that they follow orders set by their superiors. Policy was directed from Washington. I was reminded of the Nuremberg tribunals that followed World War II, where the Nazi war criminals argued that they were just following orders. I was soon overwhelmed by the outward normalcy of the base. You could describe the experience as Kafkaesque, but words do not work as descriptors here. One would have to read Hannah Arendt's *Eichman in Jerusalem: A Report on the Banality of Evil* for a comparable example of how a normal routine run by unthinking bureaucrats facilitates evil.

I assume that many of the soldiers living on the base kept themselves busy running, exercising, and drinking to block out troublesome or disagreeable thoughts. Doing whatever it takes to stay numb was the safest route to surviving each day. Not everyone had "the Gitmo experience." MC2, however, told us that "if I had to be a detainee, I would want to be a detainee here." We three visitors looked at him incredulously. MC2 continued, "Another journalist asked me whether he could quote me on this. I thought about it for a moment, and said, 'Sure, why not.'" Much has been written about the mistreatment of the detainees. Yet MC2 was not the only person who assured us of America's benevolent treatment of the detainees. Many of the bureaucrats we met, especially those at the highest level, emphasized that the detention camps were designed for "safe and humane treatment" of the detainees.

On our way to the prison library, we spotted a middle-aged detainee in white. He was bearded and his head slumped over his chest. Two guards on either side firmly escorted him to wherever they were headed, gripping him by the elbows. They waited until we entered the module that holds the library before approaching.

The library "is available to all compliant detainees," the deputy commander explained. "It provides intellectual stimulation." Those detainees who are not interested in intellectual stimulation work in the garden or play soccer, he added. Two librarians with advanced degrees supervise the library. There are some five thousand items, including magazines and picture books in nineteen languages. I spotted a handful of DVDs and videos. According to the librarian who gave us the tour, the stories of the prophets are the most popular among the detainees, followed by stories about animals. The librarians and guards inspect all books and magazines when they are returned, because the detainees, we were told, sometimes deface pictures of women. The detainees also try to communicate with each other by writing notes in the margins or by underlining words.

The military has set up a classroom in the complex to teach beginning and intermediate Arabic and Pashtu. They informed us that they were still looking for someone to teach English, which seemed odd. But there is another story here. When habeas lawyers sent English language books to their clients to help them learn English, the military explained that the detainees were not permitted to learn English. In 2007, Commander Harris considered reversing the five-year-old policy that identified English lessons as an "operational security hazard."

As we left the detention centers, we saw a Cuban iguana relaxing on a rock, warming itself in the sun. As Chris took a close-up of this prehistoric creature, the iguana proudly posed, reminding us of Tom Wilner's compelling argument in his petition to the U.S. Supreme Court in fall 2003. Chris graciously offered me the photo of the iguana.

Our guide for Camp 5 was Charlie V. Since no one wears a real name tag in the detention centers, the directors of each camp adopt nicknames. The previous director was also Charlie V. The current Charlie V predicts that that the next director will also be Charlie V. The director of Camp 6 wore a name tag reading "OIC" for officer in charge.

Camp 5 was built by KBR, formerly Kellogg Brown and Root (a subsidiary of Halliburton, where Dick Cheney was CEO before he became vice president). Cameras monitor each cell twenty-four hours a day. We were informed that Camp 5 housed the detainees considered to have the most intelligence value and to be the most dangerous. I asked the deputy commander whether Khalid Shaikh Mohammed, the alleged mastermind of 9/11, was housed in Camp 5. He answered that he did not know and did not want to know. He just did his job. We now know that Mohammed and the other high-value detainees were held at Camp 7.

We were escorted to an interrogation room. During interrogations, the detainee sits in a blue-cushioned "lazy boy." He is held to the floor with leg restraints. A table separates the interrogator from the detainee. Interrogations are conducted at night as well as during the day. An emergency call button is within reach of the interrogator. Someone asked why a monitor was in the room. "So that the detainee can watch movies," the deputy commander replied. Detainees who reveal significant intelligence matters are rewarded by being allowed to watch Arabic television shows or films.

The next day, MC2 complimented us on how easy we were as media personnel. MC2 described us as "compliant reporters." He explained that some "noncompliant reporters" would ask the same question four times in the hope that a guide would answer it differently. That was unlikely, since all escorts carry a "Smart Book" that has answers to most questions. If an answer is not in the Smart Book, the guide goes up the chain of command for the answer.

Detainee exercising (in top left corner). Photograph by the author.

We watched as a detainee dressed in white exercised in his cage by walking back and forth from one end to the other. It reminded me of the times my family and I had observed a tiger pacing his fifty-foot cage at the Oakland Zoo. I took a photo of the detainee when his back was turned. Detainees in Camps 5 and 6 exercise two hours a day. Candace Gorman told me that her client receives his two hours in the middle of the night.

Camp 6 was also built by KBR. The prefab building was brought on a barge to Guantanamo. The second tier had rails "to avoid someone falling off," the guide explained. The hallways were very dark, and as far as I could see, there was no natural light in the prison. We could hear detainees calling and even shouting to each other through the holes in the doors and floors of their cells.

Our escorts took us to the detainee hospital. There were over twelve thousand monthly interactions with the detainees, the director informed us. The medical staff supervised sick calls, routine clinic appointments, physical therapy, and a pharmacy that filled prescriptions totaling four hundred meds a day. If a detainee was seriously ill, he was seen at the base naval hospital. When I reported this statement to Candace Gorman, she commented that her client had both hepatitis

B and tuberculosis but had not been treated for either. The clinic director informed us, however, that there was no serious illness among the
detainees. He noted that the average age of the detainees is thirty-two
and that men of that age are likely to be healthy. He then stated that the
health of the detainee population mirrors that of the general population. However, the morning's PowerPoint session had indicated that 15
to 18 percent of the detainees arrived with mental illnesses.

The director showed us the tubes that were used to force-feed hunger
strikers. As many as forty-six detainees were on hunger strike when
we were there, according to habeas lawyers. The director claimed the
number was much lower, closer to a dozen.

Our escorts then drove us to interview two young prison guards. A
guard assigned to Camp 6 had been in the military for eighteen months
and was in his midtwenties. The other, formerly an aviation machinist, had been in the military for a dozen years and worked in Camp 1.
Neither guard had prior experience in prison work. The machinist said
that one day his supervisor ordered him to take a class. After a week
in the class, he realized he was being trained to become a guard. The
training lasts for one month, during which time they "are put through
everything." The guards admitted that they were nervous in their work
but tried not to show it.

Although they did not specifically mention it, their training sessions
likely exposed them to thrown feces and vomit, known as "cocktails,"
which might occur in the detention centers. The deputy commander
revealed that guards wear face masks and eye protection. "Detainees
do things to get a rise out of you," one guard explained. "They try to
get into your head," added the other.

The military rotates the guards among the detention centers. They
are not given any information about their charges except their country—
not even the detainees' names. They address detainees by numbers. The
guards are not informed of the length of their assignments; they are
only told when their tour of duty is over. The military instructs the
guards to be "fair, firm, and impartial." Picking favorites could cause
problems, they are told.

Our next stop was the food preparation facility. As I stepped from
the van to go into the building, I was approached by an escort holding
a cell phone. "Mr. Peter," he said, "have you ever done pro bono work
for the detainees?"

"What?" I responded. "No, I haven't. In fact, I do not practice law
of any kind."

"Okay," he replied, and relayed this fact into the cell phone. He hung up, turned to the three of us, and firmly directed us into the food preparation area. He then hurried off.

On leaving the food facility, I spotted the escort and inquired as to why he had asked me that question. He replied that his supervisor, the deputy of public affairs at Guantanamo, as well as the deputy's superior in Washington, D.C., wanted to know. Why? I repeated. He shook his head. He needed to wait for further instructions from his superiors.

I wondered why my presence had become an issue. When I applied to visit Guantanamo, I revealed my legal background and informed them that I had written a law review article on the illegitimate term *enemy combatant*. Why did the military now question my presence, one day after I had arrived at Guantanamo?

It is difficult to put my unease into words. I did not think that I would be detained, although that thought fleetingly crossed my mind. I had not done anything unlawful; if they had made a mistake in allowing me to visit, it was their problem. I was reminded of my earlier suspicions that conversations in our condo might be bugged or overheard by someone at the base. I phoned my wife that evening and told her about the incident. I told her that if she did not hear from me the following evening, she should contact the Department of Defense and the military officials who had approved my visit. I also asked her to contact a well-connected colleague and friend, Professor Susan Freiwald, who had attended law school with several current high-ranking administration members and had worked with Barack Obama on the *Harvard Law Review*. Perhaps I was overreacting, but in the surreal world of Guantanamo, it was difficult to find firm grounding and to fully trust my instincts. I could not be sure whether I had perceived the situation correctly and whether I was acting sensibly.

I had another fear. Knowing that the military took possession of the lawyers' written notes after they met with their detainee clients and then sent the notes to a secure facility in Washington, D.C., I feared that the authorities might demand that I turn over my notes to the military. Of course, unlike habeas lawyers, I was not privy to any classified information. However, I did not have much faith in asserting my First Amendment rights under the Constitution. Besides, if the habeas lawyers voluntarily surrendered their notes, what was to stop the military from expecting the same "voluntary behavior" from me? I intentionally did not type anything into my computer, considering that my laptop would be the most likely place for them to search. Instead, I wrote notes on little pieces of paper and stuffed the sheets in my pockets. Nothing else occurred until the following afternoon. Fortunately, having two smart and sensitive colleagues in Karin and Chris to validate my perspectives, as well as my unease, was invaluable that evening.

Guantanamo affects people in ways that are not easy to articulate. That evening, I watched Chris stride back and forth around our condo, in no particular direction, his head bent, peering out the window, then looking down again. He shook his head and muttered that this place was very weird. He struck me as acting out what other people who had been to Guantanamo had described: the feeling that we had landed on an alien planet. There may have been a familiar structure and routine in this superficially normal environment, with its McDonald's and such. But words invented on Mother Earth cannot describe this environment. There was no grounding where we stood. Interestingly, Chris echoed the same frustrations when he talked to me about capturing Guantanamo in a photograph. He mentioned that even if he returned to Guantanamo one hundred times, he could never capture its essence.

No matter how many reports on Guantanamo I read, I have yet to see words that express the intangible feelings one experiences there. In the meantime, here are the words of Nobel laureate J. M. Coetzee: "The issue for individual Americans becomes a moral one: how, in the face of this shame to which I am subjected, do I behave? How do I save my honour?"[2]

I slept fitfully that night, alternating between floating wakefulness and feverish dreams. Surprisingly, what caused my sleep disturbance was not the incident but rather an inability to escape from my observations and experiences of seeing the detention camps, the detainees, and the camp personnel "just doing their jobs."

The military may not have planned it this way, but Wednesday served to ease us out of the intensity we had experienced and to prepare us for our return to the continent early Thursday morning. We began with a visit to Camp X-ray. In early 2002, the first group of detainees arrived at Guantanamo in shackles, black-painted goggles, and earmuffs or noise-blocking headphones. Ultimately, three hundred detainees were housed in eight-by-eight outdoor cages with the look of dog kennels. The camp was originally built for Cuban boat people. MC2 read from his Smart Book as he described the camp, constantly advising us to watch out for pieces of barbed wire hidden in the tall grasses that have reasserted their place in the abandoned camp.

We visited one of the five dilapidated wooden huts that were once used for interrogations. MC2 informed us that the detainees were strapped onto stretchers when taken for interrogations, a precaution for their safety and that of the guards. There were no compliant detainees. One of our escorts pointed out what a great movie setting this corner of the island would make. The same escort told me that he had been to Iraq and hoped to return. He had a four-year-old son. "Aren't you worried about your son if you go back to Iraq?" I asked. "I want him to be proud of his father," he replied.

From Camp X-ray we headed to the Northeast Gate, the border with Cuba. A marine guide told us that every few months Cubans seeking asylum try to cross the border, but they are usually repatriated. Asylum seekers who are permitted to live on the base are not permitted to enter the continental United States. The United States had once laid landmines in the area adjoining the crossing, but all but nine mines have since been removed. Cuban landmines exist in larger numbers, and marines sometimes hear a landmine explode when an animal scampers over it.

When the border was closed in 1958, two hundred Cuban day laborers had been crossing to work on the base. At the request of the workers, Castro permitted them to continue crossing, but no new workers were allowed. Fifty years later, three Cuban workers still cross the border each morning and return each evening. They are between seventy-five and eighty-five years old, and their main job is to collect and distribute the pensions of former Cuban workers. MC2 told us that he hopes to be partying in Havana next year, envisioning that Castro will be dead and the country will return to its former festive character.

After lunch, we drove back to Camp Delta to visit the hearing rooms where the Combatant Status Review Tribunals are held to determine whether a detainee is an enemy combatant. The Administrative Review Boards that annually review each detainee's status are also held here. These boards have the authority to recommend that a detainee be released.

It was time for another round of photograph review. As we walked in, we were greeted by the deputy public affairs officer. He set his eyes on me. "You are unusual," he barked, a marked hostility in his voice and a severe gaze in his narrowed eyes. "Someone must have really spoken highly of you." He could not understand how I was approved, he began. He explained that the base needed tougher standards for visitors: "Otherwise, everyone and his mother would be down here saying that they represent media." "You are not typical," he added. He indicated that he and his superior at the Pentagon were wondering how I managed to slip in here. But it was too late. I had been approved by the commander of the base, and the chain of command trumped.

He repeated the question asked the previous day by my military escort: had I ever done "pro bono work for the detainees?" I repeated the same answer: no. I wonder what he would have done if I had represented detainees. He was a bureaucrat with limited power, but small dogs often bark the loudest.

We closed the day by meeting briefly with Brigadier General Cameron Crawford, the deputy commander of the Joint Task Force. Deputy Commander Crawford repeated what we had heard throughout the three days: the base is here for the "safe and humane care and custody of the detainees and visitors."

He then added this fanciful statement: "Soldiers and warriors dream of peace and work themselves out of a job." I wish.

That evening, Karin, Chris, and I again purchased our dinners from the Jerk House. There was something comforting about the routine. We were ready to go home. Early Thursday, when we checked in with the airline, our military escorts' jobs were completed. Two escorts said that they were heading to the beach for the day. I wished them the best. They certainly needed a "Gitmo vacation." How else could they maintain their lives among those powerful spirits lurking over and under the island they call Guantanamo?

Abbreviations

ACLU	American Civil Liberties Union
ARB	Administrative Review Board
AUMF	Authorization for Use of Military Force Joint Resolution
CAT	Convention against Torture and Other Cruel, Inhuman, or Degrading Treatment or Punishment
CA3	Common Article 3 of the Geneva Conventions
CCR	Center for Constitutional Rights
CSRT	Combatant Status Review Tribunal
CTC	Counterterrorist Center
DHS	Department of Homeland Security
DOJ	Department of Justice
DTA	Detainee Treatment Act
ERF	Emergency Response Force
FAA	Federal Administration Aviation
FISA	Foreign Intelligence Surveillance Act
FOIA	Freedom of Information Act
GC	Geneva Conventions
GC3	Third Geneva Convention
HUM	Harakat ul-Mujahideen
ICC	International Criminal Court
ICCPR	International Covenant on Civil and Political Rights
ICRC	International Committee of the Red Cross
IRF	Internal Reaction Force
JTF	Joint Task Force
MCA	Military Commissions Act
MDC	Metropolitan Detention Center
MMC	*Manual for Military Commissions*
NEX	Naval Exchange

OLC	Office of Legal Counsel
OP-SEC	Operations Security
PENTTBOM	Pentagon/Twin Towers Bombings
PTSD	Post-traumatic stress disorder
SAM	Special Administrative Measure
SERE	Survival, Evasion, Resistance and Escape
UCMJ	Uniform Code of Military Justice
UDHR	Universal Declaration of Human Rights

Notes

OPENING

1. The information regarding Padilla's experience in the cell is taken from the Declaration of Andrew G. Patel, *United States v. Padilla*, No. 046-0001(S.D. Fla. Dec. 1, 2006); from Jose Padilla's Motion in Limine to Preclude Admission of Involuntary Statements, no. 046-0001(S.D. Fla. Jan. 8, 2007); and from conversations between Jody Taliaferro, my research assistant, and Mr. Patel, Padilla's attorney, Mar. 1, 2007.

2. Conversation with Andrew Patel, Padilla's attorney, Mar. 1, 2007.

3. The brig's technical director, Sanford E. Seymour, testified at Padilla's competency hearing that a nearby paper mill sometimes caused the stink. Peter Whoriskey, "Padilla Was Deprived, Not Abused, Court Told," *Washington Post*, Feb. 28, 2007, A3.

4. "An Inside Look at How U.S. Interrogators Destroyed the Mind of Jose Padilla, Interview with Dr. Angela Hegarty," *Democracy Now*, Aug. 16, 2007, 6, http://www.democracynow.org/article.pl?sid=07/08/16/1416242# transcript.

5. Declaration of Andrew G. Patel, *United States v. Padilla*, No. 046-0001(S.D. Fla. Dec. 1, 2006), at 5.

6. Deborah Sontag, "Jailers Testify about Padilla's Confinement," *New York Times*, Feb. 28, 2007, A12.

7. Declaration of Stuart Grassian, M.D., in Notice of Intent to Rely on Expert Opinion of Dr. Stuart Grassian in Support of Motion to Dismiss for Outrageous Government Conduct at 11, *United States v. Padilla*, No. 4-60001 (S.D. Fla. Mar. 7, 2007).

8. The circumstances of a victim identifying and sympathizing with his captors has been studied and verified. The psychological condition is identified as the Stockholm syndrome. A well-known example is that of kidnapping victim Patti Hearst, who, in 1974, participated in her captors' scheme of robbing a bank and became lovers with one of the kidnappers. Erik Eckholm, "Out of Captivity; Hostage Bond to Captors Is Common," *New York Times*, July 1, 1985, A11.

9. *Korematsu v. United States*, 323 U.S. 214 (1944). In 1988, our country formally apologized to the Japanese American community and to all the Japanese American citizens and residents interned. Congress paid each person who was relocated $20,000.

10. Lindh was inhumanely treated, even tortured, for nearly two months before he was permitted to see his lawyer. See part 5.

11. "We also have to work, though, sort of the dark side, if you will. We've

got to spend time in the shadows in the intelligence world. A lot of what needs to be done here will have to be done quietly, without any discussion, using sources and methods that are available to our intelligence agencies, if we're going to be successful. That's the world these folks operate in, and so it's going to be vital for us to use any means at our disposal, basically, to achieve our objective." "The Vice President Appears on *Meet the Press with Tim Russert*," Sept. 16, 2001, http://www.whitehouse.gov/vicepresident/news-speeches/speeches/vp20010916.html.

12. Memorandum from Alberto Gonzales on the Decision Re Application of the Geneva Convention on Prisoners of War to the Conflict with Al Qaeda and the Taliban to President George Bush (Jan. 25, 2002), cited in Mark Danner, "Torture and Truth: America, Abu Ghraib, and the War on Terrorism," *New York Review of Books* (2004), 83.

13. Telephone conversation with Donna Newman, May 3, 2007.

14. In addition to mistreating detainees in Guantanamo, our leaders brutalized the detainees held in Iraq. The administration has closed its eyes to the mistreatment of its prisoners, most notably in Abu Ghraib prison. However, this book will focus on our nation's actions regarding alleged Taliban and al Qaeda detainees captured after 9/11. The issues raised by the war in Iraq are enormous but, in significant ways, dissimilar and unrelated. Iraq is best left for another work.

PART ONE

1. The administration has cited a 1942 Nazi saboteur case called *Ex Parte Quirin,* 317 U.S. 1 (1942), to justify its use of the term *enemy combatant.* In that case, the term *enemy combatant* appears only once: "The spy who secretly and without uniform passes the military lines of a belligerent in time of war, seeking to gather military information and communicate it to the enemy, or an enemy combatant who without uniform comes secretly through the lines for the purpose of waging war by destruction of life or property, are familiar examples of belligerents who are generally deemed not to be entitled to the status of prisoners of war, but to be offenders against the law of war subject to trial and punishment by military tribunals" (*Quirin,* 317 U.S. at 31). Depending on how one reads the sentence, the term is either used generically or as a synonym for the legally recognized term *unlawful combatant.* In *Quirin,* the term has no new or otherwise distinctive meaning. It was not used as a term of art.

For a thorough analysis of *enemy combatant* as used in *Quirin,* as well as an analysis of the evolution of the term from the time it was first used by the administration in February 2002, see Peter Jan Honigsberg, "Chasing 'Enemy Combatants,' and Circumventing International Law: A License for Sanctioned Abuse," *UCLA Journal of International Law and Foreign Affairs* 1 (2007), 12.

2. With thanks to my colleague Professor Reza Dibadj, who first directed me to the use of weasel words.

3. A fair trial must be equal to the trial received by a member of the armed forces of the nation holding the POW.

4. Later additions to the GC, known as protocols, have expressed presumptions that include members of some opposition groups as lawful combatants. However, although a large majority of nations have ratified the protocols, the United States is one of a handful of countries that have not adopted them as part of their domestic law.

5. Memorandum from Colin Powell on the Draft Decision Memorandum for President on the Applicability of the Geneva Convention to the Conflict in Afghanistan to Alberto Gonzalez, Jan. 26, 2002.

6. See Memorandum from President Bush on Humane Treatment of al Qaeda and Taliban Detainees (Feb. 7, 2002), available at http://www.human rightsfirst.org/us_law/etn/gonzales/memos_dir/dir_20020207_Bush_Det.pdf (last visited Sept. 17, 2007); and in Mark Danner, "Torture and Truth: America, Abu Ghraib, and the War on Terrorism," *New York Review of Books* (2004), 105–6 (including instance where Bush says that high contracting parties "can only be states").

7. GC3 Art. 4 includes additional paragraphs as to who qualifies as prisoners of war.

8. See Jennifer K. Elsea, Congressional Research Service, *Treatment of "Battlefield Detainees" in the War on Terrorism* (2006), 8–9.

9. There were a few people in the State Department who believed that al Qaeda soldiers should also qualify as lawful combatants, since they fought alongside the Taliban. Memorandum from William H. Taft on Comments on Your Paper on the Geneva Convention to Alberto Gonzales (Feb. 22, 2002), cited in Danner, "Torture and Truth," 94–95, available at www.slate.com/features/whatistorture/pdfs/020202.pdf (last visited Aug. 8, 2006).

10. See Memorandum from President Bush on Humane Treatment of al Qaeda and Taliban Detainees (Feb. 7, 2002), available at http://www.human rightsfirst.org/us_law/etn/gonzales/memos_dir/dir_20020207_Bush_Det.pdf (last visited Sept. 17, 2007).

11. Geneva Convention Relative to the Treatment of Prisoners of War art. 5, Aug. 12, 1949, 6 U.S.T. 3316.

12. There was a time when people thought that enemy combatants had rights equal to unlawful combatants. However, if that were true, there would have been no need to create the new and unauthorized category of enemy combatants. Soon, it became clear that the administration intended to distinguish enemy combatants not only from lawful combatants but also from unlawful combatants.

13. Geneva Convention Relative to the Treatment of Prisoners of War art. 5, Aug. 12, 1949, 6 U.S.T. 3316. However, in fall 2007, a military judge presiding over a military commission hearing agreed to decide whether a detainee was a POW. The judge ruled that he was not. On Reconsideration Ruling on Motion to Dismiss for Lack of Jurisdiction, *U.S. v. Hamdan* (Dec. 19, 2007), available at http:// www.scotusblog.com/wp/uncategorized/military-judge-ham dan-may-be-tried/.

14. Occasionally, commentators will use the terms *protected combatants* and *unprotected combatants* or *privileged combatants* or *unprivileged combatants,* but the most common terminology is *lawful* and *unlawful.* Through-

out this book, I will refer to the combatants as either lawful or unlawful combatants.

15. Int'l Comm. of the Red Cross, "The Relevance of IHL in the Context of Terrorism," available at http://www.icrc.org/Web/Eng/siteengo.nsf/html/terrorism-ihl-210705 (last visited Sept. 17, 2007). Quoting from the document, "[To] the extent that persons designated 'enemy combatants' have been captured in international or non-international armed conflict, the provisions and protections of international humanitarian law remain applicable regardless of how such persons are called."

16. See GC3, art 21, and Fourth Geneva Convention, art. 42. Justice O'Connor noted that there could be problems if the administration maintained that should the War on Terror continue for generations, "Hamdi's detention could last for the rest of his life." However, since active combat operations were ongoing in Afghanistan at the time of the decision, Hamdi could be held for the duration of those hostilities. *Hamdi v. Rumsfeld,* 542 U.S. 507, 520 (2004).

17. *Hamdan v. Rumsfeld,* 126 S. Ct. 2749 (2006).

18. Letter from John Ashcroft to President George Bush (Feb. 1, 2002), cited in Danner, "Torture and Truth," 92.

19. Memorandum from Alberto Gonzales on the Decision Re Application of the Geneva Convention on Prisoners of War to the Conflict with Al Qaeda and the Taliban to President George Bush (Jan. 25, 2002), cited in Danner, "Torture and Truth," 83; see also Michael Isikoff, "Memos Reveal War Crimes Warnings," *Newsweek Web Exclusives,* May 17, 2004, available at http://msnbc.msn.com/id/4999734 (last visited Aug. 8, 2006); R. Jeffrey Smith, "Detainee Abuse Charges Feared, Shield Sought from '96 War Crimes Act," *Washington Post,* July 28, 2006, A1.

David Addington and John Yoo were principal architects in drafting this memo and, consequently, in promoting this strategy. Jane Mayer, "The Memo," *New Yorker,* Feb. 27, 2006, 32. See Memorandum from John Yoo, Deputy Assistant Attorney General & Robert Delahunty, Special Counsel, to William J. Haynes II, General Counsel, Department of Defense on the Application of Treaties and Laws to Al Qaeda and Taliban Detainees (Jan. 9, 2002), in Karen J. Greenberg & Joshua L. Dratel, eds., *The Torture Papers: The Road to Abu Ghraib* (Cambridge University Press, 2005), 38–39. In the memo, Yoo and Delahunty described the Taliban government as a "failed state" and "provided arguments to keep U.S. officials from being charged with war crimes for the way prisoners were detained and interrogated." See also Neil A. Lewis, "U.S. Officials Sought Ways to Avoid POW Laws," *International Herald Tribune,* May 22, 2004, 3.

20. Memorandum from Alberto Gonzales on the Decision Re Application of the Geneva Convention on Prisoners of War to the Conflict with Al Qaeda and the Taliban to President George Bush (Jan. 25, 2002), cited in Danner, "Torture and Truth," 83.

21. *Hamdan v. Rumsfeld,* 126 S.Ct. 2749 (2006).

22. R. Jeffrey Smith, "Detainee Abuse Charges Feared, Shield Sought from '96 War Crimes Act," *Washington Post,* July 28, 2006, A1.

23. Military Commissions Act of 2006, Pub. L. No. 109–366, §§ 6(b)(2), 6(c), 120 Stat. 2600 (2006).

24. *Coalition of Clergy v. Bush,* 189 F. Supp.2d 1036 (C.D. Cal. 2002).

25. Ibid., 1048.

26. Using a Nexis search, the first time that the term *enemy combatant* appeared in the press was in the *Chicago Daily Law Bulletin* on September 20, 2001, page 6, in "Rules of Engagement," by Douglass W. Cassel, Jr. Three days later, the *Los Angeles Times* used the term in "Let Military Panels Punish Terrorists," by Neal A. Richardson and Spencer J. Crona, page 7. The first time that the case of *Ex Parte Quirin* was tied with the term in the press was on October 5, 2001, in Philip Allen Lacovara, "Criminal or Military Justice for Captured Terrorists?" *Legal Backgrounder* 16, no.43. On November 23, 2001, the *San Diego Union-Tribune* published "Terrorists Should Face Military Justice," by Joseph Perkins, page B7, which also discussed *Ex Parte Quirin* and enemy combatants. It is certainly likely that Judge Matz or his clerks could have found these and similar articles.

27. For a thorough analysis of the term *enemy combatant* and the evolution of the term beginning with its first use in February 2002, see Peter Jan Honigsberg, "Chasing 'Enemy Combatants,' and Circumventing International Law: A License for Sanctioned Abuse," *UCLA Journal of International Law and Foreign Affairs* 1 (2007), 12.

28. Military Commissions Act of 2006, Pub. L. No. 109–366, 120 Stat. 2600 (2006).

29. *Rochin v. California,* 342 U.S. 165 (1952).

30. Convention against Torture and Other Cruel, Inhuman or Degrading Treatment or Punishment, December 10, 1984, Official Records of the General Assembly of the United Nations, Thirty-Ninth Session, Supplement No. 51 (A/39/51), p. 197. See part 4 for a fuller discussion of this treaty and the related federal statutes that forbid torture.

31. Sen. Exec. Rpt. 101–30, Resolution of Advice and Consent to Ratification (1990) at I (1); Reservations of the United States of America at I (1), http://www.unhchr.ch/html/menu2/6/cat/treaties/convention-reserv.htm.

One of the purposes of this reservation was to guarantee that the United States could continue to implement the death penalty and that it would not be considered cruel, inhumane, or degrading treatment.

32. See the ICCPR, Art 7, discussed in part 4.

33. 18 U.S.C. Section 2340A (2000), which prohibits torture outside the United States. This legislation was drafted to implement the Convention against Torture. The torture of someone inside the United States had previously been outlawed by existing federal laws that prohibited brutal conduct.

34. Jane Mayer, "The Experiment," *New Yorker,* July 11, 2005.

35. Ibid.

36. Ibid. Major General Geoffrey Miller, who commanded Guantanamo from November 2002 to March 2004, apparently took many of these methods with him when he took charge of Abu Ghraib prison in Iraq. He believed in the use of behavioral psychologists and psychiatrists in "developing integrated interrogation strategies."

37. Amended Petition for Relief under the Detainee Treatment Act of 2005, and, in the Alternative, for Writ of Habeas Corpus at 9, *Zayn Al Abidin Muhammad Husayn v. Gates,* No. 07–1520 (D.C. Cir. Feb. 21, 2008).

38. David Johnston, Neil A. Lewis, and Douglas Jehl, "Nominee Gave Advice to C.I.A. on Torture Law," *New York Times,* January 29, 2005, A1. See also Dana Priest, "CIA Puts Harsh Tactics on Hold," *Washington Post,* June 27, 2004, A01.

39. *Working Group Report on Detainee Interrogations in the Global War on Terrorism,* Apr. 4, 2003, cited in Danner, "Torture and Truth," 191–92. Memorandum for Donald Rumsfeld, Secretary of Defense, from William J. Haynes II, General Counsel of the Department of Defense, Re. Counter-Resistance Techniques (Nov. 27, 2002).

40. Diane E. Beaver, LTC, Department of Defense, *Joint Task Force 170: Legal Brief on Proposed Counter-Resistance Strategies,* Oct. 11, 2002; cited in Danner, "Torture and Truth," 176.

41. 18 U.S.C. Section 2340A (2000).

42. Memorandum for William J. Haynes II, General Counsel of the Department of Defense, from John Yoo, Deputy Assistant Attorney General, Department of Justice, Office of Legal Counsel, Re: Military Interrogation of Alien Unlawful Combatants Held Outside the United States (Mar. 14, 2003).

43. Memorandum for Alberto R. Gonzales, "Re: Standards of Conduct for Interrogation under 18 U.S.C. §§ 2340–2340A," from Jay S. Bybee, Aug. 1, 2002, cited in Danner, "Torture and Truth," 120.

44. Ibid., 118.

45. Memorandum for William J. Haynes II, General Counsel of the Department of Defense, from John Yoo, Deputy Assistant Attorney General, Department of Justice, Office of Legal Counsel, "Re: Military Interrogation of Alien Unlawful Combatants Held outside the United States" (Mar. 14, 2003), 37.

46. Memorandum for William J. Haynes II, General Counsel of the Department of Defense, from John Yoo, Deputy Assistant Attorney General, Department of Justice, Office of Legal Counsel, "Re: Military Interrogation of Alien Unlawful Combatants Held outside the United States" (Mar. 14, 2003), 42.

47. Joby Warrick, "Detainees Allege Being Drugged, Questioned; U.S. Denies Using Injections for Coercion," *Washington Post,* Apr. 22, 2008, A01.

48. Dana Priest, "CIA Puts Harsh Tactics on Hold," *Washington Post,* June 27, 2004, A01.

49. Memorandum from Daniel Levin, Acting Assistant Attorney General, to James B. Comey, Deputy Attorney, "Re: Legal Standards Applicable under 18 U.S.C. §§ 2340–2340A" (Dec. 30, 2004), available at http://www.human rightsfirst.org/us_law/etn/gonzales/memos_dir/levin-memo-123004.pdf.

50. Ibid., n. 8.

51. Scott Shane, David Johnston, and James Risen, "Secret U.S. Endorsement of Severe Interrogations," *New York Times,* Oct. 4, 2007, A1.

52. Ibid.

53. Ibid.

54. Ibid.

55. Dan Eggen, "Justice Official Defends Rough CIA Interrogations," *Washington Post,* Feb. 17, 2008, A03.

56. Elisabeth Bumiller, David E. Sanger, & Richard W. Stevenson, "Bush Says Iraqis Will Want G.I.'s to Stay to Help," *New York Times,* Jan. 28, 2005; Sheryl Gay Stolberg, "President Moves 14 Held in Secret to Guantanamo," *New York Times,* Sept. 7, 2006, A1.

57. See, e.g., Dana Priest, "CIA Puts Harsh Tactics on Hold," *Washington Post,* June 27, 2004, A01; and White House, Office of the Press Secretary, "President Discusses Creation of Military Commissions to Try Suspected Terrorists," news release, Sept. 6, 2006, http://www.whitehouse.gov/news/releases/2006/09/20060906-3.html.

58. Convention against Torture and Other Cruel, Inhuman or Degrading Treatment or Punishment, December 10, 1984, Official Records of the General Assembly of the United Nations, Thirty-Ninth Session, Supplement No. 51 (A/39/51), 1465 U.N.T.S. 05, art. 2, ¶2.

59. For a very thorough and thoughtful analysis of whether torture works in the ticking bomb scenario, see Kim Lane Scheppele, "Hypothetical Torture in the 'War on Terrorism,'" *Journal of National Security Law and Policy* 285 (2005), 1.

60. Memorandum for Alberto R. Gonzales, "Re: Standards of Conduct for Interrogation under 18 U.S.C. §§ 2340–2340A," from Jay S. Bybee, Aug. 1, 2002 cited in Danner, "Torture and Truth," 142.

61. Ibid., 145–46; memorandum for William J. Haynes II, General Counsel of the Department of Defense, from John Yoo, Deputy Assistant Attorney General, Department of Justice, Office of Legal Counsel, "Re: Military Interrogation of Alien Unlawful Combatants Held outside the United States" (Mar. 14, 2003), 13.

62. Ibid., 18.

63. Jane Mayer, "The Memo," *New Yorker,* Feb. 27, 2006, 32; Dana Milbank, "In Cheney's Shadow, Counsel Pushes the Conservative Cause," *Washington Post,* Oct. 11, 2004, A21.

64. James Risen & Eric Lichtblau, "Bush Lets U.S. Spy on Callers without Courts," *New York Times,* Dec. 16, 2005, A1.

65. *Foreign Intelligence Surveillance Act of 1978 (FISA),* Pub.L. 95–511, Oct. 25, 1978, 92 Stat. 1783 (codified as amended at 50 U.S.C.A. §§ 1801–1862) (West 2003).

66. James Risen & Eric Lichtblau, "Bush Lets U.S. Spy on Callers without Courts," *New York Times,* Dec. 16, 2005, A1.

67. Christopher Lee, "Alito Once Made Case for Presidential Power," *Washington Post,* Jan. 2, 2006, A11.

68. Michael Abramowitz, "Bush's Tactic of Refusing Laws Is Probed," *Washington Post,* July 24, 2006, A05, describing an American Bar Association task force study.

69. Joyce A. Green, "List of All Bush Signing Statements and Corresponding Congressional Enactments, 2001–2008," http://coherentbabble.com/signingstatements/fullist.htm.

70. Memorandum for Heads of all Federal Departments and Agencies, from John Ashcroft, Attorney General, "Re. The Freedom of Information Act" (Oct. 12, 2001), available at http://www.usdoj.gov/oip/foiapost/2001foiapost19 .htm.

71. Memorandum for Heads of Departments and Agencies, from Janet Reno, Attorney General, "Re. The Freedom of Information Act" (Oct. 4, 1993), available at http://www.fas.org/sgp/clinton/reno.html.

72. *Youngstown Sheet & Tube Co. v. Sawyer,* 343 U.S.579 (1952).

73. "'Torture Memo' Author John Yoo Responds to This Week's Revelations," *Esquire,* Apr. 3, 2008, 3, available at http://www.esquire.com/ the-side/qa/john-yoo-responds. Near the beginning of the March 14 memo, Yoo explains the pressing need to prepare a powerful legal foundation for the military in interrogating detainees: "Because of the asymmetric nature of terrorist operations, information is perhaps the most critical weapon for defeating al Qaeda." In the same paragraph, he continues, "Interrogation of captured al Qaeda operatives could provide that information; indeed, in many cases interrogation may be the only method to obtain it." Memorandum for William J. Haynes II, General Counsel of the Department of Defense, from John Yoo, Deputy Assistant Attorney General, Department of Justice, Office of Legal Counsel, "Re: Military Interrogation of Alien Unlawful Combatants Held outside the United States" (Mar. 14, 2003), 4. When the memo was in draft, the administration was in high alert. Not only was the War on Terror prominent in everyone's mind, but the war in Iraq was about to begin. (It began five days later.) John Yoo claims that the memo was only designed for the military mission in Guantanamo, to obtain the intelligence it needed to keep America safe. "'Torture Memo' Author John Yoo Responds to This Week's Revelations," *Esquire,* Apr. 3, 2008, 3, available at http://www .esquire.com/the-side/qa/john-yoo-responds. However, commentators believe that the memo was also used to justify military interrogations in Iraq, necessarily including Abu Ghraib.

74. In February 2008, the Department of Justice Office of Professional Responsibility informed members of Congress that the office was investigating the "circumstances surrounding" the Justice Department's opinions that established the legal basis for the CIA interrogation program, including Yoo and Bybee's memos. The letter said that the office was "examining whether the legal advice contained in those memoranda was consistent with the professional standards that apply to Department of Justice attorneys." Letter from H. Marshall Jarrett, Counsel, Office of Professional Responsibility, DOJ, to Senators Durbin and Whitehouse (Feb. 18, 2008), available at http://balkin .blogspot.com/2008/02/internal-doj-investigation-of-olc.html. For an excellent analysis of the particular ethical duties and rules that Yoo and Bybee may have transgressed, see Kathleen Clark, "Ethical Issues Raised by the OLC Torture Memorandum," *Journal of National Security Law and Policy* 455 (2005), 1.

75. "'Torture Memo' Author John Yoo Responds to This Week's Revelations," *Esquire,* Apr. 3, 2008, 3, available at http://www.esquire.com/the-side/ qa/john-yoo-responds.

76. John Yoo and I debated the term *enemy combatant* before an audience at the University of San Francisco School of Law, Sept. 29, 2005.

77. Mark Benjamin, "Did Chertoff Lie to Congress about Guantanamo?" *Salon.com,* Aug. 28, 2007, available at http://www.salon.com/news/feature/2007/08/28/chertoff/print.html.

78. Jack L. Goldsmith, *The Terror Presidency* (W. W. Norton, 2007), 149.

79. *Padilla v. Yoo,* No. CV08 0035 (N.D. Cal. Jan. 4, 2008). Although individuals may file lawsuits against public officials for wrongdoing, the officials are entitled to what is called qualified immunity. That is, when the official is working in his official capacity, he is protected, unless he knew or should have known, as a reasonable person, that his conduct violated clearly established constitutional or statutory rights. The theory underlying the lawsuit against John Yoo is that a reasonable person would have known that writing the torture memos provided the justifications for violating Padilla's constitutional and statutory rights. See *Mitchell v. Forsyth,* 472 U.S. 511 (1985). Padilla had filed a similar suit nearly a year before against former defense secretary Donald Rumsfeld, former attorney general John Ashcroft, and other administration officials for similar constitutional and statutory violations. *Lebron v. Rumsfeld,* No. 2:2007cv00410 (S.C.D.C. filed Feb. 9, 2007). In addition, Yoo could also argue that national security concerns shield him from liability. See *Wilson v. Libby,* 498 F. Supp. 2d 74 (D.D.C. 2007). This case was appealed to the District of Columbia Circuit and argued in May 2008.

PART TWO

1. Joel Brinkley, "From Afghanistan to Saudi Arabia, via Guantanamo," *New York Times,* Oct. 16, 2004, A4.

2. Joel Brinkley, "A Father Waits as the U.S. and Saudis Discuss His Son's Release," *New York Times,* Oct 10, 2004, 15.

3. According to Special Advisor to the Under Secretary of Defense for Policy, Michael Mobbs. Joint Appendix I at 148, *Hamdi v. Rumsfeld,* 542 U.S. 507 (2004) (No. 03–6696) (Exhibit I—Mobbs' Declaration).

4. Hamdi and Lindh were captured together after an uprising at Qala-i-Janghi, the fortress near Mazar-i-Sharif that was controlled by notorious warlord chief General Rashid Dostum and the Northern Alliance. Tony Bartelme, "Born in Louisiana, Captured in Afghanistan, Jailed in Hanahan, Yaser Hamdi Travels Long, Strange Road," *Post and Courier (Charleston, SC),* Mar. 7, 2004, 1A.

5. Joint Appendix I at 148, *Hamdi v. Rumsfeld,* 542 U.S. 507 (2004) (No. 03–6696) (Exhibit I—Mobbs' Declaration).

6. Katherine Q. Seelye, "Threats and Responses: The Detainee; Court to Hear Arguments in Groundbreaking Case of U.S. Citizen Seized with Taliban," *New York Times,* Oct. 28, 2002, 13, available at LEXIS, News Library, NYT File; interview by Joanna Woolman with Mr. Dunham in Chicago, IL, Oct. 22, 2004 (see Joanna Woolman, "Enemy Combatants: The Legal Origins of the Term 'Enemy Combatant' Do Not Support Its Present Day Use," *J.L. & Soc. Challenges* [2005], 145) .

7. The quotes from MacMahon and the accompanying information regarding Dunham come from Jerry Markon, "Frank W. Dunham Jr.; Defended Terrorism Suspects Rights," *Washington Post,* Nov. 5, 2006, C09.

8. The three men held in the extraordinary rendition program who are most likely to have provided evidence are Khalid Shaikh Muhammad, Abu Zubaydah, and Ramzi bin al Shibh. A description of the extraordinary rendition program and these detainees can be found in Human Rights Watch, "The United States' 'Disappeared': The CIA's Long-Term 'Ghost Detainees'" (Oct. 2004), available at http://www.hrw.org/backgrounder/usa/us1004/ (last visited Aug. 8, 2006).

9. This information is from attorneys who represented defendants after 9/11. During the oral argument in the *Padilla* case, a Supreme Court justice asked the government how the Court can be certain that interrogators are not abusing the detainees. Deputy Solicitor General Paul Clement responded that the Court would have to "trust the executive to make the kind of quintessential military judgments that are involved in things like that." Transcript of Oral Argument at 20, *Rumsfeld v. Padilla,* 542 U.S. 426 (2004) (No. 03–1027).

10. Telephone conversation with Geremy Charles Kamens, Assistant Federal Public Defender for the Eastern District, Virginia, Aug. 17, 2007.

11. Department of Defense e-mail, sent December 13, 2002, Subject: Weekly Update on the Care of Detainee USCIT [blacked out]. E-mails between brig officers and others in the chain of command regarding detention and interrogation of Yaser Hamdi, Jose Padilla, and Ali al Marri at naval brigs in Virginia and South Carolina, described in "New Documents Reveal Unlawful Guantanamo Procedures Were Also Applied on American Soil," Oct. 8, 2008, available at http://www.aclu.org/safefree/detention/37083prs20081008 .html. The documents were obtained under the Freedom of Information Act by the Allard K. Lowenstein International Human Rights Clinic at Yale Law School and the American Civil Liberties Union. The e-mails are available for download at http://www.aclu.org/safefree/detention/37040res20081006.html and are also on file with the author. All grammatical and spelling errors in the e-mails appear in the originals.

12. Department of Defense e-mail, June 3, 2003, Subject: Care of Detainee USCIT [blacked out].

13. Department of Defense e-mail, April 19, 2002, Subject: Re: Care of AMCIT Detainee.

14. *Hamdi v. Rumsfeld,* 542 U.S. at 533 (2004).

15. *Hamdi v. Rumsfeld,* 542 U.S. at 536 (2004). "We have long since made clear that a state of war is not a blank check for the President when it comes to the rights of the Nation's citizens. Whatever power the United States Constitution envisions for the Executive in its exchanges with other nations or with enemy organizations in times of conflict, it most assuredly envisions a role for all three branches when individual liberties are at stake."

16. See *Hamdi v. Rumsfeld,* 542 U.S. 507 (2004).

17. Ibid., 539.

18. Plea Agreement of Yaser Hamdi, *Hamdi v. Rumsfeld,* 542 U.S. 507 (2004) (No. 2:02CV439), available at http://news.findlaw.com/hdocs/docs/

hamdi/91704stlagrmnt.html (last visited Aug. 8, 2006) and http://notable
cases.vaed.uscourts.gov/2:02-cv-00439/DocketSheet.html (last visited Aug. 8,
2006) (exhibit attached to document number 78, filed on Sept. 24, 2004
and described as "Motion by Yaser Esam Hamdi to Stay Proceedings [vwar]
[Entered: 09/27/2004]").

19. Hamdi was interviewed by phone from Saudi Arabia in the spring of
2006 for a story about John Walker Lindh. Tom Junod, "American Taliban,"
Esquire (July 2006), 113, 135.

20. E-mail from Geremy Kamens, Assistant Federal Public Defender in Alexandria, Va., Aug. 31, 2007. Kamens worked on the *Hamdi* case with Frank
Dunham.

21. Ibid.; telephone conversation with Geremy Charles Kamens, Aug. 17,
2007.

22. E-mail from Geremy Kamens, Aug. 31, 2007.

23. Joel Brinkley, "From Afghanistan to Saudi Arabia, via Guantanamo,"
New York Times, Oct. 16, 2004, A4.

24. Olivier Roy, *Globalized Islam* (Columbia University Press, 2004).

25. Much of the description of Padilla's life preceding his arrest at O'Hare
International Airport is taken from Deborah Sontag, "Terror Suspect's Path
from Streets to Brig," *New York Times,* Apr. 25, 2004, 1; and Michael Grun-
wald & Amy Goldstein, "An Unusual Odyssey: U.S.-Born Latino Turns Islamic
Terror Suspect," *Washington Post,* June 11, 2002, A1.

26. Deborah Sontag, "Terror Suspect's Path from Streets to Brig," *New
York Times,* Apr. 25, 2004, 1.

27. Ibid.

28. Letter from Paul Wolfowitz, Deputy Secretary of Defense, to James B.
Comey, Deputy Attorney General (May 28, 2004) (on file with author).

29. Padilla's Motion in Limine Regarding Money Seized from Mr. Padilla
and His Statements Made Relating to the Money at 1, *U.S. v. Padilla,* No. 46–
0001-CR (S.D. Fla. Apr. 3, 2007).

30. Telephone conversation with Donna Newman, Mar. 17, 2005.

31. *Ex Parte Quirin,* 317 U.S. 1 (1942), note 17.

32. Telephone conversation with Donna Newman, May 3, 2007.

33. Telephone conversation between student researcher Jody Taliaferro
and Andrew Patel, Padilla's lawyer, Mar. 29, 2007.

34. Conversation between Jody Taliaferro and Andrew Patel, Mar. 1, 2007.

35. Jose Padilla's Motion in Limine to Preclude Admission to Involuntary
Statements at 6, *United States v. Padilla,* No. 04–60001 (S.D. Fla. Jan. 8,
2007).

36. Deborah Sontag, "Jailers Testify about Padilla's Confinement," *New
York Times,* Feb. 28, 2007, A12.

37. Declaration of Vice Admiral Lowell E. Jacoby (USN), executed on
Jan. 9, 2003, available at http://www.pegc.us/archive/Padilla_vs_Rumsfeld/
Jacoby_declaration_20030109.pdf.

38. Ibid., 5.

39. Ibid., 8.

40. Telephone conversation with Donna Newman, May 3, 2007.

41. Telephone conversation with Professor Martinez, June 7, 2007. Similarly, the Second Circuit's decision may have influenced the Supreme Court when considering whether Yaser Hamdi had a right to due process.

42. Telephone conversation with Donna Newman, May 3, 2007.

43. *Rumsfeld v. Padilla,* 542 U.S. 426 (2004).

44. *Padilla v. Hanft,* 389 F. Supp. 2d 678 (D.S.C. 2005).

45. *Padilla v. Hanft,* 423 F.3d 386 (2005).

46. Department of Defense e-mail, sent August 22, 2005, Subject: Padilla Visit Questions.

47. Order, *Padilla v. Hanft,* 432 F.3d 582 (4th Cir. Nov. 30, 2005).

48. *Padilla v. Hanft,* 126 S. Ct. 1649, 1650 (2006).

49. Ibid.

50. See the following amici curiae briefs filed with the court: Brief of the Brennan Center of Justice at NYU School of Law and the Association of the Bar of the City of New York at 9, *Padilla v. Hanft,* 423 F.3d 386 (2005) (No.05–6396); Brief of the National Association of Criminal Defense Lawyers at 8, *Padilla v. Hanft,* 126 S. Ct. 1649, 1650 (2006) (No. 05–553); and Brief of Amici Curiae Professors of Constitutional Law, Center for Constitutional Rights, and National Lawyers Guild at 2–3, *Padilla v. Hanft,* 126 S. Ct. 1649, 1650 (2006) (No. 05–553).

51. In March 2002, the Pentagon's general counsel, William Haynes, had said, "If we had a trial this minute, it is conceivable that somebody would be tried and acquitted of that charge but may not necessarily automatically be released." Katherine Q. Seelye, "A Nation Challenged: The Trials, Pentagon Says Acquittals May Not Free Detainees," *New York Times,* Mar. 22, 2002, A13, available at LEXIS, News Library, NYT File; 2002 WLNR 4086070.

52. *Padilla,* 126 S. Ct. at 1651.

53. On August 18, 2006, the U.S. District Court for the Southern District of Florida, Miami Division, dismissed as "multiplicitous" one of the three counts against Padilla. *United States v. Padilla,* No. 04-CR-60001 (S.D. Fla. Aug. 18, 2006).

54. Neil A. Lewis, "Terror Trial Hits Obstacle, Unexpectedly," *New York Times,* Dec. 1, 2005, A30, available at LEXIS, News Library, NYT File, 2005 WLNR 19319840. The Justice Department said that he was part of a "terrorist cell that supported violent acts overseas."

55. Douglas Jehl & Eric Lichblau, "Shift on Suspect Is Linked to Role of Qaeda Figures," *New York Times,* Nov. 24, 2005, A1, available at LEXIS, News Library, NYT File; David Stout, "New Accusations Made in 'Dirty Bomb' Case," *International Herald Tribune,* June 2, 2004, 6, available at 2004 WLNR 5213392; Adam Liptak, "In Terror Cases, Administration Sets Own Rules," *New York Times,* Nov. 27, 2005, 11, available at LEXIS, News Library, NYT File; Douglas Jehl & Eric Lichblau, "Shift on Suspect Is Linked to Role of Qaeda Figures," *New York Times,* Nov. 24, 2005, A1, available at LEXIS, News Library, NYT File. In an article on Zubaydah that came out after he was transferred to Guantanamo in September 2006, the *New York Times* reported that "Zubaydah dismissed Mr. Padilla as a maladroit extremist

whose hope to construct a dirty bomb . . . was far-fetched." David Johnston, "At a Secret Interrogation, Dispute Flared over Tactics," *New York Times,* Sept. 10, 2006, 1.

56. Ibid.

57. Joint Appendix I at 148, *Hamdi v. Rumsfeld,* 542 U.S. 507 (2004) (No. 03–6696) (Exhibit I—Mobbs' Declaration, 2 n.1).

58. Dana Priest, "CIA Puts Harsh Tactics on Hold," *Washington Post,* June 27, 2004, A1.

59. Jane Mayer, "The Black Sites: A Rare Look inside the C.I.A.'s Secret Interrogation Program," *New Yorker,* Aug. 13, 2007, available at http://www.newyorker.com/reporting/2007/08/13/070813fa_fact_mayer?printable=true.

60. Katherine Eban, "Rorschach and Awe," *Vanity Fair,* July 17, 2007.

61. Motion to Dismiss for Outrageous Government Conduct at 3, *United States v. Padilla,* No. 04–60001-CR-COOKE, 2006 WL 3678567 (S.D. Fla. 2006).

62. Ibid.

63. See also Aff. of Angela Hegarty, MD, ¶11, signed Nov. 30, 2006. Dr. Hegarty observed Padilla from June 26, 2006, to June 30, 2006, and again on September 11–12, 2006. Affidavit is attached to Mr. Padilla's Reply to the Government's Response to the Motion to Dismiss for Outrageous Government Conduct, *United States v. Padilla,* Case No. 04–60001 (S.D. Fla. Dec. 1, 2006).

64. Aff. of Angela Hegarty, MD, ¶11, signed Nov. 30, 2006. Dr. Hegarty met and observed Padilla from June 26, 2006, to June 30, 2006, and again on September 11 and 12, 2006. Affidavit is attached to Mr. Padilla's Reply to the Government's Response to the Motion to Dismiss for Outrageous Government Conduct, *United States v. Padilla,* Case No. 04–60001 (S.D. Fla. Dec. 1, 2006). See also Forensic Evaluation by Patricia A. Zapf, Ph.D, dated Dec. 11, 2006, at 4, also attached to Mr. Padilla's Reply to the Government's Response to the Motion to Dismiss for Outrageous Government Conduct, *United States v. Padilla,* Case No. 04–60001(S.D. Fla. Dec. 1, 2006).

65. Phone conversation with Donna Newman, May 3, 2007.

66. Mr. Padilla's Reply to the Government's Response to the Motion to Dismiss for Outrageous Government Conduct, *United States v. Padilla,* No. 04–60001-CR-COOKE, 2006 WL 3678567 (S.D. Fla. 2006).

67. Deborah Sontag, "Jailers Testify about Padilla's Confinement," *New York Times,* Feb. 28, 2007, A12.

68. Peter Whoriskey, "Padilla Was Deprived, Not Abused, Court Told," *Washington Post,* Feb. 28, 2007, A3.

69. Madeline Bar Diaz, "Psychologist: Padilla Suffers from Disorders, but Is Fit for Trial," *South Florida Sun-Sentinel,* Feb. 27, 2007.

70. Order of Competency, *United States v. Padilla,* No. 04–6001 (S.D. Fla. Mar. 1, 2007).

71. Deborah Sontag, "Padilla Ruled Fit for Trial on Terror Charges," *New York Times,* Feb. 28, 2007.

72. Ibid.

73. Carol J. Williams, "Padilla Ruled Fit for Terror Trial," *Los Angeles Times*, Mar. 1, 2007.

74. Conversation with Andrew Patel, Padilla's attorney, Mar. 1, 2007.

75. 18 U.S.C.S. § 4241(d) (2007).

76. Nina Totenberg, "U.S. Faces Major Hurdles in Prosecuting Padilla," *Morning Edition*, NPR, Jan. 3, 2007. See *Chavez v. Martinez*, 538 U.S. 760 (2003).

77. The first charge is in 18 U.S.C.A. § 956(a); the second is in 18 U.S.C.A. § 371 and in 18 U.S.C.A. § 2339A; the third is in 18 U.S.C.A. § 2339A.

78. Kirk Semple, "Padilla Sentenced to 17 Years in Prison," *New York Times*, Jan. 22, 2008, 1.

79. Mike Clary and Vanessa Blum, "Prosecutor Calls 17-Year Prison Term for Padilla 'Unreasonable,'" *South Florida Sun-Sentinel*, Jan. 22, 2008, 2.

80. The source for al Marri's activities and the information on his laptop is a Declaration by Jeffrey Rapp, Director, Joint Intelligence Task Force for Combating Terrorism, filed in Answer to the Petition for a Writ of Habeas Corpus, *Al-Marri v. Hanft*, No. 2:04–2257–26AJ (Sept. 9, 2004). "Recently" al Marri informed his lawyers that he spells his name Almarri. E-mail from his attorney Jonathan Hafatz, April 22, 2008.

81. *Al Marri*, 378 F. Supp. 2d at 674. See also *Al Marri ex rel. Berman v. Wright*, 443 F. Supp. 2d 774, 778 (D.S.C. 2006), where the court ruled that there is a "presumption in favor of the Government's evidence," and that "once the Government puts forth credible evidence that the habeas petitioner meets the enemy-combatant criteria, the onus could shift to the petitioner to rebut that evidence with more persuasive evidence."

82. Complaint, *Al-Marri v. Donald H. Rumsfeld*, No. 2:05–2259-HFF-RSC (D.S.C. Aug. 8, 2005).

83. Memorandum of Law in Support of Motion for Interim Relief from Prolonged Isolation and Other Unlawful Conditions of Confinement, *Almarri v. Gates*, C/A 2:05–2259-HFF-RSC, (D.C.S.C filed Mar. 13, 2008). Al Marri's case based on the government's treatment of him treatment is, in spring 2008, still in its early stages of litigation.

84. Department of Defense e-mail, June 27, 2005, Subject: Question (SJA Comment [blacked out] Letter [Al Marri]).

85. Ibid., 5.

86. Telephone conversation with Jonathan Hafetz, Aug. 30, 2007.

87. Respondent-Appellee's Motion to Dismiss for Lack of Jurisdiction and Proposed Briefing Schedule, *Al Marri ex rel. Berman v. Wright*, 443 F. Supp. 2d 774, 778 (D.S.C. 2006).

88. *Al-Marri v. Wright*, 487 F.3d 160, 169 (S.C. 2007).

89. Appellants' Response to Appellee's Motion to Dismiss for Lack of Jurisdiction, *Al-Marri ex rel. Berman v. Wright*, 443 F. Supp. 2d 774, 778 (D.S.C. 2006).

90. "The Privilege of the Writ of Habeas Corpus shall not be suspended, unless when in Cases of Rebellion or Invasion, the public Safety may require it." U.S. Constitution, art. I, § 9, cl. 2.

91. Appellants' Response to Appellee's Motion to Dismiss for Lack of Juris-

diction at 39–52, *Al Marri ex rel. Berman v. Wright*, 443 F. Supp. 2d 774, 778 (D.S.C. 2006).

92. *Al Marri v. Wright*, 487 F.3d 160, 195 (4th Cir. S.C. 2007).

93. Ibid., 195.

94. *Al Marri v. Wright*, No. 06–7427, 2:04-cv-002257-HFF (4th Cir. S.C. filed Aug. 22, 2007). En banc is considered to be review by the full court, although only ten members participate.

95. Memorandum of Law in Support of Motion for Interim Relief from Prolonged Isolation and Other Unlawful Conditions of Confinement, *Almarri v. Gates*, C/A 2:05–2259-HFF-RSC, (D.C.S.C filed Mar. 13, 2008) at 3.

96. Ibid., 11.

97. Ibid., 6 n.2.

98. Motion for an Order Directing the Government to Preserve Evidence and for an Inquiry into the Government's Destruction and Other Spoliation of Evidence at 2–3, *Almarri v. Gates*, C/A 2:052–259-HFF-RSC (D.C.S.C. Mar. 20, 2008).

99. E-mail from Jonathan Hafetz to author, Mar. 29, 2008.

100. *Al Marri v. Pucciarelli*, No. 067–427 (4th Cir. July 15, 2008).

101. *Al Marri v. Pucciarelli*, No. 067–427, 2008 WL 2736787 (C.A.4 [S.C.]), at *32 (4th Cir. July 15, 2008).

102. E-mail from Jonathan Hafetz to author, Sept. 18, 2008.

103. E-mails to author from Jonathan Hafetz, Dec. 28, 2006, and June 26, 2007. As of March 5, 2008, al Marri's circumstances continued unchanged. E-mail from Jonathan Hafetz, March 5, 2008.

104. Telephone conversation with Jonathan Hafetz, Aug. 4, 2006.

105. The facts of Shakir Baloch's case are taken from *Turkmen v. Ashcroft*, No. 02 CV 2307(JG), 2006 WL 1662663 (E.D.N.Y. June 14, 2006).

106. United States Department of Justice/Office of Inspector General, *The September 11 Detainees: A Review of the Treatment of Aliens Held on Immigration Charges in Connection with the Investigation of the September 11 Attacks*, June 2003, ch. 2, at 1 (hereinafter "OIG Report"), available at http://www.usdoj.gov/oig/special/0306/index.htm.

107. OIG Report, ch. 2, p. 2.

108. Ibid., p. 5; Don van Natta Jr., "A Nation Challenged: The Detainees; Hundreds of Arrests, but Promising Leads Unravel," *New York Times*, Oct. 21, 2001, 1B.

109. OIG Report, ch. 2, p. 2.

110. Andrew Gumbel, "The Disappeared," *Independent*, Feb. 26, 2002. Before September 11, the government had to file the charging determination within twenty-four hours. On September 17, the DOJ issued a new regulation increasing the time to forty-eight hours. However, the revised regulation provided that in the event of an emergency or other extraordinary circumstances the charging decision could be made within an additional reasonable period of time. The regulation did not define "extraordinary circumstances" or "reasonable period of time." The regulation also did not provide a time period by which the INS had to notify the alien of the charges. OIG Report, ch. 3, pp. 1–2.

111. The figures mentioned in this and the following paragraphs are taken from the OIG Report.

112. David Cole, "Enemy Aliens," *Stanford Law Review* 953, 960 (2002), 54.

113. OIG Report, ch. 4, p. 11.

114. Benamar Benatta was arrested on September 11. He was cleared on November 15 but not informed of the decision. He did not know of the charges against him—false identification papers—until April 2002. He remained in solitary for five months and never saw a lawyer during that time. Michael Powell, "A Prisoner of Panic after 9/11," *Washington Post,* Nov. 29, 2003, A1.

115. Steve Fainaru, "Suspect Held 8 Months without Seeing Judge," *Washington Post,* June 12, 2002, A1.

116. *Zadvydas v. Davis,* 533 U.S. 678, 693 (2001).

117. OIG Report, ch. 2, p. 3; ch. 4, p. 4; Jodi Wilgoren, "A Nation Challenged: The Detainees; Swept Up in a Dragnet, Hundreds Sit in Custody and Ask, 'Why?'" *New York Times,* Nov. 25, 2001, B1.

118. OIG Report, ch. 2, p. 2. The process worked like this: people were interviewed by the FBI or local police. An INS agent would then determine their immigration status. They would be released if the FBI expressed no interest in them and they were not in violation of their immigration status. If they were in violation, the INS would arrest them and the FBI would decide the level of interest—"high interest," "of interest," "interest undetermined," or "no interest"—and whether to hold them with respect to the terrorism investigation. "High-interest" detainees were sent to high-security facilities. Detainees were not released until clearance investigations had been completed. The agents also requested CIA checks on the detainees. If they were cleared, they would still be subject to full INS procedures, including a "Notice to Appear," the charging document that describes the immigration laws that the detainee had allegedly violated. An immigration judge would then conduct a hearing to determine whether the detainee should be deported. OIG Report, ch. 2, pp. 5, 11; OIG Report, ch. 3, p. 1.

119. Christopher Drew & Judith Miller, "A Nation Challenged: The Detainees; Though Not Linked to Terrorism, Many Detainees Cannot Go Home," *New York Times,* Feb. 18, 2002, A1. Under a Supreme Court decision, six months is an appropriate period to hold an alien after a judge finds that an alien should be deported. However, exceptions allow for holding the alien beyond the six-month period. *Zadvydas v. Davis,* 533 U.S. 678, 701 (2001).

120. Matthai Chakko Kuruvila, "Officials: Stereotypes Help Feed FBI Probes: Report Shows How Vague Suspicions after Sept. 11 Led to Arrests," *San Jose Mercury News,* June 9, 2003, 1B.

121. OIG Report, ch. 4, p. 5.

122. Memorandum from Michael Creppy, Chief Immigration Judge, on cases requiring special procedures, to All Immigration Judges: Court Administrators (Sept. 21, 2001).

123. Tamar Lewin, "A Nation Challenged: The Detainees; Rights Groups Press for Names of Muslims Held in New Jersey," *New York Times,* Jan. 23, 2002, A9.

124. *Turkmen v. Ashcroft,* No. 02 CV 2307(JG), slip op. at 21 (E.D.N.Y. June 14, 2006).

125. See 8 U.S.C. §§ 1229–1229a (2000) for rights provided immigration detainees.

126. OIG Report, ch 3, p. 2 (Serving the Notice to Appear).

127. OIG Report, ch. 7, pp. 14–18.

128. OIG Report, ch. 7, p. 20.

129. OIG Report, ch. 7, pp. 21–30; *Turkmen v. Ashcroft,* No. 02 CV 2307 (JG), slip op. at 2 (E.D.N.Y. June 14, 2006).

130. *Turkmen v. Ashcroft,* No. 02 CV 2307(JG), 2006 WL 1662663, at *20 (E.D.N.Y. June 14, 2006).

131. *Turkmen v. Ashcroft,* No. 02 CV 2307(JG), 2006 WL 1662663 (E.D. N.Y. June 14, 2006).

132. *Id.* slip op. at *1.

133. See discussion of *Iqbal v. Hasty,* below.

134. 5 U.S.C.A. § 552(b)(7)(A) (West, 2007).

135. *Ctr. for Nat'l Sec. Studies v. U.S. Dep't of Justice,* 331 F.3d 918, 931 (D.C. Cir. 2003), cert denied 540 U.S. 1104 (2004).

136. *North Jersey Media Group, Inc. v. Ashcroft,* 308 F.3d 198, 201 (3d Cir. 2002).

137. *North Jersey Media Group, Inc. v. Ashcroft,* 308 F.3d 198, 220 (3d Cir. 2002). However, in a case dealing with access to the hearing of one detainee, the Sixth Circuit Court of Appeals issued a different decision, requiring that the hearings remain open to the media. *Detroit Free Press v. Ashcroft,* 303 F.3d 681 (6th Cir. 2002).

138. *Ctr. for Nat'l Sec. Studies v. U.S. Dep't of Justice,* 331 F.3d 918, Judge Tatel dissenting (D.C. Cir. 2003).

139. Ibid., 937–38.

140. In 2008, the Supreme Court agreed to review at least some of the issues raised by the preventive detentions of the Arab and Muslim men immediately after 9/11. The Court agreed to review a civil lawsuit brought by Javaid Iqbal, a Pakistani Muslim, against former attorney general John Ashcroft, FBI director Robert Mueller, and other officials.[141] At the time he was arrested, Iqbal had an application pending for a green card. He was deported to Pakistan after six months in the detention center and after pleading guilty to document fraud. Iqbal did not challenge the legality of his arrest or his initial detention in the Metropolitan Detention Center. Instead, he argued that his harsh and highly restrictive confinement—he was kept in solitary confinement and brutally beaten by guards—was based on his race and religion and thus was a violation of the Constitution. Ashcroft and Mueller contended in response that they had what is known as qualified legal immunity in these circumstances and that the constitutional violations were committed by lower-level officials. In June 2007 the Second Circuit Court of Appeals rejected Ashcroft and Mueller's claims of immunity at this initial stage of the litigation, allowing the lawsuit to proceed. *Iqbal v. Hasty,* 490 F.3d 143 (2d Cir. 2007). The Supreme Court will issue its decision as to whether the lawsuit can proceed in late 2008 or early 2009.

141. "Witness to Abuse: Human Rights Abuses under the Material Wit-

ness Law since September 11," *Human Rights Watch* 17, no. 2 (June 2005): 16, available at http://www.hrw.org/reports/2005/us0605/us0605.pdf.

142. 18 U.S.C.A. § 3144 (West 2000). The statute requires that the government file an affidavit alleging that the detained person's testimony is material to a criminal proceeding, that it is "impracticable to secure the presence of the person by subpoena," and that if his testimony "can adequately be secured by deposition, and if further detention is not necessary to prevent a failure of justice," he may not be detained.

143. Steve Fainaru & Margot Williams, "Justice Milking Detention Authority: 'Material Witnesses' of Terrorism Languish without Testifying," *Washington Post,* Nov. 24, 2002.

144. See also *In re Application of the U.S. for a Material Witness Warrant,* 213 F. Supp. 2d 287 (S.D.N.Y. 2002), where Justice Mukasey (he later was appointed attorney general after Gonzales resigned) agreed that a grand jury is a criminal proceeding.

145. "Witness to Abuse: Human Rights Abuses under the Material Witness Law since September 11," *Human Rights Watch* 17, no. 2 (June 2005), 48, 49, 56, available at http://www.hrw.org/reports/2005/us0605/us0605.pdf; Benjamin Weiser, "A Nation Challenged: Material Witness; Hearing Set on Charges of Coercion by the F.B.I.," *New York Times,* Feb. 1, 2002, A11.

146. Steve Fainaru & Margot Williams, "Material Witness Law Has Many in Limbo; Nearly Half Held in War on Terror Haven't Testified," *Washington Post,* Nov. 24, 2002, A01.

147. Heidee Stoller, Tahlia Townsend, Rashad Hussain, and Marcia Yablon, "Developments in Law and Policy: The Costs of Post-9/11 National Security Strategy," *Yale Law and Policy Review* 197, 202 (2004), 22; letter from Jamie E. Brown, Acting Assistant Attorney General, Office of Legislative Affairs, to Rep. F. James Sensenbrenner, Jr., Chairman, House Judiciary Committee, May 13, 2003.

148. "Witness to Abuse: Human Rights Abuses under the Material Witness Law since September 11," *Human Rights Watch* 17, no. 2 (June 2005), 3, 5, 16, 33, available at http://www.hrw.org/reports/2005/us0605/us0605.pdf.

PART THREE, SECTION I

1. An Act Making appropriations for the support of the Army for the fiscal year ending June thirtieth, nineteen hundred and two, March 2, 1901, Enrolled Acts and Resolutions of Congress, 1789–, General Records of the United States Government, Record Group 11, National Archives.

2. Agreement between the United States and Cuba for the Lease of Lands for Coaling and Naval Stations, Feb. 23, 1903.

3. Jonathan M Hansen, "Making the Law in Cuba," *New York Times,* Apr. 20, 2004.

4. Lease to the United States by the Government of Cuba of Certain Areas of Land and Water for Naval or Coaling Stations in Guantanamo and Bahia Honda, signed July 2, 1903.

5. *Johnson v. Eisentrager,* 339 U.S. 763 (1950).

6. See part 1, sections 2–3, for a detailed discussion of his involvement in the administration's torture policy.

7. John Yoo, *War by Other Means: An Insider's Account of the War on Terror* (Atlantic Monthly Press, 2006), 142–43.

8. Katharine Q. Seelye, "A Nation Challenged: The Prisoners; First 'Unlawful Combatants' Seized in Afghanistan Arrive at U.S. Base in Cuba," *New York Times*, Jan. 12, 2002, A7.

9. Katherine Q. Seelye, "Some Guantanamo Prisoners Will Be Freed, Rumsfeld Says," *New York Times*, Oct. 23, 2002, A14.

10. Mark Denbeaux and Joshua W. Denbeaux, *Report on Guantanamo Detainees: A Profile of 517 Detainees through Analysis of Department of Defense Data,* Seton Hall Public Law Research Paper No. 46 (Feb. 2006), available at SSRN http://ssrn.com/abstract=885659; Bob Drogin, "No Leaders of Al Qaeda Found at Guantanamo," *Los Angeles Times*, Aug. 18, 2002, 1.

11. Denbeaux and Denbeaux, *Report on Guantanamo Detainees.*

12. Tim Golden, "Administration Officials Split over Stalled Military Tribunals," *New York Times*, Oct. 25, 2004, A1.

13. "Bounties Paid for Terror Suspects," *Human Rights Defender*, Dec. 2006/Jan. 2007.

14. Ibid. See also Pervez Musharraf, *In the Line of Fire: A Memoir* (Free Press, 2006), 237. "We have captured 689 and handed over 369 to the United States. We have earned bounties totaling millions of dollars. Those who habitually accuse us of not doing enough in the war on terror should simply ask the CIA how much prize money it has paid to the Government of Pakistan." These amounts were substantial when compared to per capita incomes of Afghanis and Pakistanis in 2001 and 2002. The United Nations Statistics Division reported annual per capita income of $103 in Afghanistan in 2001 and $213 in 2002. Pakistan's annual per capita income was at $490 in 2001 and $561 in 2002. *Per Capita GNI at Current Prices in US Dollars* (all countries), http://unstats.un.org/unsd/snaama/dnllist.asp.

15. John Peffer, "Paper Bullets: An Interview with Herbert A. Friedman," *Cabinet Magazine* (Fall 2003/Winter 2004), 2, available at http://www.cabinet magazine.org/issues/12/pefferFriedman.php.

In an e-mail to my assistant, Jody Taliaferro, on April 18, 2007, Herb Friedman wrote that the "leaflets are classified until dropped. Once they are scattered in the millions all over Iraq and Afghanistan they are free to copy." "The vast majority of them are directly from the US government, so at the least, what you see is what they think it says. They are not always right. Others are from friendly Arabs in various countries." Thus, "the translations are either U.S. government transcripts or done locally from natives who tend to translate into their own dialect and some minor errors are to be expected."

16. *Coalition of Clergy v. Bush,* 189 F. Supp.2d 1036 (C.D. Cal. 2002).

17. Jessica Garrison, "L.A. Officials Know to Expect Attorney's Call," *Los Angeles Times*, Mar. 22, 2006, B1; Henry Weinstein, "Yagman Indicted by Federal Grand Jury," *Los Angeles Times*, June 24, 2006, B1.

18. E-mail from Erwin Chemerinsky to author, Mar. 10, 2007 (on file with author). The text of the e-mail has been edited.

19. Tom Wilner was assisted by two other members of the firm, Neil Koslowe and Kristine Huskey. Koslowe still works with Wilner on the Guantanamo cases. Huskey is now teaching at American University Washington College of Law in the International Human Rights Law Clinic, where she continues to represent people captured in the War on Terror. This former model and current human rights lawyer and teacher was profiled in the magazine *Marie Claire* (December 2006), 91.

20. Richard A. Serrano, "Detainees Launch Legal Step," *Los Angeles Times,* Oct. 16, 2002, 1.

21. Richard A. Serrano, "Kuwaiti 12's Families Elated by Decision," *Los Angeles Times,* Nov. 11, 2003, A21.

22. 339 U.S. 763 (1950). The D.C. circuit court did not think that it made a difference that the prisoners in *Eisentrager* had access to counsel and had been charged, tried, and convicted by a military tribunal for war crimes, unlike the detainees in Guantanamo.

23. *Rasul v. Bush,* 215 F. Supp. 2d 55, 68 (D.C. 2002).

24. Joseph Margulies, *Guantanamo and the Abuse of Presidential Power* (Simon and Schuster, 2006).

25. Debra Burlingame, "Gitmo's Guerrilla Lawyers," *Wall Street Journal,* Mar. 8, 2007, A17.

26. Stafford Smith wrote a book entitled *Bad Men: Guantanamo Bay and the Secret Prisons,* recounting his experiences representing thirty-five detainees (Weidenfeld & Nicolson, 2007). He now lives in London and is the legal director of the UK charity Reprieve. His book was titled *Eight O'clock Ferry to the Windward Side* when it was published in the United States.

27. *Rasul v. Bush,* 215 F. Supp. 2d 55 (D.C. 2002); *Al Odah v. United States,* 321 F.3d 1134 (D.C. Cir. 2003).

28. *The Federalist No. 84,* at 418 (Alexander Hamilton) (Clinton Rossiter ed., 1961).

29. U.S. Constitution, art. I, § 9, cl. 2.

30. See Act of Feb. 5, 1867, 14 Stat. 385 (codified as amended at 28 U.S.C. § 2254 [1982]).

31. Petition for Original Writ of Habeas Corpus and Appendix in the United States Supreme Court, *In re Abdul Hamid Salam Al-Ghizzawi,* 128 S. Ct. 347 (Oct. 1, 2007), On Petition for Original Writ of Habeas Corpus, in the Supreme Court of the United States, No. 07–6827.

32. Endangered Species Act of 1973, 16 U.S.C. §§ 1531–1544 (2000).

33. 28 U.S.C.A. Section 2241 grants the right to habeas by a person who claims to be held "in custody in violation of the Constitution or laws or treaties of the United States."

34. *Rasul v. Bush,* 542 U.S. 466, 473, 481–82 (2004).

35. Ibid., 467–68.

36. 28 U.S.C.A. § 2241.

37. 542 U.S. at 487.

38. *Hamdi v. Rumsfeld,* 542 U.S. 507 (2004).

39. See Burlingame, "Gitmo's Guerrilla Lawyers," A17.

PART THREE, SECTION II

1. For a resource on Guantanamo, including abusive practices, see University of California, Davis, "Guantanamo Testimonials Project," http://human rights.ucdavis.edu/projects/the-guantanamo-testimonials-project/index or http://tinyurl.com/299ud2.

2. Bill Dedman, "Can the '20th Hijacker' of Sept. 11 Stand Trial?" *MSNBC,* Oct. 26, 2006, available at http://www.msnbc.msn.com/id/15361462/.

3. Adam Zagorin & Michael Duffy, "Inside the Interrogation of Detainee 063," *Time,* June 12, 2005, available at http://www.time.com/time/magazine/article/0,9171,1071284,00.html; "Secret Orcon, Interrogation Log, Detainee 063," *Time,* June 12, 2005, available at http://www.time.com/time/2006/log/log.pdf.

4. Memorandum from William J. Haynes II, General Counsel, to Donald Rumsfeld, Secretary of Defense, on Counter-Resistance Techniques (Nov. 27, 2002), available at http://www.slate.com/features/whatistorture/LegalMemos .html; Philippe Sands, *Torture Team: Rumsfeld's Memo and the Betrayal of American Values* (Palgrave Macmillan, 2008), 4.

5. Memorandum from Haynes to Rumsfeld, Nov. 27, 2002; Sands, *Torture Team,* 5.

6. Sands, *Torture Team,* 5.

7. Letter from T. J. Harrington, Deputy Assistant Director of the FBI's Counterterrorism Division, to Major General Donald J. Ryder, Re: Suspected Mistreatment of Detainees (July 14, 2004), available at http://ccrjustice.org/files/TJ%20Harrington%20Ltr%20Redacted%207%2014%2004.pdf.

8. Adam Zagorin, "Detainee 063: A Broken Man," *Time,* Mar. 2, 2006, available at http://www.time.com/time/nation/article/0,8599,1169310,00.html.

9. Phone conversation between J. Wells Dixon, an attorney with CCR, and the author, Dec. 12, 2007.

10. E-mail from Gitanjali Gutierrez to the author, Mar. 3, 2008.

11. Mark Landler, "12 Detainees Sue Rumsfeld in Germany, Citing Abuse," *New York Times,* Nov. 15, 2006, A17.

12. Ibid.

13. Ibid.

14. CCR and other human rights organizations also filed a war crimes/torture case against Rumsfeld in France on October 26, 2007. Center for Constitutional Rights, "Donald Rumsfeld Charged with Torture during Trip to France," Oct.26, 2007, available at http://ccrjustice.org/newsroom/press-re leases/donald-rumsfeld-charged-torture-during-trip-france.

15. Declaration of Gitanjali S. Gutierrez, Esq., Lawyer for Mohammed al Qahtani, http://ccrjustice.org/files/AlQahtani_GutierrezDeclaration_10_06 .pdf.

16. Summary of Administrative Review Board Proceedings for ISN 063, 6.

17. Phone conversation with Brent Mickum, habeas attorney, June 2, 2008. Mickum represented three British prisoners and currently represents Abu Zubaydah.

18. Lee Ann Obringer, "How the Navy SEALs Work," *How Stuff Works,*

http://science.howstuffworks.com/navy-seal6.htm; see also Paul McHugh, "Building Elite Forces for Military of Future," *San Francisco Chronicle*, May 14, 2006, 2, available at http://www.sfgate.com/cgi-bin/article.cgi?file=/c/a/2006/05/14/MNGOBIPSBK1.DTL.

19. Phone conversation with Brent Mickum, habeas attorney, June 2, 2008.

20. Number: DOJFBI-002345. To Valene Caproni, cited in Dan Eggen & R. Jeffrey Smith, "FBI Agents Allege Abuse of Detainees at Guantanamo Bay," *Washington Post*, Dec. 21, 2004, A01.

21. Affidavit of Attorney H. Candace Gorman, dated July 25, 2007, along with the Petition for Original Writ of Habeas Corpus and Appendix in the United States Supreme Court. *In re Abdul Hamid Salam Al-Ghizzawi*, On Petition for Original Writ of Habeas Corpus, in the Supreme Court of the United States, No. 07–6827, October 1, 2007. The facts and allegations that follow are taken from her affidavit.

22. See "Do-overs and Colonel Stephen Abraham," p. 124.

23. Telephone conversation between Candace Gorman and the author, Dec. 10, 2007.

24. Ibid.

25. All the quotes in this paragraph are taken from Al-Ghizzawi's Motion for Leave to File This Reply to Emergency Motion for Rule to Show Cause and Other Relief, Instanter, in *Abdul Hamid Al-Ghizzawi v. Bush*, Civil Action No. 05-cv-02378 (D.D.C. Sept. 28, 2007).

26. Al-Ghizzawi's New Emergency Motion for Medical Treatment and Medical Records, *Al-Ghizzawi v. Bush*, no. 05 cv 2378 (JDB) (D.D.C. Feb. 5, 2008).

27. Respondents' Opposition to Petitioner's New Emergency Motion for Medical Treatment and Medical Records at 15–16, *Al-Ghizzawi v. Bush*, Civil Action No. 05–2378 (JDB) (D.D.C. Feb. 15, 2008), and attached Declaration of Captain Bruce C. Meneley, M.D. (Ex. B) at 3.

28. Reply to Emergency Motion for Medical Treatment, *Al-Ghizzawi v. Bush*, No. 05 cv 2378 (JDB) (D.D.C. Feb. 21, 2008).

29. Al-Ghizzawi's New Emergency Motion for Medical Treatment and Medical Records, *Al-Ghizzawi v. Bush*, No. 05 cv 2378 (JDB), at 5 (D.D.C. Feb. 5, 2008).

30. *Al-Ghizzawi v. Bush*, Civil Action No. 05–2378(JDB) (D.D.C. Apr. 8, 2008).

31. *Id*. at slip op. 13.

32. *Id*. at slip op. 14.

33. Status Report at 4, 5, 6, *Al-Ghizzawi v. Bush*, 05-cv-02378 (D.D.C. July 18, 2008).

34. "Back from Hell," posting of Candace Gorman to the Guantanamo Blog, http://gtmoblog.blogspot.com/ (Sept. 29, 2007, 14:38 CST).

35. Ibid.

36. Josh White, "Three Detainees Commit Suicide at Guantanamo," *Washington Post*, June 11, 2006, A1.

37. Damien Cave, "U.S. Says Inmate Legal Notes May Have Aided Suicide Plot," *New York Times,* July 9, 2006, 13.

38. William Glaberson & Margot Williams," Pentagon Files Offer Details on Detainee in Suicide," *New York Times,* June 1, 2007, A22.

39. Carol Rosenberg, "Commander of Guantanamo's Detention and Interrogation Center Talks to the Miami Herald," *Miami Herald,* May 20, 2007, 1L. "Asymmetrical warfare" has been defined by the U.S. Joint Chiefs of Staff as "attempts to circumvent or undermine an opponent's strengths while exploiting his weaknesses using methods that differ significantly from the opponent's usual mode of operations." Roger W. Barnett, *Asymmetrical Warfare* (Brassey's, 2003), 15. The term has been defined by the National Defense University, Institute for National Strategic Studies, as a version of not "fighting fair," which can include the use of surprise and use of weapons in ways unplanned by the United States. *1998 Strategic Assessment Engaging Power for Peace* (1998), chap. 11, available at http://www.au.af.mil/au/awc/awcgate/sa98/sa98ch11.htm. A suicide bomber would be an example of someone engaging in asymmetrical warfare. Dupuy et al., *Dictionary of Military Terms* (H. W. Wilson, 2003), 21.

40. "The David Hicks Affidavit," *Sydney Morning Herald,* Dec. 10, 2004, http://www.smh.com.au/news/World/David-Hicks-affidavit/2004/12/10/1102625527396.html.

41. David Rose, "How we Survived Jail Hell," *Observer,* March 14, 2004, http://www.guardian.co.uk/afghanistan/story/0,,1169112,00.html.

42. David Rose, "They Tied Me Up and Began Kicking Me," *Observer,* May 16, 2004, 2, http://www.guardian.co.uk/world/2004/may/16/terrorism.guantanamo.

43. E-mail to the author from Professor Kermit Roosevelt, University of Pennsylvania School of Law, July 7, 2008.

44. Patrick Martin, "Soldier Beaten at Guantanamo Interrogation Training," *World Socialist Web Site,* May 29, 2004, http://www.wsws.org/articles/2004/may2004/guan-m29.shtml.

45. Lt. Col. Leon Sumpter, spokesman for the Joint Task Force, cited in David Rose and Gaby Hinsliff, "US Guards 'Filmed Beatings' at Terror Camp," *Observer,* May 16, 2004, available at http://www.guardian.co.uk/world/2004/may/16/terrorism.guantanamo1.

46. "G.I. Attacked during Training," *60 Minutes,* Nov. 3, 2004.

47. Neil A. Lewis, "Hunger Strike by Detainees Goes to Court," *New York Times,* Sept. 22, 2005, A29; Joint Task Force Guantanamo, "JTF Guantanamo Updates Voluntary Fast Numbers," Dec. 29, 2005, available at http://www.southcom.mil/pa/Media/Releases/PR051229.pdf.

48. World Medical Association, The World Medical Association Declaration of Tokyo, Guidelines for Physicians Concerning Torture and other Cruel, Inhuman or Degrading Treatment or Punishment in Relation to Detention and Imprisonment. Adopted in 1975 and revised in 2005 and 2006. Paragraph 6 reads in part: "Where a prisoner refuses nourishment and is considered by the physician as capable of forming an unimpaired and rational judgment con-

cerning the consequences of such a voluntary refusal of nourishment, he or she shall not be fed artificially," http://www.wma.net/e/policy/c18.htm.

49. Tim Golden, "The Battle for Guantanamo," *New York Times Magazine*, Sept. 17, 2006, 6:60.

50. Personal communication from the clinic director at Guantanamo.

51. Mr. Wilner gave me a copy of the interview immediately after we met on Feb. 9, 2007. The copy is on file with the author.

52. E-mail from Tom Wilner to the author, July 10, 2008.

PART THREE, SECTION III

1. "Guantanamo Bay Detainees," GlobalSecurity.org, available at http://www.globalsecurity.org/military/facility/guantanamo-bay_detainees.htm. See also "Transfer of Swedish Detainee Complete," U.S. Department of Defense news release, July 8, 2004, available at http://www.defenselink.mil/releases/release.aspx?releaseid=7532.

2. Department of Defense memorandum signed by Paul Wolfowitz on an Order Establishing Combatant Status Review Tribunal to the Secretary of the Navy (July 7, 2004), available at http://www.defenselink.mil/news/Jul2004/d20040707review.pdf (last visited Aug. 8, 2006). Some objections have been raised that the tribunals were created to circumvent the Supreme Court decision rather than abide by it. See Helen Duffy, *The "War on Terror" and the Framework of International Law* (Cambridge University Press, 2005), 385.

3. Mark Denbeaux and Joshua W. Denbeaux, *No-Hearing Hearings—CSRT: The Modern Habeas Corpus?* Seton Hall Public Law Research Paper No. 951245 (Dec. 2006), 4.

4. For descriptions of torture at Guantanamo and instances where detainees were tortured or where the administration documented the use of torture in in-house memoranda, see *Treatment of the Detainees in Guantanamo.* District Court judge Joyce Hens Green wrote in the opinion that the CSRT procedures deprived "the detainees of sufficient notice of the factual bases for their detention" and denied them "a fair opportunity to challenge their incarceration." She also wrote that the hearings relied on statements obtained by coercion and torture. *In re Guantanamo Detainee Cases,* 355 F. Supp. 2d 443, 472 (D.C. 2005).

5. Department of Defense, Combatant Status Tribunal Review hearing transcript of Mamdouh Habib.

6. According to the Denbeaux Report, detainees were not able to present witnesses on their behalf unless the witnesses were detained at Guantanamo. Mark Denbeaux and Joshua W. Denbeaux, *Report on Guantanamo Detainees: A Profile of 517 Detainees through Analysis of Department of Defense Data,* Seton Hall Public Law Research Paper No. 46 (Feb. 2006), 6n7. In addition, according to a memorandum from Secretary of the Navy Gordon England, witnesses are not considered reasonably available if they decline to attend, cannot be reached, or claim that security considerations would not permit them to attend. Memorandum from Secretary of Navy Gordon England, *Implementation of the Combatant Status Review Tribunal Procedures*

for Enemy Combatants Detained at U.S. Naval Base Guantanamo Bay, Cuba, at ¶G (9)(b), (July 14, 2006), available at http://www.defenselink.mil/news/Aug2006/d20060809CSRTprocedures.pdf.

7. Ibid.

8. Telephone conversation with Mark Denbeaux, June 15, 2006.

9. Carlotta Gall and Andy Worthington, "Time Runs Out for an Afghan Held by the U.S.," *New York Times,* Feb. 5, 2007, A1.

10. Cmdr. Rick Haupt, spokesman for the JTF. Tom Brown, "US Says Guantanamo Prisoner Dies of Cancer," *Reuters,* Dec. 30, 2007, available at http://www.reuters.com/article/latestCrisis/idUSN30484972.

11. Department of Defense, Review of Combatant Status Review Tribunal of Abdullah Kamel, Unclassified Summary of Basis for Tribunal Decision, Oct. 11, 2004, 1.

12. Ibid., 2.

13. "Should any doubt arise as to whether persons, having committed a belligerent act and having fallen into the hands of the enemy, belong to any of the categories enumerated in Article 4, such persons shall enjoy the protection of the present Convention until such time as their status has been determined by a competent tribunal." Geneva Convention Relative to the Treatment of Prisoners of War, art. 5, Aug. 12, 1949, 6 U.S.T. 3316.

14. Ibid. See Order from Paul Wolfowitz, Administrative Review Procedures for Enemy Combatants in the Control of the Department of Defense at Guantanamo Bay Naval Base, Cuba (May 11, 2004), 1, available at http://www.defenselink.mil/news/May2004/d20040518gtmoreview.pdf.

15. Denbeaux and Denbeaux, *No-Hearing Hearings—CSRT,* 6.

16. Redacted Motion for Preservation of Torture Evidence at 2, *Khan v. Gates,* No. 07-1324 (filed Nov. 30, 2007).

17. Gitanjali S. Gutierrez, "Going to See a Ghost," *Washington Post,* Oct. 15, 2007, A15.

18. Gutierrez believes that Khan was there at the same time as Khalid el Masri, a German citizen and an innocent victim of the CIA's extraordinary rendition program.

19. Redacted Verbatim Transcript of Combatant Status Review Tribunal Hearing for ISN 10020, Majid Khan, Apr. 15, 2007, 1, 2, and 3.

20. Ibid., 4.

21. Ibid., 6 and 7.

22. Ibid., 37–38.

23. Carol Rosenberg, "'High-Value Detainee' Meets with Lawyer," *Miami Herald,* Oct. 17, 2007.

24. Telephone conversation with Wells Dixon, Dec. 12, 2007.

25. Ibid.

26. Ibid.

27. Andrew O. Selsky, "AP Confirms Secret Camp inside Gitmo," *Huffington Post,* Feb. 6, 2008, available at http://www.huffingtonpost.com/2008/02/06/ap-confirms-secret-camp-i_n_85382.html.

28. Ibid.

29. Telephone conversation with Wells Dixon, Dec. 12, 2007.

30. Redacted Motion for Preservation of Torture Evidence at 1, *Khan v. Gates,* No. 07-1324 (filed Nov. 30, 2007).

31. Ibid., 4.

32. Redacted Verbatim Transcript of Combatant Status Review Tribunal Hearing for ISN 10020, Majid Khan, Apr. 15, 2007, 22, 24, and 26.

33. Ibid., 22.

34. Redacted Reply Memorandum of Law in Further Support of Petitioner's Torture Motions, *Khan v. Gates,* No. 07-1324 (filed Jan. 4, 2008).

35. Denbeaux and Denbeaux, *No-Hearing Hearings—CSRT,* 37–39.

36. Ibid., 38–40.

37. Declaration of Stephen Abraham, *al Odah v. United States,* No. 06-1196 (U.S. June 15, 2007). The declaration was attached to the Reply to Opposition to Petition for Rehearing, *al Odah v. United States,* in the U.S. Supreme Court.

38. Ibid., ¶23.

39. [Written Prepared] Statement of Stephen E. Abraham, Lieutenant Colonel, U.S. Army Reserve, before the Armed Services Committee, United States House of Representatives, Concerning Upholding the Principle of Habeas Corpus for Detainees, Presented Thursday, July 26, 2007, 10, available at http://armedservices.house.gov/pdfs/FC072607/Abraham_Testimony072607.pdf.

40. [Opening] Testimony of Stephen E. Abraham, Lieutenant Colonel, U.S. Army Reserve, before the Armed Services Committee, United States House of Representatives, Concerning Upholding the Principle of Habeas Corpus for Detainees, Presented Thursday, July 26, 2007, 8, available at http://human rights.ucdavis.edu/projects/the-guantanamo-testimonials-project/testimonies/testimonies-of-csrt-officers/abraham-congressional-testimony-26-july-2007.

41. Ibid.

42. [Question/Answer Session] Testimony of Stephen E. Abraham, Lieutenant Colonel, U.S. Army Reserve, before the Armed Services Committee, United States House of Representatives, Concerning Upholding the Principle of Habeas Corpus for Detainees, Presented Thursday, July 26, 2007, at 49, available at http://humanrights.ucdavis.edu/projects/the-guantanamo-testimo nials-project/testimonies/testimonies-of-csrt-officers/abraham-congression al-testimony-26-july-2007.

43. [Opening Testimony] Testimony of Stephen E. Abraham, Lieutenant Colonel, U.S. Army Reserve, before the Armed Services Committee, United States House of Representatives, Concerning Upholding the Principle of Habeas Corpus for Detainees, Presented Thursday, July 26, 2007, 8, available at http://humanrights.ucdavis.edu/projects/the-guantanamo-testimonials-project/testimonies/testimonies-of-csrt-officers/abraham-congressional-testimo ny-26-july-2007. ARDEC is an acronym for Administrative Review of the Detention of Enemy Combatants. It is also known as OARDEC (Office for the Administrative Review of the Detention of Enemy Combatants).

44. E-mail from Candace Gorman to the author, Oct. 20, 2007.

45. See Peter Jan Honigsberg, "Chasing 'Enemy Combatants' and Circumventing International Law: A License for Sanctioned Abuse," *UCLA Journal of International Law and Foreign Affairs* 1 (2007), 12, for a review of the

many different and inconsistent definitions that the DOD and the administration have used for the term *enemy combatant* from 2002 to 2006.

46. Department of Defense memorandum signed by Paul Wolfowitz on an Order Establishing Combatant Status Review Tribunal to the Secretary of the Navy (July 7, 2004), available at http://www.defenselink.mil/news/Jul2004/d20040707review.pdf (last visited Aug. 8, 2006).

47. The word *support* also appears in the critical definitions of *enemy combatant* found in the *Hamdan* decision, as well as in the Congressional Military Commissions Act of 2006.

48. On March 3, 2004, the DOD issued a draft administrative review process memorandum that "would establish an administrative review process to reassess at least annually the need to continue to detain each enemy combatant in the control of the Department of Defense at Guantanamo Bay Naval Base, Cuba." Department of Defense, "DOD Announces Draft Detainee Review Policy," news release, *Department of Defense News*, Mar. 3, 2004, available at http://www.defenselink.mil/releases/2004/nr20040303-0403.html (last visited Aug. 8, 2006). The policy provided that "each enemy combatant would have the opportunity to explain to an administrative review board of three military offices why he should no longer be detained."

49. Department of Defense, *Administrative Review Boards at Guantanamo*, Feb. 22, 2007, available at http://www.defenselink.mil/news/Jul2007/ARB%20Fact%20Sheet%20-%20Final%20-%2022%20Feb%2007.pdf; Neil A. Lewis, "Guantanamo Detainees Make Their Case," *New York Times*, Mar. 24, 2005, A21.

50. Department of Defense, *Administrative Review Boards at Guantanamo*, Feb. 22, 2007, available at http://www.defenselink.mil/news/Jul2007/ARB%20Fact%20Sheet%20-%20Final%20-%2022%20Feb%2007.pdf.

51. Washington Post, "Names of the Detained in Guantanamo Bay, Cuba," http://projects.washingtonpost.com/guantanamo/ (last visited Oct. 28, 2008). The release of detainees appear on U.S. Department of Defense, DefenseLink News Release, available at http://www.defenselink.mil/Releases/Release.aspx?REleaseID.

52. *Associated Press v. U.S. Department of Defense*, 410 F. Supp. 2d 147 (S.D.N.Y. 2006).

53. In February 2005, Barbara Olshansky at CCR received a letter with a list of detainee names from someone in Guantanamo. However, since the list did not appear to be officially sent, she reported it to the judge who was hearing a Guantanamo lawsuit that she and CCR were filing. The judge informed her to contact the DOJ. The sender, Lt. Cmdr. Matthew Diaz, was prosecuted and convicted of disclosing secret defense information. Apparently, the Guantanamo official had wanted to give Olshansky the names so that she could provide them with representation. See Tim Golden, "Naming Names at Gitmo," *New York Times Magazine*, Oct. 21, 2007.

54. *Associated Press v. U.S. Department of Defense*, 410 F. Supp. 2d 147 (S.D.N.Y. 2006).

55. Josh White and Julie Tate, "Pentagon Releases Detainees' Names," *Washington Post*, Mar. 4, 2006, A7.

56. "Guantanamo Bay Timeline," *Miami Herald,* available at http://www
.miamiherald.com/multimedia/news/gitmo_timeline/timeline.swf

57. Amended Protective Order and Procedures for Counsel Access to Detainees at the United States Naval Base in Guantanamo Bay, Cuba, *In re Guantanamo Detainee Cases,* 344 F. Supp. 2d 174 (D.D.C. 2004) Exhibit A (IV).

58. Motion for Rule to Show Cause, *Amer Mohammon (Abdal Razak
Ali) v. Bush,* No. 05-2386 (D.D.C. Aug. 9, 2006).

59. Affidavit of Patrick M. McCarthy, Commander, JAGC, U.S. Navy at 4,
¶9 (Ex. C), attached to Respondents' Opposition to Motion for Rule to Show
Cause and Response to Court's August 17, 2006 Order, *Amer Mohammon
(Abdal Razak Ali) v. Bush,* Civil Action No. 05-2386 (RBW) (D.D.C. Aug. 21,
2006). See Candace Gorman, "Reporter Envy (or Why a Guantanamo Attorney Dreams of Being a Reporter," *Huffington Post,* Dec. 12, 2006, available
at http://www.huffingtonpost.com/h-candace-gorman-/reporter-envy-or-wh
y-a-g_b_36135.html.

60. Emergency Motion for Rule to Show Cause and Other Relief, *Abdul
Al-Ghizzawi v. Bush,* Civil Action No. 05-cv-02378, (D.D.C. Sept. 12, 2007),
at 2.

61. Amended Protective Order and Procedures for Counsel Access to Detainees at the United States Naval Base in Guantanamo Bay, Cuba, *In re Guantanamo Detainee Cases,* 344 F. Supp. 2d 174, 186 (D.D.C. 2004), Exhibit A
(IV)(A).

62. Emergency Motion for Rule to Show Cause and Other Relief, *Abdul
Al-Ghizzawi v. Bush,* Civil Action No. 05-cv-02378 (D.D.C. Sept. 12, 2007),
at 2.

63. Motion for Leave to File this Reply to Emergency Motion for Rule to
Show Cause and Other Relief, Instanter, *Abdul Al-Ghizzawi v. Bush,* Civil
Action No. 05-cv-02378 (D.D.C. Sept. 28, 2007), at 2.

64. Emergency Motion for Rule to Show Cause and Other Relief, *Abdul
Al-Ghizzawi v. Bush,* Civil Action No. 05-cv-02378 (D.D.C. Sept. 12, 2007),
at 2.

65. Ibid.

66. Letter on file with the author. Copies are also available from Mr. Stafford
Smith. The letter has been minimally edited.

67. Ibid.

68. E-mail from Clive Stafford Smith to author, Oct. 21, 2007 (on file with
the author).

69. Plaintiffs-Petitioners' Motion for Writ of Injunction, *Fawzi Khalid
Abdullah Fahad Al Odah, et al. v. United States,* 406 F. Supp. 2d 37 (filed
D.D.C. Apr. 20, 2005) (Wilner's declaration is attached).

70. Ibid.

71. Amended Protective Order and Procedures for Counsel Access to Detainees at the United States Naval Base in Guantanamo Cuba, *In re Guantanamo
Detainee Cases,* 344 F. Supp. 2d 174, 191 (D.D.C. 2004), Exhibit A (X).

72. E-mail from Candace Gorman to the author, Oct. 20, 2007 (on file
with the author).

73. Telephone conversation with Wells Dixon, Dec. 12, 2007.

74. Amended Complaint for Declaratory and Injunctive Relief, *Thomas Wilner, et. al v. National Security Agency and Department of Justice* (filed S.D.N.Y. June 28, 2007).

75. Declaration of H. Candace Gorman ¶18, Appendix to Plaintiffs' Memorandum in Opposition to Defendants' Partial Motion for Summary Judgment Regarding the *Glomar* Response, *Wilner v. National Security Agency*, Civil Action No. 07-CIV-3883 (DLC) (S.D.N.Y. May 6, 2008).

76. Ibid., ¶21.

77. E-mail from Candace Gorman to the author, May 28, 2008.

78. Declaration of J. Wells Dixon ¶22, Appendix to Plaintiffs' Memorandum in Opposition to Defendants' Partial Motion for Summary Judgment Regarding the *Glomar* Response, *Wilner v. National Security Agency*, Civil Action No. 07-CIV-3883 (DLC) (S.D.N.Y. May 6, 2008).

79. Declaration of Thomas B. Wilner ¶5, Appendix to Plaintiffs' Memorandum in Opposition to Defendants' Partial Motion for Summary Judgment Regarding the *Glomar* Response, *Wilner v. National Security Agency*, Civil Action No. 07-CIV-3883 (DLC) (S.D.N.Y. May 6, 2008).

80. Ibid., ¶6.

81. This response is known as a Glomar response, because it refers to a request for records pertaining to a ship, the *Hughes Glomar Explorer*. See *Phillippi v. C.I.A.*, 546 F. 2d 1009 (D.C. Cir. 1976).

82. Memorandum in Support of Defendants' Partial Motion for Summary Judgment Regarding the Glomar Response at 2–3, *Wilner v. National Security Agency*, 1:07-cv-3883-DLC (S.D.N.Y. Mar. 18, 2008).

83. Ibid., 19, 20.

84. William Glaberson, "Many Detainees at Guantanamo Rebuff Lawyers," *New York Times*, May 5, 2007, A1.

85. Emergency Motion for Rule to Show Cause and Other Relief, *Abdul Al-Ghizzawi v. Bush*, Civil Action No. 05-cv-02378 (D.D.C. Sept. 12, 2007), at 2.

86. Judge Leon in deciding *Khalid v. Bush*, 355 F. Supp. 2d 311 (D.C. 2005).

87. Judge Joyce Hens Green in deciding *In re Guantanamo Detainee Cases*, 355 F. Supp. 2d 443 (D.C. 2005).

88. *Detainee Treatment Act* of 2005, Pub. L. No. 109-148, §§ 1001–1006 (2005).

89. The act prohibits cruel, inhuman, and degrading treatment of the detainees that violates the Fifth, Eighth, and Fourteenth Amendments. Pub. L. No. 109-148, § 1003. See also § 1002, which requires the Department of Defense to apply the *Army Field Manual* for the standards and procedures of interrogations.

90. Pub. L. No. 109-148, Section 1004, provides a defense where the defendant did not know that the practices were unlawful and a person of ordinary sense and understanding would also not know. Good faith reliance on advice of counsel supports the defendant's position. In addition, although the provision was written to ensure that persons in U.S. control or custody, whether within the United States or abroad, cannot be subjected to cruel, inhuman,

and degrading treatment, the act seems to exempt the situation where the CIA transfers people to other countries where they would be tortured—as long as the detainees were no longer in United States custody or control.

91. President's Statement on Signing of H.R. 2863, the Department of Defense, Emergency Supplemental Appropriations to Address Hurricanes in the Gulf of Mexico, and Pandemic Influenza Act, 2006. See also Michael Abramowitz, "Bush's Tactic of Refusing Laws Is Probed," *Washington Post,* July 24, 2006, A5.

92. Section 1005(e) of the act amended Title 28 Section 2241.

93. Section 1005(e)(2).

94. *Swain v. Pressley,* 430 U.S. 372 (1977).

95. Pub. L. No. 109-148, § 1005.

PART THREE, SECTION IV

1. *Hamdan v. Rumsfeld,* 548 U.S. 557 (2006). Newly appointed Supreme Court justice John Roberts had been one of the three members of the Court of Appeals for the District of Columbia Circuit that had decided against Hamdan. Consequently, he recused himself from ruling on the *Hamdan* case in the Supreme Court.

2. On Petition for Writ of Certiorari and Writ of Certiorari Before Judgment to the United States Court of Appeals For the District of Columbia Circuit at n.1, *Hamdan v. Gates,* No. 07–5042 (D.C. Cir. July 2, 2007).

3. The Court noted that the "law of war" was included in the UCMJ discussion of military commissions. 10 U.S.C. § 821 (2006).

4. CA3 reads, "In the case of armed conflict not of an international character occurring in the territory of one of the High Contracting Parties, each Party to the conflict shall be bound to apply, as a minimum," certain provisions.

5. Section 1(d) prohibits "the passing of sentences and the carrying out of executions without previous judgment pronounced by a regularly constituted court affording all the judicial guarantees which are recognized as indispensable by civilized peoples." Geneva Convention Relative to the Treatment of Prisoners of War, Aug. 12, 1949, art. 3(1)(d) 6 U.S.T. 3316, 75 U.N.T.S. 135.

6. Military Commissions Act of 2006, Pub. L. No. 109–366, 120 Stat. 2600 (2006).

7. Ibid., § 7(b).

8. 10 U.S.C.A 950g(b) (West 2006). The review would only be on matters of law and not of facts. Thus the detainee could challenge the MCA procedures or, to the extent applicable, inconsistencies between MCA procedures and the Constitution and laws of the United States.

9. *Hamdan v. Rumsfeld,* 126 S.Ct. 2749 (2006).

10. 18 U.S.C.A. § 2441(b) (West 1997).

11. *Id.* § 2441(C)(1)(3). The Military Commissions Act of 2006 amended the War Crimes Act to define grave breaches under Common Article 3 (Common Article 3 in the Geneva Conventions does not define grave breaches) and to give it retroactive applicability to November 26, 1997. Military Commissions Act of 2006, Pub. L. No. 109–366, § 6, 120 Stat. 2600 (2006). The MCA also

gives the president the authority to interpret the meaning and application of the Geneva Conventions and provides that the president is the final interpreter of nongrave breaches under Common Article 3. Ibid., § 6(a)(3)(A)(C).

12. Ibid., § 2441(a).

13. *Military Commissions Act of 2006*, Pub. L. No. 109–366, §§ 6(b)(2), 6(c), 120 Stat. 2600 (2006).

14. There was another aspect to the MCA that affected detainees held outside Guantanamo. Since the administration was never required to provide detainees held outside Guantanamo a CSRT hearing or a hearing before a military commission, the MCA seemed to allow the government to deny all access to federal courts to aliens held outside Guantanamo. That is, even the Court of Appeals for the District of Columbia Circuit was off limits to alien detainees held outside Guantanamo.

In addition, the MCA barred anyone from raising the Geneva Conventions in any habeas or other civil proceeding in which the United States was a party. Ibid., § 5. Presumably, this provision, which has not been tested in court, includes habeas actions brought by American citizens. In addition, the MCA seems to permit the president to declare an American citizen an enemy combatant and detain him.

15. U.S. Constitution, art. I, § 9.

16. *Boumediene v. Bush,* 476 F.3d 981, 992 (D.C. Cir. 2007).

17.. Annual Review Board Submission on behalf of Lakhdar Boumediene by his Attorneys Stephen H. Oleskey, Robert C. Kirsch, Douglas Curtis, and Melissa A. Hoffer, March 31, 2005; *Khalid v. Bush,* 355 F. Supp. 2d 311, 316 (D.D.C. 2005).

18. Respondents' Memorandum Addressing the Definition of Enemy Combatant at 2, *Boumediene v. Bush,* Civil Action No. 04-CV-1166 (RJL) (D.D.C. Oct.22, 2008).

19. *Boumediene v. Bush,* Justice Breyer dissenting from the denial of certiorari, 127 S. Ct. 1478, 1480 (2007).

20. Ibid.

21. See *Hickman v. Taylor,* 329 U.S. 495 (1947).

22. Brief for Petitioners El-Banna et al. at 9, *Al Odah v. United States,* No. 06–1196 (Aug. 24, 2007).

23. *Bismullah v. Gates,* 501 F. 3d 178, 180 (D.C. Cir. 2007).

24. *Bismullah v. Gates,* 503 F. 3d 137, 142 (D.C. Cir. 2007).

25. *Bismullah v. Gates,* 514 F. 3d 1291 (D.C. Cir. 2008).

26. After its decision in *Boumediene,* the Supreme Court instructed the D.C. Circuit Court to reconsider its ruling in light of the Supreme Court decision. *Boumediene v. Bush,* 128 S. Ct. 2229 (2008).

27. U.S. Dep't of Defense, *Manual for Military Commissions,* pt. I, Preamble (g), citing to 10 U.S.C. § 948r (c).

28. Ibid., citing to 10 U.S.C. § 948r (d) (3).

29. "American Justice on Trial as Hicks Has Day in Court," *The Age,* available at http://www.theage.com.au/news/world/american-justice-on-trial-as-hi cks-has-has-day-in-court/2007/03/30/1174761752068.html?page=2.

30. Raymond Bonner, "Aftereffects: Detainees: A Drifter's Odyssey from

the Outback to Guantanamo," *New York Times*, May 4, 2003; Tom Alllard, "Prisoner of Political Fortune Set Free," *Sydney Morning Herald*, Dec. 29, 2007, available at http://www.smh.com.au/news/national/prisoner-of-politi cal-fortune-set-free/2007/12/28/1198778703367.html?page=fullpage#content Swap1.

31. *The David Hicks Affidavit*, Dec. 10, 2004, available at http://www .smh.com.au/news/World/David-Hicks-affidavit/2004/12/10/1102625527396 .html.

32. A copy of the plea agreement is available at http://www.defenselink .mil/news/Mar2007/US%20v%20David%20Hicks%20ROT%20(Redacted) .pdf, at 513–19.

33. U.S. Dep't of Defense, *Manual for Military Commissions*, pt. IV, Section 950v(25) (2007); *Military Commissions Act of October 2006*, 10 U.S.C.A. § 950v (West 2007).

34. 10 U.S.C.A. § 950p(a) (West 2007).

35. Ibid. The crimes of providing military support or resources to terrorists had been federal crimes under 18 U.S.C.A. Sections 2339(a) and 2339(b) (West 2000) prior to Hicks's arrest, although providing material support to terrorists had not been designated a war crime under federal law, 18 U.S.C.A. § 2441 (West 2000).

36. "Hicks Trial 'Could Be Derailed,'" *Herald Sun (Victoria)*, Mar. 5, 2007, available at http://www.news.com.au/heraldsun/story/0,21985,21325742–50 05961,00.html#.

37. Carol Raabus & Louise Saunders, "Major Michael Mori Humbly Accepts Award in Hobart," *Australian Broadcasting Corporation*, Oct. 12, 2007, available at http://www.abc.net.au/tasmania/stories/s2058328.htm?backyard.

38. Ibid.

39. Josh White, "Ex-Prosecutor Alleges Pentagon Plays Politics," *Washington Post*, Oct. 20, 2007, A03. Since then, several other prosecutors have quit, the most recent being Darrel J. Vandeveld in October 2008. Josh Meyer, "Guantanamo Prosecutor Who Quit Had 'Grave Misgivings' about Fairness," *Los Angeles Times*, Oct. 12, 2008.

40. Morris D. Davis, "The Guantanamo I Know," *New York Times*, June 26, 2007, A21.

41. William Glaberson, "Former Prosecutor to Testify for Detainee," *New York Times*, Feb. 28, 2008.

42. Raabus & Saunders, "Major Michael Mori Humbly Accepts Award in Hobart."

43. Raymond Bonner, "Australia Terrorism Detainee Leaves Prison," *New York Times*, Dec. 29, 2007, A7.

44. The following facts are taken from the Charge Sheet, *United States of America v. Omar Ahmed Khadr* (Feb. 2, 2007). These facts have been largely confirmed, although with some variations in dates and locations, by other sources, including those noted below.

45. Government's Summary of Evidence for Combatant Status Review Tribunal, Aug. 31, 2004, DOD, Review of CSRT, Sept. 10, 2004. The government refers to Omar Khadr by his initials, "O.K.," in this document.

46. "The Khadr Family," *CBC News Online*, Oct. 30, 2006, available at http://www.cbc.ca/news/background/khadr/.

47. "Son of al Qaeda: Inside the Khadr Family—Chronology," *Frontline*, PBS, available at http://www.pbs.org/wgbh/pages/frontline/shows/khadr/family/cron.html.

48. William Glaberson, "A Legal Debate in Guantanamo on Boy Fighters," *New York Times*, June 3, 2007, 1.

49. "The Khadr Family," *CBC News Online;* "Son of al Qaeda: Inside the Khadr Family—Chronology," *Frontline*, PBS, available at http://www.pbs.org/wgbh/pages/frontline/shows/khadr/family/cron.html.

50. Criminal Investigation Task Force (CITF) Report of Investigative Activity, Activity Number 12000040860902, Mar. 17, 2004, 2, available from the *Miami Herald* and on file with author.

51. Ibid.

52. Omar el Akkad, "Doubt Cast on Allegations against Omar Khadr," *Toronto Globe and Mail*, Feb. 4, 2008.

53. Criminal Investigation Task Force (CITF) Report of Investigative Activity, Activity Number 12000040860902, Mar. 17, 2004, 3, available from the *Miami Herald* and on file with author.

54. Ibid., 2.

55. Carol J. Williams, "Pentagon Accused of Doctoring Guantanamo Tribunal Evidence," *Los Angeles Times*, Mar. 14, 2008.

56. This paragraph is based on a conversation with Khadr's Canadian attorney, Dennis Edney, and on Edney's presentation to law students at the University of San Francisco, Sept. 10, 2008.

57. Charge Sheet, *United States v. Khadr*, Marvin W. Tubbs II, accuser, Apr. 5, 2007.

58. Optional Protocol to the Convention on the Rights of the Child on the Involvement of Children in Armed Conflict, G.A. Res. 54/263, U.N. Doc. A/RES/54/263 (May 25, 2000), entered into force February 12, 2002, with the United Nations on December 23, 2002, available at http://www2.ohchr.org/English/law/crc-conflict.htm; Defense Motion for Dismissal Due to Lack of Jurisdiction under the MCA in Regard to Juvenile Crimes of a Child Soldier, *United States of America v. Omar Ahmed Khadr* (Jan. 18, 2008).

59. See preamble, available at http://www2.ohchr.org/English/law/crc-conflict.htm.

60. Optional Protocol to the Convention on the Rights of the Child on the Involvement of Children in Armed Conflict, art. 7, G.A. Res. 54/263, U.N. Doc. A/RES/54/263 (May 25, 2000).

61. Defense Motion for Dismissal Due to Lack of Jurisdiction under the MCA in Regard to Juvenile Crimes of a Child Soldier, 2, *United States of America v. Omar Ahmed Khadr* (Jan. 18, 2008).

62. Ibid., 11–12.

63. Omar el Akkad, "Doubt Cast on Allegations against Omar Khadr," *Toronto Globe and Mail*, Feb. 4, 2008, 2.

64. Convention on the Rights of the Child, art. 1, 28 I.L.M 1448 (1989).

65. Optional Protocol, preamble, available at http://www2.ohchr.org/Eng lish/law/crc-conflict.htm.

66. Convention on the Rights of the Child, art. 38 (2), 28 I.L.M 1448 (1989).

67. Ibid., art. 37 (a).

68. Ibid., art. 37 (b).

69. Ibid.

70. Interviews were in February and September 2003, conducted by the Canadian Security Intelligence Service (CSIS). Dennis Edney & Nathan J. Whitling, Final Factum filed with the Canadian Supreme Court dealing with the extraterritorial effect of the Canadian Charter of Rights, Feb. 14, 2008, 8–9.

71. Convention on the Rights of the Child, art. 39, 28 I.L.M 1448 (1989).

72. International Committee of the Red Cross Operational Update, "Guantanamo Bay: Overview of the ICRC's Work for Internees," Jan. 30, 2004, available at http://www.icrc.org/Web/Eng/siteengo.nsf/iwpList74/951C74F20 D2A2148C1256D8D002CA8DC.

73. Petitioner's Emergency Motion to Compel the Government to Allow an Independent Medical Evaluation and to Produce Medical Records and Memorandum of Points and Authorities in Support of the Motion, *O.K. v. George W. Bush,* Case No. 1:04-CV-01136 (JDB) (D.C. Cir., Aug. 10, 2004); Dennis Edney, talk at University of San Francisco Law School, Sept. 10, 2008.

74. Military Judge Colonel Peter E. Brownback's decision, which preceded the *Hamdan* decision, was *sua sponte.* Khadr's lawyer had not raised this issue. A copy of the ruling is available on Scotusblog, http://www.scotusblog .com/wp/?s=khadr+ruling%2C+June+4%2C+2007.

75. Although it may appear that the government, by having adopted the MCA legislation, had moved closer to the actual terms used in the GC, *lawful combatant* and *unlawful combatant,* it is not really so. The MCA definitions for *lawful enemy combatant* and *unlawful enemy combatant* are not identical to the GC definitions of *lawful combatant* and *unlawful combatant.* Anything different must be different for a reason. *Lawful enemy combatant* and *unlawful enemy combatant* are weasel terms created by Congress and the administration to create a new concept that avoids application of the GC.

76. Khadr's attorneys then appealed the Court of Military Commission Review decision to the Circuit Court for the District of Columbia. On June 20, 2008, the circuit court ruled that it did not have jurisdiction on the matter. It stated that the court only has the authority to review a "final judgment." (*Khadr v. United States,* No. 07–1405, 2008 WL 2468496, D.C. Cir. June 20, 2008.) However, under the procedures laid out in the MCA, the conviction would first have to be reviewed and upheld by a military appeals court before proceeding to the D.C. Court of Appeals.

77. Umar Khadr: a meeting with, J. Gould/995-0750, Department of Foreign Affairs and International Trade, Number ISI-034, Apr. 20, 2004. The document is signed by R. Scott Heatherington, Director, Foreign Intelligence Division.

78. Ibid., 1.

79. Ibid., 4–5.

80. Ibid., 5.

81. Ibid.

82. Air Force Office of Special Investigations Report of Investigative Activity, Activity number 00444030552023, Feb. 24, 2003, 1. The statements in the text are from pages 1 and 3 of this report.

83. On May 29, 2008, the military judge in charge of Khadr's case, Army Col. Peter Brownback, was replaced by a new judge. No explanation was given. Before he was removed, Brownback had pressured the prosecution to provide key evidence to defense lawyers, threatening to suspend the case if the prosecution did not comply. "Guantanamo Judge Dismissed in Canadian's Case," *Reuters*, May 29, 2008, available at http://www.reuters.com/article/latestCrisis/idUSNASU52902.

84. *Juveniles in Guantanamo* (May 2, 2006), Reprieve Research Project (on file with author).

85. Ibid.

86. Jo Becker, "The War on Teen Terror," *Salon.com*, June 24, 2008, available at http://www.salon.com/news/feature/2008/06/24/juveniles_at_gitmo/.

87. Umar Khadr: a meeting with, J. Gould/995-0750, Department of Foreign Affairs and International Trade, Number ISI-034, Apr. 20, 2004. The document is signed by R. Scott Heatherington, Director, Foreign Intelligence Division.

88. Ibid.; Carol Rosenberg, "Afghan Tells of Sleep Deprivation," *Miami Herald*, June 20, 2008, available at http://www.miamiherald.com/news/nation/story/576870.html. Also see Amnesty International, "USA/Canada: Omar Khadr Is 'Salvageable,' Military Commissions Are Not," June 5, 2008, AI Index: AMR51/055/2008.

89. "The Kids of Guantanamo Bay," *Cageprisoners*, June 15, 2005, available at http://cageprisoners.com/articles.php?id=7880; "Transfer of Juvenile Detainees Completed," Department of Defense, Jan. 29, 2004, available at http://www.defenselink.mil/releases/release.aspx?releaseid=7041.

90. Decision and Order—Motion to Dismiss for Lack of Jurisdiction, *U.S. v. Hamdan* (June 4, 2007).

91. Opinion of the Court and Action on Appeal by the United States Filed Pursuant to 10 U.S.C. § 950d, *U.S. v. Khadr*, CMCR 07–001 (USCMCR, Sept. 24, 2007); Decision on Motion to Reconsider Dismissal of Charges for Lack of Jurisdiction, *U.S. v. Hamdan* (Oct. 17, 2007); Posting of Lyle Denniston to Scotusblog, http://www.scotusblog.com/wp/hamdan-trial-to-go-forward/ (Oct. 18, 2007, 11:09 EST).

92. Ruling on Defense Motion for Article 5 Status Determination, *U.S. v. Hamdan* (Dec. 17, 2007), available at http://www.scotusblog.com/wp/uncategorized/potential-new-obstacle-to-hamdan-trial/.

93. On Reconsideration Ruling on Motion to Dismiss for Lack of Jurisdiction, *U.S. v. Hamdan* (Dec. 19, 2007), available at http:// www.scotusblog.com/wp/uncategorized/military-judge-hamdan-may-be-tried/.

94. Geneva Convention Relative to the Treatment of Prisoners of War, art. 102, Aug. 12, 1949, 6 U.S.T. 3316.

95. Michael Melia, "Confusion Clouds Guantanamo Tribunals," *Washington Post*, Feb. 6, 2008.

96. Declaration of Daryl Matthews, M.D., Ph.D., at 3, *Swift v. Rumsfeld*, 04-CV-00777-DECL (W.D. Wash. Mar. 31, 2004).

97. Ruling on Motion to Compel Access to High Value Detainees, D 011, *U.S. v. Hamdan* (Feb. 13, 2008).

98. Carol Rosenberg, "Judge Lets Driver's Lawyers Question 'KSM,'" *Miami Herald*, Feb. 14, 2008.

99. William Glaberson, "Ex-Guantanamo Prosecutor to Testify for Detainee," *New York Times,* Feb. 28, 2008, A18; William Glaberson, "Ex-Prosecutor Tells of Push by Pentagon on Detainees," *New York Times,* Apr. 29, 2008, A12; Josh White, "From Chief Prosecutor to Critic at Guantanamo," *Washington Post,* Apr. 29, 2008, A01.

100. Glaberson, "Ex-Prosecutor Tells of Push by Pentagon on Detainees," A12.

101. White, "From Chief Prosecutor to Critic at Guantanamo," A01.

102. Charge Sheet, *United States v. Hamdan,* Marvin W. Tubbs II, accuser, Apr. 5, 2007, available at http://www.defenselink.mil/news/May2007/Hamdan_Charges.pdf.

103. William Glaberson, "Bin Laden Driver Sentenced to a Short Term," *New York Times*, August 8, 2008.

104. Mike Melia, "Gitmo Prosecutors Seek Resentencing for Detainee," *Miami Herald*, September 25, 2008.

105. Ruling on Motion for Reconsideration and Sentencing, *United States v. Hamdan,* Oct. 29, 2008, P-009.

106. William Glaberson, "U.S. Charges 6 for Roles in 9/11 Attacks," *New York Times,* Feb. 12, 2008; Sgt. Sara Moore, "Defense Department Seeks Death Penalty for Six Guantanamo Detainees," *American Forces Press Service,* Feb. 11, 2008; Charge Sheet, Criminal Investigation Task Force, Laura DeJong, accuser, Feb. 11, 2008.

107. Charge Sheet, Criminal Investigation Task Force, Laura DeJong, accuser, Feb. 11, 2008. The charges fall under various subsections of 10 U.S.C. Section 950v(b).

108. William Glaberson, "Case against 9/11 Detainee Is Dismissed," *New York Times,* May 14, 2008, A19.

109. Josh White, Dan Eggen & Joby Warrick, "U.S. to Try 6 on Capital Charges Over 9/11 Attacks," *Washington Post,* Feb. 12, 2008, A1.

110. 10 U.S.C. § 948r(c).

111. 10 U.S.C. § 948r(d).

112. *Boumediene v. Bush,* 128 S. Ct. 2229 (2008).

113. *Boumediene v. Bush,* No. 06-1195, slip op. at 5 (U.S. June 12, 2008).

114. *Military Commissions Act of 2006,* Pub. L. No. 10-366, § 7, 120 Stat. 2600 (2006).

115. *Boumediene v. Bush,* No. 06-1195, slip op. at 37 (U.S. June 12, 2008).

116. *Boumediene v. Bush,* No. 06-1195, slip op. at 7 (U.S. June 12, 2008).

117. There are two parts to Section 7 of the MCA, 28 USC 2241(e). The first part denies federal courts jurisdiction to hear habeas actions filed by the

detainees. The second part denies federal courts jurisdiction to hear cases regarding the treatment, conditions of confinement, and transfer of the detainees. Justice Kennedy struck down Section 7, ruling that it is unconstitutional. A disagreement between the government and the habeas attorneys has resulted as to whether Kennedy meant to strike down the second part of the section, since that part was not before the Court for its consideration. Kennedy did not distinguish between parts (1) and (2) in striking down Section 7. *Military Commissions Act of 2006*, Public Law 109–366, § 7(a), 120 Stat. 2600, 2635–36 (2006) (codified as amended at 28 U.S.C.A. § 2241[e]).

118. *Boumediene v. Bush,* No. 06-1195, slip op. at 82 (U.S. June 12, 2008).

119. E-mail from Stephen Abraham to the author, June 15, 2008.

120. *Parhat v. Gates,* No. 06-1397 (D.C. Cir. June 20, 2008).

121. *Parhat v. Gates,* No. 06-1397, 2008 U.S. App. LEXIS 13721, at *40–41 (D.C. Cir. June 20, 2008).

122. Ibid., *41.

123. Ibid., *42.

124. Tim Golden, "Chinese Leave Guantanamo for Albanian Limbo," *New York Times,* June 10, 2007, 1.

125. Telephone conversation between J. Wells Dixon and the author (Dec. 12, 2007).

126. Memorandum Opinion, *In re Guantanamo Bay Detainee Litigation,* Misc. No. 08-0442 (TFH) (U.S. D.C. Oct. 8, 2008).

127. Order, *Kiyemba v. Bush,* No. 08-5424 (D.C. Cir. Oct. 8, 2008).

PART FOUR

Epigraph source: Unnamed official quoted in Dana Priest & Barton Gellman, "U.S. Decries Abuse but Defends Interrogations: 'Stress and Duress' Tactics Used on Terrorism Suspects Held in Secret Overseas Facilities," *Washington Post,* Dec. 26, 2002, A1.

1. Chalmers Johnson, *Nemesis* (Metropolitan Books, 2007), 121–22; John Walcott & Andy Pasztor, "Covert Action: Reagan Ruling to Let CIA Kidnap Terrorists Overseas Is Disclosed," *Wall Street Journal,* Feb. 20, 1987.

2. Jane Mayer, "Outsourcing Torture: The Secret History of America's 'Extraordinary Rendition' Program," *New Yorker,* Feb. 14, 2005.

3. Ibid.

4. Dana Priest, "CIA's Assurances on Transferred Suspects Doubted; Prisoners Say Countries Break No-Torture Pledges," *Washington Post,* Mar. 17, 2005, A1; Human Rights Watch, "Getting Away with Torture? Command Responsibility for the U.S. Abuse of Detainees," *Human Rights Watch* 17, no. 1 (Apr. 2005): 58, available at http://www.hrw.org/reports/2005/us0405/us0405.pdf; Douglas Jehl and David Johnston, "Rule Change Lets C.I.A. Freely Send Suspects Abroad to Jails," *New York Times,* Mar. 6, 2005.

5. Jane Mayer, "Outsourcing Torture: The Secret History of America's 'Extraordinary Rendition' Program," *New Yorker,* Feb. 14, 2005, 106.

6. Johnson, *Nemesis,* 123.

7. Contrary to earlier statements, the Bush administration admitted in

2008 that it had used this British territory as a refueling stop for CIA flights. Matthew Lee, "US Fears Backlash over Terror Flights," *Washington Post,* Feb. 21, 2008.

8. Dana Priest, "Wrongful Imprisonment: Anatomy of a CIA Mistake; German Citizen Released after Months in 'Rendition,'" *Washington Post,* Dec. 4, 2005, A1. See Council of Europe, "'High-Value' Detainees Were Held in Secret CIA Detention Centres in Poland and Romania, Says PACE Committee," press release, June 8, 2007; Committee on Legal Affairs and Human Rights of the Council of Europe Parliamentary Assembly, Dick Marty, "Secret Detentions and Illegal Transfers of Detainees Involving Council of Europe Member States: Second Report," June 11, 2007.

9. Jan Sliva, "Probe of CIA Prisons Implicates EU Nations," *Washington Post* (Associated Press), June 7, 2006.

10. Sixth Declaration of Marilyn A. Dorn, *Am. Civil Liberties Union v. Dep't of Def.,* 04 Civ. 4151 (AKH), at ¶66, available at http://www.aclu.org/pdfs/safefree/20070110/cia_dorn_declaration_items_1_29_61.pdf; David Johnston, "At a Secret Interrogation, Dispute Flared over Tactics," *New York Times,* Sept. 10, 2006, 1.

11. Gerard Seenan & Giles Tremlett, "Rendition: How Planespotters Turned into the Scourge of the CIA," *Guardian* (London), Dec. 10, 2005, 9.

12. Ibid.

13. See Johnson, *Nemesis,* 125–28.

14. Elisabeth Bumiller, David E. Sanger, & Richard W. Stevenson, "Bush Says Iraqis Will Want G.I.s to Stay to Help," *New York Times,* Jan. 28, 2005. See also White House, "President's Press Conference," Mar. 16, 2005, and Apr. 28, 2005, available at http://www.whitehouse.gov/news/releases/2005/03/200503 16-3.html and http://www.whitehouse.gov/news/releases/2005/04/print/200504 28-9.html; Secretary Condoleezza Rice, "Remarks en Route to Germany," Dec. 5, 2005, available at http://www.state.gov/secretary/rm/2005/57643.htm; Attorney General Alberto Gonzales, "Prepared Remarks by Attorney General Alberto R. Gonzales at the International Institute for Strategic Studies," Mar. 7, 2006, available at http://www.usdoj.gov/ag/speeches/2006/ag_speech_060307.html.

15. Margaret L. Satterthwaite, "Rendered Meaningless: Extraordinary Rendition and the Rule of Law," N.Y.U Pub. Law and Legal Theory Res. Paper Series 44, No. 06–36 (Nov. 2006), available at http://papers.ssrn.com/sol3/papers.cfm?abstract_id=94571. For a comprehensive analysis of the practice of extraordinary rendition, see Ms. Satterthwaite's article.

16. Sheryl Gay Stolberg, "President Moves 14 Held in Secret to Guantanamo," *New York Times,* Sep. 7, 2006.

17. White House, Office of the Press Secretary, "President Discusses Creation of Military Commissions to Try Suspected Terrorists," Sept. 6, 2006, http://www.whitehouse.gov/news/releases/2006/09/20060906-3.html.

18. Jane Mayer, "The Black Sites: A Rare Look inside the C.I.A.'s Secret Interrogation Program," *New Yorker,* Aug. 13, 2007, available at http://www.newyorker.com/reporting/2007/08/13/070813fa_fact_mayer?printable=true.

19. Lawrence Wright, "The Spymaster: The New Director of National Intelligence Has a Controversial Plan to Tighten National Security," *New Yorker,* Jan. 21, 2008, 53.

20. Brian Ross and Richard Espositor, *ABC News,* Nov. 18, 2005.

21. Dan Eggen, "Justice Official Defends Rough CIA Interrogations," *Washington Post,* Feb. 17, 2008, A03.

22. Marty Lederman, "Lowering the Bar," *Balkinization,* Feb. 14, 2008, available at http://balkin.blogspot.com/2008/02/lowering-bar-well-at-least-we re-not-as.html. Lederman cites an e-mail from Darius Rajali, in which Rajali describes the various "water cures," and a personal account by "Scylla" on using saran wrap.

23. Paul Kramer, "The Water Cure," *New Yorker,* Feb. 25, 2008, 38.

24. Eric Weiner, "Waterboarding: A Tortured History," *NPR,* Nov. 3, 2007, http://www.npr.org/templates/story/story.php?storyId=16012903.

25. Lawrence Wright, "The Spymaster: The New Director of National Intelligence Has a Controversial Plan to Tighten National Security," *New Yorker,* Jan. 21, 2008, 53.

26. Ibid.

27. Greg Miller, "Three Were Waterboarded, CIA Chief Confirms," *Los Angeles Times,* Feb. 6, 2008.

28. Brian Ross and Richard Esposito, *ABC News,* Nov. 18, 2005.

29. Brian Ross, "CIA—Abu Zubaydah," interview with John Kiriakou, *ABC News,* 1:16, available at http://abcnews.go.com/images/Blotter/brianross _kiriakou_transcript1_blotter071210.pdf, attached to article by Richard Esposito & Brian Ross, "Coming In from the Cold: CIA Spy Calls Waterboarding Necessary but Torture," *ABC News,* Dec. 10, 2007, available at http://abcnews.go.com/print?id=3978231.

30. Ross, "CIA—Abu Zabaydah," 17.

31. Letter from Michael B. Mukasey, Attorney General, to Patrick J. Leahy, Senate Judiciary Chairman, Jan. 29, 2008.

32. Philip Shenon, "Mukasey Will Not Rule Out Waterboarding," *New York Times,* Jan. 31, 2008, A26.

33. Greg Miller, "Waterboarding Is Still an Option: The White House Calls the Technique Legal, Stunning Critics," *Los Angeles Times,* Feb. 7, 2008, A1.

34. Steven Lee Myers, "Veto of Bill on C.I.A. Tactics Affirms Bush Legacy," *New York Times,* Mar. 9, 2008, A1.

35. Human Rights Watch, *Off the Record: U.S. Responsibility for Enforced Disappearances in the "War on Terror,"* June 2007. The six human rights groups are Amnesty International, Human Rights Watch, Center for Constitutional Rights, Center for Human Rights and Global Justice, Reprieve, and Cageprisoners. Ibid., 19. See also Olga Craig, "CIA Holds Young Sons of Captured al-Qa'eda Chief," *Sunday Telegraph* (UK), Mar. 9, 2003, available at http://www.telegraph.co.uk/news/worldnews/asia/afghanistan/1424123/ CIA-holds-young-sons-of-captured-al-Qaeda-chief.html.

36. Letter from Paul Wolfowitz, Deputy Secretary of Defense, to James B. Comey, Deputy Attorney General, May 28, 2004 (on file with author).

37. Amended Petition for Relief under the Detainee Treatment Act of

2005, and, in the Alternative, for Writ of Habeas Corpus at 4, *Zayn Al Abidin Muhammad Husayn v. Gates,* No. 07–1520 (D.C. Cir. Feb. 21, 2008).

38. Dafna Linzer, "CIA Held Al-Qaeda Suspect Secretly," *Washington Post,* Apr. 28, 2007, A16.

39. Ibid.

40. El-Masri's story is largely taken from the Complaint, *El-Masri v. Tenet,* 437 F. Supp. 2d 530, No. 1:05cv1417 (E.D. Va. 2006).

41. Scott Shane, "C.I.A. Expanding Terror Battle under Guise of Charter Flights," *New York Times,* May 31, 2005, 1.

42. Ibid.

43. *El-Masri v. United States,* 479 F.3d 296 (4th Cir. 2007).

44. *United States v. Reynolds,* 345 U.S. 1 (1953).

45. *El-Masri v. United States,* 479 F.3d 296, 302 (4th Cir. 2007).

46. Certiorari was denied on October 9, 2007. *El-Masri v. United States,* 128 S. Ct. 373 (2007).

47. Patrick Radden Keefe, "State Secrets: A Government Misstep in a Wire-tapping Case," *New Yorker,* Apr. 28, 2008, 31–32.

48. Craig Whitlock, "Travel Logs Aid Germans' Kidnap Probe," *Washington Post,* Feb. 2, 2007, A11.

49. Craig Whitlock, "Germans Drop Bid for Extraditions in CIA Case," *Washington Post,* Sept. 24, 2007, A9.

50. "No Justice for El-Masri, Germany Drops Pursuit of CIA Kidnappers," *Spiegel Online,* Sept. 24, 2007, available at http://www.spiegel.de/international/germany/0,1518,507455,00.html.

51. See *Arar v. Ashcroft,* 414 F. Supp 2d 250 (E.D.N.Y 2006). The information regarding Arar's detention is taken from this case and from the Canadian official Commission of Inquiry report cited in the following note.

52. Commission of Inquiry into the Actions of Canadian Officials in Relation to Maher Arar, *Report of the Events Relating to Maher Arar, Factual Background, Volume I* (Sept. 2006), 52–53.

53. Ibid. See page 51 of the report for reference to Almalki. Almalki, like Arar, had been born in Syria and immigrated to Canada. He was accused of selling electronic equipment to Islamic insurgents in Afghanistan and working for a charitable organization run by Omar Khadr's father, Ahmad Said Khadr. Jim Brown, "Inquiry into Torture of Three Canadians Finally Set to Roll," *Macleans,* Mar. 18, 2007, 2, available at http://www.macleans.ca/article.jsp?content=n031808A. When visiting Syria in 2002, Almalki was detained for twenty-two months and tortured, then released without charges. Comm. of Orgs. with Intervenor Status at the Arar Inquiry (Amnesty International Canada), *Backgrounder: The pattern surrounding Maher Arar's case* (Sept. 14, 2006), p. 1. Almalki's lawyer accused Canadian officials of providing questions to Syrian interrogators. "'Canada Cannot Afford to Isolate Itself,' Torture Inquiry Hears," *CBC News,* Jan. 8, 2008, available at http://www.cbc.ca/canada/story/2008/01/08/iacobucci-inquiry.html.

54. Commission of Inquiry into the Actions of Canadian Officials in Relation to Maher Arar, *Report of the Events Relating to Maher Arar, Factual Background, Volume I* (Sept. 2006), 189, 199, 200.

55. Ibid., 171, 174.

56. *Arar v. Ashcroft,* 414 F. Supp. 2d 250 (E.D.N.Y 2006).

57. Ibid., 255.

58. *Arar v. Ashcroft,* No. 06–4216-cv, 2008 WL 2574470 (2d Cir. June 30, 2008).

59. Maggie Farley, "Canada to Compensate Torture Victim," *Los Angeles Times,* Jan. 27, 2007, 3.

60. Ibid.

61. Osama Moustafa Hassan Nasr, "This Is How They Kidnapped Me from Italy," *Chicago Tribune,* Jan. 7, 2007, available at http://www.chicagotribune .com/news/nationworld/chi-cialetter-story,1,2033270.story; see also Matthias Gebauer, "Freed CIA Prisoner Renders His Version of the Truth," *Salon.com,* Mar. 20, 2007, available at http://www.salon.com/news/feature/2007/03/20/ rendition/print.html (article provided by *Der Spiegel*).

62. Craig Whitlock, "Testimony Helps Detail CIA's Post-9/11 Reach," *Washington Post,* Dec. 16, 2006, A1.

63. Tracy Wilkinson, "In Italy, Trial of CIA Agents Begins," *Los Angeles Times,* June 9, 2007.

64. "CIA Snatch Trial Resumes," *ANSA English Media Service,* Mar. 19, 2008.

65. Phil Stewart, "Italy Judge Clears Way for CIA 'Rendition' Trial," *Reuters.com,* Mar. 19, 2008, available at http://www.reuters.com/article/topNews/ idUSL1913461200803I9.

66. Jane Mayer, "Outsourcing: The C.I.A.'s Travel Agent," *New Yorker,* Oct. 30, 2006.

67. Order Granting the United States' Motion to Intervene and Granting the United States' Motion to Dismiss with Prejudice at 9, *Mohamed v. Jeppesen Dataplan,* No. C 07–02798 JW (N.D. Cal. Feb. 13, 2008).

68. To date, 145 nations are parties to it and 74 are signatories. Convention against Torture and Other Cruel, Inhuman or Degrading Treatment or Punishment, New York, Dec. 10, 1984, http://www.ohchr.org/english/countries/ ratification/9.htm.

69. *Convention against Torture and Other Cruel, Inhuman or Degrading Treatment or Punishment (CAT),* G.A. Res. 39/46, Annex, 39 U.N. GAOR Supp. No. 51, U.N. Doc. A/39/51, 1465 U.N.T.S. 85, art. 1, ¶1 (Dec. 10, 1984).

70. Ibid., art. 2, ¶2.

71. Ibid., art. 3, ¶1.

72. *Convention against Torture and Other Cruel, Inhuman or Degrading Treatment or Punishment,* Dec. 10, 1984, 1465 U.N.T.S. 85.

73. *CAT,* Article 16, paragraph 1.

74. The most applicable human rights treaty is the International Covenant on Civil and Political Rights (ICCPR). Entered into force, May 1976. *International Covenant on Civil and Political Rights,* Dec. 16, 1966, 999 U.N.T.S. 171. Article 7 of the ICCPR requires that no one be subjected to torture or to cruel, inhuman, or degrading treatment or punishment. A close reading of this treaty, the administration argues, would permit the administration to look the

other way if someone held outside the territory and jurisdiction of the United States were tortured, even if the person had been rendered by the U.S. government to that other country.

75. Enforced disappearance is defined in the convention as the "arrest, detention, abduction or any other form of deprivation of liberty by agents of the State or by persons or groups of persons acting with the authorization, support or acquiescence of the State, followed by a refusal to acknowledge the deprivation of liberty or by concealment of the fate or whereabouts of the disappeared person, which place such a person outside the protection of the law." The treaty provides that no exceptional circumstances, including a state of war or public emergency, may ever justify enforced disappearances. Furthermore, the widespread or systematic practice of enforced disappearance would constitute a crime against humanity.

76. Sean McCormack, Spokesman, U.S. Department of State, Daily Press Briefing, Feb. 6, 2007, http://www.state.gov/r/pa/prs/dpb/2007/80158.htm.

77. Ian Brownlie, *Principles of Public International Law* (Oxford University Press, 2003), 535. See also Jennifer K. Elsea, *U.S. Treatment of Prisoners in Iraq: Selected Legal Issues* (CRS Report for Congress, May 24, 2004) (RL32395) at 8.

78. Brownlie, *Principles of Public International Law,* 488.

79. Ibid., 489–90.

80. *Restatement (Third) of Foreign Relations Law* § 702 (1987). "A State violates international law if, as a matter of state policy, it practices, encourages, or condones . . . (d) torture or other cruel, inhuman, or degrading treatment or punishment." See also Brownlie, *Principles of Public International Law,* 537.

PART FIVE

1. Unpublished manuscript by Frank Lindh.

2. Conversation with Frank Lindh, Sept. 12, 2005.

3. Frank Lindh, presentation to students at the University of San Francisco School of Law, Sept. 24, 2007.

4. Frank Lindh, unpublished manuscript, part 5, p. 14. On file with the author.

5. Jane Mayer, "Lost in the Jihad," *New Yorker,* Mar. 10, 2003, 53.

6. Rohan Gunaratna, cited in ibid., 54.

7. Ibid.

8. *The House of War* (2002), directed by Paul Yule.

9. Transcript of interview with Johnny Spann by Jen Roden, Nov. 19, 2006.

10. Luke Harding, "The Siege of Mazar-i-Sharif," *Granta Magazine* (Winter 2002), 133.

11. Conversation with Frank Lindh, June 15, 2005.

12. Harding, "The Siege of Mazar-i-Sharif," 134.

13. Ibid.

14. Interview by my research assistant, Jenn Roden, with Johnny Spann, Nov. 19, 2006.

15. In 1999, Mike told his father that he was about to undertake a secret mission in Afghanistan. Although Mike did not explicitly disclose that the hunt was for bin Laden, Johnny Spann believes that the purpose of the mission was to kill him. However, when Mike returned, he told his dad that the Clinton administration had called him back before they could successfully complete the mission. Johnny asked his son, "They called you back? Could you not locate him?" Mike replied, "No, we had him under surveillance the whole time." Johnny continued, "And I said, 'Did you all not have the people there to do what you needed to do?' Because I knew it was a small team that went in. And he said, 'No, we had the people, the snipers to get him, and we had the people there to snatch him. We were ready to do what we were told to do.' But, he said, 'the White House called us back.'" Interview by my research assistant, Jenn Roden, with Johnny Spann, Nov. 19, 2006.

16. Tony Bartelme, "Born in Louisiana, Captured in Afghanistan, Jailed in Hanahan Yaser AH: Hamdi Travels Long, Strange Road," *Post and Courier (Charleston, SC),* Mar. 7, 2004, 1A.

17. Conversation with Frank Lindh, Dec. 6, 2005.

18. Conversation with Frank Lindh, Sept. 12, 2005.

19. Conversation with Frank Lindh, June 15, 2005.

20. *Moran v. Burbine,* 475 U.S. 412 (1986).

21. E-mail from George Harris, attorney for John Lindh, July 9, 2008.

22. Memorandum for Record, Subject: Findings and Recommendations Regarding 15–6 Investigation of Photographs Taken of Mr. John Walker Lindh by 5th Special Forces Group (Airborne), Department of the Army, Feb. 3, 2003, at 1. The word *shithead* appears in the sworn statements of many soldiers who were present when the photo was taken. The sworn statements follow the investigation report.

23. Ibid., 5 and 23.

24. Proffer of Facts in Support of Defendant's Suppression Motions, *U.S. v. Lindh,* Crim. No. 02–37-A (E.D. Va. June 13, 2002).

25. Jane Mayer, "Lost in the Jihad," *New Yorker,* Mar. 10, 2003, 53 (quoting George Harris).

26. Conversation with Frank Lindh, Dec. 6, 2005.

27. Frank R. Lindh, "The Crimeless Crime: The Prosecution of John Walker Lindh," *Washington Lawyer,* May 2005, available at http://www.dcbar.org/for_lawyers/washington_lawyer/may_2005/stand.cfm (last visited Aug. 8, 2006).

28. E-mail from George C. Harris, Litigation Partner, Morrison & Foerster LLP, May 24, 2008.

29. Conversation with Frank Lindh, Dec. 6, 2005.

30. E-mail from George C. Harris, Litigation Partner, Morrison & Foerster LLP, May 24, 2008.

31. Ibid.

32. James Brosnahan, Lindh's lead attorney, said that "there was a suggestion that even if we got an acquittal that he could be declared an unlawful [did Brosnahan mean enemy?] combatant." Adam Liptak, "In Terror Cases, Administration Sets Own Rules," *New York Times,* Nov. 27, 2005, 11, avail-

able at LEXIS, News Library, NYT File. Lindh's plea agreement contains a provision that although the government forgoes any right to treat Lindh as an enemy combatant based on conduct alleged in the indictment, if the government determines that he has engaged in certain other proscribed offenses, "the United States may immediately invoke any right it has at that time to capture and detain the defendant as an unlawful enemy combatant based on the conduct alleged in the indictment." Plea Agreement of John Lindh ¶21, *U.S. v. Lindh,* 227 F. Supp. 2d 565 (E.D. Va. 2002) (No. CR. 02–37-A), available at http://www.usdoj.gov/ag/pleaagreement.htm (last visited Aug. 8, 2006).

33. Interview by Jenn Roden with Johnny Spann, Nov. 19, 2006.

34. Richard A. Serrano, "Driven by a Son's Sacrifice," *Los Angeles Times,* Apr. 7, 2005, 1.

35. Frank R. Lindh, "The Crimeless Crime: The Prosecution of John Walker Lindh," *Washington Lawyer,* May 2005, 46.

36. "Supermax: A Clean Version of Hell," *60 Minutes,* Oct. 14, 2007.

37. Michael Isikoff & Mark Hosenball, "Should He Go Free?" *Newsweek,* Apr. 11, 2007.

38. E-mail from Frank Lindh, Apr. 24, 2007.

39. Michael Isikoff & Mark Hosenball, "Should He Go Free?" *Newsweek,* Apr. 11, 2007.

40. Tom Junod, "The State of the American Man: Innocent," *Esquire,* July 1, 2006.

41. Conversation with Frank Lindh, Aug. 16, 2007.

42. Ibid.

43. Presentation to students at the University of San Francisco School of Law, Sept. 24, 2007.

44. E-mail from Frank Lindh to author, Nov. 6, 2007.

45. *Institution Supplement,* Operation & Security of the Communication Management Unit (D-Unit—FCC), THX-5270.07A, U.S. Department of Justice, Federal Bureau of Prisons, Nov. 30, 2006, 1.

46. Jennifer Van Bergen, "Documents Show New Secretive US Prison Program Isolating Muslim, Middle Eastern Prisoners," *Raw Story,* Feb. 16, 2007, 1.

47. Ibid., 4.

48. Conversation with Frank Lindh, Feb. 1, 2008.

49. *Institution Supplement,* Operation & Security of the Communication Management Unit (D-Unit—FCC), THX-5270.07A, U.S. Department of Justice, Federal Bureau of Prisons, Nov. 30, 2006, 2.

50. E-mail from Frank Lindh to the author, Jan. 14, 2008.

51. Tom Junod, "The State of the American Man: Innocent," *Esquire,* July 1, 2006.

52. Ibid.

53. Conversation with Frank Lindh, June 15, 2005.

54. Conversation with Frank Lindh, Sept. 12, 2005.

55. Conversation with Frank Lindh, June 15, 2005.

56. Alan Cowell, "The Shadowy Trail and Shift to Islam of a Bomb Sus-

pect," *New York Times,* Dec. 29, 2001, A1; Michael Elliot, "The Shoe Bomber's World," *Time,* Feb. 16, 2002.

57. Judgment for Richard Reid at 187, *U.S. v. Reid,* 206 F. Supp. 2d 132 (Mass. App. Div. 2002) (No. CR.A. 02–10013-WGY).

58. Ibid.

59. Seymour Hersh, "The Twentieth Man," *New Yorker,* Sept. 30, 2002, 75.

60. See also "Interview with John Yoo," *Frontline,* PBS, July 19, 2005, available at http://www.pbs.org/wgbh/pages/frontline/torture/interviews/yoo .html (last visited Aug. 8, 2006).

61. Neil A. Lewis, "Moussaoui's Childhood Is Presented as Mitigating Factor," *New York Times,* Apr. 18, 2006.

62. Jerry Markon & Timothy Dwyer, "Moussaoui, Shoe Bomber Link Called 'Highly Unlikely' by FBI," *Washington Post,* Apr. 21, 2006, A3, available at LEXIS, News Library, WPOST File.

63. Appellant's Contested Motion for a Limited Remand Based on the Government's Disclosure of Incorrect Declarations, Testimony and Representations at 6, *United States v. Moussaoui,* No. 06–4494, Crim No. 01–455-A (4th Cir. Nov. 27, 2007).

64. Dan Eggen and Joby Warrick, "CIA Destroyed Videos Showing Interrogations," *Washington Post,* Dec. 7, 2007, A1.

65. Matthew Barakat, "Judge to Moussaoui Jury: You Got It Right," *Richmond Times-Dispatch,* July 24, 2008, B5.

66. Appellant's Contested Motion for a Limited Remand Based on the Government's Disclosure of Incorrect Declarations, Testimony and Representations, *United States v. Moussaoui,* No. 06–4494, Crim No. 01–455-A (4th Cir. Nov. 27, 2007). See also Appellant's Reply in Support of Contested Motion for a Limited Remand Based on the Government's Disclosure of Incorrect Declarations, Testimony, and Representations, *United States v. Moussaoui,* No. 06–4494, Crim No. 01–455-A (4th Cir. Dec. 17, 2007); Appellant's Supplemental Memorandum in Support of Motion to Remand and Contested Motion for Access to Tape and Transcript, *United States v. Moussaoui,* No. 06–4494, Crim. No. 01–455-A (4th Cir. Dec. 26, 2007).

67. Appellee's Response in Opposition to Appellant's Motion for a Limited Remand Based on the Government's Disclosure of Incorrect Declarations, Testimony and Representations, *United States v. Moussaoui,* No. 06–4494 (4th Cir. Dec. 6, 2007).

68. Brief of Appellant, *United States v. Moussaoui,* Record No. 06–4494 (4th Cir. Jan. 17, 2008).

69. Ibid., 30.

70. Ibid., 17.

71. Except where otherwise noted, the information about the Lackawanna Six in this section comes from Matthew Purdy and Lowell Bergman, "Unclear Danger: Inside the Lackawanna Terror Case," *New York Times,* Oct. 12, 2003, 1.

72. "Chasing the Sleeper Cell," *Frontline,* PBS, Oct 16, 2003, 7, available at http://www.pbs.org/wgbh/pages/frontline/shows/sleeper/etc/script.html.

73. Roya Aziz and Monica Lam, "Profiles: The Lackawanna Cell," *Frontline*, PBS, Oct. 16, 2003, http://www.pbs.org/wgbh/pages/frontline/shows/sleeper/inside/profiles.html. The bios of all six men are taken from this *Frontline* piece.

74. Pursuant to 18 U.S.C. § 2339B (2000), *U.S. v. Goba, et al.,* 220 F. Supp. 2d 182, 187 (W.D.N.Y. 2002).

75. *U.S. v. Goba, et al.,* 220 F. Supp. 2d 182, 184 n. 1 (W.D.N.Y. 2002).

76. E-mail from Rodney O. Personius, Yasein Taher's attorney, to Maria Lampasona, research assistant, Mar. 18, 2008.

77. Ibid.

78. Telephone conversations between Maria Lampasona, research assistant, and William Clauss, Goba's attorney, Feb. 27, 2008; and between Maria Lampasona and John J. Molloy, Mukhtar al-Bakri's attorney, Mar. 7, 2008.

79. 18 U.S.C. § 2339B (2000). In 2007, the Court of Appeals for the Ninth Circuit held that certain terms in section 2339B, including *training* and *service,* were unconstitutionally vague and could not be enforced by the government. However, as Yahya Goba's attorney, William Clauss, pointed out to research assistant Maria Lampasona, generally when a defendant pleads guilty he gives up his right to appeals. In addition, Goba's agreement precluded him from attempting to move against the plea on any grounds whatsoever. He added that the Lackawanna Six cases were in a different circuit, and therefore the decision was not controlling on their cases. The case is *Humanitarian Law Project v. Mukasey,* 509 F.3d 1122 (9th Cir. 2007).

80. Telephone conversation between Maria Lampasona and Joseph LaTona, Galab's attorney, Feb. 25, 2008.

81. International Emergency Economic Powers Act, 50 U.S.C.A. § 1705 (West 2004).

82. Telephone conversation between Maria Lampasona and William Clauss, Feb. 27, 2008.

83. *U.S. v. Goba,* No. 02-CR-214S (W.D.N.Y. Dec. 14, 2007).

84. Phone conversation between Maria Lampasona and William Clauss, Feb. 27, 2008.

85. "Chasing the Sleeper Cell," *Frontline,* PBS, Oct. 16, 2003, 10, available at http://www.pbs.org/wgbh/pages/frontline/shows/sleeper/etc/script.html.

86. Ibid., 16.

87. Ibid.

88. Ibid., 18.

89. "No one outside the administration knows just how the determination is made whether to handle a terror suspect as an enemy combatant or as a common criminal, to hold him indefinitely without charges in a military facility or to charge him in court." Adam Liptak, "In Terror Cases, Administration Sets Own Rules," *New York Times,* Nov. 27, 2005, 11, available at LEXIS, News Library, NYT File.

90. See Memorandum Opinion from John Yoo for Timothy Flanigan, Deputy Counsel to the President on the President's Constitutional Authority to Conduct Military Operations Against Terrorists and Nations Supporting Them

(Sept. 25, 2001), in *The Torture Papers: The Road to Abu Ghraib*, ed. Karen J. Greenberg & Joshua L. Dratel (Cambridge University Press, 2005), 3.

91. John Yoo said that the "main factors that will determine how you will be charged are one, how strong your link to Al Qaeda is and, two, whether you have any actionable intelligence that will prevent an attack on the United States." Quoted in Adam Liptak, "In Terror Cases, Administration Sets Own Rules," *New York Times,* Nov. 27, 2005, 11, available at LEXIS, News Library, NYT File.

A Justice Department spokesman indicated that the factors are "national security interests, the need to gather intelligence and the best and quickest way to obtain it, the concern about protecting intelligence sources and methods and ongoing information gathering, the ability to use information as evidence in a criminal proceeding, the circumstances of the manner in which the individual was detained, the applicable criminal charges, and classified-evidence issues." Ibid. However, in reading between the lines, what these statements amount to is that the executive should be provided exclusive discretion in its decision-making process concerning these matters.

CLOSING

1. See part 3, section 2, on movements to try Rumsfeld and other American leaders who have been accused of war crimes in Germany and France.

2. E-mail from Carlos Castresana, April 18, 2008. Castresana refers to J. M. Coetzee, *Diary of a Bad Year* (Viking, 2007), 39.

ADDENDUM

1. Wells Dixon is one habeas attorney who believes this. Telephone conversation with Wells Dixon, Dec. 12, 2007. See also section 3 on challenges to government monitoring of attorneys' communications.

2. J. M. Coetzee, *Diary of a Bad Year* (Viking, 2007), 39.

Index

Italicized page numbers refer to illustrations.

Text: 10/13 Sabon
Display: Franklin Gothic
Compositor: BookMatters, Berkeley
Indexer: Sharon Sweeney
Printer: Sheridan Books, Inc.